REINVENTING MYSELF

ALSO BY MAVOR MOORE

Plays

Who's Who? (stage) 1943
The Great Flood (radio) 1947
Inside Out (television) 1974
The Roncarelli Affair, with Frank R. Scott (television) 1976
Six Plays by Mavor Moore 1989
Customs, in Cues and Entrances 1993

Plays in Translation

Yesterday the Children Were Dancing, from the French of Gratien Gélinas 1967
The Puppet Caravan, from the French of Marie-Claire Blais 1968

Opera Librettos

Louis Riel, music: Harry Somers; text with Jacques Languirand 1967
Abracadabra, music: Harry Freedman 1979

Musicals

The Optimist (radio, 1952; stage, 1956; television, 1968)
Sunshine Town (radio, 1954; stage, 1956; television, 1957)
Belinda, with music by John Fenwick (stage, 1969; television, 1976)
A Christmas Carol 1988

Verse

And What Do YOU Do? 1960

Essays

The Awkward Stage 1969
Four Canadian Playwrights 1973
Slipping on the Verge: The Performing Arts in Canada 1983
The Politics of Art 1985
My Adventures in Public Broadcasting 1986
The Folk Arts in Canada 1988
The Politics of Multiculture 1989

REINVENTING MYSELF

MEMOIRS

MAVOR MOORE

AN ARNOLD EDINBOROUGH BOOK

Published in 1994 by
Stoddart Publishing Co. Limited
34 Lesmill Road
Toronto, Canada
M3B 2T6
(416) 445-3333

Canadian Cataloguing in Publication Data
Moore, J. Mavor, 1919–
Reinventing myself: memoirs

ISBN 0-7737-2789-2

1. Moore, J. Mavor, 1919– — Biography.
2. Dramatists, Canadian (English) — 20th century —
Biography. I. Title.

PS8526.063Z53 1994 C812'.54 C94-930030-6
PR9199.3.M66Z47 1994

Printed and bound in Canada

Stoddart Publishing gratefully acknowledges the support of the Canada Council, Ontario Ministry of Culture, Tourism, and Recreation, Ontario Arts Council, and Ontario Publishing Centre in the development of writing and publishing in Canada.

To my children and their children

Contents

Preface

THIS BOOK IS about my first 50 years. There will be no book about the next 50. As biography, it is as unconventional as its subject — appearing now as document and now as recollection, now in history's past tense, and now in theatre's eternal present.

I could not have written this much had I not been a packrat, like my mother before me and her father before her. But the difficulty has been to get at the lode. I now live and teach in Victoria, British Columbia, while the James Mavor and Dora Mavor Moore Papers (including every letter I ever wrote to her) live in the Thomas Fisher Library at the University of Toronto, and my own papers are lodged in the archives of York University.

I must therefore thank the able archivists at both institutions, especially Rachel Grover and Edna Hajnal of the former and Mary Williamson and Phyllis Potnick of the latter. But since neither my mother nor I collected material with a historian's care or an eye to posterity's convenience, many clippings are undated and letters are as likely as not to be labelled "Monday." I am thus greatly indebted to Paula Sperdakos of the University of Toronto's Graduate Centre for the Study of Drama, whose fine unpublished doctoral thesis on Dora Mavor Moore (drawing on the Fisher Library papers) has provided a firm chronology for the years my mother and I worked together, and saved me many hours of research. In addition, my late brother Francis's interest in genealogy generated an invaluable family tree.

Gloria Cohen has graciously allowed me to use excerpts from the columns and broadcasts of Nathan Cohen, and Claire Coulter an extract from John Coulter's privately printed memoir In My Life. Pierre Berton, Robertson Davies, Ronald Mavor, and Herbert Whittaker have permitted me to quote from their writings. Letters from James Bridie, Alf Bell, and Cecil Clarke are quoted with the kind permission of Ronald Mavor, Dama

Bell, and Jacqueline Cundall, and those from Harry Somers and John Weinzweig with the authors' permission. The CBC Archives have been helpful with photographs. I am grateful to my longtime literary agent, Matie Molinaro, for insisting that I write a chronicle of these years; to Arnold Edinborough for persuading me to keep at it when I wanted to quit; and to editor Michael Carroll for bringing it all together. Arthur Gelber has been a source of strength throughout.

My daughters Dorothea, Rosalind, Marili, and Charlotte have caught me up on familial points, and Freeman Tovell has been of great assistance on historical matters. Three distinguished lifelong friends, Vincent Tovell, Francess Halpenny, and J. M. S. Careless, have read the entire manuscript and done their best to rid me of error. The remaining errors are mine.

Finally I must thank three forbearing wives: Darwina Faessler, who shared my life during much of the period covered in these memoirs; Phyllis Grosskurth, who taught me all I know about writing biographies; and Alexandra Browning, who puts up with me as I write this one. Reliving one's life is not an exercise I recommend. But reinventing it is another story.

Book One

If I'd Known Then

Yeh Ch'ueh asked Wang I, "Do you know for certain that all things are the same?"

"How can I know?" answered Wang I. "Do you know what you do not know?"

"How do I know?" replied Yeh Ch'ueh. "But then can nothing be known?"

"How do I know?" said Wang I. Nevertheless I will try to tell you."

— CHUANG TZE

1

Prelude

I HAD NO SAY in anything connected
with my birth. Had I known what lay ahead I might have declined the
invitation. But I was not given the option: the choice of parentage, place,
and time was already made. With a different set of ancestors, in another
country or another era, who can guess what I might have been? A black
pirate, a Hungarian pianist with a lush head of hair, a nun running for
president — the possibilities were endless but are now fanciful. As it
happened, I was born to Francis John Moore, an Anglican clergyman,
and his wife Dora (née Mavor), an actress, in Toronto in 1919.

Let us take these accidents one by one, starting with the genes.

I was conceived in England, from which my father had earlier emigrated to Canada, and to which he returned with his Canadian bride
during World War I. Before their marriage in 1916 (he at 32, she at 28)
he had been curate of Toronto's St. James Cathedral under the influential
Canon Plumptre, whose formidable wife Adelaide was a power in civic
politics long before the heyday of feminism. My mother was already an
established professional actress. The first Canadian graduate of London's
Royal Academy of Dramatic Art, she had performed on Broadway and in
Chicago and become the leading lady of Philip Ben Greet's celebrated
classical company in its North American tours. But by 1916, disenchanted with commercial theatre in the still-neutral United States, she had

returned to Toronto. A charismatic address by Laurence Irving (Sir Henry's son) on "The Drama as a Factor in Social Progress" turned her thoughts to teaching — to making theatre for others what it had been for her: a way into the art of life. Then marriage beckoned. When Frank Moore signed up as an army chaplain, she dutifully accompanied him overseas.

By coincidence, however, Ben Greet had just returned to his native London as director of the renascent Old Vic Theatre, and they met again. When the English Viola in his *Twelfth Night* became ill, he turned to his North American Viola. Already pregnant — my older brother Francis ever after claimed to be the first critic to kick a Vic actress in the middle of the play — she stepped in to become the Old Vic's earliest Canadian star. Francis (known as Fran to distinguish him from his father Frank) was born in March 1917. And shortly after the war ended in November 1918, the family returned to Canada — but not, obviously, before setting in motion the party born three months later in Toronto General Hospital.

When I tell you that my father was a Doctor of Divinity and my mother a player, you should resist the instant recall of old jokes about the Bishop and the Actress. In my parents' case the stereotypes were reversed. She was the moralist and he the operator.

From the moment I could understand the stories she read to me every night — read? radiated! — I knew she was out to uplift humanity. And every Sunday morning, as my reverend father sat at the old piano (one forefinger on his lips, the other on middle C) warming up for his sermon, I knew he was really in show business. I grew up thinking a lot about the relationship between art and religion, which may explain why I later combined the two and became a critic. There must have been some love between my parents to start with, at least enough to see them through the arrival of my younger brother Peter two years after my own; but they were fundamentally oil and water — and each was miscast as the other.

Frank Moore came from Derby in Yorkshire. His widowed mother took in washing to support her large and illiterate family, and welcomed the Church of England's offer to underwrite her oldest boy's education on condition that he enter the priesthood at the end of it. Owing everything to this Faustian bargain, including an otherwise useless degree in theology from the University of Durham, young Frank was, as it were, stuck with God. But if his indenture made him hostage to the next world, it also taught him how the wind blows in this one. Once master of the Bishop's English, he snubbed his embarrassing family and set out for Canada, aiming to leave the class system behind forever. In some ways he succeeded, turning himself into an eloquent preacher and a capable writer; but his weather vane kept showing. I often thought he would have done well in advertising, public relations, or journalism — or any of those trades in which a bit of corner-cutting now and then is seen as a badge of merit. But as a clergyman he was expected to be a moral rock. This Frank Moore was not, and he had the misfortune to marry one.

Born in Glasgow in 1888, Dora Mavor was the daughter of an internationally prominent university professor and a shy former music teacher. When James Mavor came to Canada in 1892 to accept the chair of political economy at the University of Toronto — the country's first — he was already acknowledged to be "one of the eight or ten leading British economists," and an authority on commerce, labour, politics, the arts, technology, housing, railways, and international relations. All this he had achieved without any academic degree. Even for the feisty Glasgow of his day, his track record had been remarkable.

The oldest of nine children of an Aberdeen schoolmaster, he was forced to work from his early teens. But he put himself through technical college, where he struck up a friendship with the inventor William Thompson (better known later as Lord Kelvin). Thompson's enthusiasm for science inspired James and induced all four of his brothers to become electrical engineers. Young James Mavor then went into business, where he was quickly made aware of the social consequences of pell-mell industrialization. With the town planner Sir Patrick Geddes, he was a pioneer in housing for the poor; with his lifelong friend William Morris, he was a cosigner of the Socialist League manifesto (always wary of socialism's authoritarian bent, Mavor was later fiercely anti-Bolshevik). And he edited, simultaneously, both the *Scottish Art Review* and the technological magazine *Industries*.

In England he hobnobbed and debated with the Fabians — Edward Pease, Sidney and Beatrice Webb, and the playwright George Bernard Shaw, who mockingly used his name for Candida's social-activist husband, the Reverend James Mavor Morell.[1] He rubbed brains with the literati: the editor W. T. Stead, the critic Arthur Symons, the poet W. B. Yeats and, through Yeats, Madame Blavatsky, the founder of theosophy. But the most consequential of his London acquaintances was with the émigré Russian biologist and anarchist Prince Peter Kropotkin. Later, after Mavor had settled in Toronto, it was Kropotkin who enlisted his aid in Leo Tolstoy's scheme to resettle Russia's oppressed Doukhobors·in Canada, a massive project that claimed his attention for years. Before the start of World War I, the energetic University of Toronto professor had travelled throughout much of Europe, Canada, Japan, China, and Mongolia as an adviser to governments, and written — after teaching himself Russian to research it — his classic 1914 *Economic History of Russia*.[2]

Small wonder that in Toronto, where his mania for books and curios kept his family in genteel poverty, James Mavor's name became synonymous with (a) stirring up the natives and (b) professorial absentmindedness. In the city he shamelessly lobbied businessmen, politicians, and their wives on behalf of art galleries, museums, and workers' education. On the campus he was known to leave his economics lecture notes at home and extemporize about Chinese calligraphy or Algonquian mythology. At the Arts and Letters Club, where he played master-class chess, they still tell the tale of the stormy night Mavor and five others won the draw to stay and sleep in the club's six available beds. When the others retired, Mavor was missing. He reappeared two hours later, soaked to the skin, with the explanation: "I went home to get my pajamas."

Too many things were going on in his head, and staying at home was not one of them. Despite periodic proofs of genuine affection, he was inevitably a neglectful husband and an inattentive father. Taking for granted that his two sons would match his protean example and that his only daughter would not, he understood none of the three. He produced a two-volume autobiography, *My Windows on the Street of the World*, without ever mentioning the family inside as he gazed out; such delicacy was, of course, typical of contemporary memoirs of public men, but my pawky wee grandmother Christina put it down to James's forgetfulness. Each of their offspring left the nest as soon as possible — Jim, the oldest, to study science at Cambridge and then teach biology in the United States; Dora, whose repeated academic failures he attributed to unaccountable stupidity, to run away to the theatre in search of a mission; and Wilfrid, the youngest, smallest and gentlest, to enlist in the army.

This was the family circle that Frank Moore joined when he married Dora Mavor in Toronto on November 23, 1916, and the one to which the couple returned two years later with an infant 20 months old and another on the way. The War to End War was over, the stage no longer a rival for his wife's affections, and the good life within reach. Once out of uniform and back in his old job at the cathedral, the Reverend F. J. Moore began to affect a walking stick.

TORONTO IMMEDIATELY after the First World War was hardly a metropolis, and far from becoming "possibly the most civilized metropolis in the western hemisphere," as the U.S. magazine *Art Gallery* declared 60 years later. (I base this generalization on historical accounts; I had my first, and very nearly last, confrontation with civilization at the age of 18 months, having tottered out alone onto the streetcar tracks on King Street.) But neither was it, in my later recollection, the stolid parochial backwater of post-Second World War legend. It was worse than that. It was interesting.

That is, if you understood about curtains and masks.

In those days people were very strong on curtains — on windows, in doorways, across alcoves, around commodes, and in front of stages. Like the top border of a theatre proscenium, known as the teaser, their purpose was to baffle the naive and titillate the knowing. A clause in the permit of Massey Hall, until the 1920s the only building in Canada designed specifically for music, outlawed all curtains on the ground that they implied posterior immorality. This useful principle was worked hard in the increasingly common movie houses, where the sole purpose of curtains was to screen before the show another screen on which the film was to be screened. In those days kids trying to get into the theatre were also screened by the management. I made a note that *screen* had three contrary meanings: to hide, to show, and to filter. Ambiguity was a way of life in Toronto.

After all, the city had always had a natural screen. My grandfather, arriving in this provincial capital of 150,000 in the fall of 1892, was much taken with the foliage:

> From an eminence like the tower of the University . . . Toronto looked like a settlement in a forest. Horse chestnuts, lining many of the streets and avenues, were becoming rusty; but the maples . . . gave a note of gorgeous red and yellow, while in the suburbs the sumach shrubs were brilliant scarlet.[3]

The shaded streets were only the beginning. He described the ravines formed by the gulleys of the two flanking rivers, the Don and the Humber, stretching through the city to make "natural parks of great beauty," thick with trees. The population had grown to 500,000 by the time I joined it, but the ravines were little changed. During my boy-hood, we lived in five different rented houses, all but one of them near a wildwood. The house on Lawton Boulevard backed directly onto a gore-shaped copse we called "the jungle" (long since displaced by the Yonge subway). Hidden from the world, we'd climb trees, swing on vines, and play secret games. The house on Sheldrake, farther north, was a block from Sherwood Park — known as "the forest," naturally, and full of out-laws in disguise and maids in love.

Through these wooded ravines ran sheltered bicycle paths, by which my friends and I could ride south and emerge at the other end — presto! — among pungent lumber yards or brick factories, the grand residences of Jarvis Street, the treasure-laden city dumps or the labyrinths of Rosedale, dormitory of the chronically rich — our entire reconnaissance camouflaged by friendly elms, oaks, maples, and evergreens. We could even get to the sylvan Islands in the bay by taking our bikes across on the ferries. But we seldom ventured into parts of the city accessible only by automobile (we had none) or long streetcar rides. Until I was 17 I hardly knew the Queensway in the far southwest — and then only because I had a girlfriend living there who had to be escorted from the end of the Bloor Street line through yet another forest to her home. On the long tram ride back I often reflected on the city's sudden growth.

In the winter, when the foliage grew sparse, this same landscape lay under a blanket of snow. A blanket is a horizontal curtain.

An English novelist, visiting in the 1920s, called Toronto "a sancti-monious ice-box." Let me tell you, underneath these boreal and arboreal covers was a human compost heap. The cold hello and the blank expres-sion were to keep nosy strangers guessing. For those in the know, the place was seething with passionate possibilities.

You could lose yourself in exotic enclaves like Chinatown and the Jewish district on lower Spadina, where families huddled earnestly among embracing smells and spoke in languages that hissed and sang. For every horse-drawn open carriage carrying the Misses Mortimer-Clark in their feathered hats for a Sunday drive along Lowther Avenue, there was an old nag pulling a rag-and-bone man's cart. For every single man-sion in Rosedale, there were 10 rooming houses for single men on Church Street and 20 hovels bursting with children in downtown slums. Dignity pervaded upper Jarvis Street, but its lower end was festooned with tarts parading theirs, and drunks stepping carefully in the general direction of the Salvation Army. ("High souls with low heels," the preacher Billy Cameron used to call his uptown congregation to their faces.) Birth, death, and transfiguration.

As I grew up, I had no difficulty seeing Toronto as the navel of the world. Here lived real princes and princesses — the gallant but broke Nakashidze from Georgian Russia, for one, with his pretty imitation Russian princess who peered over the heads of little boys in theatre lobbies. And there were knights like my friend the costume cutter Dick Moon, who worked for peanuts at Malabar's until one day he got a wire telling him his great-uncle once removed had died in England and he was now Sir Richard. After that he and Lady Moon had no time to talk to kids.

We had important visitors from all over, too, such as His Grace the Anglican bishop of Shanghai, Timothy Ting Fang Loo, a jolly little man unfortunately strapped for cash, who was staying with us as he passed through on his way to London to raise money for his flock. I took him around Chinatown and he made a lot of contacts. A puppeteer from Turkey whose name I've forgotten put on shows at the library. Then there was the day I opened the door of our bungalow to welcome Princess Alexandra Kropotkin, daughter of Peter, who had been at school with my mother in Brussels and now lived in New York with her fifth husband writing a gossip column for Liberty magazine. ("Linguist, friend of the famous in Europe, and descendant of the first Czar of Russia," ran her byline.) I bowed like any well-trained 12-year-old, with a "How do you do, Your Highness?" — whereupon she removed her dangling cigarette and bawled in a whiskey baritone, "Christ, darling, call me Sascha!" It was very sophisticating.

Toronto had everything a young world citizen could desire: a widely admired public library system stocked with literary masterpieces from everywhere; a fine museum filled with Greek pots, British armour, and the best Chinese tombs outside China; a gallery filled with the great art of Europe; a splendid zoo with lions, tigers, and elephants from Asia; a symphony orchestra devoted to German, French, and Russian music, annual visits from an Italian opera company out of New York; and half a dozen theatres showing hits from Broadway or London as well as world classics with international stars. We had access to everything except our own creativity.

My familiarity with the stars was such that at the age of seven I shook hands with William Shakespeare. At some function to which my mother had dragged me I was introduced to the impresario Daniel Frohman, who controlled one of the largest theatre chains in North

America. A short, bald New Yorker with a Vandyke beard and a gold watch chain spanning his ample vest, Frohman took my right hand firmly in his, removed his pince-nez with the other, and spoke gravely. "My boy, when I was a young man, I shook hands with Sir Henry Irving, who had once performed with the renowned Samuel Phelps, who learned his trade from Edmund Kean, idol of two continents, who once kissed the hand of the divine Peg Woffington, mistress of David Garrick, greatest of all actors, who apprenticed as a boy with the actor-manager Thomas Betterton, who had begun his career in a company run by Sir William Davenant, Shakespeare's godson and in all probability his illegitimate child. So I say to you, sir, you have this day shaken hands with the Bard himself." Relaxing his grip, he replaced his spectacles and turned to the goddess beside him.

Anyone who thinks a seven-year-old could not recall this inaccurate recital word for word has never experienced an epiphany. The mockery went clean over my head. I was in touch with everything — and nothing, suddenly, was beyond the reach of my little Canadian hand.

The fact was that behind its bland and proper mask, like the Phantom of the Opera, Toronto had long been plotting how it would one day burst upon an astonished world as a cultural marvel. The transformation took place behind a screen on which the legends TORONTO THE GOOD and HOGTOWN were intertwined, and the ruse was brilliantly successful.

As early as 1892, my observant grandfather had caught sight, through the foliage, of deceptively square public buildings that were monuments to neither God nor Mammon:

> Toronto is a great nest of educational institutions. . . . The whole air is full of educational administration, much of it in the agony of being born. . . . Culture seems to be a kind of craze in Canada. What they mean by it is perhaps hazy even to themselves; but they undoubtedly have a yearning for something which is not specie.[4]

I was 11 when I read that passage in his autobiography, and had to look up *specie* to learn it meant hard money. I recognized the symptom at once. I now know that the yearning for "something which is not specie" was congenital and irreversible. But at Toronto General Hospital in 1919 each baby born behind a curtain was immediately issued a respectability mask (so-called from its angelic eyes and hard nose) before being displayed. I have never been able to remove that mask. But on the whole the disguise has served me well and fooled a great many solemn asses.

So much for the place; now for the time.

"At my nativity," says the Welsh mystic Glendower in Shakespeare's *Henry IV*, "the front of heaven was full of fiery shapes, of burning cressets; and at my birth the frame and huge foundation of the earth shak'd like a coward." This was obviously hearsay, not to say hogwash. But we have the historians' word for it that 1919 was a phenomenal year. World peace, the League of Nations, Canadian independence, the Russian Civil War, women in the House of Commons, international broadcasting, the art film, Canadian painting, Canadian drama, and I all broke out at the same time. In our beginning is our end.

All of these events, understandably overlooked by me at the time, played a considerable role in my life.

Sir Robert Borden's insistence on signing the 1919 Versailles Treaty as prime minister of Canada separately from the British — an innovation bitterly opposed by the Americans — was a critical step in our emergence from colonial status. The failure of the League of Nations led to World War II, in which I finally grew up, and eventually to the United Nations, where I received my education in international politics. When Marconi obtained a federal licence in 1919 for a radio station in Montreal, like all Canadians, I automatically became a pioneer in the age of communications. Robert Wiene's film *The Cabinet of Dr. Caligari*, made (incredibly) in Germany in 1919, was the first attempt to turn cinematography into art; I saw it first when I was an impressionable 15, but it was *Dr. Caligari* that persuaded me that the motion picture was the art of our times.

When women were first admitted to the Canadian House of Commons in 1919, I was still trying to open my eyes. But I was soon exposed to the power of the women's rights movement; one of my earliest memories is of my mother returning home with her hair bobbed. After that, feminism assumed a direct importance in my life that I could not have foreseen. As our mother became increasingly caught up in the educational dimension of the movement, we three boys found ourselves helping her to mount shows in girls' schools, girls' camps, and women's clubs. Fran and I had no problem with the balance of power, but the younger Peter rebelled and took up boxing. At 14 I read John Langdon Davies's early feminist *Short History of Women* and immediately enlisted in the crusade as an auxiliary. This early training has seen me through three marriages, five daughters, two granddaughters, and countless other historic encounters with forceful women.

But of all these 1919 metamorphoses the breakthrough in radio technology haunted me the most tenaciously. I was not yet a year old when Marconi's Montreal station went on the air, at about the same time as the first stations in Britain and the United States. That is to say we all left the starting post together. By the time I was six, like most of the kids on the block, I was listening to my crystal set after lights-out under the blankets (re *blanket*, see above), fiddling with the little wire needle to pick up any channel at all. We had audio-visions of bringing in the whole world and sending back our own signals — a sort of grand cultural exchange. But the medium was already the message, although Marshall McLuhan was only in high school: the available stations and recordings seemed to be entirely American.

I was 14 and regularly acting in radio before it occurred to me to ask why. I learned that after our simultaneous launch in the early 1920s the United States had arrogated to itself every wavelength on the North American continent, and Canada had to fight for eight years to reclaim even a few. We had been sidelined by a deliberate power play. Its temporary success led to the establishment of public broadcasting in Canada in 1933, the year I turned 14; but meantime it had also led most of my contemporaries to believe they were born to be consumers of the culture of luckier souls born in a more advanced society.

Finally the consequences of the artistic renaissance in Ontario from 1919 to 1929 are still with us — even when we forget it, which I cannot. I would be the last to suggest, naturally, that this brief flowering owed anything to my arrival on the scene; but, as old Pangloss would say, there is a concatenation of all events in this best of possible worlds.

Had there been no Group of Seven prepared to stay at home and paint what they saw, had the Massey clan not built Hart House with its theatre and Roy Mitchell not put on Canadian plays there, had a few actors not stuck around to perform them while making a living selling shirts or skirts at Eaton's, had local poets not written poems and sports-writers not produced novels, had publishers not hocked their Ryrie-Birks silverware to stay in business, and had the Massey Report not maintained 20 years later that we could mount a still bigger renaissance with a television network and a Canada Council, you would not now be reading these improbable memoirs.

2

Kid Stuff

THE FIRST HOME of which I have any rec-
ollection was a dark duplex on Washington Avenue, near the University
of Toronto Schools at Bloor and Huron streets, which I later attended
from much farther away. Everything about it was dark, including my
only memory of its layout: a bedroom at the top of the stairs, with a
half-open door through which horrendous nightmares rose from hall
stands, hanging coats, brooms, and laundry bundles to carry me off to
the precipice overhanging the sea of chaos. I have happy recollections
from those years, but they are of activities elsewhere.

The best were at my grandparents' home, a rambling old house on
Isabella Street, to which they had moved when the university razed their
campus home to build Convocation Hall. The living room seemed not half
as big as the study, with its thousands of books in tall library stacks, its
prints from Japan and China, and its objets d'art from Greece and Egypt.
The dining room missed the huge sideboard brought from Glasgow, lost
when Sir Henry Pellatt went broke building his monstrous Casa Loma and
had to sell off the furniture his friends had lent him. Overnight "Sir
Henry" became "that crook Pellatt." In the sideboard's place, later on,
hung an oil portrait of the three Moore grandsons by a wretched Toronto
artist named Alan Barr — commissioned by the charitable professor out of
his wife's housekeeping allowance. My grandmother could never decide

whether to be most aggrieved at his treachery, his extravagance, or his encouragement of incompetence.

James Mavor died in 1925 — characteristically abroad — when I was only five and a half, leaving me his name and two vivid memories. The first is of a night not long before his death when he sat on my bed in a red-and-black plaid dressing gown, eyes sparkling and beard rich with cigar fumes as he read from his friend Andrew Lang's translation of *The Odyssey*. But I did not grasp the Homeric range of his mind until nine years later when my grandmother moved into a small apartment of which one room was entirely given over to the remainder of his library — the economics and Russian collections having gone to Harvard University. Because I'd worked in a library I was given the job of sorting and boxing the books, paperbacks, pamphlets, magazines, and assorted papers now piled shelfless from floor to ceiling, leaving space enough only to open the door. All around me lay the evidence of his insatiable curiosity about everything from masterpieces to muck, gradually forming a self-portrait as revealing as the recently unpacked tomb of Tutankhamen — and leading me to wonder if I hadn't incurred a similar curse.

The study in the house on Isabella Street had reeked gorgeously of cigars. In the days before vacuum cleaners, deodorants, and refrigeration each room in a house had a bouquet of its own. The basement smelled of coal, mouldy potatoes, and washing lye; the kitchen alternately of spices and gas; the single bathroom of disinfectant; the dining room of wood polish; the living room of musty upholstery, and the men's bedrooms of camphor balls, the women's of scented sachets. Those living there, too, had their own particular essence; when they entered a room, you could tell who it was with your eyes shut. When strangers approached, you could guess at their occupation, as well. But then the whole city in those days was as aromatic as a farm. The backyards stank splendidly of machine oil, chicken coops, and doghouses; the streets of horse manure; the markets of mellow apples and ripe fish; the shops of hot bread and sweet soaps; the schools of sweat; and all but the newest public buildings of spilt beer and clandestine piss. To get onto a crowded streetcar was to enter a whole sensorium of body odours.

In his backyard on Isabella Street my grandfather, in pursuance of a craze for natural milk, had even tethered a goat, which he invited my grandmother to tend. She firmly declined but agreed to investigate after a fortnight during which the poor beast had succeeded in fouling the yard but failed to produce the nectar. My brother Fran and I were there when she told him, "Y'old fool, it's a billy." My second recollection of James Mavor is of his face at that moment of truth. On crestfallen occasions I recognize it in the mirror.

But the most remarkable person in that household was the hired help. When they changed homes, the Mavors had acquired a seasonal maid-of-all-work, a tiny, illiterate, but tough Scotswoman with a pronounced harelip. Annie spent the winters at Isabella Street and the summers as cook on a grain boat on the Great Lakes. Her affection for the rough crewmen was matched, I was led to believe, only by their respect for her profanity and their fear of her cuisine.

Annie was a seer. When the oracular mode took her, she would clench her gums and mutter awesome delphic prophecies — with, in my youthful experience, unfailing accuracy. "Sing before breakfast and you'll cry before bed," she'd say, and I would. "Thursday come and the week is gone," and it was indeed. Or "Ye canna whistle while ye drink," or "If you trust before you try, you'll repent before you die." I was grateful for these precepts in later years, especially while chairing the Canada Council. But of all her premonitions the most dead-on was the one she repeatedly laid on the daughter of the house, now Mrs. Moore: "Change the name and not the letter, ye'll marry for worse and not for better."

When the spell was broken, I have no idea. Annie, who like all futurists had a vested interest in her forecasts, used to say that His Royal Highness (her favourite epithet for my father) behaved himself while the Professor was alive and then showed his true colours. HRH, however, may equally well have been ambushed by the true colours of his princess.

In the first 10 years of marriage his wife had borne and raised three children while entering vigorously into his parish activities and other community work. She had turned her theatrical skills to directing religious plays and church pageants, counselled young people, and met with the Women's Auxiliary. These ladies may have dropped stitches at her habit of presenting young brides with Dr. Marie Stopes's *Married Love*, the new birth control primer, but it aided her husband's reputation as a theological progressive. She had returned to teaching to supplement their income. Her only self-indulgence was to appear three times in three years in high-minded amateur productions at Hart House Theatre. She had been a model helpmeet.

Yet when our parents separated for the first time in 1928, my brothers and I could not think of a single instance of shared affection we had ever witnessed between the two. Too proud of his wife as an acquisition not to be jealous of her as a person, Father would wait for her to make the overture and then greet it as only his due, like the kissing of a cardinal's ring.

Nor could we recollect instances of spontaneous affection toward us. To him, home was a place to relax from God's demanding service while his family did the chores and saw to his needs: He for God and they for God in him. We could not recall his taking us out to any event except his sermons — not, at least, until after he became a father with visiting rights only — nor of his reading to us or playing games with us. I have no doubt that in his long career the Reverend Gentleman (Annie's other title for him) gave helpful guidance in the art of living to many others. But to me he bequeathed only three of life's basic survival techniques: how to stoke coal, how to shovel snow, and how to dry oneself with a taut towel.

His wife, on the other hand, knew exactly where her mission lay: with those who needed her. This was the "secret" that bound Shaw's Candida to her husband, the Reverend James Mavor Morell, when she was tempted to run off with the poetical but self-sufficient Samuel Marchbanks. And it must have astonished the hell out of the Reverend Francis John Moore to realize that his wife felt this bond less and less with her husband and more and more with her sons. If her prodigious father had failed to recognize his daughter's capability, and her insecure husband now sought to tame it, "the boys" would be its beneficiaries. These males would be her creations, validating her as a woman and vindicating her as a person. Not until decades later did she declare herself free of even this dependency. Meantime she simply took charge.

As soon as we could talk, we were taught at home, by her or by one of her large network of undervalued women friends. As soon as we could walk, we were sent to kindergarten — in those days most often a religious or neighbourhood collective run by conscientious spinsters. The single parent (which Dora Moore would soon become) was rare then and always overburdened; but single women made up an abundant and largely untapped social resource upon which she had already learned to draw for mutual aid. We were apprenticed to the best model makers and craft buffs she was able to charm into accepting our help. The one I remember best was Ruth Hahn, daughter of the sculptor Emmanuel, who worked at the Royal Ontario Museum but taught me how to carve, encrust, and paint a super wooden sword.

By the age of four and a half, owing more to my mother's initiative than mine, I had played in a piano competition and won prizes for reading, writing, and French. She wangled us into concert halls and theatres. At five I heard Jan Paderewski play and saw Anna Pavlova dance, and joined the boys' choir of St. James under the redoubtable Dr. Ham. At six I was devouring Shakespeare and dragooning the local kids into getting up shows. That same year I was cast in a Hart House production of an Indian classic, *The Toy Cart*, and made the first of my aborted debuts: I was hustled out of rehearsal when the chicken pox struck.

But I had my moment onstage a few months later when Canada's pioneer child psychologist Dr. William Blatz picked me as the guinea pig for a public experiment, at his Institute of Child Study, in the ability of high-IQ children to exercise choice. Blatz's then contentious hypothesis — in opposition to the reigning behaviourism — was that even as young humans we have considerable control over our own destiny through selection of available options; that "life is fulfilling, not fulfillment." It was not the last time I would have reason to thank Bill Blatz, but that first lesson was the most graphic: he assured me I would be controlling the interview, since my response to each challenge would dictate the next challenge. I have never since felt in such a position of command over what was to come. There sat the two of us, on either side of a desk covered with building counters, in the centre of an amphitheatre filled with a hundred judges, while I discovered the fearful intoxication of gliding on one's wits before an audience. It was an extraordinary preparation for television.

By that time Francis, then eight, had demonstrated a mechanical aptitude that was at once attributed to the engineering genius of the Glasgow Mavors. So Mother encouraged us to divide the world between us, like Charlemagne and the pope: the sciences were to be his province and the arts mine. At three Peter was too young to be anything but a general apostate. A deceptively angelic child with curly blond hair kept long by his mother, he was not about to embody anyone's idea of genetic engineering. On his fourth birthday the rebel angel hacked off his own halo and declared for the only arenas not already preempted by his brothers: sport and war. In these his only precursor had been our uncle Wilfrid ("Smoot") Mavor, a World War I hero of short stature but giant heart, whom we adored.

But by 1927 the family was already disintegrating. Mother, obviously overworked, had the foretoken of what was then called a nervous breakdown. Father, despite a salary above the average for a clergyman, refused to hire even occasional housekeeping help or to raise her allowance. In an attempt to hold things together, promoted by well-meaning friends, they rented a less claustrophobic house on Lawton Boulevard, farther north, and Father applied for the less-demanding post of director of the Student Christian Movement at the University of Toronto.

These remedies, however, were only grit for the gears. To pay for the move, he had borrowed money from a cathedral parishioner whom he had cultivated, a rich widow known to have made her pile as a slum landlord. Finding herself cast in yet another Shavian drama, this time *Widowers' Houses,* my outraged mother insisted he give it back — and borrowed the necessary sum from her brother Wilfrid, who by this time had established himself in business. The humiliated husband, seeing only a plot to prevent him from ruling his own roost, accused his brother-in-law of "intolerable interference." Countercharges such as "damn liar" and "self-righteousness" and "utterly immoral" were tossed about, rising like jetsam in a threeway quarrel we overheard at midnight from the upstairs landing.

Then, on the day following his job interview with the university's conservative president, the Reverend H. J. Cody, Father announced at dinner with great satisfaction that it had gone "wonderfully." We all cheered and applauded. Then Mother, out of simple curiosity, asked, "How did you handle the virgin birth?"

"Why bring that up?" replied Father, as if she had put salt in his tea.

"Because everyone knows Canon Cody believes in it," she said, "and you don't."

"I've no intention of discussing it just now," he said, indicating the children.

"But they know. They heard your sermon on the Virgin Mary!"

"Sure, I remember," Fran added helpfully.

"I never said I disbelieved it, not *totally,*" said Father, his bald pate blushing, a sure sign of guilt. "I said it wasn't intended to be taken *literally.*"

"Is that what you told him?"

"As long as it's taken *symbolically* . . ."

"Did you tell him you don't take it literally?"

"We're in a grey area here . . . a matter of interpretation . . ."

"You fudged it, didn't you?"

"I got the position, didn't I?"

And so on. My lifelong preoccupation with semantics, I have no doubt, began at this moment. The redder Father's bald pate became, the more blood drained from Mother's face. Eventually we three were sent up to bed, that sanctuary of whispered understandings, knowing that in their bed there would be none.

During the winter of 1928, we busied ourselves as a counterirritant. We mounted elaborate puppet shows in which everything but Fran's ingenious lighting went wrong, and Peter regularly threatened to quit as stagehand 10 minutes before show time. I read like a demon, ticking off the authors on a library list as I went: Alcott, Carroll, Cervantes, Defoe, Dickens, Dumas, Hawthorne, W. H. Hudson, Kingsley, Kipling, Lamb, Melville, Ruskin, Ernest Thompson Seton, Scott, Stevenson, Swift, Synge, Thackeray and Catherine Parr Traill. The librarian said she had never known anyone else who had read all four volumes of Alexandre Dumas's *The Vicomte de Bragelonne*, and I could see why. I began my first short story, titled "The Restoration of Kings," of which, mercifully, only the opening sentence survives: "It was getting late in the afternoon, when a very well-dressed chevalier rode into the court-yard of a very grand-looking castle, on the out-skirts of England."

I began to appear as guest soloist with various church choirs. I went to all of the visiting D'Oyly Carte productions of Gilbert and Sullivan at the Royal Alexandra, and soon knew the music and lyrics well enough to alienate half our circle of friends. Once home I made watercolour sketches of the sets and costumes in a portfolio that I still cherish as primitive art. In the spring a kind artist named Miss Milnes took me on sketching trips and taught me to work in oils. My godfather, old D. L. Carley, had a beloved wife who was dying of cancer, and after school on Wednesdays, I used to bicycle over to visit Mrs. Carley as she dwindled into a bag of bones. She was always dressed for the occasion and sat on the living room couch, with her legs tucked under her, telling me funny stories. She taught me about dying.

But we were hiding from the inevitable. After staging an enormous pageant for the Anglican Church in the spring — another attempt to show devotion — Mother immediately turned to organizing our usual summer trip to Quebec.

In La Malbaie on the north shore of the St. Lawrence, known to the anglophone colony as Murray Bay, Father had a summer congregation consisting mainly of prosperous American Episcopalians staying at the nearby Manoir Richelieu. For the first time that year we travelled in a rented Model T Ford, for which, typically, Mother had obtained the driver's licence. On the drive into Quebec Fran and I narrowly escaped being killed as Father, with plenty of swagger but no licence, lost control of the brakes descending a steep hill; it was Mother, the nervous wreck, who had the presence of mind to reach for the hand brake. Once there we lived amid surrounding luxury in a small cabin with primitive facilities, in which Mother did all the housework while Father tended the souls of his flock. I earned pocket money at the golf course and once caddied for William Howard Taft, the mountainously fat ex-president of the United States and now chief justice of its Supreme Court. The experience turned me off golf for life. I also nearly died for the second time that summer. Unable to swim, I was thrown into the deep end of the hotel pool by a spoiled lout, sank the prescribed three times, and was restored to consciousness by the ministrations of his girlfriend. To this summer in La Malbaie I trace my chronic aversion to the idle rich and respect for the useful rich. At its end we drove back to Toronto — with Mother at the wheel.

After she got us there, she had a complete breakdown. She went first into hospital — for which Wilfrid paid the bills — then to stay with her mother in Ottawa (living there to be near Wilfrid), then to New York to stay with an old friend, Dr. Mary Lee Edwards, who nursed her back to health. Father, who in her absence lost no time in hiring a housekeeper, claimed she had abandoned her family. He began to preach sermons alluding to the heavy burden carried by those of us charged with loving and caring for the mentally disturbed. Mother consulted a lawyer, who advised her that she had no justifiable cause for divorce — adultery being then the sole legal ground — and in the event of separation might not, since she was the one to leave, be given custody of the children. She returned in March, just in time for Fran's 12th birthday and my 10th. Peter was then seven and a half.

THE YEAR 1929 is notable for many events, including the crash of the stock market, the Pact of Paris at the League of Nations, and the arrival of the talkies — probably in reverse order of lasting significance. But there are more important things in life. Nineteen twenty-nine was the year my pet squirrel died, and I wrote my "Ode to Skippy":

> Ah, do you know of squirrels that sit upon
> Your shoulder? Sleep, curled up, in open palm?
> That ride for miles inside your hat or on
> Your bicycle with perfect, unflushed calm?
> We had a squirrel that could do it.
> But now, wee Skippy's dead; yet living still

In our o'erburdened memories. Oh what a joy
He gave us with his squirrel-like antics, till
One morn we found him dead. Unlike a boy
I wept: we all wept — he was gone . . .

I can't go on.

Nineteen twenty-nine was also the year of my first encounter with a microphone — as a singer. CFCA, one of two private radio stations then in Toronto, presented our choir in a program of Christmas music, in which I sang Healey Willan's "Huron Carol." This was the station's bow to native talent. The motive for the Canadian content was the same then as it has been ever since: beating the rap. In its 1929 report, Canada's first Royal Commission on Radio Broadcasting, led by 73-year-old Sir John Aird, chairman of the Canadian Bank of Commerce, had just recommended the establishment of a publicly owned and operated system, and the political battle for control of the nation's communications was on. The commission had pointed a finger at the poor public service record of commercial stations affiliated with the U.S. networks, so the pirates had all rushed to put on holy orders for the duration. This flummery fooled few at the time, although it has succeeded in fooling many since.

But radio was only one crest of the 1929 revolution in arts technology that rearranged my options. The advent of talking pictures meant the abrupt decline of professional theatre across the entire continent. Since 1916, when the first silent feature films appeared, live theatre had been blithely painting itself into a corner with two popular dramatic forms better served by its upstart rival: naturalism and spectacle. When the sound track opened the way for full exploitation of the cinema's potential for both, theatre was deposed by its own gods. Little remained of its commercial empire in North America except the bastion of Broadway, and little of its artistic pretension except the scorned half-academic Art Theatre movement.

Its epitaph was written in 1929 by a Canadian, the same Roy Mitchell who had been Hart House Theatre's first director. His *Creative Theatre* was once called "maybe the best book ever written about the American theatre."[1] Published in the United States after Mitchell had moved there for good, it vigorously attacked both the "traders" who had debased theatre and the artists who had sold out to them. It cried for "a theatre keyed to the minds of those whose preoccupation in life is to make, leaving the cheaper, more prolific motion picture to serve those whose prevailing itch is to have." Foreshadowing many of the later approaches of Bertolt Brecht, Antonin Artaud, Tyrone Guthrie, Peter Brook, and Jerzy Grotowski, Mitchell saw drama as "the first of the methods of revelation . . . powerfully sacramental because it deals in communion, and . . . uses the cumulative power of the audience to perform its task." He also believed that theatre begins at home: "The most ancient principle of the arts is that it is better to use what you have, to build with native stone, to carve in native woods."

I was 20 before I met Mitchell, but by 1929 he had already mapped the decade in which I grew up. In that year Toronto's half-dozen resident stock companies collapsed. The directors, actors, and technicians went south (where things were not much better), found what other jobs they could in Toronto or, like the great Jane Mallett, turned amateur. I remember Alex McKee, a Canadian veteran of the North American stage, coming to our door peddling Bibles. Aside from vaudeville at Shea's Hippodrome and Loew's Uptown, road shows at the Royal Alex and Yiddish companies visiting the Standard on Spadina Avenue, the professional theatre vanished so swiftly that newcomers such as Lord Bessborough, when he became governor general in 1931, assumed it had never existed. In its place, in Toronto as elsewhere in Canada, arose an amateur movement of such impressive scope that in 1933 Bessborough founded the Dominion Drama Festival, giving official sanction to the growing belief that amateurism represented the very best Canadians could do. By the time I arrived at university in 1936, Hart House Theatre had become not a crucible for a new theatre, as Mitchell had wanted, nor even an experimental opportunity for students, but a vehicle for prominent amateurs who intended to keep it that way.

In 1929, however, there was still hope that from the ashes of Toronto's commercial theatre would rise a sacramental, mythic theatre of the sort envisioned by Roy Mitchell. Its prophet was the young high school teacher Herman Voaden, devotee of Eugene O'Neill and student of the European art theatre, who taught a three-nights-a-week course in modern drama in the University of Toronto's extension program. Inspired by the nationalist fervour of the Group of Seven painters, Voaden established a playwriting competition that led to the publication of Six Canadian Plays, and later to the Symphonic Theatre experiments of the 1930s, which made his name. Our paths had not yet crossed, but they were soon to cross and recross in the fields of both theatre and cultural politics, and finally to meld.

At home, where a nervous truce had reigned since Mother's return in the spring, I was aware of only a little of all this and understood less. In the long, hot summer of 1929 the domestic tension grew. We three boys were sent away to Camp Onondaga, run by an old Ridley School connection of Wilfrid's, on some sort of working holiday basis. Released from the strain at home, we energetically joined in every activity, drinking in the clear air, revelling in the water, exploring the trees — bristling spruces, white birches, red maples, dogwoods, fine elms, and basswoods — and ate like horses. We returned in August to find a considerable change in store.

Friends had persuaded Father it was time he took the initative in providing for his family's health and education. Perhaps inspired by the lifestyle of his tourist flock in Murray Bay, he had decided to go from one extreme to the other. He would show the Mavors what he was made of! Nothing would do for it but his sons had to attend the best of private boarding schools, and his wife become a lady of leisure. Of course, there was no money for such prodigality; but there were at that time certain school fee discounts available to children of the clergy, and he had another of his conscience-money schemes in mind. My godmother, the wealthy and devoutly Anglican Miss Marion Laidlaw of Queen's Park Crescent, had done little for her godson since receiving that honour; I seem to remember once having awkward tea at her mansion. Father proposed that she atone for this neglect by sending Francis and me to Upper Canada College. Peter was to bide his time.

The deal was struck, generously on my godmother's part, and after new outfits and caps and much labelling on mended shirts and socks, off we went in September to UCC Preparatory School, and sheer hell. The Prep was several cuts above Dotheboys Hall in Dickens's *Nicholas Nickleby*, I must say at once, and I have met graduates who ascribe my misfortunes there to bad luck. But the plots have certain similarities.

I had been used to a life full of enthusiasms and activities where self-discipline was a necessary ingredient and clothing, so long as it was decent, immaterial; here I was met with smothering routine, discipline imposed for its own sake, and judgement by uniform. Every morning the boys were paraded and inspected by the headmaster, Somerville by name and the Duke by nickname, a gentlemanly bully with a slight limp, for which he carried a cane known to be used for less amiable purposes. The matron, Mrs. Caddenhead by name and Cabbagehead by nickname, was tough, good-natured, and thoroughly intimidated by the Duke. The single friend I had was my form master, Mr. Beausire, a recently arrived and not yet disenchanted young Englishman who wrote short stories. I gave him ideas for several.

On rainy mornings we were expected to wear our rubbers for the parade. One day my left rubber was not to be found; the matron said not to worry, she would speak to the head, and to get on out there. The Duke stopped in front of me, pointed his cane at the missing article as if I had stepped in a cowpie, and invited me to visit his study immediately after parade. There without prelude he selected a birch rod and ordered me to lower my trousers. I protested that Matron had promised to explain. "Blame it on someone else, would you?" he said as he laid on. My chums laughed at the incident, and Cabbagehead said I must learn to accept injustice because life was full of it.

But two weeks later I got my own back. Put to bed in the infirmary with a fever that Cabbagehead suspected might mean influenza, I had a high old nightmare about fishing up north — suggested to my overheated brain by the dark green of the room, the thin wooden picture rail, and the pale blue wall above it, which became respectively water, fishing rod, and sky. My delirium caused such a panic that the Duke himself was called in to calm me and walked straight into the dream: I took him for a strong-arming gamekeeper and lit into him. Before waking up, I had given him a black eye in front of half a dozen boys and several of his staff. This popular and unpunishable feat made me the hero of the Prep for at least 24 hours.

The victory, however, was pyrrhic. In October 1929 Fran and I went gratefully home one weekend, and at dinner on Saturday night Father — obviously primed by the Duke — scolded us for failing to appreciate our good fortune in being at such a school. Peter made the mistake of thinking that was funny, which brought on all three of us a heated reminder of the sacrifices he was making to see that we were properly brought up. Mother wordlessly started taking plates into the kitchen. Father stormed upstairs to the bathroom. On his way back he kicked the terrier all the way downstairs, and Peter and I simultaneously cried, "You bastard!"

When all of us misbehaved, he would punish the oldest for not keeping the other two in line, and he went after Fran, who had said nothing, with his heavy walking stick. The dog's yelping, Fran's howls of denial, and Father's matching shouts of "Liar!" brought Mother from the kitchen. She marched across the room, seized the stick, and began to beat the astonished beater. He retreated, indignantly proclaiming his duty as a man of the cloth to teach boys to tell the truth, respect their elders, and fear God. Whereupon she reached into the bookshelf containing his precious *Encyclopedia of Religion and Ethics* and pitched volume 1 at his head, followed by volumes 2 through 10, until in self-defence he opened the front door and fled. She threw the stick after him and locked the door.

He returned early the following morning, Sunday, still keyless, and stood on the front lawn, demanding to be let in to get his clothes. She opened the second-floor bedroom window and one after the other tossed out his suits, shirts, underwear, and accessories — ending with his clerical collars — and a pair of old suitcases to put them in. I answered the telephone when he called later to say curtly, "Tell your mother I have taken a room at the university."

On Monday, after Fran and I had left for UCC, Mother had the lock changed. And soon after that — having allowed him back under treaty to clear out his effects — she closed the house and took Peter up to Ottawa to stay with his grandmother.

I was caned twice more — once, as I recall, for daydreaming — and Mr. Beausire had a row with the Duke over me that ended in his dismissal. I was desolate. In late November I became sick again and was still in bed when the school, including its infirmary, closed for the Christmas holidays. Fran had already left for Ottawa on his own. The Duke, by now convinced I was either a lunatic or a clever facsimile, allowed his wife to ensconce me in an alcove off their dining room until my removal could be arranged. I can remember only reading, reading, reading — anything in the bookcase by the bed, but especially a long, small-print edition of Charles Kingsley's *Hereward the Wake* with woodcut illustrations. By the time Mother came down from Ottawa and called in a doctor, I knew the Norman Conquest like the back of my spotted hand. It turned out that I had the mumps as well as the measles and a temperature of 105. Against all regulations, but to the infinite relief of the Duke and his Duchess, she immediately called a taxi and smuggled me onto the train to Ottawa, where I survived Christmas and stayed for the rest of the winter.

Just after my father left home, in October, the stock market had crashed. I failed to notice it. By the end of 1929, so far as I could see, the times had mightily improved.

3

In All Directions

SPRING HAD NO SOONER returned to Ottawa in 1930, bringing with it restored health, than it dawned on us that we were broke. The Great Depression was clearly worsening, but that was only half of the economic vise. My father — referred to thereafter by the initials P.A., as in Personal Appearance (rare) or Public Address (preaching as opposed to practice) — was also refusing to send any money. His justification, even after he changed his ways, was that withholding an allowance was his only means of enforcing access to his sons. The recently married Wilfrid was facing new responsibilities, and my grandmother had only a small apartment and a smaller pension. It was clear that Mother would have to find a job, and in Toronto.

The theatre profession she knew did not exist. The only other possibility was teaching, for which she had neither degree nor training. But when her Uncle Sam, the last of her father's engineer brothers and now head of the heavy equipment firm of Mavor & Coulson, invited her to Glasgow, she saw an opportunity to visit London and consult old contacts about recent theatre training methods. When Fran finished his year at UCC, we three boys were once more off-loaded on Onondaga Camp, to our great delight, and off she went. There, with the help of two dedicated swimming teachers, the West Indian McCatty brothers, I finally overcame the aquaphobia that had plagued me since the near-drowning in

Murray Bay and became an avid swimmer. The best source of strength, I was to discover, is often one's own weakness.

In the fall of 1930 we rented a duplex on Sheldrake Avenue while Mother sought to make ends meet. She taught drama in schools and directed student plays, and led courses at the YWCA in "Etiquette," which she hated, and in "The Art of Living," which she relished, perhaps because she was fast becoming an expert in it. Reviving her rusty French, she gave classes at Windy Ridge, the innovative primary school founded by the same Dr. Blatz for whom I had once played guinea pig. That autumn Herman Voaden in the University of Toronto extension program was looking for an acting coach and found that Dora had returned to town; they later formed the Hart House Touring Players to take Shakespeare into the high schools.

For all of these activities she conscripted "the boys" as elves. We typed out lists, stamped envelopes, made props and costumes, toted lighting equipment, and applied makeup to actors even less practised than we were. I have never forgotten being "head of props" when she and Healey Willan, in June 1931, mounted the North American premiere of Rutland Boughton's opera The Immortal Hour in a garden setting at the university; nor have its songs ever left my head.

But we had to earn our own money, as well. We made garden ornaments (brightly painted wooden birds on white sticks) and sold them door-to-door; we cut lawns and shovelled snow and delivered papers; and we charged admission for the bumbling puppet shows we put on, often involving neighbourhood chums such as the two lively McNaught kids, Kenneth and Lesley. On Sundays I sang in nearby St. Clement's Church ("Stainer, The Crucifixion: Master Mavor Moore") for 50 cents and played dibs along the hymnbook racks for penny bets during Dr. Nicholson's sermons. I sang with the Toronto Symphony Orchestra and the Mendelssohn Choir, among others, in Bach's St. Matthew Passion, conducted by Ernest MacMillan before he was promoted to Sir. For $10 I gave a Christmas concert at Ardwold, Lady Eaton's mansion near Casa Loma, where the changing room turned out to be a library of fine books with — to my gradually dawning horror — all their pages uncut.

The pages of the books at the Deer Park Public Library, where I worked after school on weekdays, were well thumbed. In love with romantic fiction, I here discovered the whole wide world of nonfiction — biography, history, philosophy, nature — to which I have remained attached. My guide was a veteran librarian, Miss Belcher, whom I

27

sometimes inadvertently addressed as Miss Burpee. This was the first symptom of a memory deficit in the name bank that has plagued me all my life, often bringing responses less good-natured than hers. ("Can't even remember my bloody name!" an indignant senior civil servant once shouted at me; he shall be nameless.) Had I, or psychiatry, been further advanced at the time, this flaw might have been flagged as a minor but telling sign of an obsessive-compulsive personality in the making.

For one year I attended the evolving St. Clement's School, run by Miss Conway and Miss Waugh — Laurel and Hardy in appearance but Gandhi and Churchill in character — which then still accepted a few boys in the junior grades. Dear Mrs. Hanley taught English literature with a soft Yorkshire accent and a hard ruler, and cast me in my first character role: Mr. Bennett in *Pride and Prejudice*. Mrs. Bennett was played by a splendidly wholesome classmate, Betty Sumner, whose name I shall never forget because I was directed to hold her hand for an entire scene, the lines of which have escaped me ever since. At the end of the year St. Clement's, possibly prompted by my intrusion, declared that it would take no more boys and be henceforth a school for girls only. That is how I came to be a St. Clement's Old Girl.

In July 1931 I returned to Onondaga as a junior counsellor, teaching handicrafts and staging plays. Mixing every day with six-year-olds, I discovered the unnerving ability of the very young to parody their elders, which I later used in writing topical comedy. And for the first time, singing the female role of Yum-Yum in *The Mikado*, I experienced the perverse thrill of finding oneself the object of helpless laughter.

That fall, thanks to Grandmother's pension and a small allowance from Wilfrid, we rented a frame bungalow on Walmsley Boulevard that became our first real home. The house itself was tiny, but it had a garden with an apple tree and a grapevine, and a shack where we kept rabbits and white mice while the dog and/or cat lived in the basement. We papered and painted every room with inexpert affection, and in these bohemian quarters welcomed, along with friends and neighbours, many a bewildered foreign visitor. Sir Barry Jackson brought along half his Birmingham Repertory Company, then performing at the Royal Alexandra, including a florid young narcissus named Donald Wolfit. There were two written rules of the house: "No wrestling in the living room!" and "Projects off the table before dinner!" — and one unwritten: "When Mum has one of her spells, let Meem cope." Meem, deriving not from Wagner's dwarf but from Fran's early attempts to pronounce Mavor, was my first and only nickname. Mother's occasional depressions required only a gentle talking-out from the dark cave; but the therapy, as so often happens in amateur psychoanalysis, compromised the therapist. In time these rules became redundant, although the dining room table long remained the scene of heavy industry.

Across the street lived a parody of bourgeois families, with a beer-swilling sausage of a father, home like clockwork at 5:30 to start drinking, and a henna-haired mother who shortly afterward would storm onto the porch in her bursting corset, negligee flying, to scream at her vagrant daughters: "Doreen! Francine! Get back in here or you get the hairbrush!" Up the street on the same side, in a dark old town house, lived a childless couple straight out of Chekhov: he a retired colonel up to nothing more strenuous than daily walks; she a once-upon-a-time aspiring actress unwilling to let him forget the day 20 years ago when she turned 18 and gave it all up to marry a handsome soldier, and look at him now. "I could have set Broadway on fire!" she would say dramatically as she passed the sandwiches, and he would nod in silent confirmation of their mutual tragedy. Across from the town house, in a second-floor bachelor flat, lived the exotic William Manifold Gibson, reporter for the *Globe*, only son of a chief justice of Ireland, penitent roué, impenitent literateur, who played an oddly influential role in our lives for a few years.

As a youth, Gibson had been kidnapped by the Irish Republican Army, with whom his father refused to treat, and rescued from a firing squad by the British Black and Tans. Later he left Oxford University under a cloud — a scandal connected with a murder committed in his rooms by a friend — and was dispatched to the colony with a small monthly remittance that went on fine wines and finer clothes. Otherwise he scraped by on his meagre journalist's salary, subsisting with mortifying frugality while tucking his immaculate handkerchief up his left sleeve. In Toronto he was a resident alien, unhappy when his eccentricity was ignored and equally unhappy when it was noticed. At our place, where eccentricity was taken for granted, he felt at home.

He was a dozen years her junior, but we all knew that Willie Gibson was hopelessly in love with Mother. She treated him gratefully and thoughtfully in return, but as a prodigal son, not a suitor. He was expected to earn his return passage to Respectability by making himself useful, like many another lame duck, in her various good causes — teaching, for example, at the Workers' Educational Association. To her, in the light of her failed marriage, all men were on probation. A liaison was out of the question and remarriage out of court. She and Father were merely legally separated, and never thereafter divorced. Adultery being the only actionable fault, he had no cause to divorce her and she, with or without cause, had no intention of ruining a clergyman. Her sense of betrayal was acute, but she was uninterested either in compensation from another man or in vengeance on men in general. She had three sons to raise and became very clever at finding surrogate father figures for them — most often upright teachers, camp counsellors, and the like. But as a role model for young teenagers, the sophisticated Willie was quite another matter.

He would disappear on benders and then regale us with his misadventures — except for the winter night he tried to drown himself off the Bay Street docks, which we learned about only because the police who hauled him out found Mother's name and telephone number in his pocket.[1] He would present us with smart New York or London magazines and urbane bestsellers (publishers' copies, I now realize, from his newspaper reviewing), take us to exhibitions of avant-garde paintings, and bequeath us his stylish suits to be cut down and taken in. In 1939, after we had moved to another part of town and our paths had diverged, the aristocratic William Manifold Gibson went off to war as a private. He sent us witty postcards from Britain. He was killed in the first assault on the beach at Dieppe, in a heroic dash that a comrade described as deliberate suicide. He left me something of his brittle sense of humour, his love of risk, his itch for new ideas, and his old suits. Together they saw me through high school, and beyond.

The University of Toronto Schools, called UTS to distinguish the offspring from the parent, is a peculiar institution designed to give hands-on classroom experience to teachers-in-training at the university. It also differs from other public high schools in requiring an entrance examination and token fees, and when I went there in the 1930s, it was still for boys only, perhaps on the dubious premise that an apprentice teacher of either sex able to handle a roomful of teenage boys could handle anything. Staffed by master teachers under a principal understood to be next in line for dean of education, it maintained a demanding academic standard and a curriculum with unusual emphasis, for the times, on the arts and innovative areas such as sex education. Far less subject than the boys' or girls' private schools to economic and racial favouritism, let alone religious bias, it also boasted a student body more representative of the cosmopolis Toronto was becoming.

When St. Clement's said goodbye to its boys in 1932, Mother applied to get both Fran and me into UTS, warning me before the entrance exam that she could not afford even the token fees for two boys, and as I had the better chance to win a scholarship, I had better do so. The combination of flattery and blackmail worked. And here I found, at 12, an environment sufficiently settled and stimulating to emerge from my coccoon and start (as a later generation would say) to get my act together — a process still incomplete as I write. Fran's brief experience there was less happy, and Peter, who felt about schools as foxes do about hunts, entered UTS later only to feel trapped.

Before the fall term commenced I finished my first complete one-act play — and the first to be produced. Mother, seeking a play for the Eaton Girls' Dramatic Club, had complained about the lack of works with all-female casts. "I'll write you one," said I, with the megalomania befitting a recent scholarship winner. I was much taken at the time with the legend of Pandora's Box and had a vision of the Eaton's salesladies in diaphanous shifts traipsing wraithlike out of a huge trunk to something by Ravel. The preface, here abridged for humanitarian reasons, will give you the picture:

> In this play no property or scenery is used. The words are said entirely by the chorus and their leader, a sybil. The others say to her, "Speak, for thou seest where we cannot see." The parts of the Mortals and of the god Hermes (*obviously a Hermaphrodite. Ed.*) are shown in mime. The ball with which he tempts Pandora, and the Box, you must picture in your imagination. When the troubles are freed and all despair, the leader says, "Evil must dwell with good, ere it can pass, but it will pass!" . . . She tells Pandora to open the Box again. This time Hope appears, there is a Dance of Happiness, and the play ends with these effective words:
>
>> "But Hope will live 'midst worldly grind,
>> The last resort of Human Kind."[2]

The single performance was greeted with great acclaim by its audience of hopeful friends and relatives. I mention *Pandora*, however, not to rescue genius from well-deserved oblivion but to show at what a tender age I had already become a shameless optimist, gambler, and plagiarist.

At UTS all three of these bad habits were confirmed.

To E. L. Daniher, who taught Canadian history with an affectionate sense of its comic possibilities, I owe my lengthy addiction to optimism — only now in remission. Until then my life had been nothing if not a worldly grind; but Daniher argued from our country's history that even the worst can turn out for the best, otherwise we would not be there in his splendid classroom listening to his pearls of wisdom.

Canada, he explained — at a time when the explanation was heresy — had always been a nation of losers. The natives lost to the French, who lost to the English, who were outsmarted by the Scots, who were outnumbered by the losers fleeing the American Revolution, who gave way to the losers from war-torn Europe. But this desperate pact among failures, claimed Daniher, is a beacon of hope to a disjointed world, proving that the most illogical of federations — one divided by geography, climate, ethnicity, language, religion, culture, and economy, and run alternately by jackasses and crooks — can become a successful modern state. Even if the present Canada were to fall apart in the distant future, another equally illogical solution will replace it; and in the meantime our history stands as an enduring testimonial to the triumph of implausibility over expectation. Many years later, when I heard about the British historian who sneered at the Canadian historian, "And what do you do in the afternoons?" I imagined Danny replying, with a sweet smile, "Shoot snobs."

It was Joe Gill, the redheaded, red-faced young modern history and English teacher, who made a confirmed gambler out of me. He did this by demonstrating the advantages of poker as a teaching method. I have used it ever since. Gill's strategy, even when he was dead sober, was to lie with a straight face and dare you to catch him at it. Not that he hadn't learned his subject the hard way; he was just damned if you were going to learn it the easy way.

"Now when Wellington defeated Napoleon at the Battle of Austerlitz . . ." he would say, with a breath's pause to allow hands to shoot up, then, "Yes, Campbell?"

"It wasn't Austerlitz, sir. It was Waterloo!"

"Who told you that?"

"Everybody knows that, sir."

"Don't be a smart-ass, Campbell" — this to Ross Campbell, destined to be head of Atomic Energy of Canada and ambassador to NATO. "Have you looked it up?"

"It's right here somewhere — "

"Tell us when you've found it, not before. And never listen to what everybody says. Everybody's wrong half the time, including me. Anyway, when Wellington beat Napoleon at the Battle of Whatever in 1812 — What's biting you, Grange?"

"With respect, sir, it wasn't 1812!" — from Sammy Grange, later a justice of the Supreme Court of Ontario.

"Then when was it? Oh, shut up, Grange. Careless, when was it?"

"I think it was 1815."

"You *think?* Not good enough, Careless. Look it up!" — this to Maurice Careless, soon to be a legend among Canadian historians for his accuracy. "Anybody know the month?" No hands raised. "I'll lay you a nickle it was March. What's Spain like in March? All right, Campbell, what's it say?"

"Waterloo, sir, and it's not in Spain. It's in Belgium."

"Well, there you go. Now after his defeat Napoleon was sent to the Isle of Able."

"No, sir! Elba, sir!" Heated interjection from Bob Rogers, future lieutenant governor of British Columbia and chancellor of the University of Victoria.

"Simmer down. I just got it backward. Anyone know what a paradrome is?"

"Pal-in-drome, sir!" — from Barry McKelvey, future world-famous heart surgeon.

"Don't get fancy with me, son." Then, picking up the chalk, Gill would ask, "How do you spell that?"

This was enlightenment by disinformation. He was teaching not facts but critical thinking — leading the shy to question the premises of the confident and the confident to check their own. None of us would ever forget Waterloo, Belgium, 1815 — but that was only the beginning. Those tricked into looking up the weather would get sucked into astronomy, military tactics, European history, political philosophy, *War and Peace.* "Able was I ere I saw Elba" drew many of us into more complex linguistic and literary games, and all of us learned how to use reference works. And, of course, how to play poker and a mean game of bridge.

As for plagiarism, it was also at UTS that I first became aware of the possibilities inherent in *Bartlett's Familiar Quotations* and other anthologies of profundities. I invented a system for passing exams that consisted of memorizing enigmatic aphorisms from arcane authors ("As Simonides of Ceos used to say . . .") and working them into the answers. Although

useless for Johnny Workman's math tests, the quotations worked splendidly almost everywhere else, especially when given in the original Latin
or Greek, which I had begun to study. Since they were accurate, in the
unlikely event that the teacher had the time or inclination to check them,
the scheme was almost foolproof — and at year's end I was skipped
ahead one grade despite dismal marks in the maths and sciences. I got
away with this ruse until one day canny old Charlie Phillips, our ancient
history teacher, failed my paper with the blunt inscription: "Ignorance
dressed in silks and velvets." But I have never been able to shake the habit
altogether. My later essays are often garnished with others' epigrams,
and now that my own appear in books of Canadian quotations I have
taken to stealing from myself.

The truth is that even then I recognized the gambit, uneasily, as one
of my father's. Was I really free to choose my own path, as Bill Blatz had
assured me?

In the winter of 1931 Father was still working with the Student
Christian Movement at the university and taking us out on occasional
weekends. We usually proposed a movie, as it limited the time available
for conversation. Then, after the show, he would hand each of us a $2
bill, while still sending Mother no allowance. My own earning power had
markedly diminished since Sunday, June 20, 1931, when my voice broke
on the high G of Handel's "Angels Ever Bright and Fair" in the full glare
of the congregation. Despite such makeshifts as delivering papers and
earning lunch by working in the school cafeteria, I was hard up. That fall
Father left for Cincinnati, Ohio, where he had secured a position at Christ
Church Cathedral, an Episcopalian shrine supported by the influential Taft
family, whose acquaintance he had cultivated during summers at Murray
Bay. Back in Toronto we were selling off the remaining pieces of Mavor
family silver at Ward Price, the auctioneers. They charged a fee to erase
the initial "M." *Change the name and not the letter* . . .

Early in 1933, 16-year-old Fran, whose mechanical bent was now
irreversible, left for Glasgow to become an apprentice engineer at Mavor
& Coulson, living under the care of his great-uncle Sam and three maiden
great-aunts. Mother was grateful for their beneficence, hopeful she was
doing the right thing for Fran, but fearful of the gap in generations and
cultures. In order to raise at least some funds for the rest of us in Toronto,
her brother Wilfrid took the drastic step of suing the Reverend F. J. Moore
for his sister's substantial medical expenses. The Reverend Mr. Moore then
lodged a countersuit for "alienation of affection," a rare if briefly fashion-

able form of litigation, alleging that Major Wilfrid Mavor, while pretending to mediate, had, in fact, poisoned the wife's mind against the husband. When both cases came to trial in Toronto, just after my 14th birthday, I made my first appearance in a courtroom scene.

I must let my father speak from his own memory of the event, in a letter he wrote to me in 1946, the last word in the last exchange we ever had:

> All I asked of you in my last letter was to consider that a fuller knowledge of the facts might conceivably broaden your point of view. . . . In [your] last letter, however, you specify a particular instance which comes within your own direct experience. Here you are entitled to an answer, and you shall have it. I have regretted, ever since it happened, that an action of mine should have led to your being brought into Court, with Peter. I did not bring you into Court; but I was the cause, unintentionally, of your being brought in. It was only at the last moment that I knew you were to be there; and I should have called the whole thing off then, and accepted the situation. That I did not, I have always, as I said, regretted, and have been sorry for it. I express my sorrow now, and especially for the suffering which it caused you.
>
> Why did I not say so before? First, because there was an agreement in the separation agreement that neither side should discuss the situation with the children; and I felt, rightly or wrongly, that if I said anything at all I might say too much. Secondly, you yourself caused heartbreak that day. You spoke of me in such a bitter way that made even the judge look up, and that would have been agony even for the worst father on record to hear. I need not remind you of what you said. [Under cross-examination I apparently said, " He can go straight to hell."] Afterwards, if I had spoken at all, I could not have helped but remind you of that. And I dared to hope that some suffering word might come from you. But neither you nor I said anything, and time went on. . . .
>
> You are kind enough to say that, like Francis and Peter, you are grateful for what I am doing now. [The separation agreement resulting from the trial obliged him to set up a $1,000 trust account for his children and send his wife a small monthly allowance.] I have always wanted to do what I am doing now, and hope to be able to keep on doing it.[3]

And he did until he died in 1968. But what is one to do with a man who has to be forced to do what he says he "always wanted to do?" At the time I doubted that he would maintain a bargain made under duress, so I denied him the benefit of the doubt. So did my darling grandmother, Christina, who died before the trial ended, blaming herself for having talked Dora into marrying him in the first place.

THE MAIN REASON I made so bold at the trial was that a few weeks earlier I had become financially independent, in a manner of speaking. My school chum Douglas Hicks and I won auditions to play the teenage heroes in The Crusoe Boys, a daily adventure serial on a private radio station, advertising a cereal of the other kind. For a dollar a day, Monday to Friday, we dashed to rehearsal after school and performed the show live, in fierce competition with the U.S. networks and under constant threat of cancellation by the nervous sponsor. To encourage him Doug and I spent hours on the phone dunning our friends' mothers to buy the cereal and mail in the box tops.

This tough commercial mill was my first training ground in radio, and in 1933 I knew no other. What I cared about was that The Crusoe Boys was written and produced by Canadians for Canadians and we were going to make it work. My awareness of the long parliamentary battle over publicly financed broadcasting was vague. Within two years I was performing for the newly established Canadian Radio Broadcasting Commission; but I evenhandedly applauded all efforts, public or private, to give Canadians access to production as well as reception. Many of our proudest early programs, symphonies as well as sports, were launched by sponsors such as the Canadian Pacific Railway and Imperial Oil. On the face of a Crusoe Boys script I jotted down: "The first rule of art is to get it DONE. Who pays for it hardly matters as long as SOMEBODY does." This sensible proposition, openly stolen from Robert Browning's The Pied Piper, is one I still support. Doing so has earned me the censure of political dogmatists of both left and right, and the scorn of the self-anointed realists who believe society should pay now and fly later, maybe.

We were learning to fly, moreover, by inventing the rules as we went and racing to improve them before they hardened into rulers. More than any other, this early experience convinced me that the most exciting challenge in life is to break new ground. The earthy figure of speech is far from accidental; I had spent the previous summer as a farmhand on Colonel D. H. C. Mason's spread near Georgetown, Ontario, where I began to understand the Latin root meaning of *culture* — preparation for growth, as in *agriculture*. This is a sense of the word now subverted by the anthropologists, who have adopted it as a synonym for civilization, the sociologists, who use it to mean lifestyle, and the business community, who abuse it to mean company practice. But it is one still preserved in the school, the laboratory, and the farm, where the virtue of fertilizer is appreciated. *The Crusoe Boys* was fertilizer. Ever since I have had no patience with those who maintain that culture occurs spontaneously. Any farmer knows that culture is the way you make things happen.

In Canada during the Depression, moreover, it was obvious that plenty had to be made happen. Broadcasting and writing were among the most auspicious cultural mediums — no one then used the umbrella plural *media*, now widely used as if it were singular — but all the arts held possibilities, and several of them were already productive. Unsure which field I most wanted to enter and, in fact, seeing no necessity to choose yet, I emulated Stephen Leacock's hero and rode madly off in all directions.

When my voice broke, I had given up on singing (or vice-versa), but not on music. And I was lucky enough to have at St. Clement's Church a choirmaster alert to my need to find another instrument. Dugald Henderson was a giant of a Scot with huge hands, who had studied piano in London under the virtuoso Mark Hambourg, the oldest of four remarkable musical brothers. The second was the violinist Jan. The two youngest had already landed in Toronto: cellist Boris to join the new Hart House String Quartet and found the Hambourg Conservatory, and pianist Clement, always in the shadow of the mighty Mark, to drift into the nightclub scene and emerge as one of the fathers of Toronto jazz. Henderson's Presbyterian father, foreseeing a similar slide into the pit for his piano-playing son, had insisted he learn an honest trade; so the young man left his concert career to become a civil engineer, married and emigrated to Canada. By the time I knew him he was in charge of Toronto's sewer system. On weekends he escaped from the sewers to play the church organ.

Henderson took no regular piano pupils; his hours at home with his piano were a communion rite inviolable by others, even his wife. When we began our weekly sessions, he made it clear there would be no fee; I was to repay him by becoming an acolyte in his ritual. He knew of my basic training under a sound conservatory teacher, and of her impatience with my impatience: I neglected Czerny's exercises in favour of my own songs, understandable in a singer newly robbed of his voice. Henderson came at it another way. He encouraged me to make my own music, but showed me how much better it could be if I did thus and so — in order to do which, of course, I must master keys, scales, and fingering, and that was where Czerny might help, so let's try him. Afterward I would sit and listen, while in a transport of joyful torment the master played the most delicate Mozart or the most crashing Liszt until he bowed his head and said, "Thank you," and I knew it was time to leave.

But too many ambient challenges distracted me. I lacked the single-mindedness necessary to master a musical instrument, and to this day envy those who have it. Instead I had a sort of pattern-mindedness, attached more to composition than components. I went to study composition with Mrs. Healey Willan, the less celebrated wife of Toronto's most celebrated composer-teacher, who did her good best to focus my efforts. But when Gladys Willan showed Healey a composition of mine grandly titled *Capriccio*, he scribbled a snort on the manuscript: "Even a caprice must have form of a sort." It was an epitaph for my youth. Perhaps for my life.

Prodded by Willie Gibson, I had submitted an intense short story and several hilarious jokes to *The New Yorker*, and blamed the ensuing silence on the editors' failure to appreciate Canadian sensibilities. I became an instant convert to nationalism and sent the same story to *Maclean's, Saturday Night*, and *The Canadian Forum*, from all of whom I received at least the courtesy of prompt rejection slips. In 1934, needing a summer job, I phoned the *Maclean's* editor who had signed the slip and asked to interview him for the school magazine on Journalism as a Career. He fell for it and, during the interview, I delicately inquired about other, perhaps less dignified, employment opportunities — in fact, anything going. No Gallup Poll then existing, I was hired on commission to make a house-to-house survey in Guelph, Ontario, to establish for the magazine's advertisers the buying patterns of its middle-class subscribers. My assignment was to list the cars, radios, refrigerators, washing machines, et cetera, at given addresses. I have paid little heed to polls ever since.

This is not due to mistrust of pollsters. My first finding among the good citizens of Guelph was that when questioned about their personal possessions, habits, and tastes most people like to lie — from vanity, shame, suspicion of the questioner's motives, or the sheer fun of dangling strangers on a string. My second was that human targets are moving targets; households are hotbeds of comings and goings, additions and subtractions. My third was that for an honest, up-to-date profile of a person or a family one must ask not the subject but the neighbours.

After a walking canvass of 40 or 50 homes, many of them unattended, I hit upon a marvellous shortcut — the corner storekeeper. For a handful of small change and an hour of small talk I could learn all I needed in one place. One such mine of information was an old fellow who had, he said, helped Edison invent the telegraph and watched Strathcona drive the last spike of the CPR. Between my arrival and that of the Jehovah's Witness lady who preempted the conversation, he put his boots up on the counter and filled me in as he pared his fingernails with a pocketknife:

> Mrs. Bennett? She got no car. Nephew Fred's got a car, '29 Ford, lives over to Kitchener? No radio, calls it a sin. She got a old gramophone, I think it's bust now. Her daughter Lou, she's in 142? She got the sewing machine. Number 63 . . . that's Wuppert? . . . they split, twenty-fourth a May. She got the house, the fridge and the kids. He got the car, the radio and the boat? a bargain. Art Frewer at 101, he'd be on your list. Died last week, liver? He got a car, old blue Pontiac, '26. You wan it?

I made a story out of him, including his scant courtesy to the Jehovah's Witness and her biblical quotations ("You know that place where it says, 'And Judas went and hanged himself'? — and you know where it says, 'Go thou and do likewise'?), but *Maclean's* showed no interest. The story would have sunk the survey.

The following summer, 1935, I tried another field. Dissatisfied with my random drawing and painting, I had been attending the classes of Arthur Lismer, the most notable pedagogue among the Group of Seven, and at 16 had a portfolio varied enough to talk myself into a job at the Art Gallery of Toronto. My two-month task, at $5 a week, was to catalogue its largely unsorted print collection, which owed more to chance donation than to selective purchase. My ignorance of art history was outstanding, but thanks to Grandfather's battered 1911 encyclopedia, the public library, and the reference works in the adjoining Grange (once home to Goldwin Smith), I managed to identify three rare works by the 17th-century French engraver Claude Lorrain that the gallery was unaware it had. This feat engulfed me in a wave of celebrity unequalled since the night I gave the headmaster of the UCC Prep a black eye. It also led to the first of the big forks in the pilgrim's road.

AT SCHOOL, MEANTIME, there was a variety of extracurricular activities, including the usual handball, cosmic debates, and kissless dates with friends' sisters. Sisterless myself, I was accustomed to girls as companions at work and play, but as an opposite sex found them beyond me in both senses: hard to read and hard to reach. It was not just that I was severely nearsighted; in the presence of these inner-directed deities I felt like a fish, unable to see anything above or ahead but only below or to the sides. Intimacy with them, I assumed, was possible only when they were conned into taking leave of their wits, and I wanted no part of such dirty tricks. The nobler excitement of literary and dramatic affairs was quite enough for me at the moment. And apart from the school magazine, The Twig ("As the twig, so the branch"), for which I wrote and was later an editor, the most stimulating of all affairs at UTS was the annual classical play.

If my experiences to date had left a few internal scars, the new lot were highly visible. In successive years I managed to get my left hand skewered by a rapier during a fencing match in The Rivals, my right thumb almost severed on a broken bottle in Henry IV, Part I, and my skull cracked open in Macbeth. A decade later it occurred to me that somebody had been trying to tell me something. But at the time these wounds were battle honours, and I would never have pleaded the truthful excuse, which was that without glasses I was too myopic to see them coming. How often since then have I tried to rekindle Faulkland's surprise at the intrusion of actuality into his make-believe duel, the roar of laughter at Falstaff's double take when he saw red wine coming out of his hand instead of the bottle, or the tumultuous curtain call greeting Macbeth's slow realization that the liquid trickling into his eyes and his mouth was not sweat! Without any formal training as an actor, having imbibed all I knew from working with others, from visiting classical stars such as England's Martin Harvey and America's Walter Hampton or from watching Hollywood films, I was certain of only one thing: I had tasted blood.

UTS, under Joe Gill's spur, was not the only Toronto school to mount such ambitious productions in the 1930s. For a time there was as much rivalry between the theatre teams as the hockey teams. At nearby Harbord Collegiate, conductor Brian McCool presented annual Gilbert and Sullivan musicals with great comic flair. Do you mean to tell me you missed The Gondoliers and the debut of Johnny Wayne (then Lou Weingarten) and Frank Shuster as the Duke of Plaza Toro and the Grand Inquisitor? It was the birth of a notion: what New York Times critic Jack

Gould would later designate "literate slapstick." Upper Canada College also had a lively tradition of all-male Shakespearean revivals. And if you failed to catch young Robertson Davies's Malvolio, you will never fully understand the quintessence of his novels.

From these and other productions in public and private schools, both boys' and girls', emerged a generation of actors, musicians, and technicians to lead the transformation in Toronto theatre, radio, and television that followed World War II. But they also greatly increased awareness of the arts among future lawyers, business and labour leaders, physicians, and politicians. My UTS programs are yellow with age, and many of the cast there listed died in the war that followed their graduation. But imagine! *The Rivals'* apoplectic Sir Anthony Absolute was only the steelworkers' smooth union negotiator Murray Cotterill in disguise! My diplomatic Julia, Douglas Hicks, became a diplomat. Her friend Lydia Languish was none other than Charlie Walker, distinguished economist, while her handsome Captain Absolute, Harry Tattersall, really did become a soldier. My seductive Lady Macbeth, compulsively washing her hands, was Robert Cameron, who went into advertising. The Macduff who split my skull, Ralph Sturgeon, appropriately became a surgeon. The heroic Malcolm mellowed into federal mandarin Tom Fletcher. The First Murderer transformed himself into that eminent barrister John Clarry, Q.C., and that incompetent old general Siward developed into the resourceful entrepreneur, politician, and Chief Boy Scout of Canada, Donald Deacon! To know this is to grasp the deep roots of the cultural transformation in the wider community.

Many of my close companions in these UTS ventures were in the year ahead of mine, and were soon due to graduate and go on to university. I wanted desperately to go with them. In February 1936 I approached the principal to see whether I could possibly matriculate a year early. I learned that such a thing had never been suggested before, and that consequently there was no rule against it. The main penalty would be the loss of any university scholarship at which, with longer preparation, I might have had a chance. The question was only whether I was up to it — whether in less than four months I could master more than a year's work.

For me to do so in the maths and sciences would have been impossible. Since childhood I had resisted with all my being the imperious certainties of both numbers and natural law. Algebra I saw as a labyrinthine trap. My fury at the constraints of geometry compelled me once to spend a whole week and a hundred crumpled pages trying to disprove the theorem about the hypotenuse of right-angled triangles. To my impatient imagination physics was far less interesting than metaphysics, which may have been the reason I once led the affirmative side in a school debate: "Resolved that numbness is a feeling." As far as I was concerned, the hole was always worthier of attention than the doughnut.

But I found that I could cover the necessary nine subjects without a single math or science, although that, likewise, had never been done before in Ontario: two English (language and composition), two French, two Latin, two Greek and modern history. Of these I was weakest in the classics, and sought the advice of old Daddy Mills, the classics master, who shook his head in all directions, said dryly, "Moore, you can do anything you want if you want to hard enough," and offered to coach me.

I have since recognized this homily as one of the most foolhardy ever coined. It usually leads straight down the garden path to one of those catastrophes we afterward call a learning experience. But at that age I swallowed it whole. My plan to sit all my senior matriculation examinations in June 1936 was officially approved, and on March 5, just before I turned 17, I confided to my diary: "Tuition started with Mr. Mills. Very hard work from now on." The strength of my determination may be gauged from the previous entry, only four nights earlier: "School dance! Beth!" Apparently I put all other pursuits aside.

In early May, however, I received a letter from H. O. McCurry, the assistant curator of the National Gallery of Canada in Ottawa, with an astonishing proposition. In the half century since its founding in 1880 the National Gallery had acquired a large number of old European masterworks in addition to its growing Canadian collection and was now faced with the problem of maintaining them. McCurry, apparently informed of my work the previous summer at the Art Gallery of Toronto, asked if I would consider, upon graduation from high school, an offer from the National Gallery to put me through an entire education in art restoration — the University of London, the famous Courtauld Institute, postgraduate studies in Paris and Boston — on the sole condition that I join the National Gallery at its conclusion.

I could not decide whether this intervention was divine or — like the Faustian indenture that bound my father to the Anglican Church — demonic.

4

Awakening

EARLY IN 1936 I started to keep an occasional diary.[1] The year had not begun well. My first note, under January 21, was: "King George V dies. World mourns & even I feel depressed. Edward VIII proclaimed King." I no longer know whether this meant that all people, including the humblest, lamented this blow to monarchy, or that even a republican must mourn the loss of George because the thought of Edward was so depressing. But the double solipsism — the world and I sharing the same political focus — lasted exactly three days or until the next entry: "Read *Mazzini* last night."

For some reason, possibly hormonal, the 19th-century Italian patriot's struggle to align differing cultures in a single frame shattered my simplistic lens. I began to think furiously about diverse points of view and how they challenge politics (of whatever colour) to accommodate them. This was the first intimation I had of the unfashionable theory that politics wait on culture, not vice versa, which I have since upheld. It obviously reflected, at the time, a subconscious need to come to grips with my own diversity of interests. Other influences were driving me into the same centrifugal frame of mind. I had acquired a taste for black jazz and Japanese calligraphy. My close encounter with *Macbeth* aroused curiosity about my Scottish heritage. The Witches' curse (diary, February 16: "Macbeth — 11 stitches") naturally gave me a keen interest in alternative religion. In short, I developed an international itch, along with a common symptom of disenchanted nationalism: the pinched nerve. Under March 14 the diary has: "Saw Voaden's Play Workshop — something to think about but rather poorly acted." Not for the last time, I wondered whether the local garden was worth all the effort Voaden and others were putting into it, and wanted out. This was before I had read Voltaire's *Candide*.

At a less disoriented moment I might have declined the National Gallery's generous offer at once. But my first thought was that I could not afford to. My second was that I could not bear separation from my friends heading for the University of Toronto to change the world from that unlikely base. My third drove me back to the first; short of the miracle of winning a prize with my premature ejaculation from high school, I had no means to pay for a university education anywhere. But then it dawned on me that the decision was premature. There was, after all, a critical path involved — on which the first hurdle was to pass the Ontario exams that lay like sleeping gorgons only six weeks away.

To complicate matters further, Mother was concocting a plan to transport us all to Britain that summer. Fran had now been in Glasgow for three of the four years of his apprenticeship; the combination of on-the-job training, unfamiliar schooling, and domestic life with spiky if benevolent senior relatives had sapped his health. Mother, convinced that the best tonic was not withdrawal but the satisfaction of completing his final year, proposed that the family pick him up in Scotland and go down to London for a holiday. As usual, she had figured out the finances with great ingenuity — aided by the news that my athletic brother Peter, now 14, had won a place on a schoolboy cricket team subsidized to attend the 1936 Berlin Olympics. She arranged a London–Toronto house swap with her friend Margaret Hayes, recently divorced from the actor George Hayes, who was leaving her Twickenham flat to return to Canada with her son and daughter.[2] I was attached, for the voyage only, to the Overseas Education League's exchange students. And on June 26 — the dreaded exams over but the results unknown — Mother and two sons set sail on the *Duchess of Atholl*, bound for Glasgow.

MY GRANDFATHER'S GENERATION OF MAVORS was now reduced to a brother and three sisters, living in a handsome old terrace house in Crown Gardens. All but one of James's four younger brothers had predeceased him, including the youngest, Alfred, a brilliant charmer who had run off to London, made a mint from inventing a freewheel bicycle, married a rich beauty, squandered both fortunes, and died of malaria after attempting a comeback as a tea grower in Ceylon. By 1936 the surviving brother, now patriarch, was 73-year-old Sam, a short, genial engineer with vested corporation and trim beard, whose past included a stint as a captain in the Japanese navy and exotic travels in the South Pacific. He was a confirmed bachelor — a condition stemming, apparently, from a promise made to his dying mother to "look after the girls." (Sam was as good as his word; on his death in 1943 he left a substantial bequest to a Mrs. Black and her daughter, both of them said to be faithful and kind, who lived modestly on the outskirts of the city.)

"The girls" were Isabella, Mary Ann (Nan), and Jessie. They were well-travelled and vital women. Nan was a linguist, Jessie a musician. As a young missionary in Africa, Isabella had caught typhoid fever and lost all her hair; now 75 she wore an ill-fitting wig and was supposed to be more than slightly potty. Fran always maintained she was the sanest of the three, pretending idiocy only to confound the tyranny of her younger sisters. He once observed her reading, when on Jessie's approach she deliberately turned the book upside down and skewed her wig. This daft behaviour gave her sisters a cross to bear for which, having so few, they must have been privately grateful. Nan and Jessie had long since come to terms with living comfortably at home, because no man offering an alternative had ever been found acceptable. Like many of their contemporaries, they had grown bossy from uselessness; but their hearts were in the right place, and there we found them.

The summer residence in which we stayed with the Aunts was a mansion on the Black Douglas estate in Dumbartonshire, parts of which dated back to 1300. Outside of the movies I had never seen anything like it. In Ontario any building a quarter as old was a historic site. Standing amid smaller lodges like a manor house with pups, The Mains was surrounded by velvet lawns, ancient trees, and magnificent flower and vegetable gardens. A child could tell it was haunted. The entrance hall was guarded by suits of armour and the stairwell by portraits of the mighty dead. "My bedroom is palatial," Mother wrote to a friend in Toronto. "The bed itself is a four-poster with drapes so big I feel as if at least three other people ought to be sharing it with me! Peter says his room is 'spooky' and wants to sleep with me. Needless to say we are all on our best behaviour and trying out our best party manners — I hope to goodness we can last out till the end of our stay."[3]

The visit began awkwardly, with Uncle Sam being taken off to hospital, from which he later returned to convalesce. Meals, with their constant corrections ("Don't shovel peas with your fork, Francis — you're not in the backwoods now!"), were a great strain on Mother's loyalty and our lips. But a bigger problem was the laundry. Not allowed to do our own and reluctant to ask more of the overworked maids, we solved the dilemma one dark night by lowering a bundle from an upstairs window into the waiting arms of Dixon, the chauffeur, a longtime accomplice of Fran's in circumventing the rigours of the household. This unsung hero sneaked it into the village in the black Daimler, if such were possible, and returned it the following night by the same route.

I also recall a crisis to do with my breaking the tip off a wooden croquet post. There were fortunately no witnesses, but I could hardly ask for the glue without admitting what it was needed for and precipitating some dire medieval punishment. So I took a needle from my sewing kit, pushed both ends of it into the matching pieces until they fitted together, stuck the post back in the ground, and looked innocent when it later snapped under one of Aunt Jessie's formidable drives.

At the time this immersion in well-bred ways, even those of the newly rich, aroused every red corpuscle in my democratic arteries. But in retrospect I began to see it as an invaluable inoculation. For years after, whenever I found myself hobnobbing with personages of royal or comparable rank, I simply imagined them as the Aunts and looked innocent. It has often been no great stretch of the imagination.

But it was with succeeding generations that the lasting links were forged.

Osborne Henry Mavor, who was known as O.H. and signed himself OH!, was Mother's first cousin and almost exact contemporary. He was also the only one of her Glasgow relatives connected with the theatre. Already a distinguished physician, he had acquired a second reputation as a dramatist under the pen name "James Bridie" — a disguise at least partly dictated by the senior Mavors' dim view of any such louche connection. As an army medical officer during World War I, he had travelled widely in the Middle East, and on his return became active in Glasgow arts and letters. He helped to found the Scottish National Players. In 1930, with The Anatomist, based on 19th-century Edinburgh's notorious Dr. Knox and his body snatchers, he broke into London theatre and gradually gave up medicine in favour of playwriting. In the six years between then and our visit to Glasgow he had turned out a series of wise and witty hits, including *Tobias and the Angel* (directed by Tyrone Guthrie, who had played its first Angel), *Jonah and the Whale*, *A Sleeping Clergyman* (with Robert Donat), *Mary Read* (directed by Guthrie, with Flora Robson and Robert Donat), and *Storm in a Teacup* (made into a film with Rex Harrison and Vivien Leigh). And he was already a pillar of the Malvern Festival, dedicated to Bernard Shaw, where despite charges of dramaturgical inconsistency he was hailed as the Shavian heir apparent.

It took no time at all, when we visited the family's summer place in North Berwick, for me to realize I had found a kindred spirit:

> MM: Why don't they do your plays in New York?
> OH: Because I won't let them.
> MM: Why not?
> OH: Because they'd bugger them up. They want to translate them.
> MM: You don't think that would work?
> OH: Let them write their own bloody plays.

I immediately abandoned my plan to adapt Bridie for Canadians, and made a note to tell them to write their own bloody plays.

OH's son Ronald Mavor, in his turn another physician turned dramatist (and for a time a Scot turned Canadian), has written of the split personality that haunts so much Scottish writing: "From Hogg's *Confessions of a Justified Sinner*, through Stevenson's *Dr. Jekyll and Mr. Hyde* to the psychiatrist R. D. Laing's *Divided Self*, the Scot has shown an obsession with what Gregory Smith, in 1919, called 'the Caledonian antisyzygy,' meaning an attempt to unite opposites."[4] From his own attempt to unite opposites, Dr. Mavor/Mr. Bridie struck a creative light and generated a personal warmth that charmed even his critics. It will come as no surprise, then, that a 17-year-old votary from Toronto, his idol a dead Scots grandfather, his interests fragmented from the time he could remember any, his quest for roots cut off from his father's, and now in a total fog as to his future direction, should find a new idol in this other antisyzygistic Scot.

On the morning of our arrival in London we moved into the Hayeses' flat, then in the afternoon saw Peter off to Berlin for the Olympics. That evening, thanks to the good offices of Mavor/Bridie, we attended Komisarjevsky's electrifying Russian-style production of *The Seagull* by Chekhov (the first Chekhov play I had ever seen) with a cast headed by Edith Evans as Arkadina, John Gielgud as Trigorin, Peggy Ashcroft as

Nina, and Stephen Haggard as Konstantin — all of them in their morning glory. (Haggard knew no other; he was killed in the war.) After the performance, we were welcomed backstage, where half the remaining luminaries of the British stage seemed to have congregated with an excitement no less than ours. This was my introduction to the fabled theatre of London. And I was too drunk on the experience to grasp the 1896 play's exquisite relevance to the world of 1936. The evening of the very day I see my brother off to Adolf Hitler's Germany, I find myself in a British theatre filled with glitterati applauding a play about self-centred artists and impoverished aristocrats on a rundown estate, totally oblivious to the gathering apocalypse. I was living out the irony, for God's sake — and I missed it! But I was not alone. So far as I remember, the entire audience was caught up in Chekhov's reverse dramatic tension — action avoided instead of action taken — without noticing that we held one end of the rope.

From then on, while the shilling seats and the meagre savings lasted, my whole visit to London was one continuous artistic toot. In 30 days, commuting daily by train from Twickenham, sometimes *en famille*, sometimes on my own, I contrived to attend 21 plays, nine films, three operas, two ballets, and five concerts, not to mention museums, galleries, assorted historical sites, and Kensington Gardens.

At the little Mercury Theatre in Notting Hill Gate I saw the first production of T. S. Eliot's *Murder in the Cathedral*, which sparked the modern revival of poetic drama. In the West End I revelled in the high comedy of Gilbert Miller's all-star *Pride and Prejudice*. I saw Emlyn Williams's thriller *Night Must Fall* with Williams himself, and Terence Rattigan's first hit, *French Without Tears*. I had my introduction to classical chinoiserie at S. I. Hsiung's *Lady Precious Stream*, with its symbolic costumes and onstage property man and musicians. I saw Shakespeare indoors at the Old Vic, outdoors in Regent's Park, and at Stratford-upon-Avon — and watched the German actress Elizabeth Bergner ("canned elf," Guthrie once called her) shrink Rosalind in a film of *As You Like It* with a young Laurence Olivier as her justifiably bewildered Orlando.

Many of the seeds planted then bore fruit. Komisarjevsky's *King Lear* at Stratford-upon-Avon introduced me to the less familiar quarto version, which I later twice made use of. Seeing *Mother Goose* led Mother Moore and me to revive the pantomime tradition at Toronto's Royal Alexandra in 1950. I was enchanted by Dodie Smith's very English domestic comedy *Call It a Day*, while the London production of Mazo de la Roche's

Whiteoaks — the first Canadian play to become an international hit — infuriated me with its anglicization of the Ontario milieu. I had a dubious sort of revenge when I Canadianized *Call It a Day* to launch CBC Television drama in 1952. I roared with laughter at Aldwych farce masters Ralph Lynn and Tom Walls, and later, as a director, often tried to coax their deadpan timing from actors who, never having seen them, had no notion of what I meant. I relished Herbert Farjeon's topical revue *Spread It Abroad*, with Nelson Keys, Cyril Ritchard, and Madge Elliot, and had in mind the high style of its low comedy when the supposedly indigenous *Spring Thaw* was sprung in 1948. I marvelled at the Drury Lane spectacle-with-music mounted by writer-composer-actor Ivor Novello (the true begetter of Andrew Lloyd Webber), which boasted both a burning building and a sinking ship. Twenty years later I stole both stunts when I adapted Stephen Leacock's *Sunshine Sketches of a Little Town*, in an attempt to create a Canadian musical.

What I failed to notice was that this dazzling array was largely retrospective — a celebration of tradition. I can remember few signs of the kitchen-sink realism, gritty film, agitprop art, or other innovations to come within a decade. The lone piece of grim naturalism I saw was D. H. Lawrence's *My Son's My Son*, with the intrepid Sybil Thorndike as wife and mother of coal miners; but this was an unfinished work from an earlier period now belatedly surfacing. And the only political drama on hand was the documentary *Semmelweiss*, about medical anti-Semitism in turn-of-the-century Vienna. The cries of revolt against the status quo came not from an avant-garde but from a rearguard urging a return to past greatness: the poetic drama, the classic roles, the well-made play, the comedy of manners.

There was experimental radio drama (soon to be exported to Canada), but experimental meant fiddling with the art form, not reflecting social upheaval. British films sought the light entertainment market. Television was in its infancy. Marxism was more evident in the bookstores than in the art galleries, where the latest discovery was J. M. W. Turner and modern painting was European. Henry Moore's nonobjective sculpture was only emerging from the studio. Les Ballets Russes de Monte Carlo, with its British dancers disguised as Muscovites, was enthroned at Covent Garden while elsewhere Marie Rambert struggled to persuade audiences that British names did not spell mediocrity. I heard exchanges at parties about creativity versus commercialism (the Arts Council of Great Britain was 10 years away), and harangues at Hyde

Park Corner about too few opportunities for the working classes and too many for the perverts and the bloody immigrants; but there was no foretaste of impending cataclysm. In the depths of the Depression, it seemed, the established arts were at their highest polish since the turn of the century, and the public wanted to look back in pride, not in anger.

But all this is hindsight. There at the feast I was more eager to eat than to analyze, to collect the experiences of new acquaintances than to sort out my own.

There was, for example, Frederick Hudd, an indestructibly English fixture in Canada House, later deputy high commissioner, who worked as diligently for Canada as for his flower garden in Kent. Freddy Hudd had been best man at my parents' wedding, and gave me avuncular lessons in diplomacy both domestic and global. He remained as devoted to both parents as he was to both countries — a juggling act that I found hard to master but very useful to catch onto.

There was Gwen Cates, an American heiress who preferred the name Phoebe, a year my junior in age but light-years my senior in sophistication. Her mother and mine had briefly attended Radcliffe College in Massachusetts together, recognized each other in Piccadilly Circus, and quickly brought each other up-to-date. The American friend had married a millionaire New York Republican ("Hitler? A honey compared with that son of a bitch Roosevelt!") and produced the statutory son and daughter. The two families went to the Cateses' luxurious hotel for cocktails. Then Mother took Fran off to buy him a suit at the Thirty Shilling Tailors, Sonny went off with an Italian Contessa, and the Republican parents off to a dinner engagement. Phoebe and I were It. Perhaps you have never had occasion to take out an American heiress on half a crown, which is what I had in my pocket. But Phoebe rose to the occasion. The moment I opened my wallet and swore I'd lost a £10 note, she offered to treat us to a film and supper. Afterward she shrewdly let me pay the shilling busfares back to her place, leaving me sixpence for the underground back to the railway station. As we parted, she confided that she was a Roosevelt Democrat. Thus began, in England, my protracted education in the American way of life.

We went to Haslemere in Surrey, where the early-music enthusiast Arnold Dolmetsch had set up his antique instrument factory. The Swiss-born Dolmetsch had learned his trade at the Chickering Piano plant in Boston, where he met my grandfather, who invited him to Toronto after discovering a mutual passion for goat's milk. Dolmetsch believed that all artifacts should be made out of natural materials, and all music performed on the instruments for which it was written. That evening, when the whole family played their early instruments in the garden, the two ideas became one. Beside the drawing in my sketchbook I doodled: "Art has something to do with harmony in ourselves AND nature." It was not a bad guess.

Then there was dance pioneer Marie Rambert. No choreographer nor dancer but an inspirer of both, Rambert was in the circle of Mother's London friends devoted to high art on a flat purse. She and her husband, the playwright Ashley Dukes, had converted an old suburban parish hall into a small gem of a theatre, the Mercury, where she started the Ballet Club, the first permanent home of British ballet. The so-called club was both a company and a school, where with minimal resources Rambert nurtured a whole generation of notable dancers, choreographers, and designers. To see this vital little enterprise challenge the London establishment was a lesson in faith. Rambert and her two lively daughters invited the Moores for a day at the beach, and there on the Sussex sands we had an animated discussion about a similar base for Canadian theatre. I hesitate to count the old church buildings in Toronto we later investigated as possibilities for a theatre, even after we started one four years later in a more symbolically Canadian space — a barn.

Finally there was Dorothea, Lady Butterworth, who became an important woman in my life. She was yet another great-aunt, but of a different provenance. Even in her late fifties, when I met her, she personified what Matthew Arnold once called "that constellation of beauty, wit, and riches that makes every man an astronomer."

When Alfred Mavor married Dolly Ionides in London in 1896, the bicycle genius from Glasgow was 30 and she was 18, the daughter of a Greek-born tobacco importer and his elegant wife. Alfred's proposal was the 13th she had received in the year since her debut, and the superstition was vindicated when the unlucky couple lost first his fortune and then hers on dud inventions. Divorce left her with a teenage daughter and no income. She became secretary of the Rhodes Foundation, running its international scholarship system from her London office, in which, among other unorthodox habits, she secretly smoked a pipe. The outbreak of war in 1914 caught her in Europe, and before she could get out she was stricken with sleeping sickness. A wealthy friend of her father's hired a yacht, obtained safe conduct from the German government, and sailed to Bremerhaven to rescue her. The friend was Sir

Alexander Butterworth, chairman of the London, Midland, and Scottish Railway, a diminutive but energetic widower 25 years her senior; his son George, the most promising British composer of his generation, had just been killed at the front. Having adored Dolly since her childhood, he married her in her wheelchair and took care of her for the rest of her life, which she spent in bed.

But what a bed! On one side was a telephone switchboard that allowed her to chair the board of a London hospital and keep in touch with her friends. On the other was a complicated arrangement of swivelling decks and drawers accommodating meal trays, a radio, books, periodicals, the latest newspapers, and equipment for writing, sewing, and leatherwork with her one good hand. At the foot of the bed was a television set. Beyond it, on the wall, hung a photograph of Dolly at 18 — a deliberate source of ironic merriment for the lively mind now trapped in an increasingly inert body. But neither nostalgia nor immobility impeded her social life. In the adjoining room she would hold parties, cleverly cast to throw oil and water together, from which the guests would detach themselves in twos and threes to visit her bedside. And there Lady B., up-to-date on world affairs, stocked with intellectual arcana, bursting with gossip and avid for more, would hold her maverick court.

At one of these I was introduced, as a shining example of modern Canadian youth, to a tall lady of generous proportions and courtly manner who had spent five years of her youth in Ottawa as daughter of a governor general, the earl of Aberdeen. Holding a cup of tea in one hand and a cream puff in the other, I grew so agitated at her condescension that when I bit into the pastry the cream cascaded out the other side, making a white skunk's stripe down the front of her long black gown. I had no recourse but inadequate apology, but Aunt Dolly afterward shared my secret glee.

There were cryptic rumours, both at home and abroad, that Dolly's incapacity was more convenient than real; that her insatiable demand for attention made deserters of her doctors and reluctant saints of her family. But she unfailingly gave me more than I gave her. She became my closest confidante, and for years to come we exchanged letters, articles, and clippings in a conspiracy of interests.

On August 10 word arrived that I had passed the Ontario examinations. My marks were wildly uneven, but thanks to Daddy Mills I had got through. I was in such a state of jubilation, and so enamoured of London, that I immediately wrote to Ottawa accepting the National

Gallery's offer to turn me into an art restorer if it would keep me there. Two weeks later McCurry, the assistant curator, replied: "I think your decision to stay in England and take what time you can at the University of London and the Courtauld Institute is a wise one. . . . I think the program as outlined will work out very well."[5]

We were both overconfident. The University of London declined to accept an Ontario matriculation and insisted I take their entrance examinations. These included one in mathematics, at which I was a dunce, and one in Greek, far beyond my level. I inquired about tutors, but their fees punctured that balloon. Daddy Mills, I decided, was a fool. I wrote the National Gallery to cancel the plan and wired the University of Toronto for information about bursaries for penitent prodigals with good marks in English.

Peter arrived back from Berlin full of stories about Adolf Hitler and a black runner named Jesse Owens. Once in Toronto, he faced yet another change of hated school. Fran was to return to Glasgow to complete his apprenticeship, but having been reunited with his family was reluctant to part from them. Mother decided on a radical solution: for one year she would move to Glasgow, where the cost of living was less, give Fran a home, and entrust Peter to the more highly structured Scottish schools. We left Peter with cousins in Paisley, and in mid-September she and I sailed for home to put the furniture in storage and abandon house. For the first time in my life I was to be completely on my own.

5

Learning

"MY DEAR MAVOR," my father wrote from Cincinnati in mid-November 1936, "I heard, indirectly, the other day, that Peter is in school in Scotland, & that you are in residence in the University of Toronto. I need not say that I was surprised. But I should have felt rather better about it if I had heard of it from you or Peter. . . . I should appreciate a line from you as soon as possible, telling me where Peter is; how you like Gate House; what you are doing in the University, etc. . . . I shall be coming to preach in Trinity College on Jan. 17, & shall hope to see you then."[1]

I sent him the address of the unheated, cold-water bungalow that Mother had rented in a Glasgow suburb, and a brief rationale: "Peter agreed that a year in school abroad would do him a world of good. . . . I calculated that I could live in residence on the $50 a month which you send for me, if not luxuriously at least keeping body and soul together. . . . I am at University College in English Language and Literature, a new course that includes English, Latin, Greek, Ancient & Medieval History, Anthropology, Philosophy, Psychology & Fine Arts. I went into residence at Vic [Gate House, Victoria College] because the rooms are far better than Trinity, and the crowd is much nicer than Knox."[2] This was a collage of public information and private smoke screen.

Peter was, in fact, a reluctant recruit to Scotland's famed educational system. When Mother pleaded with one headmaster to make allowances for her rambunctious North American 15-year-old, he replied, "Madam, this school was founded by John Knox in 1565, and what was guid enough for John Knox is guid enough for your boy." The new boy stoically endured the sneers of classmates and teachers about snowbound log cabins in impenetrable forests, until it occurred to him to tell lies of Munchausean proportions about his exploits as a Mountie scout among the Red Indians, after which he was treated with deep respect. But he hated writing anything longer than a postcard and had asked me to "deal with P. A." I was being equally evasive about my own situation. The "if not luxuriously" was bravado: I had managed to get a bursary to cover tuition fees, but the room and board would eat up all but $5 of the monthly allowance. I had registered at nonsectarian University College precisely because of Father's connection with Trinity, the Anglican centre; and I had taken a room in the Victoria residence only because there were none left at UC. If it must be one crowd or another, I told myself, better the eclectic United Churchers than the pietistic Anglicans, the dour Presbyterians, or the tyrannical Catholics. If there had been a Buddhist residence, I would have gone there.

Near the entrance to University College, a Neo-Romanesque edifice from the 1850s, I found a legend: "Here was realized a major nineteenth-century aspiration: the establishment of a non-denominational institution of higher learning supported by government." This inscription suited my iconoclasm and my appetite for diversity. But it also showed that a government could do for the community what self-seeking factions would not. In later years I became accustomed to American astonishment at Canadian reliance on government funding for culture and education, and at our faith in government's impartiality; in the U.S. tradition these are provinces of commerce or private philanthropy that government enters only to politicize. To most Americans the notion of government as a defence against the procurement of culture, not as its procurer, has always seemed chimerical. To me it seemed eminently practical.

But the defence, I came to see, had vast holes in it. The bursary that enabled me to attend university came from an endowment established in a burst of Christmas generosity by Colonel Reuben Wells Leonard, an engineer convinced that "the preservation and development of civilization along the best lines are primarily functions of the White Race," the future of which depends on "the stability and prosperity of the British Empire" and "the Christian religion in its Protestant form."[3] Its bigoted terms have since been altered by the courts; but in my time eligible students had to be British Protestants, with preference given to "the sons and daughters respectively of the following classes . . . (a) clergymen, (b) schoolteachers, (c) officers, NCOs, and men" — and so on down a long list of the privileged poor, a profile that fitted me perfectly. Not for the last time, however, I neglected to read the small print in a contract. Perhaps I thought ignorance was bliss. To my eternal discredit, I simply took the money and ran.

I ran for everything. The term was not yet a week old when some optimist nominated me for first-year treasurer of the Literary and Athletic Society, and I ran. The end of the whirlwind campaign was noted in my diary: "Lost — thank God!" Concurrently I turned out for the Players' Guild and appeared as old Esdras in Maxwell Anderson's *Winterset*, then as another ancient in Eugene O'Neill's *Rope*, which went on to win the intervarsity competition at Hart House Theatre.[4] I began to think I was born old. To make some cash I put my library skills to work buying and selling used textbooks. Aiming to change the course of world events, I joined the Historical Society. Within a month I was on the editorial board of the college literary magazine, *The Undergraduate*, and found myself writing songs for the annual U.C. *Follies*, surrealist poetry for the annual undergraduate contest, and dramatic criticism for the campus newspaper, *The Varsity*.

My first journalistic assignment was to interview the same John Gielgud I had encountered backstage in London, now making his American debut in *Hamlet*. Guthrie McClintic's production was opening in Toronto because McClintic considered Canada psychologically midway between London and New York. "In his dressing room the other night," I boasted, "John Gielgud gave *The Varsity* some of his ideas about the Prince of Denmark. . . . 'We put in all the little dirty bits for the benefit of the New Yorkers,' he said with a self-conscious beam. . . . His insistence on using a sword [instead of a foil] resulted in a gash in his left arm during Monday's dress rehearsal."[5] This blood bond alone would have secured him a rave review, but there was more to it than consanguinity. When Maurice Evans's *Hamlet* later came to town in Margaret Webster's handsome production, the two versions taught me the elusive difference between elation and catharsis in the theatre. At the end of Evans's performance the audience stood and cheered, lingered in the lobby with loud praise for the acting, the direction, the music, the sets and the costumes, and went home jubilant. At the end of Gielgud's performance the audience applauded voicelessly, passed soberly through the lobby with muttered good-nights, and went home shaken.

For *The Varsity* I also first tried my hand at the no-turn-unstoned school of criticism then led by George Jean Nathan in New York and James Agate in London. I gave short shrift to an original farce by a Toronto journalist: "*Down the Rainpipe, Darling* was the title, substance, and, we presume, the fate, of last night's offering." In the true spirit of the game, I composed this conceit while waiting for the curtain to rise. When Toronto's St. Lawrence Centre for the Arts was launched 35 years later, that same dirty trick was played on me.

Although most of the UTS mates with whom I arrived were from the year ahead of mine and bound for different faculties, we met regularly at all-campus activities and a nearby café, the redolent Campus Coffee Shop. With the addition of instant recruits from other schools, primarily congenial women, we formed a band of two dozen that lasted throughout our university years, mutually identifiable even at a distance by our shrill code cry "Oy!" We were devoutly interdisciplinary: in medicine, engineering (including the trailblazing Sally Macdonald, "The Female Engineer"), modern languages, English, philosophy, history, economics, political science, law, commerce, art history, and even theology. By the standards of the day we were also considered bohemian, although this was not difficult. When I returned to the academic fold in 1970, students dressed down to avoid the imputation of respectability; in the 1930s even the poor tried to achieve it. Disdaining either convention, we wore whatever we liked and relished the ensuing puzzlement.

We travelled in packs, comparing books, records, and films — as much a reconnaissance of the self as of others. We read D. H. Lawrence and Virginia Woolf, and H. G. Wells's *Experiment in Autobiography*. We exchanged notes at the Prom concerts at Varsity Arena, organized by hardup musicians under the rhapsodic baton of handsome Reginald Stewart. We saw Gypsy Rose Lee in *George White's Scandals*, and the even more popular Ruth Etting at Shea's Hippodrome, singing, in a prototypical miniskirt, "What Will the Men Be Looking at a Hundred Years from Now?"

Our most brilliant companion, by common consent, was Graham Sanderson, only son of Toronto's chief librarian and his jolly Lancastrian wife. Unlike most of us, he knew exactly where he was going: through medicine to become a psychiatrist to become a novelist. Looking like a short, genial chimpanzee unconvinced that Homo sapiens had improved the stock, at UTS he had played a savagely funny Mrs. Malaprop, edited *The Twig*, and introduced his friends to *Brave New World* and *Ulysses*. On a leaf of my notebook, during a long-winded 1938 Hart House debate ("That this House would rather fight with Eden than go fascist with Chamberlain"), he improvised a sonnet:

> Beautiful to sit and hear sweet tones
> filling the air from nowhere and to talk
> in peace of human wrong. My friend, we mock
> ourselves so we may live. From Death's white bones
> we shrink, the better to love Saint-Saens' The Swan.
> We cannot live alone; but they won't miss
> the one that died. What is the road to bliss?
> The happiness that might have been is gone:
> passion in any ugly form it loathes.
> (Take note, M. Moore, that the world knows no real love.)
> Strife is man's happiness — the urge to move
> past merely reproduction, food and clothes.
> Philosophizing half the weary night,
> Outside, a starving man: a startling sight.[6]

If Sanderson was to be our Tolstoy, our da Vinci was a lanky droll named John Terrace, only child of a mismatched Scots merchant and his urbane American wife. We allowed "T" to draw anything, no matter how insulting, on anything, which he did regularly on paper, books, envelopes, tablecloths, napkins, and the occasional shirt. Since T and I attended many of the same classes, we became inseparable sparring partners. The poet Earle Birney taught us Anglo-Saxon, good for hours of competitive punning. E. K. Brown introduced us to 17th-century literature, where our minds were far too comfortable, and also to what little Canadian literature was taught. Sanderson had just shown us *An Experiment with Time* by J. W. Dunne, a British mathematician convinced that all times and places coexist, leaving the mind free to roam in dreams. Since neither of us felt at home in the here and now, T and I made a compact to sneak up on our contemporaries from the past and the future.

Except, that is, in the theatre. Our whole gang — humanists, artists, engineers, scientists, social scientists — met most often in the pocket theatre on the second floor of the Women's Union, where the UC Players' Guild, with the assistance of faculty members such as Victor Lange (rumoured, in future years, to be a German spy), mounted the first Canadian productions of plays by Eugene O'Neill, Maxwell Anderson, T. S. Eliot, W. H. Auden, and an assortment of then obscure Europeans. We even pioneered the form known later as the happening. During the cocktail party in Eliot's *Sweeney Agonistes*, we drank neat Scotch onstage instead of the customary ginger ale. My piano playing, if I remember correctly, was never more fluid, and the whole exercise, we estimated at the time, marked a new high in naturalism. Certainly that was the view of the dean of women, Marion Ferguson, who met us on the landing on our way out. Gallant Jack Maybee, happening to be nearest to her, said, "Thank you, Miss Ferguson," with a deep bow that became a nosedive down the stairs. Ever since I have regarded happenings as traps for the self-indulgent.

It was in the breaks between performances, rehearsals, elections, meetings, debates, *The Varsity*, *The Follies*, movies, concerts, and other pressing engagements that we found time for lectures and essays. Having learned medieval history from Ralph Flenley, who covered the blackboard with incomprehensible diagrams, and renaissance history from Dicky Saunders, an American who squeezed puns out of the most unlikely material ("Let me tell you about those dirty burghers in Amsterdam!"), I continue to find history either confusing or funny. As for essays, I had great difficulty getting a decent mark out of J. R. MacGillivray, who taught Restoration poetry, until the night I abandoned all hope and wrote an essay on Robert Herrick's poems in praise of the grape while drinking a bottle of port. It earned an A.

Shakespeare was taught by the warm-hearted principal of University College, the gravel-voiced old Malcolm Wallace ("'Dost thou not see my baby at my breast?' — Beautiful, in'n it!"), and Trinity's intense young G. Wilson Knight, champion of the fallacy of imitative form — that mysterious texts require mysterious explanations. But Knight had at least the courage to put his ideas to the test, staging and appearing in several of the plays despite a right elbow that stood out like a shelf bracket and a speech impediment that made Hamlet say, "Peuchance to dweam, ay, theh's the wub." After his return to England and subsequent ascent to the highest rank of Shakespearean scholarship, Knight misled generations of readers by citing his Toronto productions as validations of his theses. I remember his tragedies as comic and his comedies as tragic. They proved only that criticism without creativity produces charts. Had I learned that axiom then it would have saved me from tripping over it 20 years later.

But the giant Shakespeare was an old friend. New literary acquaintances were harder to gauge. "You seem to have some difficulty making up your mind among so many critics," Birney wrote in the margin of my essay on Chaucer. He was right, and about more than Chaucer; I had discovered Euripides, Machiavelli, Marlowe, Donne, and others whose revived reputations were matters of considerable controversy. The mind I was making up as I went along told me, in an interim report, that too many other minds were already made up; that critics who claimed exclusive possession of the light were more likely sitting in the dark illuminating their own faces. My growing scepticism about religious dogma was clearly spreading to other areas, abetted by two minor courses of unexpected interest.

One was Oriental literature, in which the Old Testament was taught as a Jewish text, with Buddhism, Taoism, and *The Bhagavad Gita* to come. I began an essay on the Bible — I could quote the King James version by the yard — with a blast of sheer hubris: "To talk of the Bible as literature is as fatuous as to talk of Beethoven's Ninth as music." The book could be nothing else, I argued, and owed its power to "the cadence and rhythm of the imagery, rather than to the logical content, often sheer nonsense." This piece of impudence earned me an A+, encouraging me to think I was onto something. Soon I learned that a young Victoria College professor named Northrop Frye had been onto it for some time.

The other crucial minor course was anthropology, taught by C. W. M. Hart, a caustic Australian for whom little was sacred except John Stuart Mill's dictum: "Of all vulgar modes of escaping from the consideration of the effect of social and moral influences upon the human mind, the most vulgar is that of attributing the diversities of conduct and character to inherent natural differences."[7] To Hart all racial or national stereotypes, complimentary or derogatory, were forms of fraud. His favourite example of artificial beautification was the self-flattering portrait of Homo sapiens then being extrapolated from the meagre remains of Pithecanthropus erectus. His favourite example of intentional uglification was the damning of Joan of Arc by medieval ecclesiastics, each according to his political affiliation. His favourite example of multiple fraud was the pseudo-biology of the Nazis, by which they consigned themselves to the head of the evolutionary parade and everyone else to the tail.

This compulsive categorizing, with the aim of putting up one's own agenda while putting down everyone else's, seemed to me exactly what most literary and artistic critics were engaged in. I might well have become a dogmatic anti-dogmatist before reaching the age of consent had it not been for F. H. Anderson's Plato course.

Fulton Henry Anderson, tall, bald, potbellied, and gay, was most famous for his invariable opening line in first-year ethics. "Now," he would boom, scanning the coeds fresh from high school in their perms and sweater sets seated like pigeons along the front row of the amphitheatre, "what *is* ethics?" Stunned silence. "Well, you go out, and you *sin* . . . ehm?" Involuntary blushes; instant interest. Socrates rides again. "Poetry," I wrote confidently in my first essay for Anderson, "began with music and dance and drama, in the religious Dionysian festivals of fertility, where revellers (to quote Havelock Ellis's happy and famous phrase) 'joined in the cosmic rhythm of the universe.'" In the margin Anderson demolished both me and Ellis: "Are you quite sure the universe has a rhythm, and that it is Dionysian? Is it syncopated, or isn't it? Etc." Alongside my lament that "Sometimes Plato pushes the point beyond necessity (why does he go beyond common sense!)," Anderson put: "He'd be a damned fool if he didn't."

I was determined not to become a damned fool, which is to say one without a compass. And by the end of November, despite recurring problems with dead languages, I was beginning to feel I had a fix on worldly wisdom. With a firm comic hand I was directing the last play of the term for the Players' Guild. On the afternoon of Friday, December 2, backstage at the little theatre in the Women's Union, I kissed a girl for the first time and he who knew everything suddenly knew nothing.

IN THIS MORTAL CRISIS I did what Canadians always do in a crisis: I set up a Royal Commission. In close confidence I consulted every expert around, including, for lack of a father, fathers-substitute past and present. They told me either that it was about time, which I already knew, or that I must work harder than ever, which was only to restate the problem. I sought the advice of my beloved doctor, J. Z. Gillies, to whose generosity I owed the weekly injections that kept my chronic bronchitis at bay; he recommended half an hour of deep breathing every morning. I wrote thick letters to Aunt Dolly in London, begging for guidance on female psychology. She replied that there was no such thing, and that if I wanted a reading of one particular female, my description of this specimen as "divine" and "glorious" lacked something in specificity. I consulted Mrs. Pohl, the immigrant Earth Mother who had been our cleaning woman, to whose home on McCaul Street I now regularly delivered my weekly laundry. Mrs. Pohl, I knew, was both illiterate and very wise; the Wednesday ritual in her parlour with homemade wine and Polish pastry was an oasis in my hectic life, especially when her drunken tinker of a husband absented himself. But when she stopped crying it was only to tell me to follow my heart, which to her eternal regret she had chosen not to do before settling for the tinker.

I even told my mother about it, as an excuse for failing to write more often. "I shall never forgive myself for leaving you," she replied in alarm: "Remember that and make all the effort you can to pull yourself together."[8] A second letter was more specific: "Go about in a group. And for the girl's sake as much as your own, do not single her out more than you can help. . . . You ought to have your experiences, but . . . it is bad to isolate a girl." Neglecting to say how I could have one without doing the other, she added — to my alarm — that things were not going well in Glasgow, and "it would take very little for me to pack up and come home anytime."[9] The soundest counsel came from my brother Peter on a postcard I received on New Year's Eve: "Feeling awfu' homesick. Reasons: 1. I ain't heard nothing but Scotch. 2. I ain't seen no snow. 3. I ain't seen no sun. I hope you have recovered from your Christmas binge. I hope you had one."[10]

No binge was in sight, however, and thus no recovery. For months I was in a state of combined perpetual motion and suspended animation. The battle of life went on, but on its most pressing front I could neither advance nor retreat, being too green to know what steps to take in either direction. Should I conquer my passion or the lady?

Things took a turn for the worse when I was almost thrown out of residence for having a woman in my room at night. Ralph Sturgeon, the Macduff who nearly killed my Macbeth, was now a medical student and enamoured of an energetic coed known as "Tarzan" in residence at Victoria College. He and she had decided to liven up a college dance by switching clothes, and would I allow him to change in my room on campus and make him up appropriately? He arrived after supper with Tarzan's dress and floppy tam in a box, left his own gear with me to be retrieved in the morning, and departed, as her. At about 1:00 a.m. I was roused by furious banging on the front door and let in the dishevelled transvestite. It appeared that while dancing past the dean of women he had made the mistake of winking at her; the masquerade was exposed, and he had had to outrun half the enraged women at the dance to get here. I handed him the box containing his own clothes and told him to get lost. The following day I was hailed before the dean of men, who said, "Moore, a woman was seen leaving your room in the small hours this morning in a dishevelled condition. Would you care to explain yourself?" The more I tried, the less credible the truth sounded, until I found the presence of mind to refer him to the dean of women. But it was clear from the nudges and winks my fellow students gave me that the story was widely hailed as a brilliant invention.

I buried myself in study, but a head full of fantasies has no room for irregular verbs. I wrote the final examinations in a feverish sweat, and while awaiting the results found a job in the periodicals section of the public library to pay off my debts.

The grades arrived just after I had sealed a long confessional letter to Terrace in Portland, Maine, where he had gone to spend the summer with his American grandparents. I wrote a single word on the envelope flap before posting it. "Goddammitt," he wrote in reply, "why in hell did you put that word FAILED on the back? Jesus Christos! I'm a man of iron, but at the sight of that word I reeled in my tracks & clutched feebly at the wastepaper basket for support. My hand is still shaking." He is writing the next day, after learning that he himself has passed. He plans an idyllic summer listening to records, reading, painting and playing tennis. He wants half a dozen of the gang to "chuck your collective jobs, take Graham's car, and stay down here for a month or so. You can pay a buck a week for food, etc. . . ." He went on to write:

> I'm sitting up in my room overlooking the sea. We're on top of a hill, so the sea is a goodish bit below, although but 300 yards away. From a line of foaming & crashing on rugged rocks, it sweeps up to the horizon, where there is a thin band of lovely pale green sky — the rest is a lowering blue-grey. Add to that a nice breeze and a salty tang to the air, and there you have it. . . . The rest, as far as I can make out from where I stand, is silence. Oh — how's Toronto, old chap? You may use this letter for advertisement if you wish, sirs.[11]

It was Greek I had failed. But since I passed out before finishing the exam and my other grades were acceptable, I was given an *aegrotat* (excused by illness) that allowed me to proceed into second year with a grade known as Below the Line. For all the world to see, I had now been officially declared Below the Line. I looked in the mirror and my spirit sank. How could any self-respecting woman want that? The noble Mavor nose was still there. But behind the thick glasses the Moore moon face, epicanthic eyes, and big ears were having their way, and for the first time I was sure my hair was quickly thinning. Good God, was I going to look like my father? Even the periodicals room at the library conspired to depress me, as the old, the unemployed, and the lonely trooped in to read up on real or manufactured disaster. While Spain erupted in civil war, the *Regina Leader-Post* (as I remember) sported the headline SOMETHING WRONG SOMEWHERE SAYS WICKSTRAND. Wickstrand, whoever he was, had it right. At the end of June I quit my job and hitchhiked to Maine.

Terrace's step-grandfather Alexander Bower, an exuberant 80-year-old seascape painter turned gallery curator, greeted me in an undershirt and a voice like a Brooklyn trucker: "Ha wah yuh, luvaboy! Sankchuary awaits!" T's diminutive grandmother laughed scornfully. "He's only the cook. Stay at your peril." I did, for six weeks, and the only thing that suffered was my self-pity.

The house that Bower built stood high on Cape Elizabeth, its back a two-story wall of glass facing the ocean. Through this on wet days T and I watched the play of light on rock and sea as we sketched, wrote, or played abusive card games to recordings of Bach, Franck, Tchaikovsky, Rachmaninov, and Billie Holliday. We swam in every kind of weather. On fine days we enlisted Top, the boy next door, and his sister (whom T, mimicking Sanderson, found "ra-a-a-ther interesting") for an inept game of tennis, or piled into Top's old convertible and tooled down the coast through Kennebunkport, Portsmouth, and Salem to Boston, taking in the summer stock theatres and outdoor concerts. We left our mark in puritan Boston, where the public library's grand lobby, with its imposing John Singer Sargent murals, sported a sign saying ONLY LOW CONVERSATION PERMITTED until our hysterical misbehaviour caused its removal.

At the Bowers' place, example outranked precept. Alec Bower was more than the cook; he was a passionate gourmet. It was this old man's appetite for life that restored mine. He rose at 4:00 a.m. daily to paint for four hours before breakfast; from ten until one he attended to his Portland Art Gallery; after lunch he napped for an hour, then read — at the moment Jakob Burckhardt's monumental *Renaissance in Italy* — until dinner, which stretched until midnight if the Bowers stayed home. Self-educated, he had travelled the world like Peer Gynt, collecting experiences that he would relate at the drop of a cue in his Brooklynese translation. ("I was sittin atta window wit de Rajah, watchin dis intoiminable weddin procession of elephants wid howdahs on to-ap, okay, an go-angs an awlat, when he toins to me an says can you beat it, Bowah? All dis fuss an fedders over a coupla nice kids takin up sexual relations!") Eventually he had found his Solveig — and in time for them to enjoy each other. I never knew T's grandmother's first name because even her husband, with elaborate pride, called her Mrs. Bower. It was Mrs. Bower who persuaded me that love letters, like letters to the editor, seldom satisfy any indulgence but the writer's.

IN LATE AUGUST the family returned from Glasgow — Fran bound nervously for Toronto University's School of Practical Science, and Peter for a cram school. We had little enough time to find a house, get our furniture out of storage, and move in; but after my year of freedom the dark box we rented on Sherwood Avenue proved to be a nightmare. Terrace, now back in Toronto with his silently embattled parents, had escaped to an off-campus rooming house and invited me to share it. Mother was plunging once again into every teaching and directing job she could find, and agreed to my departure in exchange for a promise to help with the productions. To pay my share of both rents I knew I would have to take on every radio job available.

Dora Mavor Moore, as she now began to call herself, was almost 50. Not for the first time she had deliberately interrupted whatever career she had managed to fashion for herself; and the bitter winter in Scotland had taken its toll in varicose veins and added weight. But it had also given her time to take stock. The professional theatre in Toronto was nonexistent and the amateur theatre self-serving. The best hope, she knew, lay in education: in persuading the next generation to raise its sights. Before leaving Britain she had taken the precaution of going back to school herself, studying at the Central School of Speech and Drama. She went to the Malvern Festival to see a new Bridie play and was introduced to Bernard Shaw, then 80, who clasped her hand in both of his and said sheepishly, "I took your father's name in vain." She went to Dublin and visited the Abbey Theatre, a prime model for Canada, in the company of W. B. Yeats and his wife.

Once home she found a job supervising dramatics for the Toronto Playground Association and set to work establishing groups and classes in several schools. She developed an especially close bond with Forest Hill Collegiate, where I and Fran, with his new electrical skills, worked with her in mounting scenes and plays that were more experimental than the participants knew. The population of Forest Hill Village, in the city's northwest, was undergoing a radical change as immigrant families moved north from their downtown ghettos; its schools were bursting with talented children, mostly unencumbered by WASP continence, from whom their upwardly mobile parents expected much. DMM was counting on them to form the vanguard of her cultural revolution. But not even she expected the revolution to be so imminent.

I was the one who should have seen it coming, because while studying at university I was learning to swim in the rising tide of radio.

By 1938, when Rupert Lucas was appointed head of CBC drama and young Andrew Allan left his commercial drama experiments at CFRB to visit England, colonies of professional actors, writers, and technicians had formed in Montreal, Toronto, and Vancouver. Those with experience in local series such as *The Farm Show* were in demand when the more ambitious network programs came along, often with guest directors or stars from London or New York. The most dazzling of the directors was the BBC's Lance Sieveking, who made up in flamboyance what he lacked in sense of humour; for one epic he used the washroom as an echo chamber with riotous on-air consequences. That winter I played Lysander in *A Midsummer Night's Dream* for the Scots-born, New York-based director John MacDonell ("Make love to the microphone, laddy. It's closer than the girrl"), and Edgar to Walter Hampton's *King Lear*. The great American tragedian was so carried away in one scene that he lowered his script and recited from memory, restoring the cuts as he went. I also sang the Lord Chancellor and other patter roles in the CBC's first Gilbert and Sullivan series, proving that my singing voice would henceforth be more notable for agility than quality.

Occasionally all hands would be summoned from across the country for a gala performance. When Rupert Lucas promised the rising Broadway star John Carradine that he could play *King John*, the Toronto acting stable was augmented by Eleanor Stuart from Montreal, Frank Willis from Halifax, and Frank Vyvyan from Vancouver. Sir Ernest MacMillan and half the Toronto Symphony were hired to provide the music, and a special studio was set up to accommodate cast and orchestra. But in the break between dress rehearsal and live broadcast, Lucas took Carradine, Willis, and two or three other colleagues and their wives out to a dinner at which they drank toasts to William Shakespeare, the king, President Roosevelt, the queen, Mrs. Roosevelt, Prime Minister King, his dog, and each other. The pace of the ensuing broadcast was funereal. Directing from the booth, Lucas was throwing cues a full five seconds after the actor targeted had begun to speak; MacMillan, beet-red with angry sobriety, compensated by conducting everything as if he had a train to catch, which I am sure he wished he had. Carradine, accustomed to acting on a full quart, anyway, tried to stem the surrounding anarchy by making frantic speed-up signals to his fellow drunks every time they took a deep breath. When Willis began the Papal Legate's long peroration, sounding like a submerged tuba, Carradine loudly whispered from the sidelines, "Speak up, for Chrissake, speak up!" As Philip the Bastard, I had the play's famous last speech, beginning "This England never did, nor never shall, yield to the proud foot of a conqueror . . ." It was never snappier. And as I rattled off its final sentence, "Naught shall make us rue, if England to itself do rest but true," *King John* went off the air with neither coda nor credits — only the announcer's embarrassingly accurate tag, "This is the Canadian Broadcasting Corporation."

All of this stimulating extracurricular activity, however, was calamitous to my studies. And to my romance: before spring my affair of the heart had dwindled to its humiliating conclusion. Somehow I found time to keep up with my best subjects, but at the cost of slipping behind in my worst. The year once skipped returned to haunt me. When examinations came, in the spring of 1938, my failure was total, and this time I had no excuse.

SIR WILLIAM MULOCK, 94, waved me to a dining chair beside his own as he tucked into eight o'clock breakfast: a bowl of hot porridge, a separate bowl of cold cream, and a bottle of Scotch. Laurier's bearded postmaster general, the mentor of Mackenzie King, former chief justice of Ontario, and now chancellor of the University of Toronto, had summoned me from summer camp in Haliburton, where I was working as a counsellor while sending out job applications to the department stores. There were no full-time jobs in the performing arts in Canada, and I knew I had to face it. University was finished with me and I with it. What on earth had this to do with the venerable Sir William? It was a very strange conversation:

SW: It has come to my attention, sir, that you have failed.

MM: How is that, Sir?

SW: Never mind. You should not have failed.

MM: No, Sir.

SW: But I am told you headed the pack in English and philosophy.

MM: That's news to me, Sir.

SW: You will repeat your year, sir, and get it this time.

MM: Sir, I'm broke.

SW: A bursary will cover your fees. The rest is up to you, sir.
     Telephone the registrar tomorrow morning. You may go.

MM: Yes, Sir. (*exit, tripping over chair*)

And that is how I came to find myself back at university, repeating my second year but in a different course: philosophy with an English or history option. To give me a familiar base, I took the English option, sadly buried the dead languages, and sailed nervously into the quicker waters of logic, metaphysics, aesthetics, semantics, politics, psychology, and modern criticism.

"The more you do," runs the old tonic, "the more you find you *can* do!" I had reason to know this was rubbish; but the times called for heroic measures. And I was, so to speak, a sinner on parole. On and off the campus I became busier than ever, especially when I discovered I had low blood pressure and was forced to abandon my plan to die young of a heart attack. There was an apocalyptic smell in the air. On the first of July 1938, the national birthday, our family moved into an old log farmhouse that was already historic and quickly became more so, changing Canadian theatre in the process. The following year World War II changed the whole planet — making education, communications, and the arts, already my professional interests, matters of growing national and international concern. Before graduating in 1941 I had also become a schoolteacher, a radio playwright, a professional stage actor, a theatrical manager, and an army officer.

Some sort of regeneration clearly took place in my second try at second year that enabled me, for a time at least, to cope with the volatile universe around me and in me. It may have been only the realization that I'd received more than my share of luck and had better start delivering. But I remember it as much more dramatic than that. Three Furies made a simultaneous landing on my id, my ego, and my superego (about which I had just learned in Psychology II). I fell deeply in love and almost became a parent. I discovered the mighty verses of William Blake and immediately enlisted with the rebels. And I came under the spell of G. S. Brett, a Merlin who taught philosophy as if my life depended on it.

My only direct experience of psychology until then had been as a guinea piglet for Dr. Blatz; it was an intelligent game, I concluded, like chess. If psychology were any more scientific, surely, it would be as insufferably certain as mathematics. At university our first textbook was The Psychology of Insanity, and I promptly wrote and circulated a travesty titled The Insanity of Psychology. The appreciative laughter had scarcely dried when a disturbed high school friend committed suicide, the gentle wife of a couple close to our family was driven mad by her husband's persistent public jibes at her expense, and at the ancient Queen Street asylum, through one-way glass, our psychology class observed interviews with the inmates, among them an old syphilitic desperately trying to communicate his pain in an indecipherable code of his own invention. He was alone in hell. After that I took psychology seriously.

At least as a clue to the behaviour of others. In my own case, naturally, the creative tension between id, ego, and superego was in perfect balance. To start with id and ego, here I was, learning about love from a talented, beautiful, and cosmopolitan young woman at the same time as I learned about romantic poetry from a brilliant but monastic pedant.

Arthur Sutherland Piggott Woodhouse's knowledge of life outside the academy seemed to come almost entirely from books about it. "Now," he would ask, as if barely able to dangle both the scandal and the cigarette from his lips at the same time, "what was it that changed Milton's poy-etry? Why, he was in lawve! He was in lawve!" — a subject in which most of us guessed him to be less experienced than we were. Aside from his mother and his star postgraduates, the sole object of ASP's affection, as far as anyone could tell, was the literary canon. And he guarded it jealously. After weeks spent on the pontifical John Dryden (who blamed Shakespeare's popularity on audiences "content with acorns before they knew the use of bread") and the bilious Alexander Pope (for whom Man is "Fixed like a plant on his peculiar spot, To draw nutrition, propagate, and rot"), Woodhouse had scheduled a single hour on the visionary, life-affirming, shit-disturbing William Blake ("You never know what is enough until you know what is more than enough"). That was when I rebelled. Determined to sacrifice myself on Blake's iconoclastic altar, I climbed into my chariot of fire, raised my shield of seven-times-beaten-brass and, in a polemic read aloud in Woodhouse's seminar, assaulted the whole reactionary English department. Instead of martyrdom, however, I once again had to settle for the applause of my peers, including my lady friend, for punching authority in the eye. Authority was stoical.

This joint (if empty) victory of love and licence might have turned me into a prehistoric hippy had it not been for the timely intervention of a superego.

George S. Brett was then 60, of average height and plain dress, so physically unremarkable that I once guessed he was made entirely of intellect. Even at home he read standing up at a lectern because, he claimed, the mind was clearer. Oxford-educated and India-trained, Brett had arrived in Toronto before the First World War to teach classics, but soon moved into broader fields and chaired the department of philosophy at University College until his death in 1944. His widely quoted *History of Psychology*, written between 1912 and 1921, was the last to treat psychology as an intellectual rather than a physiological subject. Brett was a polymath, as well informed on recent movements in the humanities, arts, and sciences as he was on those of the past. His lectures, dry only in their wit, were exercises in mental alertness, in spotting relationships between ideas across disciplines, time, and space. He led me to Bertrand Russell and C. E. M. Joad, the pattern tracers.

In my third year, 1938–39, when I was president of the Philosophical Society, I persuaded Father Phelan, the distinguished head of Toronto's Pontifical Institute of Medieval Studies, to lead a discussion on "The Social Ethics of the Roman Catholic Church," and asked Brett to attend. As the eminent priest traced his faith back to "what I learned at my mother's knee," the eminent philosopher sat cross-legged on the floor like a kid at a magic show, then started the discussion by asking amiably, "Father, did you believe everything your mother told you?" For Brett the given was never more than a starting place for examination of the alternatives.

But neither was he about to damn the wheel because there was no such thing as a perfect circle. After exhausting the possibilities of reason, he insisted, we had no option but to take a leap of faith. He seconded the deity's nudge to the bewildered Arjuna in *The Bhagavad Gita*, to the effect that no one gets to heaven (or anywhere else) by wishing or by reading how-to books. You must eventually make the leap yourself, but only after a firsthand reconnaissance. It was this habit of mind, this linkage of faith and scepticism, this marriage of heaven and hell, that made George Brett's philosophy course by far the most practical of all my university courses. I have since found this fact difficult to explain to some of my friends in business.

I thought of Brett one dark night in London in 1944 as it rained buzz bombs, and wrote to thank him for all that his guidance had meant to me. The reply came from his widow, telling me that my letter was the last he ever read. In my mind's eye he stood at his lectern, pale but erect, as I watched him read my note between the pages of Whitehead, or possibly Wittgenstein, and then, having exhausted the possibilities of reason, die in a standing leap.

THE PLACES I LIVED IN while attending university, I now realize, were as much a part of my conditioning as any school. The house that we bought in the summer of 1938 on the outer edge of Forest Hill Village was one of the oldest in Toronto. Built in 1815, it stood at the corner of what is now Bathurst Street and Ridelle Avenue, several blocks north of Eglinton Avenue (unpaved west of Spadina), with only one other roof in sight. Without electricity, gas, plumbing, or water supply other than the hand pump in the backyard, it had been the farmhouse for the area, and was said, on firm if minimal authority, to be the house where William Lyon Mackenzie, fleeing his failed 1837 rebellion, disguised himself as a woman to reach the U.S. border and freedom. The original log cabin had since been enlarged and stuccoed, but the old divided cow door still stood — it stands as I write — leading into what used to be the kitchen. And near it, flush with the original pine floor, is the runged trapdoor that once led to the dug-out basement. It had a wood stove in the kitchen, three fireplaces on the main floor, and no heat on the second. West of the house there still towers the ancient elm tree, with one branch, according to local legend, bent horizontal by the Mohawks as a trail marker. The property cost us $3,500, most of it put up by Wilfrid and his brother James, doing well as a biologist in the United States. Beside it, on a lot we neither owned nor could afford to buy, stood a small barn, sheltering, for as long as anyone living could remember, only a two-holer outhouse. Despite its lack of everything conducive to public use, including accessibility, it was this abandoned barn that Dora Mavor Moore recognized as the theatre of her dreams.

The story of that theatrical cradle belongs with its postwar sequel, which I shall get around to. Here I need only say that in addition to everything else, I found myself performing, directing, and managing stage plays and tours in a weird combination of professional ends and amateur means. But the renovation of the old farm played an important role in my education, providing my brothers and me with on-the-job training in waste disposal, plumbing, carpentry, plastering, and other useful trades such as rat slaughter and starling hunting, not to mention bodybuilding opportunities such as chopping wood, toting water, endless snow shovelling, and 200-yard dashes in pursuit of a bus. We had no car, and missing the last bus from St. Clair and Bathurst meant a three-mile hike home. Mother relied on friends with cars and a neighbouring cabdriver, Mr. Roots, an ingeniously earthy Cockney ("Pedestrian? 'E's loik a fart in a colander — dunno which 'ole to get aht of!") who would do anything for her but considered our late-night calls a damn nuisance.

The study of philosophy by coal oil lamp, however, seemed irresistibly appropriate — until the night the Philosophical Society met at our place and George Edison said the light was too murky to read the notes for his paper. Some of us thought it was his paper, but let that go. It took this social calamity to make me admit that, aside from all the other inconveniences, my own eyes were worsening. In March, with exams coming up, I rented a room on Huron Street near the university.

The rooming house was owned, it turned out, by a Canadian theatrical legend, Pat Rafferty of *The Dumbells*, that durable World War I army revue. In 1921 *The Dumbells* had given Canada its one and only Broadway hit, and for a decade afterward its only cross-country success. Rafferty had been unemployed since then and was now an embittered elf. Mrs. Rafferty, who ran the establishment and everything else in sight, was a big blonde with a loud laugh and a fund of theatre stories. It was these that first awakened my interest in the history of popular theatre in Canada, about which almost nothing had been written. I much respected her critical acumen:

NEIGHBOUR:	You seen that movie at Loews' Uptown?
MRS. R:	What's its name?
NEIGHBOUR:	*Gone with the Wind.*
MRS. R:	That's not a name. It's a condition.

I had the downstairs front room with the bay window through whose lace curtains I could observe, unseen, the human comedy on Huron Street.

Here it was that I gave myself an education in baroque music, listening to records while I studied. And here it was, with the understanding Mrs. Rafferty as chaperone, that I received my lover and my long-postponed initiation into the mystery of sex. It was all the easier when she confided that an internal operation had left her unable to bear children.

For the summer of 1939 Doug Hicks and I found jobs as head counsellors at a new camp, sharing responsibility with a magnificent relic of *The Dumbells'* war, a Welsh-born classics and math teacher from Halifax named Gwynne-Timothy. From his years as track-and-field runner, pugilist, tennis player, soldier, and aviator, G-T had acquired a steel rod in one arm, a metal plate at the back of his head, a bad heart, and asthma, none of which dissuaded him from energetic diving, hiking, football, volleyball, or hockey. "G-T it," an injunction coined by his stoical wife Dorothy and adopted by the camp, meant "Make the most of what's left!" There are moments, now multiplying, when I still repeat it to myself. When the war came, G-T assured us, he'd be back in uniform. "You'll be back in bed," said Dorothy.

When the war did come that September, I was playing Sir John A. Macdonald in a historical pageant at the annual Canadian National Exhibition, squeezing in a two-week job before the fall term at university commenced. The producer and star was Kate Aitken, celebrated broadcaster, cook, fashion expert, advertising magnate, and director of Women's Affairs at the CNE. "Mrs. A." was a maternal dynamo, warm as toast and hard as nails. Like many another capable and energetic woman of the time, she had long been held back by conventional notions of a woman's role. One fine day she demoted her husband to handyman, took over the family's affairs with the help of two daughters, and built a business empire on her knowledge of women's needs. Her show in the Women's Building at the CNE drew 3,000 adoring spectators three times a day. In the breaks between these shows I used to visit the adjacent Canadian Press booth, with its teletype machines spitting out the latest news.

On the afternoon of September 3, 1939, with the second show started, I had time to kill before my entrance and wandered over to the CP machines. Britain and France had just declared war on Germany; Canada might follow. I dashed back to catch Mrs. A. before her next entrance. "Don't tell them," I said. "They'll panic!" "Nonsense," she replied. "They'll all have a good cry and then sit back and enjoy the show." And that was exactly what they did. Here endeth the First Lesson in promoting the war effort.

That fall I enlisted in the University's Officers' Training Corps. Poor eyesight was only the most obvious of my handicaps for active service; without my glasses I could never find the trigger, let alone the target. I was acceptable, however, to the militia. And like many of my friends, I was as much interested in being in on the fight as I was in the cause. Insufficiently attached to either God or Country to say Thy Will Be Done, I nevertheless wanted a share in the eternal battle between good and evil.

This inchoate drive to do one's duty — whatever it was supposed to be — was about to become the worst of my bad habits. The compulsive pattern was already forming. I see it now (I could not then) as a form of idealistic gambling, a surrender to whatever irresistible bet came along. In this fall of 1939 I was about to return home and settle down to studies and apprentice soldiering when I was offered a part-time job as resident housemaster in a boarding school. I had no crystal ball to tell me this was the beginning of a teaching career. It simply looked like an interesting path to take at that moment: independence with pay while I continued at university.

Crescent School for Boys (of 6 to 12) was then a small private school newly relocated in splendid quarters on the former Massey estate, known as Dentonia Park, in the city's east end. The buildings, baronial in style, housed a heated indoor swimming pool, a 200-seat theatre, an assembly room, a small gym, a tiny hospital, a billiard room, and accommodation for up to 100 boarders. The main mansion boasted several large rooms with high ceilings, among them two very grand washrooms, in one of which stood the first urinals I had ever seen in a private home. These were clearly designed to accommodate important men and intimidate small boys. The headmaster was W. R. E. Williams (M.A., Cantab.), a ruddy and genial don inseparable from his pipe, his academic gown, and his wife, the school matron, known as "shrinking Violet" on account of her size, not her amiable personality. Most of the staff were British, and Williams needed some Canadians. On the recommendation of his fellow Welshman Gwynne-Timothy, now teaching there, he hired Doug Hicks and me — Hicks to teach history and live out, Moore to teach arts and crafts and live in.

From fall to spring I lived there, every weekday making the hour-long streetcar ride to university after a morning class, and returning in the afternoon to teach another class or two. In reality the students taught me. From them I learned the thrill that comes with igniting the creative imagination of the young, convincing them that tomorrow's reality depends on what they do with today's. (This axiom is not always easy to get across. Years later I put it into a teaching capsule in Miss Stacey's song, "Open the Window!" for the musical *Anne of Green Gables*.) Best of all were the weekends when the school was deserted except for me, the cook, and the handful of boarders who had nowhere to go, whose families lived thousands of miles away, or had gone on distant vacations, or off to war, or were no longer a family.

Over the Christmas holidays, which were snowless in 1939, I had two such charges, aged six and seven. They had been invited to Christmas dinner at the homes of friends' parents, but lunchtime found the three of us alone in the dining hall with a long afternoon ahead. The older boy asked if we could play football. I explained that two teams required at least four players. The younger, who had been silent during the meal, suddenly asked me a gentle question that made me spill my tea: "Sir, who is Jesus Christ?" It was the same question I had asked my reverend father one Christmas long ago, receiving a flustered reply about a man who was a god, or a god who was a man, but not really, because he didn't have a human father, really a holy ghost, so to speak, who rose from the dead to save us all, or some of us, perhaps. I said simply, "Many people believe he was the son of God." Then the little bugger said, "Sir, who is God?" My courses in Oriental literature had not prepared me for this. Ignorance I could have coped with; innocence was unfair. After waffling as badly as my father ever did, I took refuge in the doctrine of immanence and announced that God, if you believed in Him, was right here in this room with us. That was when my inquisitor sprang his trap. "Then, sir, couldn't God be fourth for football?" It was an extraordinary game we had that afternoon in the middle of a world war in which God, according to His earthly representatives, was already very busy on both sides.

When spring came, my brother Peter dropped out of cram school to enlist in the infantry; our Uncle Wilfrid, back in uniform, was already a brigadier and in charge of army ordnance in Ottawa; and Francis, with his rare combination of British shop training and North American technical education, was plucked out of university and sent to New Jersey as a liaison officer between the British and American aircraft industries. Only I, of the men in the family, was still at home. When the university and school terms ended, I tenderly parted from my lover and reported for my first professional theatre job, playing summer stock in a converted town hall over a jail where senior German prisoners of war were being held. It was the summer of 1940, and I was 21.

The story of the Actors' Colony in Bala, Muskoka, the only professional theatre then operating in Canada, belongs in a chapter to come. But there is one part of it that belongs here, because it grew me up, as they say, in short order.

We had been performing for about four weeks — four plays in as many weeks; I had never been worked so hard in my life — when I received a letter from my lady telling me that she thought she was pregnant. Understanding this to be impossible, I wrote back with what must have seemed an insensitively sensible suggestion: to see a doctor. She replied that she would prefer to await my return when we could discuss the situation. Unable either to leave in mid-season or to do anything further by proxy, I could only get through the days while at night proliferating scenarios, as I felt sure she must have been doing, any one of which would radically alter both our lives. When at last we met, nervously sitting astride our bicycles at the edge of a familiar park, she said that her guess had been correct. Instead of putting aside the damn bicycle and taking her into my arms, I blurted out a bewildered, "But you said you couldn't!" She replied, as if to an idiot, that although she had been told she could not *bear* a child, there was no reason she could not *conceive* one. I was still trying to sort out the implications of this, lost in the Witches' quibble about "born of woman" that doomed the unfortunate Macbeth, when she asked if I wanted to marry her. Taking my hesitation for reluctance, she abruptly rode off.

I never saw her again. But unbeknown to me, her parents had been sending her for counselling to my old mentor Dr. Blatz. Handling the affair with rare understanding, they involved him as intermediary. Knowing both parties intimately, Blatz wasted no time on exploring options:

> WB: Neither of you should marry the other. It would be a disaster
> for all concerned. We do things differently these days. The
> child, if there is a child, which is problematic in view of the
> mother's condition, will be put out for adoption. You are
> going to pay all the medical expenses. Can you find the dough?
>
> MM: Somehow.
>
> WB: Then open a separate bank account and keep your mouth shut.
> There's no sense in hurting others. This is your responsibility.
> I'll be in touch.

The experience was strangely like my interview with Sir William Mulock two years before. Again my life was being taken out of my hands — in my own interest, I was assured. But then her life was also being taken out of her hands, as a mother's always is. To meet the obligation my only recourse was to steal time: to drum up all the well-paying radio work I could without letting anyone, either at the university or at home, know how much time was missing. In this stolen-time-frame I felt I was playing out a tragedy — one definition of which is that everyone can see it coming but no one seems able to stop it. In due course there was a child, born dead. Its mother married soon, but died not long afterward in her sleep. It is survived by its father. Youth ends, I see now, when you begin to confront what might have been.

My checkered career as a university student had a happier ending. I redeemed Sir William's bet, other quondam losers will be glad to know, by heading my final year, before which I was nominated for a Rhodes Scholarship. Entering the committee room for the famous gruelling, I overheard the end of Principal Malcolm Wallace's benediction: "Yes, but he learns from his mistakes!" It still mocks me from the wall above my desk.

Book Two

The Real World

You dream you are the doer,
You dream that action is done,
You dream that action bears fruit.
It is your ignorance.
It is the world's delusion
That gives you these dreams.

— *THE BHAGAVAD GITA*

6

The Propaganda War

"FLOUR-BOMB," said the militia manual, "a brown paper bag filled with flour; on impact explodes visibly but harmlessly." From an ancient Moth biplane piloted by a brother officer I dropped one after another onto our fellow part-time soldiers below. And as I did so, I began to think of myself as a "flour-bomb": all fizz and no effect. A substitute for the real thing. Not an explosive but something exploded. This was not the stuff of military epic. Nor was skiing with dud rifles on the low slopes of High Park, nor bouncing on armoured carriers along the farm roads of Richmond Hill. These happened to be milestones to me because, until I became recruiting officer for the Second (Reserve) Battalion Royal Regiment of Canada, I had never flown in a plane, used a pair of skis, or driven a car. But they had considerably less to do with military training than with publicity opportunities in the campaign to recruit volunteers. SKI TROOPS INVADE HIGH PARK, ran the headline in the Toronto Telegram.[1]

It was the winter of 1941, and most of my close high school and university friends were on active service, or headed that way — Doug Hicks, Jim George, Freeman Tovell, and Eric Atkinson in the navy; Francess Halpenny and Elizabeth Stone in the air force; and Terrace, who was half American, in the U.S. Air Force. Sanderson was doing his internship in the army Medical Corps. Other good companions of both sexes were in either the services or the Red Cross. Some of the promising lives were already wasted. Dashing Harry Tattersall, Captain Absolute to my Falkland in *The Rivals,* had hardly made lieutenant when he was killed in a training exercise 50 miles from home. Ralph Sturgeon, the Macduff who broke my skull and had since become a surgeon, had been blown up with his London hospital shortly after arriving overseas. Popular Paul McGillicuddy, the campus politician who signed up early with the Royal Air Force because, he said, "After the war, a politician without a medal will be a dead duck," won his medal in the Battle of Britain posthumously.

But the lives of the quick and the dead meant something, while mine was a floundering search for meaning. In the months after graduation I was running a circus with four rings between which I saw no connection except that they were all in a circus. I was working up recruiting stunts for the regiment, writing articles, appearing on radio (still my main source of income), acting in amateur stage shows for the Arts and Letters Club, and directing for Mother's penurious Village Players — who in the grand old wartime theatrical tradition were upholding the flag of high culture while entertaining local troops with fluff. On top of everything else I was studying toward a master's degree in semantics — looking for the meaning of meaning.

The immediate catalyst for the postgraduate plan had been a lecture in Hart House Theatre by the venerable U.S. Shakespearean scholar E. E. Stoll. Like most academics of his generation, Stoll spurned the microphone, and his frail voice and pursed articulation scarcely carried to my seat in the 10th row. On the way out I ran into Principal Wallace, who ebulliently embraced me with a "Well, Moore, what about *that,* eh!" "I don't know, sir," I said. "I couldn't hear him." "Ah, yes, Moore," came the reply, "but what a mind! *What a mind!*" At that very moment the problem of communication between minds — the ultimate connection — seemed to me of transcendent importance, and one that urgently needed attention. As a beginning, I conceived a thesis on the symbolic codes long used in the theatre arts — language, mime, myth — as an approach to the conveyance of meaning.

Much of the rest of my life, I see now, has been a wistful attempt to complete the thesis that got crowded out of it then.

"CBC Features Department," the *Radio Times* for December 1941 announced, "has accepted for presentation the first script of Mavor Moore, a young artist who is one of the leading character actors in many of CBC's Toronto dramatic originations." The script was a wartime version of Charles Dickens's *A Christmas Carol*, with Scrooge as "a hard-boiled 20th-century businessman, who is taken in hand by the Spirits of Christmas Past (in a London air raid shelter), Christmas Present (in German-occupied countries), and Christmas Yet-to-Come (if Canada loses sight of the value of her precious heritage of freedom)." Fifty years later my conscience prompted me to make amends with a stage musical as true to Dickens's ghost story as I had once been false. But at the time I hoped the plagiarism would be redeemed by the originality of the technical effects, of which I felt sure Dickens would approve.

The experiment would not have been at home in the CBC's drama department. The head of drama, Rupert Lucas (director of the ill-fated *King John*), was a onetime light opera singer and bon vivant with a lazy mind, a flabby soul, and an ambition exceeding his endowment. A product of theatrical convention, he was ill-equipped to explore a new approach to drama through the ear alone, with original text, music, and sound score — especially at a time when documentary and other mixed formats were scrambling the traditional categories of both entertainment and art, allowing us to invent our own. He was also intellectually incapable of grasping the importance of radio as a communications medium in a compartmentalized country such as Canada. These shortcomings loomed large in the midst of a war demanding continual demonstration to Canadians of what they themselves could achieve.

Lucas's contribution to the war effort was *Theatre of Freedom*, a series of adaptations of established British, European, and American stage plays connected with the struggle for democracy, starring famous British, European, and American actors, with the addition of a few Canadian expatriates anxious to show their colours such as Walter Huston and Raymond Massey. It was only at the insistence of other producers, notably Andrew Allan in Vancouver and Rupert Caplan in Montreal, that the series also included contemporary radio plays by the Americans Arch Obler, Norman Corwin, and Archibald MacLeish, and a new play by the Irish-Canadian John Coulter. "The supporting casts are Canadian," the advertisements boasted.

Other CBC departments were looking further ahead. By the end of 1941 a National News Service was being set up under veteran journalist Dan McArthur, with five newsrooms across the country and a London headquarters for war correspondents. To meet the wartime demand for documentaries and special occasions, the CBC had also set up a department of feature programs under J. Frank Willis, a Haligonian of prodigious provenance. Chronicler of the 1936 Moose River Mine disaster (the actuality that first bonded the nation by radio), onetime first mate of *The Bluenose*, rumrunner, northern explorer, actor, painter, poet, reporter, Willis had imagination and talent to burn. He often drowned them instead, but the vision held. Until the appointment of Andrew Allan as Lucas's successor in 1943, Willis was at the centre of the rapidly expanding creative circle in CBC Radio, and it was he who drew me into it.

On December 7, 1941, the day the Japanese attacked Pearl Harbor, I received two job offers as a director — one from Willis at the CBC for $35 a week, the other from John Grierson at the new National Film Board for $30 a week. My school and university chum Tom Daly, already at the NFB, urged me to join him. Still in debt, I took the CBC job because it paid $5 a week more.

The Corporation's first Toronto headquarters, a former private station, was in a run-down industrial complex on Davenport Road near Bathurst Street. I was given a desk in an open area that accommodated, in the fashion of newspaper offices, about 10 producers and a few secretaries. Only section heads rated closed offices, the flimsy walls of which failed to muffle the interior ribaldry and recrimination. Down the corridor was the sound effects department, crowded with vegetable and mineral junk from which three leprechauns coaxed unlikely noises at all hours. Past this were the soundproof studios, and master control with its primitive banks of intricately wired walls, panels, and recording machines. As a sign of intense mental activity, almost everyone smoked, and the single most prevalent object was the ashtray.

On the day I reported for duty my desk was stacked with homework — on top, the Corporation's revealing *Annual Report*:

> Even in time of peace, national radio has played an increasingly important role in welding together the diverse elements of our population; in wartime it serves also to . . . sustain morale by means of programs that adequately interpret the will of the whole Canadian people to prosecute the war to a vigorous conclusion by every means in their power.[2]

The fact was that only the advent of war had roused the parliamentary rear guard to notice that broadcasting could be a nation builder as well as an advertising medium. And even then they saw nation-building as a form of advertising. To wage war on the homefront they needed to reach the people, and by 1941 radio reached almost 90 percent of them. Once aboard the bandwagon, of course, they tried to hijack it as a conveyance for government policy. What had inspired the public broadcasting movement in Britain and Canada in the 1930s was precisely the opposite notion: that government must serve culture. These small minds saw radio as their windfall, not the country's.

I wrote to Sanderson, overseas, marvelling at "how deeply our leaders' heads are in the sand." If radio had suddenly emerged as the nation's primary means of expression, it was because radio was filling a vacuum. In 1941, as he and I knew well enough, there was little else — and that little owed less to political encouragement. Aside from the province of Saskatechewan and the city of Montreal, grants, subsidies, and tax breaks for the arts and letters were unknown. Constitutionally education was a provincial preserve, and culture was seen as the handmaid of education; in most communities the only theatres were the inaptly designed and ineptly equipped school auditoriums. Canadian writing, music, theatre, and painting, even where recognized and admired, owed more to social grace and local pride than to general popularity and national concern. They were present, but marginal to the pervasive American presence. It was *faute de mieux* that CBC Radio had become Canada's national theatre, newspaper, magazine, sports arena, comic strip, concert hall, town hall, school, and farm exchange combined.

The opportunity was breathtaking. But the report I read reflected only its authors' patronizing insecurity before the Corporation's political masters: "During the last year Canadian plays of a very even quality have been produced; they demonstrate that some Canadian authors and playwrights now have a competent knowledge of this new medium." There was no hint that Canada had entered the radio age at the same time as Britain and the United States, that its failure to stay abreast was due to lack of political will, and that our broadcasters might soon be acknowledged as innovators. Caution reigned.

My first meeting with the general manager left me thinking I had joined a lost cause captained by a stoned ostrich. Gladstone Murray, a courtly graduate of the BBC brought back to initiate public broadcasting in his homeland, was about to address a Canadian Club luncheon on *The Impact of Radio on Youth* when he was introduced backstage to his youngest producer. He smiled affably. At the head table he smiled through the usual fulsome prologue, slowly stood, said "Thank you!" and slid straight down and out of sight. The chairman proclaimed him overcome with fatigue and called for a medical volunteer, but everyone there could see the man was fu' as a coot, as they say in Glasgow. I was told the event was frequent if not always so spectacular. But I learned to respect Gladstone Murray's acumen about everything except himself, and was sorry when he left soon afterward. Sober three days a week, he ran the Corporation better than some of his successors sober for seven.

In Toronto Murray had surrounded himself with accelerators and brakes in dangerously equal proportions. When the Canadian-American playwright Merrill Denison wrote from New York asking for a current who's who, I sent him the following reply:

> *Ernest Bushnell*, general supervisor of programs: ex-pop singer. Ablest executive in the Corp. Always frank and demands frankness of others. His artistic humility earns support of those whose ideas he solicits and backs. *George Taggart*, assistant supervisor: also a pop singer, but forever. A smooth, conceited, buyable pusher. Desperate to marry the small mind and the big ego. *Charles Jennings*, supervisor of program planning: former announcer, smart, university-educated. Recognizes traffic control as the key to power: nothing happens without his knowing.

> *Dick Claringbull*, regional supervisor for Ontario: Accountant, bigot and self-appointed bottleneck. *Ira Dilworth*, regional supervisor for B.C.: nice guy. Former English prof, friend of Emily Carr, Ned Pratt et al. An intellectual who understands creativity. Great raconteur. *Charles Delafield*, head of institutional brdcsts: ex-secretary Hart House at U. of T. Damn nice chap, but knows nothing about broadcasting and never will. *Harry Boyle*, farm brdcsts: the hick exterior hides a deep thinker. Could be important.

> *Elizabeth Long*, supervisor of women's talks: One of only two female department heads. This is Misogyny Hall. A knowledgeable old hand, but jealous of her position. *Mary Grannan*, supervisor of children's brdcsts: the other female head. Flamboyant, warm ex-teacher from Maritimes. Squelches opposition to her programs by simple expedient of allowing none but her own on the air. *R. S. (Rex) Lambert*, adviser on art & education: ex-editor BBC Listener, old crony of Murray's. Would like Grannan's job or bigger, but knows he's too old & too English. Also a warlock: speaks intimately about everything from libel laws to poltergeists.

The drama producers you know, but maybe not our best music man John *Adaskin*, a fine musician turned director of music and variety shows. Champion of young talent. Adaskin, announcer Lorne Greene and Montreal producer Rupert Caplan are CBC's only Jewish staff members. Fed up with the local anti-Semitism, he intends to quit and freelance.[3]

Joining this group, happily unaware of my role as Merrill Denison's mole, I was given a dog's breakfast of programs to direct, including *The Farm Show*. Cumulatively the experience was inuring. But the biggest challenges were the war shows, which for lack of models we had to invent. There were three categories: recruitment for the military, uplift for the civilians, and Victory Bond promotions for everybody. Beginning as Willis's assistant, I soon found myself producing and directing all three on my own.

The weekly *Comrades in Arms* saluted the spirit of cooperation animating the three armed services — a premise frequently in greater danger than the country. The navy, army, and air force each assigned contributing officers, whose rank and qualification varied widely. Bill Strange of Naval Intelligence ("*Commander* Strange to you!") was John Bull personified. His bulk, seniority in the British navy, and successful prewar career in broadcasting and advertising lent him a dignity that reduced his critics to practical jokes. During one broadcast, the performers systematically undressed the veteran actor Frank Peddie as he stood narrating a long Strange epic, while the author turned a helpless purple in the booth. The army adviser was Major Dick Diespecker, a Vancouver broadcaster, artilleryman, and poet. With his pal Dorwin Baird, an unjustly eternal sergeant, he wrote documentaries so plodding they seemed real, and one of my jobs was to prevent his fake Longfellow from ruining the effect. ("Do you think I have something to say to posterity?" Diespecker once asked Ira Dilworth, who replied evenly: "To posterity, perhaps.") The RCAF link, Flying Officer Andy McDermott, was a former advertising executive whose main aim was to get equal airtime with the senior services by fair means or foul. His assistant, a lowly aircraftsman named Fletcher Markle, recruited from Andrew Allan's radio drama crew in Vancouver, wrote rings around all of them.

Aside from the night a 10-ton truck started up in the middle of the Atlantic and Willis tore the door off the booth to get at the soundman responsible, our reenactments of war were not so much inaccurate as highly selective. Dialogue was severely restricted; I was the first director to get "Christ!" on the air as a soldierly oath, and it raised hell. Obscenity was best drowned out by a burst of gunfire. In radio the prize moments were necessarily those when something could be heard. Before television, newsworthiness depended on noiseworthiness. Long before Marshall McLuhan pronounced it "hot," we understood that radio provided the imagination with a key rather than an inventory. Certain sound effects became so evocative of entire campaigns — the air raid siren, the police van, the jungle cries — that recordings were regularly worn out. But for establishing place, occasion, nationality, mood, and tension nothing could rival music.

It was conductor Sam Hersenhoren who persuaded Willis that our documentaries for the home front needed original scores. Anxious to upgrade my clumsy grip on music theory, I resumed studies with the most advanced of our young composers, John Weinzweig. Once a week, in the Weinzweig parlour, the master patiently drilled his backward pupil while his wife Helen made tea and (I realize in retrospect) quiet mental notes of male bonding rituals that would later inform her perceptive novels. Without those lessons I would not, I think, have gone on to write my own musicals or librettos for other composers. But the lessons bore more immediate fruit in my ability to integrate the texts of our CBC Radio series with the incidental music of Weinzweig and the other composers — Lucio Agostini, Morris Surdin, Howard Cable — who gave them such emotional authenticity. *New Homes for Old* (true refugee tales), *Canada Carries On* (good deeds), *Our Canada* (identity), *Nazi Eyes on Canada* (paranoia), and other disposable wartime series owed much of their impact to original scores. On July 10, 1941, the *Globe and Mail* reported that the CBC had set off a bombing scare with a program dramatizing a mock Nazi attack on Halifax. The music, which should have been a giveaway, was widely criticized for being too effective.

The incident delighted Orson Welles, one of the stars donating their talents to the Canadian war effort, whose 1938 *War of the Worlds* had caused a panic in the United States. He was only four years older than I when he came in October 1942 to appear in an episode of *Nazi Eyes on Canada* directed by me, and refused to work for "this kid." Willis, who was to play the villain, took over the direction and I stepped into his acting role. Welles was then at his grandest. He had a secretary named Miss World whose sole function, aside from keeping him supplied with cards and other paraphernalia for magic tricks, was to interrupt rehearsals with telegrams and messages. "Mr. Welles," she once carolled in mid-scene, "Miss Del Rio is on the line from Hollywood!" "Oh God," sighed Welles, "tell her I love her!", and turned back to the microphone. Merle Oberon, in another episode of the same series, accepted my direction but responded to none of it, simply repeating a two-note inflection that I gathered was the only one she had. But when she was brought an egg sandwich instead of a chicken sandwich for lunch, she lay on the studio floor and screamed over a range of three octaves.

Other celebrities — Cedric Hardwicke, Anna Neagle, Herbert Marshall, Paul Muni — gave me lessons in both skill and generosity. Oscar Levant, then as legendary for his wit as for his piano playing, gave me an unforgettable lesson in the power of expectation when he convulsed his Massey Hall audience for two minutes by strolling to the microphone and saying, "Ummm . . ." I was learning that in the communal arts the commune is as important as the art.

Some of my teachers were local. Don Henshaw was in the advertising business. Clever and unscrupulous, he had grasped a trend that escaped most economic and social theorists of the day, occupied as they were with fascism, socialism, capitalism, and other moralities. Henshaw foresaw that advertising, which serves any master, would one day become the power behind the throne of every domain — business, media, government, sport, art, education, even religion. In the Age of Information it would be public relations, not love, that made the world go round. To promote the sale of Victory Bonds, the federal government and the advertising agencies had jointly established a War Advertising Committee. Don Henshaw was its ambassador to the CBC.

Neither government nor the crown corporation, I think, recognized the slippery slope on which this collaboration had launched them. Henshaw's CBC colleague, assistant program supervisor George Taggart, was only too ready to go along; having reached the limit of his incapacity, he was about to leave public radio for a job in advertising. He and Henshaw were the coproducers of the weekly series *Highlights for Today*, designed to boost the Victory Bond campaign. I was its director. This euphemistically titled sales pitch, scheduled on Sunday nights for maximum impact, called for all the nous I could muster. Its speakers were among the most distinguished, its pundits among the most learned, its entertainers among the most renowned in the land. Brain surgeon Wilder Penfield rubbed airwaves with soprano Pierrette Alarie, aviation pioneer John McCurdy with actress Marie Dressler, parliamentarian

Agnes McPhail with runner Percy Williams. Merely assembling it every week was a logistical nightmare, even without Henshaw and Taggart breathing their oleaginous countermands down my neck.

Finally came the Sunday night when the dress rehearsal ran a minute short. The gap could easily have been filled with theme music, but Don Henshaw had one of his epiphanies. In the control booth, where veteran production assistant Grace Athersich, the engineer, and the conductor were awaiting instructions, Henshaw whispered to Taggart, whose face lit up, then turned to me. "Give 'em the Lord's Prayer," he said with sly reverence. "Thirty seconds flat. Top it with 'God Save the King' — half a minute on the nose. It'll knock 'em dead." The engineer stared at the wall, the conductor at the floor, Grace at the ceiling. Astonishing myself, I said, "No." Taggart turned red, cocked his uneven teeth, and shouted, "Who's running this show?" I said, "You can, if you like, George, but one of us is leaving right now." On a nod from Henshaw, both of them left the booth.

Before this insubordination had been dealt with, I received word that my brother Peter had been seriously wounded overseas. I applied for active service again. This time the army's reach was far enough down in the barrel to find my myopia acceptable, and I quit the CBC. But before leaving town I wrote and staged for the Arts and Letters Club a one-act play called I Know You, about an advertising man who goes to war and is killed in battle, leaving a question for the family and friends who knew him only too well: Does death in the cause of truth atone for a life of casuistry?[4]

THE JOB OF GENERAL STAFF OFFICER III (Intelligence and Security) for Military District No. 3, HQ Kingston, Ontario, allowed me to sport a red armband and brought me face-to-face with saboteurs, spies, the Royal Canadian Mounted Police, and the governor general — all of whom proved toothless. But to get there I had to pass through basic training in Trois-Rivières, officer training in Brockville, commando training in Camp Borden, an RCMP security check, and the intelligence course at the Royal Military College in Kingston. ("Strip yourself of all inhibitions and worries and be prepared to go full out mentally and physically.")

The "I" school at RMC was run by Colonel R. O. Macfarlane, a Winnipeg historian whose chaotic moustache concealed a constant smile at his charges' naivety. He had a great respect for candour and a firm grasp of its antithesis: psychological warfare. Our chief instructor was a crack I and S colonel on loan from the British who rejoiced in the Anglo-Saxon name of Cuthbert Skilbeck. In impeccable Oxonian, Skil taught us to how to break locks, codes, laws, and hearts in the pursuit of information.

At his suggestion I followed my appointment as the new district security officer with a calling card: an unannounced visit to a nearby barracks, where I posed as an emissary from the chief of staff in Ottawa and made off with their personnel records and weapons inventory. It was one of my finest performances, but went unreviewed since the adjutant could hardly admit he had no idea what was in either. On the strength of this success I was allowed to visit RCMP headquarters in Ottawa to view the secret files on individuals in my district. These included some of my close friends from school and university, whose only common error seemed to be a penchant for joining causes; this explained how I had slipped through the net. The files' contents were mere filler; their power came from being secret and being there.

All of these events went to my head, and when I caught the new Ronson Flamethrower on public display at an army demonstration in Brockville, I felt it was time to let the local brass know they were under highly sophisticated surveillance. As I reminded Int. HQ, Ottawa (copy to the commanding officer, Brockville), "the marginally noted weapon is on the secret list." Unfortunately the weapon I had listed in the margin was "Ronson Lighter." A deadpan reply came from the chief (copy to the commanding officer, Brockville), commending my vigilance but pointing out that the marginally noted weapon was readily available in any cigar store.

I lectured recruits on Nazi theories of race, and defended conscientious objectors against overzealous recruiters. But my outstanding feat was the trapping of a German spy. Our platoon's sergeant and chief censor, an aristocratic Czech 20 years my senior, flagged a curious letter addressed to a private in Camp Petawawa asking for the names of other Saskatchewan boys in the unit, with reply requested to a mailbox number. The bulb went on. A whole regimental battle order, by God, could be deduced by adding up provincial numbers! A watch on the mailbox netted a corporal in the Women's Army Corps with a German name. I had Sergeant Woolner arrest her in my jeep, bring her into my office, and stand by to throw in German phrases to catch her off guard. The little corporal, terrified when she realized how much we knew, said she was "only doing it for the party." Scenting big game, Woolner and I hammered her in both languages (she seemed to understand neither) to tell us who her boss was. Finally she blurted out, "Tommy Douglas!" What was this? The Great Prairie socialist parliamentarian a Nazi spy? "You're in trouble," I said hard, and she started to cry. "All right, I'll tell you! I know it's illegal to politick in the army, but we gotta win the provincial election!" As I drove her home — Woolner with his arm around her in the back seat muttering "Now, now, don't cry" — I assured her no word would pass our lips about politicking if none passed hers about false arrest.

The truth is that my mind was not on counterespionage. I was now a married man.

For a year I had been courting Darwina Faessler, who preferred the nickname Dilly to the feminized tribute imposed by her father. Charles Faessler, an industrious Swiss-born grain merchant and free thinker, was resolved to name his children after the scientists he idolized; his Canadian wife, Isabella, preferred simple first names to go with the uncommon surname. As a compromise, they agreed that she would name the girls and he would name the boys. After Elizabeth came Haeckel; and after Anita there should, in an orderly Swiss universe, have come Darwin. So the third daughter became Darwina, who at the age of 20 married a scientific ignoramus.

I first saw her five years earlier, the summer Doug Hicks and I, with a day off from camp counselling in Muskoka, tried to think of any girls we knew within hitchhiking distance. Hicks remembered our fellow student Anita Faessler, whose family had a cottage near Huntsville. We got there by serial inquiry, only to find Anita absent — out in the canoe, as it happened, with her prospective fiancée Walter Tovell — and her mother away shopping. Guarding the cottage was a 15-year-old faun with her dark Titian hair up in braids, her bright conversation unaffected, and her laughter golden. What a splendid girl, I thought, for my brother Peter in a year or two! Three years later, after she had joined the Village Players and shown her mettle as a singer and designer, I forgot Peter and marvelled at how the four-year discrepancy in our ages had shrunk. Perhaps she had grown wiser faster — or perhaps I, in the army with an overseas posting ahead, felt neither of us had any time to lose.

On October 16, 1943, we had a modest Unitarian ceremony at her home. As pillars of Toronto's Unitarian community, the Faesslers shared my discomfort with orthodoxy. To avoid army church parades ("RCs 0845 hrs, Prot. 1000 hrs") I had identified myself as "Unbeliever"; but it was the great monolithic creeds I objected to. Unitarians pray To

Whom It May Concern, which made sense to Dilly and me, and the minister allowed us a hand in writing the ritual. In the photographs Dilly looks radiant, I pompous, with my Sam Browne belt on backward. Afterward we went off by train to the cottage in Muskoka, now russet and chilly in mid-October. We had a five-day honeymoon before I returned to Camp Borden for advanced training. When I was posted to Kingston in the spring, we moved into our first flat. A letter from my mother awaited us:

> Yesterday I telephoned Mrs. Sanderson. . . . She told me that Graham was still in England so far as she knew and that he had seen Terrace a week before he was missing, also that T. was the only one of the bomber crew that had not been heard from — three were prisoners — and that they did hope that he might get away somehow. . . .[5]

While I lived in connubial bliss in Kingston, Ontario, the Allies had launched the Normandy invasion.

Had I not been so disoriented, being in heaven one week and feeling guilty about it the next (how little I knew then about manic-depressives), I might have been more receptive to the assignment that came almost immediately. I was summoned to Ottawa for an interview with the eponymous General Mess, in charge of Army Public Relations and Entertainment. What he had in mind, said the general, was to send me overseas in command of a unit of the Canadian Army Show, and for this to promote me to captain. I indignantly refused the bribe. Was I to desert my bride, only to let my fighting comrades down by going back into showbiz?

It was at this moment that my completely ad hoc career — to which you may all bear witness — took on the appearance of a carefully planned trajectory. Chastised all my life for aimlessness, I was about to be commended for foresight. With the Army Show a dead issue, I received orders to proceed overseas to join a new psychological warfare section attached to Canada House. My former teacher Colonel Skilbeck, now back in Britain, had apparently advised the Canadians that I was a natural for the job. "My dear fellow," Skil said to me three weeks later over a brandy in London's Automobile Club, "could anything less than sheer prescience have led you to accumulate systematically all five essential qualifications for fighting a propaganda war? The skills of several arts, a stint as teacher of impressionable minds, a theoretical background in communication, practical experience in the media, and a nodding acquaintance with the utterly insane world of military intelligence!"

THE CONVERTED BOMBER LANDED us in London on a late afternoon in July 1944. Reporting to the Allied Officers' Club for the night, I went straight to sleep in a double room. I was awakened after dark by the sound of oncoming buzz bombs and nearby sobbing. On the bed across from mine sat a white-haired Australian brigadier, fully dressed but with his red-tabbed tunic unbuttoned, shaking with fear. "Are you all right, sir?" I asked. "No! Been through seven campaigns in five countries. Never met anything like this. The bloody things are unaimed, you see." He talked all night to keep them away.

Like the buzz bombs, some deeds belong to the dark — not because they are dreadful but because their effectiveness depends on illusion. I still have a copy of Psychological Warfare Document No. 25, our Kingston training guide:

> Propaganda is a weapon, wielded either on behalf of one's country or on behalf of oneself, as in the competitive advertising world, and successful practitioners are unwilling to endanger their success in the future by revealing the methods they have used in the past. That is why there are practically no books on propaganda worth reading. It is also the reason this paper is graded SECRET.[6]

Since those days there have been books galore claiming to expose the principles and techniques of wartime propaganda, using the label SECRET only as a lure. But in 1943 the injunction was still taken seriously by both sides.

The first principle, I observed, is that someone has to conquer while others stoop.

At Canada House I was one of two army captains seconded to Thomas Stone, newly appointed counsellor on security affairs to High Commissioner Vincent Massey. The patrician Massey knew the advantages, in such a role, of keeping his hands impeccably clean. The wartime High Commission housed a dazzling diplomatic staff whose last names included, at one time or another, Vanier, Pearson, Léger, Ignatieff, Lemieux, Holmes, Ritchie, LePan. But when it came to patronage and media-grubbing, Massey passed the spade to one Campbell Moody, who had traded in his major's uniform for a cutaway and striped pants, in which array he became awesomely expert at shovelling low soil at high levels. And where really covert strategy was concerned — the grey links between the official and the unmentionable — the senior Stone was his man. These dispensations allowed Massey to assure the Canadian government, Parliament, and people that he was (a) completely in charge and (b) not responsible for mistakes.

Tommy Stone was a widely travelled diplomat who had married a wealthy American Southerner and after her death married her equally wealthy sister. He had emerged from an understandably early retirement to organize Canadian participation in the shadowland of propaganda policy. At university I had acted with his talented niece Elizabeth. He was a reincarnation of the Scarlet Pimpernel: a charming dandy, gone prematurely white, given to piano playing and singing at parties, but able to metamorphose instantly into a man of action. I and my fellow officer, a dashing Québécois journalist who spent his off-hours trying to beat Casanova's track record, were welcome at the parties but expected to snap to attention on cue.

My colleague's job was to produce leaflets to be airdropped over enemy units inviting them to surrender. That these worked we knew from captured enemy documents. "The morale effect of these tactics," one German commander reported, "is beyond all doubt. On July 13 a corporal deserted who had been decorated with the Iron Cross, Class II, the Close Combat Medal, the Infantry Storm Medal, and the Medal for the Wounded."[7] My job was to represent Canada on the joint committees masterminding psychological warfare in each of the theatres of war, and to conspire with the BBC's medium-wave and shortwave European services, which had closer links to Allied Intelligence than officialdom was prepared to admit.

At such weekly meetings I learned the second principle of propaganda: Someone has to stoop while others conquer.

The argumentative experts on the Central European Committee knew the continent like the back of their hands, and some wore skulduggery like a glove. My favourite was Major Fine, a former judge from Detroit, nicknamed "the Fixer." With a wave of his cigar he could rustle up a plane, a jeep, or a commando unit to heist enemy prisoners from the front lines into a London radio studio in nothing flat. When Fine was through with him, the prisoner would thank him, on air, for his benevolence. As patriotic as he was dishonest, the Fixer was deeply grateful to his country for giving him the chance to lie and cheat in its defence. No one, at least in my hearing, ever asked him how he did it or what he disbursed in bribes. Everyone knew he could be counted on to perjure himself on a friend's behalf and tell the truth about a rat.

The Far Eastern Committee was more relaxed, perhaps as a result of Asian conditioning. The legendary Oriental scholar Arthur Waley, now in his fifties, whose translations of the Japanese Noh dramas I already revered, appeared each week in the same broken spectacles held together by the same safety pin. Canada had little to contribute. The chairman was a red-maned, red-moustached Burma specialist from Cambridge whose interventions were rendered unintelligible by the pipe clamped between his teeth. The only time he ever removed it to open his mouth, as far as anyone could recall, was the first time I opened mine — to inform the committee that as a consequence of enemy losses at sea the Canadian navy was now the world's fourth largest. "*Really, Canada?*" Burma said, agape. "Yes, sir," I said. "Good God!" he exclaimed, then replaced the pipe and turned to the next item on the agenda.

In his 1980 *A History of the British Secret Service* Richard Deacon often invokes national character as a factor in espionage, "For a Canadian," he says, "William Stephenson was singularly unobtrusive."[8] I never met the man called Intrepid; when I arrived, he had already moved to New York to act as the Secret Service's North American link. But what Canadians, aside from imperious Lord Beaverbrook, could have inspired Deacon's odd stereotype? In Bush House and MI5, where the great eccentrics of British Intelligence held court, the Canadians moved like country mice, recognizing their hosts only from the crumbs they dropped. The genial Jack Wheeler-Bennett allowed us a few, but Ivonne Kirkpatrick, who interrogated the Nazi Rudolf Hess after his strange flight to Scotland and discussed the incident with Stone in my presence ("Hess is quite mad, you know!"), gave us no hint that MI5 had, in fact, engineered the whole caper. I chatted with Major Anthony Blunt about art restoration but not politics. I was introduced to Kim Philby, head of the Secret Service's new Soviet section, who asked if I were related to the Mavor whose *Economic History of Russia* he knew. But I had no idea who they really were, and they had no intention of enlightening me — or anyone else, as it turned out. It was not until years later that Peter Dwyer, the retired British Secret Service officer who became the Canada Council's first director, told me of his part in exposing Philby as a mole and failing to implicate the nimble Blunt, who became surveyor of the queen's paintings and a knight before his eventual padded fall. In 1943 I was an innocent abroad.

But I was learning. In the BBC I spent time with producer Lawrence Gilliam (later a colleague at the United Nations) and poet Louis

MacNeice, then a director. In the European Service I worked alongside Michel St-Denis, destined to play a notable role in Canadian theatre, and Pierre Shaffer, who became head of Radiodiffusion Française after the war. St-Denis once briefly introduced me to General de Gaulle, whose celebrated 1967 intervention in Canadian affairs (*"Vive le Québec libre!"*) would one day save me from becoming president of the CBC.

At the time, my main connection with the CBC was to make occasional broadcasts to Canada about life in wartime London. Under it all ran the bass continuo of the rocket attacks: the long crescendo of the approach, the cutoff, the eerie pause, the detonation. This sound had become such a crucial symbol of wartime Britain that the CBC asked RCAF Sergeant Fletcher Markle, late of *Comrades in Arms*, to make a new recording of a V1's impact. The next raid caught me near RCAF headquarters in Lincoln's Inn Fields, and ducking into the ancient buildings, I found Fletcher perched on a windowsill with his wire recorder. As one rocket putt-putted ever nearer, we laughed in triumph until its motor cut off, whereupon we raced for shelter, leaving the recorder to its own devices. I used this on-mike *crumpf* as the signature for my initial broadcast to Canada in November. "In spite of a paper shortage," I reported, "the really popular gift is a book. Stores sell biographies, thrillers, war books, even poetry as soon as published."[9] The use of books as an answer to bombs, I thought, neatly caught the difference in attitude between London and Toronto.

"There was a whole gang of us listening," I heard from Mother in a letter that said much about three people whose lives were now intertwined:

> I heard it all & as if you were in Toronto. Your voice has changed a bit. In spots you were quite English and in others purposely Canadian, I fancy. Your attack has improved greatly. Dilly was very funny about this when I remarked to her that it had "improved." She thought I was criticizing you and rose to your defence like a flash. . . . She is such a loyal little person! You have something very precious in her adoration and devotion and *loyalty*. Don't ever let her down, darling. She'll go through hell for you! When I say loyalty, I don't mean just physical loyalty — oh well, I think perhaps you can understand what I mean. It was feeling that my loyalty was running out of a sieve that crushed my spirit, and when I saw the same quality in Dilly I could not forbear a word of advice. I don't often do it, do I! — Give advice, I mean, so perhaps you will excuse it this once.[10]

The fact was that she seldom hesitated to give advice, especially about transgressions that had not yet occurred to me. Robertson Davies once called her, respectfully, "a witch."

Despite the loving letters from home — almost daily from Dilly — life in London with its random rockets, hyperactivity, and exotic intrigue was oddly disconnected from both Canada and the Continental war. The fog, when it came, wrapping streets, cars and people in impenetrable shrouds while seeping through doors and kerchiefs into eyes and lungs, was no mere fact of life but a vast symbol of oblivion. Identity was masked in a uniform, changed in the darkness or lost in the confusion. Information was either mobilized into press releases ("The American president says . . .") or atomized into snippets rising out of the mist ("And then, my dear, he *ate* it!"). News of the war was plentiful, but news of family and friends was hard to come by.

There was no further word of Terrace. By the time I got to London, Sanderson had already left for a field hospital in Normandy, and my brother Peter was in Italy with a reconnaissance regiment, the Princess Louise Dragoon Guards. I heard from Mother, who had heard it from her brother Wilfrid the brigadier in Ottawa, who had first seen the report in code, that Peter had been seriously wounded again. Lacking further details, she telegraphed me — I was in Intelligence, wasn't I? — "in the hope that you might be able to get more information for me." Years later, when the fog lifted, I got the gist of it from the official history of the assault on Tomba di Pesaro:

> As they were returning [from a reconnaissance] they were caught in the open by shell fire and Major J. B. Lawson was killed, when Lieut. P. M. Moore took command of "B" Squadron. . . . As soon as the leading elements of the Battalion crossed the starting line, they ran into sniper fire from both front and flanks. . . . The unit reached its objective, the last 50 yards literally on hands and knees. . . . Casualties had been very high. . . . Lieut. P. M. Moore was wounded at the starting line, leaving "B" Squadron without officers.[11]

But this is too tidy. "Caught in the open" meant trapped between their own artillery barrage and the enemy's, as I eventually learned from Pete, who attributed his survival to "an empty cartridge in my heart pocket, my sergeant's regrettable refusal to leave me for dead, and a surgeon who just loved sewing."

A similar plea came from O. H. Mavor/James Bridie in Glasgow: "I don't know whether you heard that my son Robert has been posted missing in Normandy. It seems probable that he is a prisoner, as his tank was found burned-out with evidence that the crew had got out of it safely. . . . We have moved Heaven and Earth to trace him. If a lucky wind blows any information through your office, perhaps you will let us know."[12] The wind, when it blew, was unlucky.

Amid this anxiety — indeed as its counterpoint — there was a good deal of *carpe diem* and *gaudeamus igitur* among the military. I went to parties with new American friends (where my blank Canadian face proved a great asset at poker), to long lunches with British colleagues that liquidated the afternoons, and to impromptu congresses of fellow Canadians whenever birthdays or unbirthdays provided an excuse. We often met at the Beaver Club, known as "Mother Massey's Hash House" because there the high commissioner's wife, Alice, tended the lunch counter. "The bizarrely hatted lady herself so takes my attention," I wrote to Dilly, "that I am rarely able to notice or taste anything else, including, thank God, the rabbit stew."

Canadian officers in London had a reputation for almost indecent consanguinity. Dilly was related to the Massey clan through her sister Anita's marriage to Walter Tovell, whose mother Ruth was Vincent Massey's cousin. Walter's younger brother Freeman, a navy lieutenant, lived in the same South Kensington digs as I. Freeman and I often went out on the town with Dilly's sister Betty Faessler, our mutual sister-in-law, who was second-in-command at Canadian Red Cross HQ in Burlington Gardens, just off Piccadilly. (On cold winter nights, we were given to understand, the CRC girls often treated the local tarts to hot chocolate and curiosity.) My old friend Douglas Hicks was at Navy HQ, and his wedding to Flying Officer Elizabeth Stone, niece to my boss Tommy Stone, caused a terrible dent in her uncle's diplomatic liquor supply and the following day's naval and air operations.

But London life was more than military. Through Earle Birney (now a major) I met some female British poets so intense I considered giving up poetry forever. The National Film Board's Joe Golightly, an unabashed egghead both physically and professionally, introduced me to British film-makers achieving daily miracles in the teeth of crippling shortages. I took Russian classes at the Foreign Office. Between galleries, concerts, operas, and ballets I saw the Marx Brothers' *A Night at the Opera* 14 times. A new play starring Helena ("Pixie") Pickard, Cedric Hardwicke's vivacious wife, with whom I'd performed in Toronto, drew me backstage. Now that Cedric was based in Hollywood, she announced, they were separating; but since he was in town at the moment, they were dining together, and would I like to come along? I found myself seated between these two highly civilized thespians at a small table in the dining room of the Savoy Hotel, pecking at an undercooked flounder while they shredded each other in finely modulated stage whispers. By the time the crème glacée arrived, they had settled on divorce, and I had lost all appetite for an acting career.

I had regular lunches at Simpson's-in-the-Strand with the BBC's Gilbert Harding. The hyperbolic Harding — broadcaster, scold, Catholic convert, pederast, and master of the ornate insult — was back in London after a stint as BBC representative in Toronto, where we had become firm sparring partners. It was after such a lunch that Harding delivered himself of one of those notorious public diatribes soon to make him famous on *The Brains Trust*. When a departing American major at the next table dropped a U.S. $10 tip for the waiter, Harding rose like an apoplectic basilisk.

GH: You swine! Don't you realize what you're doing? You should be taken out and shot at the earliest possible dawn!

MAJOR: What are you talking about?

GH: Suborning a British waiter! And don't pretend you don't know what I'm talking about, sir. I'm talking about corruption. I'm talking about buying souls.

MAJOR: Now wait a damn minute —

GH: You Yanks come over here flush with blood money from armament sales, vulgarity oozing from your every gonad, and flaunt your tainted loot before those who've done the fighting for you! Do you imagine that the lackey who gets *that* from you will take *half a crown* from me or my friend here? You, sir, and your unhappy ilk, are wrecking the British economy, tearing apart the fabric of English society, undermining the Allied war effort — Come back! I haven't finished yet!

MM: Gilbert, sit down, for God's sake. Everyone's watching.

GH: (*surveying his audience*) Listening, too, I hope!

The London theatres were packed. Dr. Johnson's dictum, "We that live to please must please to live," is never more apt than in a great city under siege. Both visiting legions and resident Londoners had to be catered to. They mingled at the topical revues such as *Sweeter and Lower* (successor, naturally, to *Sweet and Low*), in which singer Hermione Gingold, fruitlessly disguised as a fire warden, addressed her nightly plea to whatever American officer had the misfortune to sit in the upper box on stage right: "Is Your Stirrup-Pump Still Working, Colonel Hop-Hop-Hopkins?"

Did the visitors want English classical drama? There was Gielgud at the Haymarket with a concise history of it: *Hamlet, Love for Love, The Importance of Being Earnest,* Maugham's *The Circle.* Did Britons want to wring laughter from their wartime predicament? There was James Bridie ready with two successive comedies, *Mr. Bolfry* and *It Depends What You Mean,* witty parables of the here and now for audiences out to outface calamity. Bridie/Mavor was one of their own, one of the unsinkable bereft. Refusing to mourn the now certain death of his elder son Robert, he would periodically descend on London from Glasgow to join the laughter in the theatre as if public merriment were the antidote for private sorrow. We used to pub-crawl after the show and visit his friends, including the star and director of both plays, Alastair Sim. Sim's ripe English accent turned out to be a comic mask for his natural Scots, and he easily wore the Bridie plaid: bright lines crossed with dark irony.

Black comedy thumbing its nose at tragedy also gave an unaccustomed edge to Laurence Olivier's *Richard III* and Tyrone Guthrie's production of *Peer Gynt,* both in the Old Vic season at the New Theatre. Shuffling onto the forestage with a glint in his eye, Olivier got a laugh with Richard's opening line: "Now is the winter of our discontent . . ." When misfortune drives the middle-aged Peer, played by the middle-aged Ralph Richardson, to fall on his knees in prayer for the very first time, Peer's frustrated "God, you're *not listening to me!*" brought sympathetic applause from the house. I had lunch with Richardson at a bistro beside the theatre before a matinee of *Peer,* and worried aloud when he stayed so long, leaving only 10 minutes to make himself up as a 19-year-old for the opening scene. "Makeup? Oh, no, dear boy, only the wig. Youth's all in the mind. When they *want* you to be young . . ." The performance, I realized, owed as much to the audience's need to believe as to Peer Gynt's.

And the need to believe was paramount. The guiding principle of this theatre was not escapism but affirmation. On every stage in London a small red light went on at the start of an air raid, alerting those who wished to go to a shelter — but few ever did. The act of staying, like the act of coming, was a declaration of faith.

At a performance of *Macbeth* starring Donald Wolfit and his wife Rosalind Iden, the little red light came on just after Duncan had been murdered offstage. We could hear a V1 approaching, but no one moved, perhaps because Lady Macbeth was at that moment taunting her husband about his cowardice. As she left to return the bloody daggers to the scene of the crime while Macbeth soliloquized, the rocket came closer, closer. As she reentered saying, "My hands are of your colour, but I shame to wear a heart so white," the familiar putt-putt stopped dead. In the silence Macbeth groaned. And then it struck — so near that the theatre trembled and the painted castle buckled. Undeterred, Lady Macbeth went straight on with her next line: "I hear a knocking at the south entry!" The theatre exploded with laughter and applause, not at the accidental pun but at the triumph of civilization over destruction.

We also saw chaos routed by a single concentrated intelligence.

On an autumn evening in 1944 Freeman Tovell and I were at the Churchill Club when the three famous Sitwells, Edith, Osbert, and Sacheverell, gave a reading of their poetry. "This attraction," the editor John Lehmann reported, a decade later, "had drawn almost the whole of the smarter literary and artistic world. There seemed very little room indeed in the hall for the ordinary members of the Allied forces for whom the Club was supposed to be run."[13] Edith, then almost 60, had just begun to read when a V1 was heard approaching and the club alarm sounded. Standing as erect as the Elizabethan queen she so strongly resembled, the poet paid no attention whatever to the intrusion. As the doodlebug kept chugging in until some of us could see the flare reflected on the windowpane, she scarcely raised her voice as she read through the cutoff, through the silence, through the nearby crunch, to the poem's end. It was *Still Falls the Rain*, written after the first air raids in 1940:

> Still falls the Rain —
> Still falls the blood from the Starved Man's wounded Side:
> He bears in His Heart All Wounds . . .

Not until she dropped her head did anyone stir. Then we applauded, for a long time.

In my case, obviously, all this activity was a substitute for action. I felt guilty at being marginalized, at playing Falstaff, once again, as he encouraged the valiant from the sidelines — "On, bacons, on!" The sense of shame reached its nadir on the day of my war wound, as it came to be called.

I awoke with a fierce abdominal pain. Unable to get out of bed, I rolled onto the floor, but when I tried to stand up, I found myself bent over as rigidly as a T-square. I struggled into my uniform, made my way down to the street, and hailed a taxi to the Canadian army medical station in Trafalgar Square. The medic on duty ordered me into hospital without delay, and I was put aboard a transport bound for our base at Wolverhampton, where I was bedded down in a large ward amid casualties from the front — men with bandaged heads and encased torsos, elevated legs, missing arms, and tubes attached to what was left. The healthiest of the lot were a teacher I knew from Ottawa, turned bright yellow from jaundice, and me, with a stomach ache. The doctors decided I had gallstones, but before they could operate the pain disappeared as abruptly as it had come, and they were faced with an insoluble medical mystery. While my wretched companions lay neglected, my bed became the scene of a daily conclave of specialists comparing notes and meaningful glances. A week later one of them asked me, as an afterthought, if I'd eaten anything unusual the night before the attack. "Oh, yes," I said helpfully. "I went out to dinner with my uncle [the brigadier, who happened to be in London] and ate oysters." "On top of Scotch?" asked another, knowingly. I nodded, and they all looked out the window. "Captain Moore," asked a third, "has no one ever told you not to eat oysters on top of Scotch?" "No, sir," I said. "Why?" "They petrify," said number two, adding, to his colleagues, "He's obviously passed them." "Captain Moore," said the first, "get the hell out of here."

I need hardly say that as my health improved my conscience worsened. The depression deepened when Campbell Moody, Canada House's devious troubleshooter, summoned me from my cubicle into his magnificent front office and announced that he had arranged for me to be promoted to major. I had felt for some time that Moody disliked me, but had never considered the possibility of being kicked upstairs. "I've been talking to headquarters," he said smoothly: "They want you to take command of the overseas Army Show." This was almost the same offer I'd turned down before leaving Canada. Refusing the second bribe as indignantly as I had the first, I went off to drown any second thoughts in Scotch without the oysters.

But my spirits were soon raised by an unexpected call from the U.S. consul in London, a Mr. Tandy, who wished to see me on a confidential matter. Something was in the wind! Had "the Fixer" put them onto me? What was Stephenson up to in New York? Before the appointed meeting

I had a call from a second notable American, the bishop of Ohio, who announced himself as chairman of the U.S. Fight for Freedom Committee and invited me to dinner at the U.S. officers' mess. I should, of course, have recognized the bait. But it was not until after we had discussed God for half an hour that His Grace got around to my earthly father in Cincinnati, the jewel in his diocese. "Your father loves you. Why do you not write to him?" Consul Tandy, it turned out, was yet another emissary from Cincinnati.

Had I mastered psychological warfare only to become the *object* of a propaganda pitch? Was it from the Reverend Francis John Moore that I was to receive my graduation papers in the devil's golden rules: *Concealment of Object, Maximum Authority, Appearance of Truth, Repetition?* When the renewed campaign produced no response, he wrote to me himself:

> I have been distressed and perplexed by your silence. I can only think that there is some connection between this and the visits of Mr. Tandy & Bishop Hobson to you in London — that is to say, my suggesting that they should call on you. But, my dear Mavor, if in doing that I displeased you, surely the punishment scarcely fits the fault! Besides, in explanation of the innocently-committed error, I can at least say that when I made the suggestion to Mr. Tandy, it was not certain that the Bp. would be going, or when. And the Bp. knew you were in London, for he asked from time to time where "the boys" were. And I did no more than give him your address, nor do I know what you talked about when you met. He enjoyed seeing you, & gave a good report of your looks — that is all I know. . . . You misjudge me if you think I had some ulterior motive. . . . Please do send me a line, & let us have some contact with one another.[14]

But by the time his letter reached me I was back in Canada, where I wanted only to be rid of what I considered his problem. I never replied. What could I say that he did not already know? He was 60 years old, for God's sake! How could a man reach 60, I asked myself at 26, without having taken a good look at himself in the mirror?

Early in January 1945 Tommy Stone called me into his office to show me a signal from Ernest Bushnell at the CBC. The Corporation was setting up a shortwave International Service in Montreal to cover Europe, the West Indies, and Canadian Forces overseas. Would Canada House, and the army, please release me to come back and organize programming for the troops? In any case, as Stone pointed out, the European war was into its martial coda. The Allied powers were preparing to meet in Yalta to divide the spoils, and the psychological warfare front was shifting to the Pacific, where the United States had started its heavy bombing of Japan. On January 17, 1945, the day the Russians marched into Warsaw, I telegraphed Bushnell: "Am returning by air at an early date."

On my first night in London, back in 1936, I had seen Chekhov's *The Seagull*. In 1945 I spent my last night in London at the dress rehearsal of the Old Vic's *Uncle Vanya*, thanks to Ralph Richardson. He was the Vanya, Olivier the Astrov, Sybil Thorndike the Marina, with a cast so mutually supportive it could hardly be called supporting. Once again I was hooked by Chekhov's magic trick: boredom on the stage transformed into tension in the audience. Being driven frantic not by action but by aimlessness. Like a doodlebug. Like my war.

Terrace was presumed dead. Sanderson, like Terrace an only child, had been found dead, run over by a tank. Many other good friends had been killed and many more wounded. And I was going home to keep up, by remote shortwave, the spirits of those still at it.

I even felt guilty about returning to my family and the friends who were left. At the first opportunity I telephoned Sanderson's mother and father and was invited to visit them that evening. When I arrived, no one answered the doorbell. I went around to the back of the house and found the kitchen door open. I crossed into the living room, the scene of so many of our youthful parties, and called out. I could hear their voices in conversation upstairs, low, fragmented. I called again. Silence. I waited for some time and then left. When I telephoned later, there was no response.

7

Finding Canada

"AFTER THE EXCITEMENT OF ARRIVAL," I wrote to Bert Powley, the old newshand at CBC's London office who saw me off, "I have spent a week in a complete coma, and am now in Montreal pending my retirement from the cloth. As you possibly have heard, arrangements are still going forward for the opening on the 25th [February] notwithstanding that the second transmitter will not be functioning. My title is Producer of U.K. Broadcasts while Arthur Phelps of the U. of Manitoba is Supervisor. I think it is going to be extremely interesting."[1]

I thought, I suppose, that we would be inventing the future in the footsteps of Marconi, who sent the first wireless signal across the Atlantic from Newfoundland to Cornwall in 1901 and founded a company in Montreal. But I knew very little about the new point of departure.

Montreal in early 1945 was a volcano looking for an eruption. The wily right-winger Maurice Duplessis had just been reelected premier of Quebec, and Camillien Houde, the shrewd clown who owned the circus, had been reelected mayor of Montreal after spending time in prison for counselling his fellow Québécois to defy the conscription laws. Under the snows and behind the eyes one could see the pent-up resentment, aggravated by the war, against the anglophone establishment. Dilly and I met it the day we moved into our second-floor flat on downtown Bishop Street and were greeted by our landlady, not unkindly, as *"les anglais"* with *"le gouvernement fédéral."* Half-Canadian, half-Swiss (and more at home in French than in her father's native German), Dilly had never considered herself particularly *anglaise*; and as half Scots, I was licensed to object to having a Sassenach father. But there was no denying the other label. The CBC in Quebec was a federal presence, and with its new International Service, Ottawa was staking out a claim.

The IS — what was it about these initials: first Intelligence and Security and now International Service? — was situated two blocks away in a renovated brothel on Crescent Street, just off Ste-Catherine, the main street. This did not signify civic reform, however. Houde's Montreal was changing but not planning to go straight. Now and then a former client would appear, asking for Jeanine or Jacqueline, only to be handed a leaflet announcing the establishment's change of policy. He could not have found a less likely madam than the new boss, Peter Aylen, a cool-headed 30-something in a three-piece suit, with reticent hair, well-bred voice, and rain-check handshake. An administrator with the CBC from its inception, Aylen was one of the first to identify himself as a career broadcaster, which he had recently taken to calling "the youngest profession." Committed and shrewd, he was assembling a team of skilled technicians, alert European expatriates, and impatient Canadian programmers. The plan was rightly ambitious; the shortwave transmitters in Sackville, New Brunswick, were the world's most powerful. But the building's racy origin was not entirely inappropriate. The new owners had also to hustle for patrons.

The known audience consisted of the Canadian forces still in Europe. We gave them daily newscasts in English and French, the weekly magazine program *Canadian Chronicle*, and the big, bilingual musical variety series *Canadian Party* — all unabashedly uplifting and nationalistic.

The newscasts delivered the facts, nothing but the facts, and all the facts except the downers. For *Canadian Chronicle* we hewed and skewed the week's events to fit a single entertaining theme with a bloody-mindedness worthy of Procrustes. *Canadian Party* became a showcase for sentimental songs by Ruth Lowe, Félix Leclerc, Johnny Cowell, Norman Campbell, and other Canadians — and even weightier works by serious composers. John Weinzweig, arm-twisted into contributing a symphonic suite from his incidental music for *Our Canada*, wrote afterward:

> Mavor, you are a genius. Or maybe a cad. I couldn't figure out how I got invited to *Canadian Party*. For most of the show I sat tense, wondering how I could fit in with such company (congenial, of course) as Alys [Roby, the chanteuse] and Oscar [Peterson, the jazzman]. Then you did it! I am full of humility. In fact I am humid. That piece started out as gold-mining music. But it sure takes a train-ride beautifully.[2]

The futility of my nationalist crusade became evident when *Canadian Party* was reviewed in *Radio World*: "This broadcast, under Mavor Moore's direction, has verve, it has dash. It has all the qualities of New York or Hollywood."[3] This prepared me for the reception awaiting Canadian musicals in years to come: both praised and damned for matching the American competition.

The response from the troops was encouraging, and we had letters from English-speaking civilians in various countries. The unknown quantity was the number of potential listeners. I wondered why the government had risked such a huge expenditure on so uncertain a venture, especially with the British and the Americans already in the field. Then came a long letter from Klaus Goldschlag, a young German-born Jewish refugee I'd recommended to the army, now with Canadian counterintelligence in occupied Germany. (Thirty years later Corporal Goldschlag was back in Germany as Canada's ambassador.) "Fraternization is rampant," he wrote, "and even I am following that policy, though strictly from motives of re-education. . . . The civilian population is quite unexpectedly cordial."

The reason, he guessed, had less to do with Canadian charisma than with a process of elimination.[4] Betrayed by their own radio systems, listeners in Axis-controlled Europe were turning to shortwave reports from elsewhere. It was not so much that the big lies were being routed by the truth, as that our liars had taken the precaution of establishing their credibility in time of adversity. Now that the tide had turned in their favour the Atlantic Allies could exploit this carefully cultivated trust. The trust did not extend eastward to the Russians, however, since Marxists, like fascists, have always made the strategic error of flaunting their confidence in the power of propaganda. And of the other Allied powers, the self-effacing Canadians — untainted (it was said) by British self-righteousness, French pride, or American grandiloquence — were seen as the least propagandistic and therefore the most trustworthy.

But where was their voice? No government alert to postwar possibilities in diplomacy, international trade, and immigration could ignore such an opening.

With talk in the air of a political link between Canada and the West Indies, the English-language Section established a shortwave signal to the Caribbean. We heralded the arrival of this new service by distributing, free, a calypso record entitled "Tune your radio with me / And hear the news on the CBC," which I produced. This rare disc featured Lord Caresser, a Trinidadian singer living in Montreal, and a backup group under young Oscar Peterson with a mercifully unidentified chorus consisting of Stuart Griffiths, head of information at the IS, his secretary, and me. It was so successful that our supervisor Arthur Phelps, with a bravado as bushy as his eyebrows, decided it was time to take on American audiences, as well. So I developed *The Beaver's Tale*, 10 records covering our version of North American history, which we gave away free to U.S. stations. It was the first Canadian radio series ever carried in the United States, and had no effect whatever.

The more I tried to explain Canada to others the more I realized how little I knew about it. Even in university I had had only a few lectures on Canadian literature (from the zealous E. K. Brown), tucked into a course on American literature. I had never been north of Algonquin Park (canoeing), east of Trois-Rivières (army camp), or west of Windsor (smuggling cigarettes).

If necessity is the mother of invention, shame is the father of education. Dilly and I listened to Quebec radio, pored over local newspapers, visited art galleries and francophone night clubs, and went to every possible play. Seeing Les Compagnons de St-Laurent, the remarkable amateur troupe founded by Father Emile Legault to revive the classical tradition, we first encountered Jean Gascon and Jean-Louis Roux, soon to form their professional Théâtre du Nouveau Monde. From Les Compagnons, also, sprang the imaginative Pierre Dagenais, whose career took off like a comet with a magical French *A Midsummer Night's Dream* and burned out almost as quickly.

Acting and design skills were plentiful here, but original plays reflecting Quebec life were rare. The only harbinger of the coming efflorescence was the annual satirical revue *Fridolinons*, named after its star, the lippy street urchin Fridolin created by Gratien Gélinas. In his battered cap, sneakers, and moth-eaten Canadien sweater, Fridolin carved up the Québécois family as only a member of the family could. I missed much of the *joual*, but what I did understand brought me closer to Gélinas's family and gave me ideas about carving up my own.

Among the gems in *Fridolinons '45* was a sketch about a plucky little army recruit, a bastard whose overseas posting spikes his plans for marriage and a legitimate family. It was from this seed that Gélinas developed the 1949 play Tit-coq, which marked the arrival of Quebec theatre on the world stage. But the sketch that made a direct hit on my conscience was La vie édifiante de Jean-Baptiste Laframboise, "dedicated to all the little Canadiens who don't want to screw up their lives."[5] Gélinas played Jean-Baptiste from cradle to grave. This born poet is relegated to the priesthood by family and teachers; the seminarians find him unfit even for that so he settles for notary, lives right, and works hard until he dies, mourned as a pillar of the community. As he stands before God justifying his existence, his sins of omission — spectral columns of all the books of poetry he might have written — rise around him. The little man protests, "Father, I thought that could never happen to a Canadian!"

In that moment I grasped the Canadian identity. But I had not yet discovered Canada nor found myself. My life, it seemed, was being assembled for me out of anything handy, like a bird's nest.

By the end of summer I was feeling both inadequate and restless. In May the finale of the European conflict brought many of the troops home, diminishing our audience. In June delegates of 50 nations meeting in San Francisco produced a United Nations charter. In July Stalin, Truman, and Churchill (succeeded by Clement Attlee) met at Potsdam to engineer peace for the rest of us. On August 6 the atom bomb was dropped on Hiroshima, and within a month Japan capitulated. In this last act of the war Canada was a bit player, its loud shortwave voice little more than an echo.

Toronto, meantime, was taking off. Andrew Allan, back at CBC Radio with a group of his Vancouver disciples, had launched the weekly Stage series that galvanized anglophone radio drama and its audiences from east to west. In anticipation of the coming bonanza, announcer Lorne Greene was assembling faculty for his Academy of Radio Arts and invited me to join it. The Arts and Letters Club, spurred on by Herman Voaden and John Coulter, had generated a movement to lobby the federal government on behalf of a national theatre. The club's membership of distinguished artists, academics, professionals, and businessmen made a potent combination; but my mother thought it a pipe dream. "You don't start national," she said. "You become national." She thought more highly of the plan for a self-sustaining civic theatre hatched by Roly Young, the Globe and Mail's "anti-arty" theatre critic.

Young wanted "a permanent home that would provide an opportunity for our most talented artists to make a living here in their native land. This would apply not only to the acting end of the business, but also to designing, playwriting, singing, dancing, etc."[6] After the organizational meeting DMM scribbled me a note:

> He is nearer the mark than the Arts & Letters. Was impressed by his sincerity. [But] groups represented certainly not promising for such a scheme. . . . Cannot get connection with Royal [Alexandra Theatre] and Young straight. Suspect something behind venture. No need for anxiety — feel this will not receive sufficient backing to put it through.[7]

The reason for this last reassurance was that she had embarked on a similar venture of her own. She was already 58 and had been working toward it for much too long to sit around waiting for consensus.

How had theatre in Toronto reached this crossroads? Let us backtrack.

PAY WAS UNHEARD OF IN THE VILLAGE PLAYERS, formed in 1937 by graduates of the collegiate in Forest Hill Village where, in the mid-1930s, "Mrs. M." had inflamed students with a passion for theatre. Their plan was twofold: to present experimental plays and to tour Ontario high schools with the annual Shakespeare curriculum drama. To their mentor, a revival of the Hart House touring tradition might have seemed like old joy; but the Hart House group had consisted mainly of older amateurs bound to regular jobs, while the younger Players were willing to commit themselves to theatre first, supporting themselves with whatever jobs appeared. She found a similar commitment among students she directed at the university, and among the eager freelancers converging on Toronto to seek their fortune in radio. It was this converging commitment that prompted her to turn our old house into a production centre and, in 1940, the barn into a summer theatre.

A more unpromising launching pad for the revival of professional theatre would have been hard to find. It was miles from the city's centre and hard to reach. The stage (formerly the stables, transitionally an outhouse, then a storage space for scenery) was 18 feet across, eight feet deep, two feet off the floor, and about three feet higher than the tall actors. The rest of the small barn held some 80 spectators, counting those draped among the rafters of the hayloft. Our first lighting, supplied by coal oil lamps and candles, was as hazardous as it was dramatic; but once the house was electrified in 1942 — the year after we got indoor plumbing — we ran lines out to the barn and my brother Francis, in his periodic visits home, supervised the installation of a rudimentary switchboard. Since it was unheated, the place was unusable in winter. Legally speaking, it was unusable as a public theatre at all, which was why passed hats replaced tickets. Every movable in the house was fair game for sets and props. Costumes were constructed on the spot, the old wood stove in the kitchen serving as the centre of the dyeing industry and the dining room table as a sewing circle.

Rehearsals took place downtown, but it was here that the ambitious Shakespeare plays were prepared for their tours. At first the cast and crew were merely listed alphabetically: "The Following Ladies and Gentlemen Are Taking Part in this Evening's Performance." I performed Jaques and Falstaff (again) and bullied Mother into mounting a modern-dress *Macbeth*. "Of all *Macbeths* seen here the most unusual," wrote the *Toronto Star*'s elliptical critic, Augustus Bridle.[8] Our *Henry V*, staged by the newly arrived English actor-director Earle Grey, was well reviewed, except by a neophyte wrecker named Frank Rasky in *Canadian High News*: "I'm sorry to report that their effort tasted strongly of half-baked ham. . . . As the Chorus, Mavor Moore bounced back and forth with over-emphasized face-making, huffing-and-puffing and arm-waving like a busy traffic cop on Yonge Street."[9] The busy traffic cop was an apter image of my situation than young Rasky knew. I was earning a living from radio, studying for examinations, performing and directing at university, working with the VPs in the touring productions, and acting in the elaborate amateur productions mounted by Earle Grey at the Arts and Letters Club. But about theatre as a full-time occupation I knew next to nothing. One acted on the stage, I assumed, as a sort of tithe to the Muses.

My professional initiation began in 1940 with a letter from John Holden confirming my summer job with the Actors' Colony in Bala, Muskoka:

> Bring along all the clothes you have that you might use. Also sheets, blankets and towels. . . . We have some but with changes every week sometimes we're short. I still haven't my ingenue, and have to do some more interviewing. . . . Strange, last year there were dozens of girls; this year I haven't found any I think have 'it.'[10]

Holden's summons was unmistakably different from Roy Mitchell's call to holy orders or my mother's to social service.

Like Mitchell, John Holden had been born in the United States, raised in Toronto, and trained in New York before returning to Canada

— in 1929, just after Mitchell left for good. But in aspect and philosophy he was the old lion's opposite: a short, natty, sassy product of the same commercial theatre Mitchell fulminated against. Having earned his spurs at the Shubert Organization as a production manager with a knack for remounting Broadway hits, he set out to revive the commercial stock company in Canada. In the summer of 1934 he formed a cooperative for a weekly "straw hat" season in the tiny Muskoka resort town of Bala, and between 1936 and 1939 also mounted a winter season at his Walker Theatre in Winnipeg. Seen in context the achievement was remarkable: in those Depression years his was the sole professional stock company operating year-round in all of North America.

Many of my radio colleagues of the 1930s — Jane Mallett, Budd Knapp, Babs Hitchman, Grace Webster, Alex McKee, among others — were veterans of the John Holden Company in Winnipeg. Holden also hired what he called "comers." Robert Christie and Grace Mathews had just returned from training in England; his summer ingenues in Bala had included my talented fellow students Helen Gardiner and Elizabeth Stone; Eric Atkinson, William Needles, Peter Mews, and Jean Cruchet (Killer) had acted with the Village Players. A weekly pay cheque was their certificate of professionalism.

Everyone pitched in at everything — acting, scenery, lights, props, costumes, box office. Unions and job descriptions were unknown. All 15 lived in two large adjacent cottages on the lakeshore. Facing a different play every week, we rehearsed the new one all day and performed the old one every night except Sunday when we dress-rehearsed its successor. On Mondays we went by car, truck, and ferry to Bigwin Inn to perform for the idle inebriates at that fashionable resort. (This was known as "running the play," since the stage in the ballroom was twice as wide as the Bala stage.) We returned on Tuesday to open the new production on Wednesday. Before dinner at six came the sole daily break: 90 minutes for swimming, sunning, and learning lines. Socializing came after the show — at one's own risk. Breakfast was at eight sharp the next morning and the previous night was the prime topic.

Induction into the family was summary. The playhouse in Bala was the upper chamber of the old town hall, with the jail below. The dressing rooms consisted of a single space divided by a curtain, directly over the stage, from which our voices were always in danger of being heard out front. It was also the only backstage crossover. When I shut my eyes to go through the women's half, the ladylike Kathleen McVicar hissed,

"Good God, boy, if you haven't seen it yet it's time you did!" Later when I was changing in mid-show, a strangled "Help!" came from the other side of the curtain; the ingenue — that year a Detroit policeman's daughter loaded with the required 'it' — was alone and trapped in a girdle. With the family honour at stake, I did not hesitate.

This was summer vacation country, filled with wealthy cottagers and their restive offspring, tourists from Michigan and Illinois, students bound for adventure, and the usual local infrastructure of seasonal support for cars, boats, camping, dancing, and dry throats. The plays reflected John Holden's notion of his public's taste: comedies, thrillers, and melodramas such as The Milky Way, The Alarm Clock, Coquette, Spooks, Ten Nights in a Bar Room. All were American except the season's opener, St. John Ervine's British comedy of manners The First Mrs. Fraser, which was Holden's nod to art. His credo was simple: "It's hard to make money on art, noble to lose money on art, okay to make money on crap, but a terrible sin to lose money on crap."

Already balding at 22, I learned my trade as a character actor. In The First Mrs. Fraser I was cast as the mature James Fraser, opposite veteran Isabel Price as his abandoned ex-wife. On opening night I was so stunned by her intensity that when she gave me the cue to deliver the repentant Fraser's reproposal, not a word came out. "Are you making me a delicate offer of marriage, James?" Isabel asked coyly. I nodded helplessly. As she kept on feeding me my own lines, I kept on nodding until the tears came. Five minutes later, having proposed to herself, she took the bull by the horns and rejected me. I managed to get out a single indignant "Well!" and fled the stage. But I also learned to ad-lib at length. One night old reliable Alex McKee failed to return from the cottage for his reentrance, leaving four of us floundering onstage. Somebody remembered the pack of cards planted in a drawer for the next act, and we played a riotous game of poker while the stage manager ran to get him.

The most telling lessons were those Holden administered himself in full public view. Playing Simon Slade, the perfidious barkeeper of Ten Nights, I faced the audience from behind the bar. Holden, as a drifter, entered and ordered a drink, his back to the audience. When I asked, "What'll you have, stranger?" he lowered his eyelids to expose a second set of eyes painted on them. At that moment I figured a straight face was worth about $10 a second. In Spooks I played a detective who solves the case by offering a slice of pie to each of the eight suspects, of whom only the murderer believes it poisoned. One night Holden, as the butler, cut the pie into seven sections before handing me the plate, retreated upstage, and waited. I had distributed five before I spotted the trap. Knowing the game by then, I turned to the butler and said, "Go get another pie." Holden calmly produced a knife and divided the last piece in two.

But what a research opportunity I was missing! Working in radio had separated me from a live audience, the very ingredient I recognized as essential for my grand graduate study in the semantics of theatre. Here, where much the same audience came every week to share in the ritual, I had a priceless laboratory in which each performance was a fresh experiment. At one Saturday matinee, when Simon Slade snarled at his long-suffering wife, "One would think, to hear you talk, that I had committed every sin in the Decalogue!" a small boy ran up to the foot-lights and yelled, "And so you have, you dirty old bugger!" I burned to interview this biblical scholar after the show, but he had vanished. I was too busy doing things to take notes, and too preoccupied with my personal crisis to do more than hang on.

One factor in the mutual relationship of artist and audience I could hardly miss: their attitudes toward each other changed radically when both knew the company was professional. From the artists' point of view it was a question not so much of quality or remuneration as of putting oneself on the line; from the audience's point of view it was a question of dedication to their entertainment. I began to understand my mother's scorn for the Little Theatre/Drama Festival approach ("playing at instead of playing"), and her unflagging efforts to form an ensemble, a company. Only in that way, she believed, could the artists have a focused livelihood and their audiences a reliable expectation — and the two went together. Her closest friendships, I noticed, were less likely to be with the intelligentsia and the culturati than with the old hands who had paid their professional dues — theatre manager George Keppie, opera singer Nina Gale, vaudevillian Jack Arthur — and the Young Turks in search of a profession to pay dues to. In 1940 she had no company yet, but she developed greater respect for John Holden, who had, than for any number of dilettantes cocking a snoot at commercial junk in the Ontario boondocks.

Two years later, when I was working at the CBC, the brave theatre in Bala was reduced to showing movies. But the Village Players were flourishing in the Barn on Bathurst Street. When I went into the army, Dilly, who had become their main costume designer, kept me abreast of their activities, which now included light entertainment for the troops as well as more serious endeavours. And every letter from my mother was filled with details of new productions and new recruits:

> The VPs are doing *Night of January 16th* on August 7th & 8th. Vincent [Tovell] has taken over the direction. I think it's an excellent cast, but the lad is worried and has yet a lot to learn in handling people. Still he's doing very well. I've had Mr. Stevenson put a gallon of tar on the roof of the barn — it was leaking. Fran's electrical fixtures are swell, but Sally [Macdonald, "the Female Engineer"] still blows fuses — what a girl! Last night it rained cats and dogs.[11]

It was in this makeshift theatre, as the war ended, that Canadian audiences were introduced for the first time to Bertolt Brecht, Federico García Lorca, Thornton Wilder, half a dozen Canadian playwrights, and a new generation of actors and directors. To the original band of enthusiasts, students, and radio freelancers had been added war veterans, trickling back from the army, navy, and air force shows with experience under their belts and a career on their minds. The Village Players were now the only theatre company in Toronto matching CBC Radio's new *Stage* series in dedication to plays by contemporary writers, Canadians among them. It seemed to me inevitable that a professional company would follow, although not all the Village Players shared this hope.

But in 1945 this had not yet happened, and a return to Toronto was not, at that moment, my idea of expanding one's horizon.

I WAS NOW 26, DILLY 22. We wanted a family, for which our Montreal flat was too small. For five years I had been making propaganda while plays, stories, and poems piled up in drawers; I needed desperately to talk in my own voice. I was not sure what its tone might become, but I was certain of one thing: I could no longer go on touting Canada while knowing only a fraction of it.

One of those scolding me on this account was Ira Dilworth, the urbane head of the CBC's Pacific Region; and it was at this pivotal moment that Dilworth approached us to move to Vancouver, promising creative freedom, a house, and a horizon unequalled anywhere on earth. This was terra incognita. Our only West Coast talisman was a painting by Emily Carr, a large oil sketch of sea and rock shoreline done on cardboard when she was too poor to buy canvas, bought for a song at her first Montreal exhibition. On the strength of our fascination with the world of Klee Wyck — a world Carr's friend Ira Dilworth had helped to bring to light — I agreed to make a recon-naissance trip west by train. To justify the expense I stopped off to produce news reports and editions of *Canadian Party* in Winnipeg and Vancouver.

After crossing the sullen Ontario Shield and the icy north shore of Lake Superior, I naturally mistook Winnipeg for the West. I visited the cel-ebrated Walker Theatre (built in 1907, converted into a cinema only months before my arrival), from which C. P. Walker had turned the tables on the American theatrical syndicates and run the entire midwest circuit out of Winnipeg. (Twenty years forward, when the Walker was once more a playhouse, I was to present *Spring Thaw* there.) Inside the CBC I found the management as dull as the talent was sharp. Outside, the unaccustomed dryness of the bright cold weather fooled me into euphoria. I walked a short block from the Fort Garry Hotel to a drugstore in search of tooth-paste, only to be asked by the chemist if I realized my nose was frozen and would I like a wee snort of Highland Remedy. It was thus I learned about Prairie cold and Prairie warmth at the same time.

I stopped off in Calgary to record a commentary on Castle Mountain, which had just been renamed Mount Eisenhower. As stolid and grey as the general-president, the mountain has since reverted to its original name, inadvertently memorializing the transience of glory. The scar of the ghost town known as Silver City, still there on its flank, gave me my first taste of the tough old Wild West. I returned to sample the hot springs at Banff. After floating in the steamy water for half an hour with the snow drifting down on my face, I concluded that civilization had made remarkable strides and in all probability could go no further.

I have since made many trips across the Rocky Mountains by air, but none has matched that first train ride. When seen from above, through the eye of an eagle or a god, the Rockies are a magnificent quilt embossed with impressive miniatures. To the human eye moving among them at earth level, they are the pillars of the universe itself. When I emerged in Vancouver the next morning and telephoned Dilly in Montreal, the move west was quickly agreed upon.

My career in psychological warfare closed as ineptly as it had opened. I began by arresting an imaginary spy, and now ended by over-looking a real one. Quebec scientist Raymond Boyer, whose shortwave commentaries to Europe I sometimes put on the air, soon went to prison for interlarding them with messages to Russian scientists. Apparently he believed that by helping an ally he was helping science. The awkward question for the dutiful is always which duty to place first.

"DAHLING," said the whiskey contralto behind me to someone else, "who is that chahming young man leaning on the mantelpiece?" Since I was the only person of any description leaning on the mantelpiece, I turned around. The speaker, I learned, was the party's hostess.

"Torpedo" Corbett was sixtyish, not much over five feet tall, slight with mannish white hair, and dressed in navy blue silk pants and vest over a white satin blouse with black-and-white accessories: pearl choker, pearl earrings, jet bracelets, a monocle, a foot-long cigarette holder. There was a single dash of colour on her left breast: striped ribbons supporting two full-size medals. She was, I learned in the first 30 seconds, the daughter of English nobility. The Canadian soldier she regretted having married during World War I had become a prosperous Vancouver lawyer. In time he became so fed up with her eccentric parties that he bought her a mansion on Vancouver Island ("He knows I *loathe* crossing water, dahling!"), along with the adjoining lot as a catchment for the empties. The medals, which she reputedly wore night and day, were all that remained of her two sons, killed in action with the Royal Navy. She said I reminded her of the younger.

Torpedo's parties brought out a vivid sample of local society and its visitors: artists, lawyers, natives, sailors, physicians, writers, politicians, musicians, teachers, and rolling stones. Her guests seemed to have no qualifying political creed, but their hostess would tolerate no criticism of the Royal Family. Whenever a hint of it arose, she would pointedly excuse herself for a moment, then descend the staircase draped in a Union Jack. As a young woman, Torpedo had gone to dances with Winston Churchill and his aristocratic friends, and now watched over their conduct of world affairs like a sister hawk. One midnight, alarmed at some peace proposal or other, she silenced us all while she telephoned the British statesman to give him a piece of her mind. But like many during the war, she shared a party line, and her attempts to reach London were thwarted by a local farm gossip. On her third attempt Torpedo exploded, "Get off the line, you common bitch! I'm calling Winston Churchill!"

Such incidents were emblematic. Vancouver in the spring of 1946 was a cauldron crossed with a teacup, its volatile ethnic and class mixture simmering under a lid of British gentility. Like most ocean ports, it must always have been both rough and sophisticated; but the war in the Pacific had thrust the West Coast from a distant rear echelon into the front line. In the ensuing panic militia troops had been hastily mobilized against invasion, Japanese Canadians herded off to internment camps, and British Columbia suddenly elevated from lumber colony to citadel of Empire.

British Columbia's newer citizens, however, took no more kindly to hurry than did its sidelined aboriginal owners. Nearby California lent the West Coast an air of Nirvana — even if only as a temporary residence. This was the farthest west, the end of the Canadian line, double-or-nothing time, or simply time out before going south or dying. After a week on the coast, Dilly and I felt a compulsive rallentando. Human endeavour, however useful as a time filler or a time binder, was mocked by the eternal. The artificial lawns, imported gardens, ribbon roads, giant tankers, and surgical clear-cuts were minified by the scale of nature and the patient threat of earthquakes and tidal waves. Even the newcomers' sacred myths were challenged by those of the aboriginal gods, and their imported arts upstaged by a highly creative Native culture they had dismissed as primitive.

Despite this massive inertia — or perhaps because of the solid footing it implied — the place was jumping with cultivation and expectation. Great emphasis was put on education and the arts. During the war, the University of British Columbia had augmented its inadequate quarters with military huts and extended its reach into the community. At war's end degree courses in theatre were instituted by Australian-born Dorothy Somerset, while Sydney Risk, her predecessor at the university, was forming the professional Everyman Players to tour the western provinces. There was a rich musical life: fine choirs, competent orchestras, a stylish jazz scene. Dance schools were full. The Andrew Allen-led exodus to CBC Toronto had depleted the freelance acting colony, but the expertise of the remainder, like that of the local technicians, was formidable. Actors, singers, musicians, and technicians worked together in the elaborate *Theatre Under the Stars* musicals in Stanley Park, staged by Hollywood's demanding Aida Broadbent.

The literary scene in 1945–46 was equally lively. Pierre Berton was writing for the Vancouver *Sun*, Eric Nicol for *The Province*, and several novelists for posterity. Alan Crawley's *Contemporary Verse* gave voice to such West Coast poets as Dorothy Livesay and Malcolm Lowry; and just after I arrived, my old mentor Earle Birney returned to teach creative writing at UBC, bringing with him the editorship of the Toronto-based *Canadian Poetry Magazine*. He included some of my poems alongside those of Livesay, Al Purdy, Miriam Waddington, James Reaney, and P. K. Page. In return I worked with Birney on some radio plays, especially a comedy based on the army court-martial of a feckless private, which became the centrepiece of his picaresque war novel *Turvey*. Turvey and I were to meet again.

The West Coast nationalism I encountered, however, was far from narrow. Links with Canada's allies had been greatly strengthened during the war, and there was a growing awareness, prompted by increased immigration from Asia and elsewhere, of other international connections. The general assumption seemed to be that the wind in our sails could carry us anywhere. The whole world was suddenly within reach. The Russians, long mistakenly identified in the popular mind with the Sons of Freedom, an extreme Doukhobor sect given to arson and parading in the nude as a means of protest, were now literally landing at the dock, fully clothed and in quest of friendship.

The *Orel* was the first Soviet ship to visit North America since God knew when. Dilworth, convinced I had Russian connections ("Your grandfather knew Tolstoy, didn't he?"), insisted I record a news interview with the captain, who was said to be fluent in English. A meeting was arranged for the afternoon by a Canadian navy officer, who joined me and announcer Bill Herbert for a fortifying lunch before we went aboard. Herbert was a former sailor; and thanks to my beginner's Russian course at the British Foreign Office, I was able to exchange greetings with the captain in his own language. But as Blackbeard ushered us into his quarters, snapping rebukes at his crew as he went, we realized that his English was like my Russian: two dozen words and half a dozen phrases. I was about to receive a lesson in cultural diplomacy that proved extremely useful when I later worked at the United Nations.

From photographs standing on his dresser or winkled from our wallets, we were able to exchange domestic situations. With the help of a wall map and gestures, we established the size of the boat, the length of the trip, and the weather in Vladivostok. The wire recorder was produced, greeted by laughter, and put away. Pushing a button, the captain summoned a brawny female sailor, who saluted and left. Seconds later the intercom blared "I Can't Give You Anything but Love, Baby!" Blackbeard recalled and blasted her, after which we got Rimsky-Korsakov's *Coq d' Or*. Pressing another button, he whipped out a bottle of V.O. ("No vwodka!") and four shot glasses. Like sprites out of *The Tempest*, three Amazons appeared with a folding banquet table and chairs, set them up, laid a cloth, covered it with platters of cold meat, salad, and cheese, and vanished. "Sit!" the captain ordered, and we sat. "E-at!" he commanded, but having just eaten we could only pick while he ate. "Drink!" he ordered. "Down de khetch!" We were trapped.

BLACKBEARD:	To Canada! (*all toast, down the hatch: refill*)
WE THREE:	To the Soviet Union! (*all toast: refill*)
BLACKBEARD:	To de kink! (*all toast His Majesty: refill*)
WE THREE:	To the president! (*all toast: refill*)
BLACKBEARD:	To de prime yinister of Canada! (*all toast: refill*)
WE THREE:	To the Soviet prime minister! (*all toast: refill*)
BLACKBEARD:	To de Canaddian pipple! (*all toast: refill*)
WE THREE:	To the Russian people! (*all toast: refill*)
BLACKBEARD:	To Breetitch Clombia! (*all toast: refill*)

It was at that point, as well as I can recall, that the stalwart Herbert raised his hand and pitifully mouthed at me the word "Bathroom." Even if I could have thought of it, a translation was unnecessary, but the captain was deeply hurt. "Khwy you no e-at? Canaddians drink, drink, no e-at!" On a throat-cutting signal from our navy colleague, I decided to cut our losses while we could still count. "*Spasibo! Spasibo!*" I repeated gratefully as we bowed our way onto the tipsy gangplank, which we negotiated on the ropes as in a storm at sea. As we headed for a taxi, Blackbeard's plaintive cry followed us: "Khwy you no e-at?"

The *Orel* interview was easily the most instructive I never held. But for sheer excitement it ranked below another 1946 event I missed: Vancouver's Silver Jubilee.

The finale was to be a spectacular fall pageant in Stanley Park, with its lofty trees, on a vast outdoor stage with a full symphony orchestra beneath it and the snowcapped mountains behind it. I represented the CBC on a local committee struck to work with the producer, an imported heavyweight from the U.S. Midwest named Harkrider. Harkrider was so important that he was unavailable on the telephone, to anyone; he could only be reached by telegram, even from the next room in the Hotel Vancouver. Having no time for meals, he nibbled on carrots all day. His mind, he told the first meeting of the production committee, was occupied day and night by "concepts" — and the concepts he worked up for that pageant were awesome.

The show, with a cast of thousands, is to tell the story of Canada's West Coast, starting with the forest primeval and ending with World War II. After the overture, the orchestra sinks out of sight. In the dark we hear the sound of an axe felling a tree. Then two axes and two trees, then three — and so on till we get to 100.

    TECH. DIR.:   But Mr. Harkrider, when you get past about five,
                        through the loudspeakers you really can't tell how
                        many trees.
    HARKRIDER: Don't bother me with details. Then the lights come up,
                        and a lone Indian comes onstage, portaging a canoe.
                        Over his head. He's followed by a second Indian with a
                        canoe over his head, then a third, and so on, Indian file
                        — maybe some women — till we get 100 canoes all
                        snaking their way across the stage to form a giant
                        salmon. Okay?
    NATIVE REP.:   Mr. Harkrider, I don't know if you've ever portaged a
                        canoe, but you can only see about three feet ahead of you.
    HARKRIDER: No problem — walkie-talkie.

And so it went, down through Canadian history — never a problem — until we reached what Harkrider called "the climax before the climax."

He had, he announced, engaged his close friend John Charles Thomas, the famous American baritone (whose larynx was only slightly more legendary than his liver), to sing The Lord's Prayer. Kneeling in front of Thomas was to be a trio of supplicants: the Anglican primate, the Catholic archbishop, and the United Church moderator, with the chief rabbi as standby in case any of the former declined the honour. To top this, as the climax after the climax, he proposed a spectacular onstage World War II battle, accompanied by Tchaikovsky's 1812 Overture with its triumphant coda boosted by the guns of four destroyers moored in the inlet beyond, firing in tempo — and beyond them, ignited on the downbeat of the final chord, a 100-foot burning cross on the forward slope of Grouse Mountain.

I could hardly avoid comparing this extravaganza with the modest theatrical step reported from Toronto. My mother, beavering away in her barn with the Village Players, got word in August that a small auditorium in the Royal Ontario Museum would be made available for public use. It had seats for only 425, no wings, no overhead space, no dressing rooms, and no proper lighting. But the following morning she appeared at the ROM to negotiate its lease for the nonprofit professional company she and her disciples were determined to launch. With no money for a down payment, she used her father's contribution to the museum's founding to argue that they owed her this opportunity, and offered to equip it for use as a theatre. She had no money for that either, but no matter. She cashed in two Victory Bonds bought for her by her sons, worth $2,000, and immediately announced the opening in mid-October of *The Playboy of the Western World*, to be followed by five other plays before Christmas. The Village Players had given birth to the New Play Society.

I was not sure whether her enterprise or Harkrider's was the more foolhardy; but I knew which one better deserved The Lord's Prayer.

Before either opening night, however, our situation abruptly changed. Dilly and I had been in Vancouver for six months and were expecting our first child. We loved the place and had gained many friends. But our furniture, winter clothes, and other effects were still in storage, the CBC having failed to deliver either the promised chief producer's position or (in the face of a severe housing shortage) a place to live. While we moved our suitcases from one sublet to another, Ira Dilworth dithered.

He did his best to make us feel at home by inviting us frequently to his own, which was handsome. He introduced us to kindred spirits, including Native artists, and showed us the unpunctuated notebooks of Emily Carr, which he himself had rendered into stylish prose. He shared with us his remarkable repertory of learned jokes, such as the one about the old Irish boatman who rowed the American poet Longfellow across the river to kiss the Blarney Stone:

BOATMAN: An' where d'ye come from, Mr. Longfellow?
POET: I live in New England.
BOATMAN: More's the pity. An' what do ye do for a livin'?
POET: I write poetry.
BOATMAN: An' how do ye do that, sir? What is poetry?
POET: Ah, my friend, for centuries the great minds of the
                  world have been seeking the answer to that question.
BOATMAN: Tell me in a word or two.
POET: Impossible! I can only say that a poem has lines of a
                  certain length, usually with a rhyme at the end of them.
BOATMAN: Could ye give me an example, Mr. Longfellow? One o' yours?
POET: "I shot an arrow into the air / It fell to earth, I knew not
                  where."
BOATMAN: Now let's see if I got it straight. How's this? "There was
                  an old lady who lived in a punt: / She sat on a nail an'
                  sure it went straight up her backside." Now will ye tell
                  me, Mr. Longfellow, is that poetry?
POET: (in great distress) No, sir.
BOATMAN: Ah, but ye got to admit, I come pretty damn close!

The Blarney Stone, however, has its 200-mile limit. I had no hint that we were approaching it until I received a laconic note from Lorne Greene in Toronto on his new Academy of Radio Arts letterhead: "Should you find the situation out there not entirely satisfactory, I would be interested in hearing from you." Did the hub know more about the road than the rim did? In early October, over a gourmet lunch at the Devonshire Hotel, Dilworth confessed he couldn't bring himself to force the terms of our agreement on his second-in-command, program director Kenneth Caple — a provincial fixture in both senses, geographical and intellectual — who had his own plan and his own man. If a house were made available, Dilworth wanted to know, would I stay on under someone else? Hadn't he come pretty damn close?

That weekend I had a crash course in introversion. What did I want to do with my life — with our lives — now? What in hell was I doing at the moment, getting up variety shows for a dwindling overseas army, directing radio plays for a regional audience, and downing drinks with incomprehensible visiting sailors in the pursuit of news! In less than a year, running counterclockwise to the rest of Vancouver, I had gone from international to national to parochial — growing backward, like shrinking Alice. Even if I could reverse the process, where and what did I want to be?

Was I an actor trying on straw costumes, intending someday to spin gold from the straw? Then better sooner than later. Was I a writer, collecting experiences and characters for stories and plays? Then I should forget salaried jobs and get down to the works in my head or my notebook. Was the lack of Canadian theatres and publishers a valid alibi for not doing either? Then why not head for New York or Los Angeles? Why stick around where you're not wanted? But wait: why would Americans be interested in what interested me? Go there and you must act American, write American, become American. Was I ready to give up on Canada?

Why not instead join DMM's crusade for a Canadian theatre, the noncommercial temple of art envisaged by Roy Mitchell (who had just died, for his sins, in the United States)? Before we could get our plays performed, there had to be theatre companies to perform them. That was the necessary first step: found a theatre. But how to make a living while doing it? It was all very well for my mother to work for nothing, but what would happen to the monthly allowance she was counting on from me if I became part of the deficit? I could always freelance and teach, as before. But could I make enough to support an extended family and a theatre? And where did my first duty lie? Was it to my wife and children (however many), to my art (whichever it was), to my career (wherever it led), to my mother's dream (postponed, after all, to raise her sons), to society, to the country, to world peace . . . ?

Wherever else, I figured, I owed no debt here. I gave the CBC two weeks' notice and in a fit of folly announced that we would pay our own way back, furniture and all. We would return flat but free. I telephoned Frank Willis and Andrew Allan to tell them I would be available for casting. I wired Lorne Greene to find out if he still needed a janitor. He wired back: JANITOR'S POSITION OPEN AND YOU'VE GOT IT. WILL EXPECT YOU ON FACULTY OF ACADEMY THE MOMENT YOU ARRIVE — WONDERFUL NEWS. I wrote to Mother and asked if we might rent a room in the old house until we found a place to live, and offered to help with the New Play Society.

The company name, one of several considered, had been invented by Dora's old friend Jean Atkinson to signify a new society for putting on plays. Its purpose, according to a flyer soliciting members, was "to promote interest in good drama and give young Canadians an opportunity to create a living theatre in Canada." If it was too late to change the tame title, I thought, there was still time to nudge it into a braver meaning: a society for putting on new plays. Whether my mother foresaw where all this would lead, I have never been sure. I thought then that she was as much swept along as sweeping. What neither she nor anyone else could predict was that her little enterprise would be the only action in town when the town exploded.

This was the postwar Toronto to which Dilly and I returned in October 1946, just in time to catch the dress rehearsal of the Society's second production in the Museum Theatre: Strindberg's The Father. It reminded me that I had forgotten all about my own father.

8

Canada or the World?

WHEN WE MOVED into the ancient log house on Bathurst Street eight years earlier, the only neighbourly sight from its windows was the distant chimney of Roots the cabdriver. We could rehearse a full-scale battle in the field outside the barn without arousing attention, and none but the profane Roots and his long-suffering wife shared our concern at the prevalence of rats and the annual infestation of skunks.

By 1946 the old house with its well on one side and its septic tank on the other was being crowded by fashionable brick homes with swimming pools. In the gully across the street some fast operator had built a golf driving range from which the rodent population fled in justifiable terror. The roads were paved and buses ran in every direction — which was just as well. My two brothers were also back from the war and back in the house, and until I bought a secondhand Austin Mini, none of us owned a car. In sprawling Toronto it seemed everyone else did. The postwar shortage of housing led developers to snap up every vacant suburban lot, including the one between us and Bathurst Street that we could never afford to buy. Now relegated to a side street, the grandly numbered 2600 Bathurst Street became the lowly 8 Ridelle Avenue. Soon even its view of the thoroughfare was blocked by a characterless high-rise apartment building. Then we learned that our beloved barn, half of it encroaching on an adjacent lot to the north, would have to be demolished if that lot were sold. Within a month the barn came down, its weathered planks of yellow pine sold for reincarnation as designer furniture.

The city's population was heading for a million (twice that, with the suburbs), and its personality for a transformation. Young families from the downtown wards were moving into the stylish houses in our northwest enclave — among them the Greenes, the Hersenhorens, the Waynes, the Shusters — while our place with its long, low verandah and Indian marking tree became a solitary remnant of the pioneer past. The old wards to the south were quickly refilled with newcomers — Italian, Polish, Ukrainian, Hungarian, German, Greek, Portuguese — whose arrival enhanced overnight the restaurants, the variety of merchandise in the stores, and the general conviviality. If civic politics still squirmed in the straitjacket of the Orange Order, civic morality had already slipped into something more comfortable. Everyone said Toronto was going places.

The long oaken lunch tables at the Arts and Letters Club, where I was the first third-generation member, skirled with demands for government aid to the arts. The old hall had heard nothing so rousing since Grandfather's heyday — not even the traditional Christmas dinners when everyone dressed up in medieval tabards to sing carols and my reverend father made his annual Toronto appearance to pronounce the benediction, giving advance dispensation for profanities spoken in drink. Defying the old guard's taboo against both politics and notoriety, concerned writers, artists, musicians, lawyers, doctors, merchants, and academics were agitating for the club to lead a national lobby for the arts and letters.

In 1944 the Arts and Letters Club and 15 other cultural groups had sponsored a march on Ottawa, with Sir Ernest MacMillan, sculptor Elizabeth Wynn Wood, and Montreal architect Ernest Cormier as field marshals. Their campaign for a national arts body, tax breaks for patrons, and a network of arts centres had drawn little blood on Parliament Hill but plenty of ink in the newspapers, and all were agreed the momentum must be maintained. Now Herman Voaden, the teacher, dramatist, and president of the newborn Canadian Arts Council (renamed the Canadian Conference of the Arts when the Canada Council was founded 10 years later), was plumping for a second march. At the parallel women's Heliconian Club, where I sometimes went to give my mother a hand with events, teacups rattled and wineglasses clinked with schemes to promote art among the culturally deprived — a class that included a regrettable proportion of men and thus nearly all politicians.

But it would be a gross mistake to reduce this movement, as some recent historians have done, to the machinations of a privileged elite determined to foist their own high European culture on the masses. The passion for individual and collective development through education and the arts was fiercest among the have-nots. Labourers, women, farmers, natives, and immigrants were determined to find and use their voices. For every brouhaha at the Arts and Letters Club or the Heliconian Club (in both of which, in any case, the iconoclasts outnumbered the icons), there was a class at the Workers' Educational Association or a course at the YWCA, where my mother taught Theatre and the Art of Living to eager groups of self-improvers. In isolated northern Sudbury, lecturers and theatrical attractions were sponsored by the Communist Mine, Mill, and Smelter Workers' Union. It was the poorer Prairie provinces that generated a Canadian Association for Adult Education, a movement welcomed in all parts of the country. Far from conspiring to entrench an existing tradition, high or low, this populist army and its allies were out to learn everything from anywhere in order to build new traditions. Their aim was growth, personal and communal. They saw education and the arts as crucial means to this end; and lacking private philanthropists on the American scale, they turned, in the Canadian fashion, to government. Their common targets were ignorance, cynicism, and sloth — however well disguised as common sense, scepticism, and the status quo.

Such heady activism, however, was more than a Canadian phenomenon. It was a function of the times.

The United Nations Organization, pending completion of its permanent home in Manhattan, was forging a brave new world in temporary quarters at Lake Success on Long Island. Member countries were setting up commissions on the peaceful uses of atomic energy, the recently decanted genie expected to redeem the world instead of destroying it. The United Nations Educational, Scientific, and Cultural Organization (UNESCO) was gearing up to reduce illiteracy, foster communication, and promote understanding through the universal exchange of art and research. Television was arriving, with an entourage of audiovisual inventions including the kinescope and the photocopy machine, to herald the Age of Information and its sibling Era of Communications. Everywhere optimism held the stage, or at least the main stage. Pessimism was relegated to off-Broadway, where I saw Eugene O'Neill's dark play The Iceman Cometh, appropriately set in the End of the Line Café. "O'Neill," one critic wrote, "seems to conclude that, for those who face

up to reality, all hope is lost; for those who keep their cherished illusions
. . . there is at least the illusion of hope." Lake Success was only an hour's
drive away.

For the next four years I was to divide my time between these two
centres of optimism: the awkward teenager Toronto and the worldly
burgher New York City. Soon after my return home, a letter came from
Peter Aylen, recently appointed head of radio at the United Nations.
Would I be interested, now that I'd left the CBC, in writing and directing
some programs for the United Nations? But in the coming months I had
commitments to the New Play Society and radio and film engagements.
Would the New Year be too late? Not at all. A contract would be in the
mail at once.

The moment I signed that contract I saw myself as a citizen of the
world — "resident in Canada," as I wrote to the all-wise Aunt Dolly,
"but at home everywhere." She sent back a two-word postcard: "Good
luck." I was too euphoric to catch the irony.

NOTHING IN TORONTO's booming arts scene boomed louder than radio. I
was grateful for this, because my theatre activities were proving both time-
consuming and costly. While Dilly and I lived at 8 Ridelle, I cadged a lift
three days a week with my neighbour Lorne Greene to teach acting at his
Academy of Radio Arts. It was, we agreed years later, the start of a very
Canadian friendship: between one who stayed and one who got away.

Lorne, as the world later discovered from *Bonanza*, was a big man with
a deep respect for the power of speech and the voice to prove it. Less well-
known were his deep affection for his native land and his social conscience
— both sorely tried once he became an American "billionaire." His
Russian-born parents had sent him to Queen's University, then to study
acting at New York's famous Neighborhood Playhouse School. On the outbreak of war he returned to enlist, but the army relinquished him to be
chief announcer for the CBC *National News*. His nightly broadcasts and ring-
ing narration for National Film Board morale boosters earned him the
name the "Voice of Doom," a role he relished but often mocked. ("There
are two kinds of Russian place names, Mavor: long ones like O-O-O-OMSK
and short ones like DnieperpetrOVSK.") At war's end, offended as much by the
CBC's parsimony as its lingering anti-Semitism, he left to freelance and to
found his academy in a renovated mansion on upper Jarvis Street.

It stood directly across the road from the CBC's new headquarters, a
former private girls' school abandoned as the tenderloin district crept

north. During the war, it had been a much joked about billet for service-women. Recalling the history of the International Service in Montreal, I mentioned to Lorne the curious connection between broadcasting houses and bawdy houses. "Well," he said, "there goes the neighbourhood." The whole country was by then caught in a whirlwind of postwar uplift. The rescue of culture from commerce had become a national crusade with the CBC as spearhead. Ten years earlier a young person of either sex rooming on Jarvis Street below Wellesley would have been considered aimless, desperate, or worse. With the advent of the CBC, the Academy of Radio Arts, a couple of union offices, and other omens of respectability, Jarvis Street's boarding houses teemed with career-minded students on parental allowances and demobilized veterans on government retraining grants.

Despite the growing Canadian film industry and the availability of U.S. television to the south, our education systems had continued to regard theatre, music, and dance as gentrified avocations. But the performing arts were fast becoming sought-after vocations, and the urgent question was how to keep the liveliest talents from seeking training — and subsequent careers — where the action already was. Greene saw that radio was the one established medium offering creative youth an entrée to the future, a decent living, and a chance to stay in Canada at the same time.

By 1946 the profession had grown so fast that many of its elders were still in their twenties. Those of us rash enough to teach at Greene's academy, flipping experience into pedagogy overnight, were training our own executioners. Fortunately most had not yet made up their minds what to do. Of the few who continued as actors, Leslie Nielsen achieved international stardom while others became pillars of the national scene. The rest made their mark in television and allied fields — Elsa Franklin as producer, Fred Davis as moderator, Gordie Tapp as comedian, Drew Crossan as director, Bernard Trotter as radio executive and later as cultural historian, others as announcers, agents, advertisers, and assorted auxiliaries. The great-hearted Mohawk singer Jim Buller, who became a close friend of mine, converted his frustration at the lack of opportunity for Native performers into a movement to provide it for his successors.

What made radio their common conduit was not only the still slim pickings in Canadian film and theatre but the character of the medium itself: simultaneous, ubiquitous, and inexpensive — an ideal mass medium for a dispersed and disconnected people. We already had at our disposal the world's most extensive radio network. There was in the air —

and we were on the air — an Arthurian sense of having been given a sword with which to seize the day.

In the case of drama day was night and Arthur was Andrew. The CBC's Sunday evening series, launched with *Stage 44*, was designed by drama supervisor Andrew Allan to put Canadian radio on the world stage — not vice versa, as his predecessor Rupert Lucas had tried to do. Two years later, when I arrived, Canadian radio was already playing the unaccustomed role of trendsetter.

On Saturday mornings at ten o'clock sharp Mister Allan (invariably so-called in the studio) would call to order the cast and crew assembled in the dilapidated theatre of the CBC Concert Studio on McGill Street. In better days the midtown building had been part of the Margaret Eaton School, my mother's training ground. I knew it first as the Eaton Girls' Club, where she directed my juvenile *Pandora's Box* — not a bad metaphor for radio, I have thought since. The CBC then bought it as a studio for *The Happy Gang* and other live audience romps. In short, the place's lineage was noble if a bit frayed. A new ritual was about to elevate it, briefly, to the status of temple.

At a small table on the forestage the elegant Andrew, in double-breasted suit and French cuffs, his pale blue eyes beaming with anticipation, sat beside his devoted script editor Alice Frick. To one side sat Bruce Armstrong (or another engineer), with the rumpled author of the week defensively draped over a nearby chair. The actors occupied the front seats below them. Rank thus established, scripts were dealt out, parts assigned, and the week's play introduced. The reading was at sight and concentration intense — broken only by an occasional late arrival, most famously the irresistible Jane Mallet with the alibi that she had been "cornered by a squirrel in Queen's Park," or the dark jester Tommy Tweed harrumphing that he had "just run over a fool of a boy," or the late-risen John Drainie with no excuse but his talent. After the reading, we would move as required to the microphones onstage while the soundman set up his gear and Mr. Allan invited Miss Frick, Mr. Armstrong, and Mr. or Miss Author to join him in the control booth. The talkback crackled with civil exchanges.

> "Miss Scott, would you . . . ?"
> "Mister Allan, am I . . . ?"
> "May I suggest, Miss Scott . . . ?"

When these proved insufficient, he would emerge for a chat.

The single live performance meant a single chance to get it right. Instant invention was compulsory. Between scenes, all the regulars (except Ruth Springford, who flew by the seat of her unerring instinct) marked their scripts with diacritical doodles — Drainie's code being by far the most elaborate — to preserve inflections for performance time. While there was plenty of joking, the process, whether for tragedy or comedy, was fiercely earnest. To break up on mike was a cardinal sin, and but for Holden's tutelage in straight faces I would have been a frequent offender. (My worst moment came in *East Lynne* when Barry Morse, after opening an imaginary locket, delivered the line "Ah! A lock of my first wife's hair!" as "Ah! A lock of my wife's first hair!") Allan forgave lapses but not timidity. His direction was always courteous, but when a performer repeatedly failed to respond, the courtesy turned to ice.

The ritual left no time for bumbling, however pardonable. While the actors broke for lunch at Little Denmark, a block away on Bay Street, composer-conductor Lucio Agostini rehearsed his orchestra on the remaining half of the stage. Agostini was a conductor's son and a perfectionist, but his musicians were equal to the challenge. A generation of string players trained at the Toronto Conservatory by the renowned Kathleen Parlow — Albert Pratz, Hyman Goodman, Maurice Solway, Paul Scherman, Percy Faith — had already made a reputation abroad. The return of some fine instrumentalists from the military bands had given the brass and woodwinds a new brilliance, and the lively local jazz scene produced some formidable percussionists. It took a pickup band of this calibre to master a new score a week in a lunch break.

The afternoon was taken up with the interweaving of words, music, and sound, then a run-through for timing. (Allan's skill in trimming was often parodied, if only slightly, in the dictum "Cut the next three pages and substitute 'but.'") On Sunday evening came the dress rehearsal, then the performance, "live to network." Its unseen audience was huge — second, at its height, only to *Hockey Night in Canada* — but the auditorium was empty except for actors awaiting their cue, moving in and out of the antiquated seats with deep respect for the unscripted squeaks of vengeful ghosts.

By the time I got to know him, Allan appeared to be a highly polished enigma, proud and secure in his mystique. He was older than most of us, especially the young women he continually cast as Galatea to his Pygmalion, and effortlessly magnetic. But inside I recognized another tormented son of the manse, forever oscillating between idealism and guilt, caught in the spiritual equivalent of a pincer movement.

Born in Scotland, he accompanied his clergyman father and family to Australia, New York, and Boston before arriving in Canada at 17, already a cosmopolitan. At the University of Toronto, a dozen years ahead of me, he acted with distinction at Hart House and edited *The Varsity*. The uproar caused by one of his editorials, a cheeky survey of student atheism, was followed by his sudden departure from university. He afterward denied any link between the two events and with heavy irony blamed the Depression: "I cannot afford to go through life with the stigma of a university degree." (Allan remained an ironist: 40 years later when he was made an honorary Doctor of Letters by York University — Toronto failing — his evident amusement upstaged my delivery of the citation.) He won a job with private radio station CFRB as an announcer-operator-producer, and a reputation as a clever dandy.

In 1938, with dreadful timing, he went to Europe to seek his fortune in commercial radio. When war loomed, Ernest Bushnell invited him to return home as drama head for CBC Vancouver; and on September 1, 1939, Allan, his father, and his actress fiancée Judith Evelyn embarked for Canada on the liner *Athenia*. They were at dinner two nights later when the torpedo struck. He and Judith were among the exhausted survivors, after he had seen his father, in the same lifeboat, chewed to death by a propeller; the news finished his ailing mother, and Judith soon afterward left for Broadway. He found a source of regeneration in Vancouver's dynamic radio community, and in 1943 was made national supervisor of CBC drama. By the time I returned to Toronto in 1946, the clever dandy had become a serious artist.

In *A Self-Portrait* Allan described his approach: "My idea of being 'definitive' (which I had been told we must be) was to give the *writers* their head — to let them write what they wanted to write, and in the way they wanted to write it. The subtitle on the early *Stage* series was 'a report on the state of radio playwriting in Canada.'"[1] Marian Waldman, Harry Boyle, Alan King, Robert and Rita Allen were Toronto regulars, but writers from everywhere were drawn to Toronto by this rare flowering of Canadian boastfulness. Fletcher Markle, Lister Sinclair, and John Bethune came from Vancouver; Joseph Schull and Hugh Kemp from Montreal; Len Peterson, Tommy Tweed, George Salverson and W. O. Mitchell from the Prairies. Four seasoned Canadian playwrights, the feminist Patricia Joudry, the intellectual Gerald Noxon, the firebrand Ted Allan, and later the radical Reuben Ship, returned from the United States.

Even before the program grew from half an hour to an hour, from intensive sketches to extended stories, Stage had filled the role of national theatre for anglophone Canada and attracted international awards. Within 10 years it was notorious. In 1954 a bootleg recording of Ship's satire on un-Americanism, The Investigator, with Drainie's uncanny evocation of Senator Joseph McCarthy, was circulated anonymously in the United States and proved instrumental in the senator's downfall. Its pedigree was eventually revealed by the New York Times's Jack Gould — the critic who had sparked the American reputation of the series in the first place with a 1945 review of Lister Sinclair's A Play on Words: "Radio was grown up last night in Canada. . . . Sooner or later, our own writers must be allowed to write as they choose within the normal bounds of propriety and have their say at a good hour when it will mean something."

Gould (and Allan) notwithstanding, the claim that Stage's dramatists were allowed to write as they chose was fanciful. Allan was a meticulous producer, editor, and director who had his way as all three. He did not so much give writers their heads as cultivate and reap what was in them. He was even known to plant ideas in the first place. He needed writers for his cause, one fully embraced by a renascent CBC under its first full-time chairman, the deceptively boyish journalist Davidson Dunton.

Unlike the commercial U.S. networks, the CBC had a purpose for radio greater than the medium itself: to help the country grow up. While there was still time. One way or another the airwaves would be used — either by Canadians for their agenda or by the neighbours for theirs. In the area of drama, Allan believed, the best defence was offence — and the strategy came straight out of his own psyche: the pincer movement. Instead of aping the competition he would go around it to left and right, giving Canadian audiences precisely what they could not get elsewhere: reflections of their own lives plus international masterpieces shunned by the commercial networks. This double thrust, involving both original plays and adaptations of world classics, could hardly be called either chauvinistic or anti-American. He was out to get Canada into the international club — and as a producer, not a mere consumer.

The first step was to persuade Canadian listeners to support such a radical idea. To woo them Allan employed every propaganda tactic known, from direct flattery ("You, the listener") to the avoidance of profanity or obscenity — a habit often wrongly attributed to puritanism on his part. His motive was quite different. "He held," his editor Alice Frick says, "that if there were no words in a play which might immediately offend a listener, then ideas which might be shocking or unacceptable to some could be presented."[2] When a scandal arose in 1949 over Lister Sinclair's *Hilda Morgan*, about an unmarried mother, one listener complained of the use of the word "pregnant" — but the debate in Parliament was about illegitimacy and censorship.

The second step was to convince the artists they were up to it.

Allan's actors had to be versatile to the point of anonymity — to appear "as cast" and to accept (at least in the beginning) a standard fee. He was building on existing strength. From constant work in British and American plays our actors had become expert chameleons. They needed only the chance to become equally expert at playing themselves to become peerless among English-speaking chameleons — as Christopher Plummer later proved. But this required a constant supply of Canadian plays, which Allan knew would take time to develop. Meanwhile he saw no reason why Canadian audiences should have to listen to foreign-language plays through the double filter of English–English or American–English translations — a practice, he once told me, as absurd as "watching the Moscow Circus through your aunt's binoculars." In what was then a daring departure he challenged writers and actors to translate Ibsen, Chekhov, and Giraudoux into Canadian–English. Even more impudently, he argued that since Canadian speech is more intelligible to the British than American speech, and vice versa, we should perform English-language classics in our own accents for both.

Whatever the idiom, Allan insisted on accuracy. One week he would have me act Sweeney Todd, Demon Barber of Fleet Street, the next an Alberta farmer, then a Greek demigod followed by a Scots laird, a Quebec priest, and Marlowe's Mephostophilis. Once the *Stage* series gained its Sunday beachhead, Allan introduced Dickens's *Pickwick Papers* on Mondays, in a 36-episode adaptation by Tommy Tweed. Next came *Nicholas Nickleby* — driving the magazine *Saturday Night* to hyperbole: "Mavor Moore, who portrayed lovable, laughable Mr. Pickwick, now portrays the vicious, sadistic school-master Wackford Squeers, and does it with equal brilliance."[3] How could the writer know what a model I had in the cane-crazed "Duke" at UCC Prep?

After playing Phileas Fogg in *Around the World in Eighty Days*, I became a one-man United Nations. As a German-Jewish refugee in a fact-based documentary directed by Esse Ljungh, I almost fooled my old International Service colleague, German-born Eric Koch:

> Where on earth did you learn it? Your acting was so authentic that I
> am sure you did it with the aid of the Supernatural. . . . If your name
> had not been announced at the opening I would have sworn
> Rosenberg was played by a genuine Rosenberg — I was really quite
> shaken by your performance.[4]

I was shaken by Koch's letter, since I knew my acting to be mostly artifice.
But on one occasion my identification with a role was terrifyingly complete.
A visiting English director cast me in a new drama by Tyrone Guthrie, *The
Flowers Are Not for You to Pick*, a replay of the fantasies of a drowning youth.[5]
"What made the play real and affecting," the critic John Watson wrote, "was
the superb performance of Mavor Moore, which carried conviction in every
line and every stammer."[6] How was he to guess that I had once drowned?

But you must not be misled when I make an example of myself. Our
troupe, while it lasted, had formidable strength in depth — those mentioned plus Bernard Braden, Barbara Kelly, Budd Knapp, Alice Hill, Lloyd
Bochner, Aileen Seaton, Don Harron, and more — and we paced each
other in the big or small roles in which we alternated.

Our undisputed champion was a Vancouver high school dropout,
with a nondescript voice and a limp from a boyhood accident that left
him in constant pain. John Drainie was possessed by a creative demon.
Through unrelenting self-criticism, hard study, and a towering capacity
for sticking at something until he got it right, he learned to transform
himself into a mouse, a slot machine, or a giant as occasion demanded.
When the magic worked, he would laugh triumphantly. This was not a
salute to his own artistry — he laughed equally at another's triumph —
but a celebration of the human capacity to make wonders happen. Adept
at any accent, he nonetheless made classical verse sound musical in his
native Canadian; and he read prose with a clarity born of sheer, concentrated honesty of mind. Considered by many (including his leading rival,
Orson Welles) to be the world's finest radio actor, Drainie personified the
dilemma of stardom in Canada: What do you do for an encore? Leave?

Not until the announcement of a *CBC Wednesday Night* series for 1948
did I begin to write for CBC Radio again — partly because acting was a
sure source of cash while I worked without salary for the New Play
Society, partly because I was constantly dashing off to concoct documentaries for the United Nations. But *Wednesday Night* was inviting.

Capitalizing on the success of the *Stage* series, program director Ernest
Bushnell envisaged — in his bath, he told me, although others attribute the

inspiration to Ira Dilworth's bath, or Davidson Dunton's — a weekly three-hour period devoted to the performance arts: drama, music, opera, literature. Some say the seed was imported from the BBC's highbrow *Third Programme* by that earlier transplant, Rex Lambert; others credit Harry Boyle, the imaginative general director of the series. Whatever its patrimony, CBC *Wednesday Night* was also a response to the desire of other directors to get in on the action. Allan's appointment as drama supervisor had caused some resentment among his seniors, especially Montreal's Rupert Caplan and Winnipeg's Esse Ljungh, who moved his ebullient Nordic id to Toronto to play Dionysus (as Len Peterson had it) to Allan's Apollo. The gentlemanly Caplan was a master craftsman; Ljungh was more evocative than Allan as a director of actors; Frank Willis — his nose less out of joint since he was already supervisor of features — was more alert to the shifting borders between drama, documentary, and actuality. In addition there were freelance directors, myself included, eager to experiment with new ideas.

Since I was out to save both Canada and the world, it will come as no surprise that I had in mind something both quintessentially Canadian and unmistakably universal. Returning on the train from New York one night, after completing an edition of *The U.N. Review* on obstacles to world peace, I dreamed of the Huron legend of the flood (a version of which I had come across in James Mavor's memoirs) as a sort of Swiftian allegory for the atomic age. There was a precedent for the destruction of the world.

That summer of 1948 Dilly and I and 15-month-old Dorothea retreated to the Faessler cottage in Muskoka. This chalet on the shore of Fairy Lake, which gained Charlie Faessler the nickname "Baron von Elfensee" among his Swiss friends, had just acquired a boathouse with a screened loft ideal for cloistered creativity. There, between swims and paintings, I wrote *The Great Flood*, telling how Chief Kopi's search among the animals for his vanished brother, Glooskap the idealist, is impeded at every turn by the priests, the politicians, the newshawks, the merchants, the physicians, the artists. At length he finds Glooskap at the bottom of the sea, imprisoned by the Great Sea Lions who control the waters. When Kopi kills their King, the Sea Lions invoke the flood that destroys the world. But Kopi builds a raft on which a band of faithful creatures survives to start a new world from the debris of the old. John Weinzweig added music based on aboriginal forms, and I directed the whole for CBC *Wednesday Night*, with Lloyd Bochner as Kopi and John Drainie as the Shaman (who bore more than a passing resemblance to my reverend father). I was appropriating every voice familiar from my childhood — human, animal, and divine — in an effort to find my own.

Fortunately *Saturday Night* critic John Watson was on my wavelength: "Mr. Moore is a completely adult kind of humorist, a relatively uncommon species in this land. His humour is universal in appeal, compounded of wisdom, optimism, anger, and pity."[7] But when *The Great Flood* was nominated for the first annual Canadian Radio Awards, one of the three drama judges — a priest — found it far too blasphemous for the top prize proposed by the other two, so it was listed as a "runner-up." (I was in no position to complain, being chairman of the committee of the Canadian Association for Adult Education responsible for the awards.)[8] The compromise winner was Ibsen's old shocker *Ghosts*, adapted by Lister Sinclair and directed by Esse Ljungh. Having thus learned that subversion can be sanctified by time and fame, I next adapted two seditious classics: Schiller's *William Tell* and Voltaire's *Candide*.

Plundering my feeble German and five existing translations, I rendered *William Tell*, in toto, into English blank verse. To the great delight of that free thinker Charlie Faessler, who suggested it, *Tell* became the centrepiece of a CBC *Wednesday Night* devoted to Switzerland. According to the CBC *Times* of that week, I said I "aimed to achieve a version devoid of archaisms or fustian." Missing the target by a mile, I fell headlong into both. But the eminent German scholar Barker Fairley found it "pleasant to see how easily the play went into modern English,"[9] and got to work on his translation of Goethe's *Faust* into similarly accessible English prose. Twenty-three years later we premiered Fairley's *Faust* at Toronto's St. Lawrence Centre.

Inspired by events at the United Nations, I turned *Candide* into a musical comedy — long before the version by Leonard Bernstein and his various colleagues (which we shall come to later) — for which I also wrote the music. Broadcast in 1952, with orchestration and incidental scoring by Howard Cable, *The Best of All Possible Worlds* was the first Canadian musical comedy carried by the CBC. It received the best of all possible reviews from Chester Duncan on *Critically Speaking*:

> That irreverent broadcast should give a kick in the pants to one of our most deep-seated illusions; I mean the lingering Canadian legend that all the best brains leave home. This was an enterprise that combined intelligence with professional skill of the highest order. Mr. Moore's musical comedy was as witty as it was charming. It was an eruption of Canadian talent that shook the walls around this bulwark of our culture, the CBC![10]

How could Duncan know that long before then I had decided to leave both the CBC and Canada for good?

"UNTIL THE REST OF THE WORLD can afford television," said U.N. Assistant Secretary-General Ralph Bunche, losing another length of cigarette ash to his mottled vest, "we rely on radio. So work your ass off." In the absence of Secretary-General Trygve Lie — we are back in May of 1947 — Peter Aylen had taken me to meet the senior U.N. bureaucrat available, the senior black U.S. diplomat, and his favourite wiseman.

In his mid-forties, bulging behind his executive desk like a lambent watchdog, Bunche exuded two auras often considered mutually exclusive: absolute authority and amused detachment. His expensive but tousled clothes told anyone interested in costume that he owed his rise to self-assurance masquerading as modesty. He spoke of a new world order with a dash of bitters, as if mocking his own obvious mastery of world affairs. Was that crack about working my ass off a threat or a joke? (When Bunche won the Nobel Peace Prize three years later for his work as U.N. mediator in Palestine, I knew the secret of his success: he kept them guessing.) I decided to take no chances. My arrival at the embryonic radio section, after all, coincided with the traumatic pregnancy of Israel, riots over the partition of India and Pakistan, and the inflammatory Universal Bill of Human Rights. My ass and everyone else's.

I had come to New York early to lease an apartment, while Dilly followed later by train, bringing baby Dorothea in a wicker bassinet. At Pennsylvania Station she emerged from the coach with the other end of the basket and half her luggage upheld by a muscular stranger — Canadian, obviously, since before vanishing he took pains to assure me his motive was entirely chivalrous. The cabbie welcomed us with the usual gritty Manhattan spiel, but added such an affecting tale of his heroic struggle to pay for a small daughter's eye operation that I gave him a $10 tip. Dilly kicked me, and I kicked myself when I got the same story from another cabbie within the week.

Our three-month sublet in New York — the first of several — was a third-floor walk-up on Fifty-seventh Street, owned by a concert pianist absent on tour. It had two beds, two pianos, and two locks — one more of each than we were accustomed to. The windows, sealed against airborne pollution, proved no barrier to the pigeon caucus that woke us every morning at six. Tedde, as Dorothea came to be called, was a model traveller, whether asleep in her basket or alert in her collapsible stroller. With her as safe-conduct we explored Central Park, cased the galleries, studied window displays and restaurant menus, investigated the second-hand dealers, and made friends with the grocers. To the south lay the many-splendoured stores of mid-Manhattan, and within walking distance the marquees of Times Square, then still safe to amble in.

The most novel experiences for us were the great public galleries, especially the Museum of Modern Art, where we lingered in astonishment. Like most Canadians (and most Americans at the time), we knew little about American painting, which seemed to swing between homey realism and European surrealism. But immigrants named de Kooning, Gorky, and Rothko were leading the forces of abstract expressionism, and we soon saw we had strayed onto a battlefield. The music scene, from Louis Armstrong and George Shearer to the Philharmonic and station WQXR, was equally exciting. And we bought cheap theatre seats for plays such as All My Sons, by the young radical Arthur Miller, Finian's Rainbow, and the Rodgers and Hammerstein Carousel, directed by Rouben Mamoulian, designed by Jo Mielziner, and choreographed by Agnes de Mille. Carousel confirmed my hypothesis, framed after seeing the same team's Oklahoma in 1945, that the serious musical was the operative form of modern theatre. In my notebook I wrote: "Why no Canadian musicals?"

But nights on the town were necessarily few, even when we could enlist friends to baby-sit. At Lake Success, to which I commuted by serial subway, I was assigned to develop a regular U.N. Daily Review, which turned out to be a priceless opportunity to learn the ropes at the navy's expense. Secreted in the English-language radio booth overlooking the General Assembly or the well-equipped studios below, I followed and edited the day's proceedings, incorporating news from related agencies and commentary by myself and others. Recording technology had reached new heights, with tape bringing an unexplored potential for arranging fact and exploiting fantasy, and the "transcription" disc, bringing a revolution in distribution. It was dangerous work. In my second week I precipitated a diplomatic incident by reporting, during a vote, that "someone has just gone to dig up the representative from Ecuador."

My gaffes, however, were no more frequent than those of the politicians and diplomats, although I began to suspect that theirs were seldom as naive as mine.

In the course of the Palestine debate the U.S. delegate, silver-maned Senator Warren Austin of Vermont, declared that the whole tragic problem could easily be resolved "if only the Jews and the Arabs would come at it in a Christian spirit." During the India–Pakistan wrangle, the laconic British ambassador, Sir Alexander Cadogan (who talked in short bursts of five or six words), dismissed New Delhi's claims as "rot," which prompted India's Sir S. Radhakrishnan, onetime professor of philosophy at Oxford, to rise like a cat offered a morsel at a banquet. After apologizing for his English, he showered Cadogan with elaborate compliments to the special genius of that language for articulating complex spatiotemporal processes such as *decomposition,* the effects of which, on persons no less than nations, his honourable friend had regrettably failed, perhaps due to overwork and the lateness of the hour, to take fully into account before rising to speak, or whatever it was he was doing. On another occasion, with China's Quo Dai Chi in the chair, the arrival of a shock-haired elder in striped pants and cutaway caused a stir in the visitors' gallery. Quo turned from the microphone to ask an aide, "Who is that?" Behind his hand the aide replied: "Sir Julian Huxley, director-general of UNESCO." Quo banged his gavel and had welcomed "the brave representative of that gallant little country" before the aide could make a fist around the microphone.

The meetings of the Economic and Social Council and its branches were studded with gems. As the Commission on Human Rights drafted its charter, the patience of Canadian umpire John Humphrey, its divisional director, was in great demand. In the chair was the eminent U.S. delegate Eleanor Roosevelt, her genteel New York tenor in full flight. In the vice-chair was the French delegate, a neatly bearded professor from the Sorbonne who also spoke in English — not out of gallantry toward Mrs. Roosevelt but because (to the alarm of the Belgians, Swiss, Canadians, and others) he shared her view of multilingualism as a recipe for civil discord. When the agenda came to white slavery (transportion of prostitutes between nations), Mrs. Roosevelt, speaking as the U.S. delegate, moved that prostitution be outlawed everywhere. Her motion was seconded by the professor from France. But the moment she resumed the chair he raised his hand to move, as I remember it, an extraordinary amendment:

MRS. R: A seconder *may* move an amendment, I believe, Professor, but only if it is not in conflict with the original motion. May I ask what you have in mind?

PROF: Of course, Madame. I propose that all prostitutes be licensed.

MRS. R: But how can they be *outlawed* and *licensed* at the same time?

PROF: There is no difficulty, Madame. Prostitution is a terrible evil, and of course it must be outlawed. But of course that will not work, so the prostitutes must also be licensed.

This is pure Voltaire, I thought — the best of all possible worlds is a musical comedy.

The powerful Security Council, designed as a lightning rod, was just as often used as a wet blanket. Simultaneous translation into the five official languages (English, French, Russian, Spanish, Chinese) not yet being available, all speeches had to be rendered into the "international" tongues, English and French. During one of the frequent Balkan crises, the Yugoslavian representative launched an attack on Greece in French, only to be interrupted by the U.S. delegate, Herschel Johnson, asking the chair in English if this tirade against a fellow member was in order. Before the chair could reply the tirade had to be translated into English and the interruption into French. Then the Soviet Union's Andrei Gromyko asked, in Russian, if Johnson's interruption was in order. His intervention was repeated first in French and then in English. Johnson said he refused to recognize the right of the Soviet delegate to tell him when to speak and when not to speak, and this was repeated in French. Gromyko said in Russian that it was not up to Johnson to say what was in order and what was not. This was repeated in both French and English, all before the chair had said a word — and the communal coitus interruptus continued for the better part of an hour.

"By any standard except that of Victorian melodrama," I wrote for *Saturday Night* after my return to Toronto three months later, "this little exchange was vastly insignificant. Yet out of a whole day's important debate this molehill was chosen to be made into a press mountain. The least of the colorations had Mr. Gromyko 'shouting'. . . . I can never remember the Soviet delegate raising his bovine tones, and I defy anyone to maintain heat in an argument punctuated by translators who could make cold prose out of *The Song of Solomon*." I begged readers "not to sink into the pessimism which prophesies doom and in doing so brings it on. Constructive measures are going forward in many fields. The grave danger is that differences between the great powers, however minuscule, receive enormous publicity while these positive agreements and achievements are sceptically ignored or suspiciously dismissed as meaningless."[11]

Assembling a daily program of U.N. initiatives around the world in a dozen different fields had convinced me that activists could influence the political agenda. I had before me the daily example of Raphael Lemkin, the lone campaigner who haunted the corridors at Lake Success, pestering delegates until genocide was made an international crime. After chatting to Lemkin, I would catch myself mumbling old Daddy Mills's canon,

"You can do anything you want if you want to hard enough," at that time being recycled by the Reverend Norman Vincent Peale as the Power of Positive Thinking. Our *U.N. Review* won a Peabody Award, and a memorable accolade from *Variety*, the journal of showbiz: "Sock public service."

But was the sock connecting? In the English-language service alone we were putting out 45 to 60 hours a week; but U.S. listener ratings for public service programs were generally low, and abroad we had few ratings to go by. On bad days we fell back on Pascal's wager: the necessary gamble that to win is possible. At Lake Success I developed an undying respect and affection for my fellow gamblers.

They came from every corner of the globe. We had the wisest of the wise, divine Ma Than E from Burma (the adjective is now debased, but how else does one describe a goddess?), and the shrewdest of the shrewd, the wondrously hatted Dorothy Lewis, our liaison with the U.S. commercial networks she knew like the back of her bejewelled hands. There were veterans of wartime radio like the BBC's brilliant Gibson Parker, everything trim and trig except in his sexual closet, and Dutch-born Hans van Stuwe, kindness itself to everyone, including his septuagenarian French mother-in-law Fifi, who flirted with every male under 50. There were graduates of the Voice of America, among them Michael Hayward, head of English-language programming, and the innovative producer Gerald Kean, my first boss. I cherished my bridge partners: Afghan philosopher Muhammed Malek, Marguerite Clark from everywhere, George Movshon, the Afrikaaner who hated apartheid, Stephanie Dinkins, who fled American comfort to report from the world's plague spots, and Hungarian Emery Kellen, whose sharp political cartoons (at everyone's expense) gave him a head start in television.

Colleagues with axes to grind I avoided. I once found myself wedged between two smiling Soviets in the back seat of a limousine en route to Manhattan, playing eye Ping-Pong as one insisted that my grandfather's Russian books were widely admired in the Soviet Union (he could not have read them) while his mate kept asking where I had learned Russian. How else could I tell anecdotes like the one about the *Orel* docking in Vancouver, which he overheard in the cafeteria, with such a flawless accent? I had a single thought, lying somewhere between pride and sweat: they had a file on me.

Most of my international associates were neither nationalists nor ideologues. They approached other cultures with curiosity and respect, seldom hesitating to make jokes at the expense of their own. They saw themselves as public servants to humanity, and all of humanity as equally threatened by the new atom bomb. If they had a common belief, it was in the mathematician's "butterfly effect" — that air disturbed by an insect in Nagasaki can lead to a cyclone in Rome. They were global villagers before McLuhan discovered the place. To them, nationalism and ideology were mere growing pains. "Brotherhood," said one of the most articulate, U.S. playwright Norman Corwin, "is not so wild a dream as those who profit from postponing it pretend."[12]

I found much the same attitude among the prominent well-wishers of all nationalities who volunteered their talents. One of my directorial responsibilities was a series of recordings of the Preamble to the U.N. Charter, read by international stars: Charles Boyer, John Gielgud, Luise Rainer, Laurence Olivier, Paul Muni, Charles Laughton, Madeleine Carroll, Fredric March, and the like — including Orson Welles, now claiming to have predicted my rise in the world. Aside from Gielgud — who revealed himself as a man interested in little but acting and as an incorrigibly mannered actor when forced to play himself — they read with personal conviction: "We, the peoples of the United Nations, determined to save succeeding generations from the scourge of war . . . to reaffirm faith in fundamental human rights . . . "

These public servants and public figures made a formidable alliance of yea-sayers. Yet in its attempt to spread the alternative vision, it became clear, the United Nations was at the mercy of existing networks and cultural systems. In Communist countries these institutions were part of the government; in most others they were party to the prevailing dogma — the religious fundamentalism of the Middle East, for instance, or the advertising-driven commercialism of the United States. Independents prepared to buck the trends anywhere were few and by definition ill-organized. Could the nonpartisan unifying message be delivered before catastrophe struck again? This was the uncertain frame of mind in which I left for home after three months in New York, and dreamed, on the train, of the cautionary fable that became The Great Flood.

What kept me coming back to Toronto was the belief that in Canada we had a rare chance to avoid this choice of evils, to develop, out of the eye of the storm, new uses for broadcasting and new forms of art free of both governmental and commercial tyranny. At the same time it was the challenge of effecting changes in the larger sphere that drew me to the United Nations again and again over the next three years, until there came a day when I was no longer sure from where to where I was commuting.

The two arenas were close but contrary. In Toronto I spent the winters birthing a shoestring theatre while supporting my family on freelance earnings from radio acting, periodic teaching, and parochial journalism. In New York I spent the spring or summer months as a director, writer, and (eventually) producer first in radio, then in television, working with a peerless international talent pool and the latest technology. I did no acting beyond accidentally starring on U.S. prime time radio when Fletcher Markle, newly installed as director of CBS's *Studio One*, cast me as Dr. Stockmann in *An Enemy of the People* after his American star fell ill.[13] I was turning out two regular series, *The U.N. Story*[14] and *The U.N. Today*, preparing features for global distribution, lecturing on U.N. affairs at the New School for Social Research, and mounting combined operations with the American networks. In the NBC and CBS studios John Daly and Mike Wallace inoculated me with a strain of hypertension so effective I have since remained proof against it. It killed Daly, but Wallace seems to have thrived on it.

Before our return to New York for a second summer I had read *Mutual Aid* by James Mavor's friend the anarchist Peter Kropotkin, with its anti-Darwinian thesis that cooperative species survive best; and I had discovered *The Human Situation* — Scottish philosopher Macneile Dixon's prophetic plea to "open the windows" to knowledge. So I was well prepared for an event reported by the Canadian Press out of Adelphi College, New York, in August of 1948:

> A Canadian is taking a prominent part in an international seminar attended by representatives of 23 countries . . . on how to teach school children the setup, methods and the accomplishments of the United Nations. Mavor Moore, 29-year-old Canadian freelance radio artist from Toronto, leads the discussions on radio and recordings which are one feature of the five-week meet sponsored by the UN Educational, Scientific and Cultural Organization.[15]

The 45 teachers from all over met with a pride of lions — from Secretary-General Trygve Lie and Eleanor Roosevelt to Dwight D. Eisenhower (recently installed, in error, as president of Columbia University) and Professor Lyman Bryson (soon to leave Columbia University for the more lucrative presidency of CBS). Lie was his usual pompous self, but Eisenhower had a neat trick for suggesting instant friendship. As Mrs. Roosevelt introduced each of us from her list, Ike would listen to the name but look keenly at the person approaching; when my turn came, he shot out his hand and said, "Hya, Mavor!" as if he remembered me perfectly from the last time. We also heard from experts on audiovisual aids, linguistics, and other international specialties, including the U.S. State Department's Alger Hiss, whose deep-set blue eyes gained him a place on the honour roll of possible spies I failed to spot. But neither old rhetoric nor new technology was a match for the teachers' reality.

The Italian delegate described her students as too hungry and too nervous to concentrate on the alphabet, let alone the universe; she considered vitamin B more urgent than filmstrips. A Yugoslav principal said his problem was not so much to expound on the ethics of international amity as to introduce his teenagers to ethics; as children they had survived the war by thieving and whoring and later received medals for betraying and killing. The Greek teacher had no school; 70 percent of classes in Greece, she said, were held outdoors or in someone's parlour, while the 30 percent housed in buildings (or reasonable facsimile) had no heat, no desks, few books, few pencils, and little paper.[16] The most sought-after book at the seminar was *The Teacher and the Post-War Child in War-Devastated Countries* by the farsighted American educator L. W. Kenworthy, containing instructions for making blackboards, chalk, charcoal, balls, pipes, pens, and other necessities out of found materials.

This was all very well, offered an African teacher, but these European countries were literate societies with long educational traditions merely interrupted by war. What about the illiterates? How did one sell a new world order to societies totally ignorant of world history, unable to read books, and deprived of alternatives? Remembering old George Ade's sensible advice, "In uplifting, get underneath," I felt suddenly weak. A cloud of resignation hung over the whole group, but not for long.

One of life's recurrent surprises is the persistence of fleeting encounters that pop up from the recesses of the memory, on cue, to illuminate a crossroads. When J. R. Chao, the University of California philologist who was directing the seminar, fled occupied China with his physician wife, Buwei, they abandoned everything except his almost completed Mandarin translation of *Alice's Adventures in Wonderland* and *Through the Looking Glass*. Their ship was torpedoed in the Pacific and the priceless manuscript lost. The first thing Chao did on arrival in the United States was to begin it again. By the time we met he had got as far as *Jabberwocky*. I wish I could explain how the reading aloud of a nonsense poem, filled with puns in a language nobody there understood, could become an unforgettable lesson in regeneration. I cannot, but it did. Each of the participants went home with a specific project for local use.

The seminarians also agreed that broadcasting, the economical mass medium, should be a prime means of promoting literacy everywhere. I took the liberty of suggesting to Ottawa that the Canadian broadcasting system, now available to 97 percent of listeners in the country, offered the federal government a unique opportunity to study the use of radio to reach illiterates. I was informed that this was an educational and therefore a provincial matter. Or a case of falling between nine stools.

In an odd way the international organization's promotion of its programs, even though Canada shared in them, was seen in Ottawa as foreign infringement on Canadian territory. UNESCO, in particular, was regarded in some quarters as either a waste of time or a cultural Trojan horse. In my sojourns in Toronto, where I sat on the executive committee of the United Nations Association, I had firsthand experience of the government's procrastination in signing the UNESCO agreement permitting duty-free movement of educational, scientific, and cultural materials. Even U.N. radio transcriptions were taxed — on the acetate in the disc.

A similarly cautious Canadian reception awaited what was on the discs.

While most of our English-language output was carried in the United States, Australia, New Zealand, South Africa, and often Britain, I had the impression that my friends in CBC public affairs did not like to import free propaganda programs, no matter how noble the source or how compelling the production. The excuse usually given was that U.N. programs were "too popular" in tone, which struck me as hilariously perverse: the better they worked the worse they must be. In the eyes of the alternative private stations, on the other hand, the programs were "too highbrow" or "too controversial." The few carried by either network were slighted by the press. Even when I persuaded producer Gerald Kean to mount one of our productions in Canada — a drama about displaced persons jointly sponsored by the the CBC, NBC, and the CIO[17] — the sole Canadian review consisted of two sentences from *Toronto Star* columnist Gordon Sinclair: "Kean handed Canadian customers an awful dog. Herbert Marshall was brought here to star in some meaningless jumble."[18]

The reception in the United States was markedly different. Our programs were noted in advance and critically analyzed in major newspapers and magazines. "From Lake Success," Saul Carson wrote in *The New*

Republic, "still come the most successful documentaries on our air." Of the drama dismissed by Sinclair, Carson wrote: "The secret of *Tomorrow's* success . . . was the production given it by Canada's Mavor Moore, the superb acting of a couple of young Canadians whose names were new to me [John Drainie and Diane Foster], and the music by a young Canadian composer, Louis Applebaum."[19]

Between 1947 and 1950 at Lake Success we produced documentaries on narcotics control, world health, the International Bank, industrial development, and several U.N. agencies. All of them had famous stars as narrators. Gary Cooper pronounced nuclear "nucular," as I learned from having to edit out the 97 times he got it wrong and substitute, throughout, the one time he got it right. (I now realize Cooper was only a pioneer.) I survived the celebrated tongue-lashings of John Garfield, who addressed me as "Wonderboy," "My good fellow," and "You little twit." On better days I worked again with Cedric Hardwicke, now parted from his Pixie in London, and directed Melvyn Douglas, Joan Crawford, José Ferrer, Rex Harrison, and Lili Palmer — about whose marital or other arrangements I made it a point, as a practising Canadian, to know as little as possible.

The exception to this rule was Franchot Tone, who was part-Canadian. He narrated *This Is the U.N.*, a historical series I codirected with Robert Lewis Shayon for an independent company. At the end of each day's taping Tone would be picked up in a different sports car driven by a different blonde. He would introduce me to her, and the next day ask for an assessment — a recurring embarrassment since I had trouble telling them apart. Whether Tone's companions were mere chauffeurs or look-alike mistresses, however, his work in the studio was dazzling. Never having met such a gifted actor so prodigal of his gifts, I began to speculate about the connection between talent and dissipation. I concluded that we elect actors as surrogate sinners, just as our ancestors once elected sacrifical kings, allowing them great leeway for a period of seven years with the option of self-destruction or ritual death at the end of it. Franchot Tone took the first option.

This Is the U.N. received wide distribution and an enthusiastic welcome in the United States. The *New York Times's* Howard Taubman called it "stirring stuff";[20] the Association for the United Nations called it "magnificent"; the editor of the *Christian Science Monitor* predicted that it "will take its place among the great historical archives of our time"; it won several international awards.[21] No Canadian network wanted it.

Our most significant breakthrough to a larger public, however, came with *Year of Decision* (1950), an hour-long program on atomic energy prepared for the Mutual Broadcasting System, which made headlines all over the world. "The [U.N.] team," noted *The New Republic's* Carson, "included Gerald Kean as supervisor; Mavor Moore as writer-director; Jeff Sparks and Michael Hayward as the radio reporters who interviewed scientists; Antonia Gordon, who did much of the basic research; and Louis Applebaum, a Canadian composer, who for the second time in five or six months contributed distinguished and effective music to a U.N. show. Professor Albert Einstein was on the program."[22] This was the only review in which Applebaum preceded Einstein, who had never before allowed his voice to be recorded.

We had worked on the program for a year, with J. Robert Oppenheimer as our consultant. As the script developed, Gordon, Sparks, and I would take each revised version to Oppenheimer's office in the Institute for Advanced Study at Princeton. Close-cropped and tweed-wrapped, the atomic scientist looked more like an anorexic leprechaun than a Public Figure. He spoke sparely and softly. Reading the script, he turned pages at the rate of a slow tennis rally, giving each about as much attention as you or I might give a phone number, neither speaking nor making notes. Then he would hand the script back and begin a commentary with his eyes closed: "On page 2, line 14, the narrator says . . ." — and so on throughout the 100-odd pages.

We had plenty of homework to do between classes. The program covered military and peaceful uses of atomic energy in the realms of power, medicine, and materials, as well as the East–West deadlock over international control. We sent investigators to universities, hospitals, and other research centres, and interviewers to talk to human guinea pigs. We looked at the icon "atomic" in everyday life: its sudden popularity as a subject for songs and as a name for every sort of company from laundries to publishers; the vogue for "fission" and "critical mass" jargon in intellectual circles; the widespread fear of an atomic Armageddon. But the headlines generated by *Year of Decision* were all versions of the one that appeared in the *New York Times* the next day: WORLD ATOM RULE URGED BY EINSTEIN.[23]

We used a trick on Einstein. Oppenheimer had asked him to allow an interviewer to record a brief statement urging on all nations the "nonparticipation" creed of Mahatma Gandhi. When Einstein and his wife graciously invited a U.N. representative to tea, we sent our most experienced interviewer, a popeyed monomaniac named Jeff Sparks who could charm the pearl out of an oyster. After tea Sparks produced his tape recorder and microphone, into which Einstein read his short statement about Gandhi in slow and heavily accented English:

> We should strive to do things in his spirit — not to use violence in fighting our cause, but by nonparticipation in what you believe is evil.

Ostentatiously setting his recorder aside, Sparks then casually asked Einstein what he thought should be done with the supply of bombs already stockpiled. Einstein shrugged. Without naming the United States or the Soviet Union (the only nations known to have atomic bombs), or the United Nations, he then replied:

> Give it into the hand of a supernational organization. During the interval of peace, one must have some protecting power. One-sided disarmament is not possible. This is out of the question. . . .

Sparks pressed him: "Was the current atomic armament race a way to prevent war or the way to another world war?" Einstein shrugged.

> Competitive armament is not a way to prevent war. Every step in this direction brings us nearer to catastrophe. . . . Armament is no protection against war, but leads inevitably to war.

It was soon after this that Sparks, making his farewells, stooped to retrieve his tape machine and discovered that it had been left on. It was all terribly embarrassing, et cetera, but since the remarks inadvertently recorded were so crucial to peace, so important to humanity, would Dr. Einstein really want to deprive the world of this chance to *hear* him — not to read what some reporter quoted him as having said, but to hear him actually saying it? Einstein shrugged. Here, of course, I am only quoting Jeff Sparks. But I know that the day after the broadcast the world's press and radio quoted all 90 seconds of Einstein's answers, with Sparks's questions edited out.[24]

In August 1950 *The Canadian Forum* published an essay of mine, sent from New York, that began with an apology: "It is four months since the *Forum* asked me to do an article on the Canadian theatre. At the time I was too involved in helping the Canadian theatre to exist at all to take time out

James Mavor (1854–1925) at the Arts and Letters Club. Sketch by Arthur Lismer. (Mavor Moore Collection)

Dora Mavor Moore (1888–1978), c. 1922.
(Mavor Moore Collection)

Francis John Moore (1885–1968), c. 1922.
(Mavor Moore Collection)

Brothers-in-law: Major Wilfrid Mavor (left) and Captain the Reverend Francis Moore in World War I. (SASHA MAVOR ARMOUR COLLECTION)

Visiting Dr. O. H. Mavor ("James Bridie") in East Berwick, Scotland, summer 1936. "OH!" sits on the left beside his cousin Dora, with (from left) my brother Peter, Robert Mavor, and me. (RONA MAVOR/THOMAS FISHER LIBRARY)

Meem (left) and Fran in the hated UCC Eton suits in 1929. (FRANCIS W. M. MOORE COLLECTION)

President of the University of Toronto Philosophical Society, 1940. (YORK UNIVERSITY ARCHIVES)

The lieutenant marries Darwina Faessler, with his Sam Browne belt on backward, October 16, 1943. (YORK UNIVERSITY ARCHIVES)

My mother and I holding up the only known picture of the "barn," in a painting by actor-artist Hedley Rainnie. (MERV LITTLE/YORK UNIVERSITY ARCHIVES)

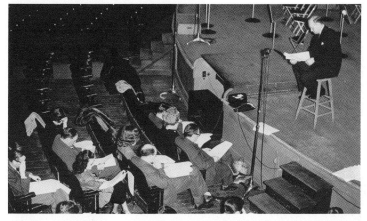

Andrew Allan giving notes to the cast of *Stage* in CBC Radio's McGill Street Studio in Toronto, 1948. The bald head is me. Others among the assembled include Jane Mallett, John Drainie, Lloyd Bochner, and Tommy Tweed. (THOMAS FISHER LIBRARY)

The first *Spring Thaw* in 1948. Holding hands are Frosia Gregory and Don Harron, with Jane Mallett under the table. (YORK UNIVERSITY ARCHIVES)

My mother directing in the Museum Theatre. (THOMAS FISHER LIBRARY)

As Bolfry in James Bridie's *Mr. Bolfry*, with Pegi Brown (left) and Babs Hitchman, New Play Society, 1947. (YORK UNIVERSITY ARCHIVES)

As Louis Riel in John Coulter's *Riel*, New Play Society, 1950. (YORK UNIVERSITY ARCHIVES)

With Jane Mallett in *Spring Thaw '51*. (R. S. MACPHERSON/YORK UNIVERSITY ARCHIVES)

As Judge Brack in the CBC-TV production of *Hedda Gabler*, with Joan Greenwood in the title role, 1957. (CBC-TV)

As Caesar in Shaw's *Caesar and Cleopatra* at the Crest Theatre, 1962, with Toby Robins as Cleopatra. (ROBERT C. RAGSDALE/YORK UNIVERSITY ARCHIVES)

Directing John Garfield at Lake Success, with U.N. producer Gerald Kean (*right*), in 1950. (YORK UNIVERSITY ARCHIVES)

Hyde Park, New York: Eleanor Roosevelt (*centre*) hosting the August 1948 UNESCO Conference on Education. I'm sitting on the grass, wearing sunglasses. J. R. Chao is at Mrs. Roosevelt's left. (YORK UNIVERSITY ARCHIVES)

CBC-TV Toronto, opening night, September 8, 1952. Giving notes to pianist Glenn Gould (*centre*) is director Drew Crossan; chief producer Moore (*far right*) is checking the script. (CBC-TV)

Nathan Cohen on CBC-TV's *Fighting Words*. (CBC-TV)

With program director Stuart Griffiths in an early CBC-TV studio, 1953. (CBC-TV)

Talking to Tyrone Guthrie in the tent at Stratford, 1954. (PETER SMITH & CO./YORK UNIVERSITY ARCHIVES)

As Sir Wilfred Robarts (centre) in Agatha Christie's Witness for the Prosecution at the Crest Theatre, 1957. (ROBERT C. RAGSDALE)

Norman Campbell's 1955 CBC-TV production of Sunshine Town. Robert Goulet (second from left), Paul Kligman (centre), Robert Christie (far right). (PAGE TOLES/YORK UNIVERSITY ARCHIVES)

Barbara Hamilton as Cacambo, Robert Goulet as Candide, in The Optimist, opening the Avenue Theatre in 1955. (McKAGUE/YORK UNIVERSITY ARCHIVES)

The ecumenical "Togetherness" from Spring Thaw '61, with Dave Broadfoot (left), Jack Duffy, Peter Mews, and Bill Cole. (YORK UNIVERSITY ARCHIVES)

As Bob Edwards in the National Film Board's *The Eyeopener Man*, 1957. (NATIONAL FILM BOARD)

Directing *Spring Thaw '64*, first national tour, with Dave Broadfoot (left), Marylyn Stuart, and Dean Regan. (YORK UNIVERSITY ARCHIVES)

The *Wayne and Shuster Show* in rehearsal, Charlottetown, 1964. (CHARLOTTETOWN FESTIVAL)

Kate Reid and Eric House, with Don Harron (centre) up to no good, in my play *The Ottawa Man*, Charlottetown Festival, 1966. (GEORGE WOTTON)

Bernard Turgeon in the title role of *Louis Riel*, Harry Somers's 1967 opera, with my libretto.

(CANADIAN OPERA COMPANY)

The 1967 Centennial Committee studying a model of the National Arts Centre, Ottawa, 1966. To my left: Secretary of State Maurice Lamontagne, Doris Anderson, and Roland Michener. (YORK UNIVERSITY ARCHIVES)

In all directions, 1967. Cartoon by Lewis Parker. (*Maclean's*)

I give the picture to Mayor William Dennison. The St. Lawrence Centre problem as seen by Franklin in the *Toronto Star*. (MAYOR MOORE COLLECTION)

to write about it; but I offered to do so as soon as I left Toronto [for New York] in May. . . . I became involved at once in writing and directing a special U.N. program on control of atomic energy. . . . A few days after this broadcast, the Korean incident occurred, and at the moment of writing we at [the] U.N. are still wreathed in the battle-clouds of its depression."

I proceeded to unpack my heart: "This preamble is not an excuse . . . as if to say that my mind has been occupied with greater things. It is rather the most pertinent fact in the article itself, for I believe *King Lear* to be as important as the relief of Seoul. I believe the creations of the human mind to be as important as the conduct of human affairs — in fact I wonder to what end the latter are carried on at all if not to make the former possible. Yet . . . most of my fellow-Canadians disagree with me, and demonstrate their disagreement daily by placing the conduct of affairs so far above creative achievement that one is allowed to smother the other."

Then I lit into my compatriots:

> My experience in Canada, from schooldays up, has been that concern with the creative arts stamps one as a lightweight, or queer, or both. And concern with the drama (that most basic, graphic and revealing of the arts), above all marks one as removed from the sphere of practical life almost to idiocy. Only an equal concern for making money out of it can restore regard for one's sanity.

> Promising actors are begged by their families to become lawyers, or at least clergymen; nascent designers and painters are guided into architecture or interior decorating or poster-making; incipient writers are persuaded that the cheapest advertising blurb is a worthier pursuit than saying what they honestly think; young women with talent are beguiled into believing it should be quashed in favor of the respectable frustration of an unhappy marriage. If all else fails, they can teach.

Finally, denying that my anger was due to "disappointed idealism" or "lack of appreciation," I made odious comparisons. "I know of no country, including Afghanistan and Tibet, where the dramatic arts and artists are held in such low esteem as in Canada; and if we take into consideration [Canada's] importance in the modern world, any other nation's philistinism pales into obscurity. Almost any of us, workers in the Canadian theatre, are regarded by the public at large (not the initiated theatregoers) as 'amateurs'; yet in London and New York — the world centres of theatrical activity in our language — we are accepted as accomplished professionals, as has been proved time and again by those of us who wished to do so. . . . It is not the Canadian artist who is not good enough; it is the Canadian public which is not good enough for the artist."[25]

Anyone might guess from this tirade that I had no intention of returning home — especially anyone overhearing what I had just told my wife on the telephone: CBS had offered me a job directing *Studio One*, America's leading television drama series.

9

Toward a Canadian Theatre

"From Mavor Moore, who probably knows more than anyone else just how much progress our native theatre has made since Canadians became aware of themselves as a nation — which is to say since 1939 — this kind of indiscriminate maligning causes perplexity and dismay. . . . When Moore decries the ingratitude and apathy of the Canadian public, he is in effect refuting the facts of his own experience."

The forthright voice from 1950 could only be that of Nathan Cohen, responding to my *Canadian Forum* article in an early issue of his new periodical, *The Critic*.

I first met Cohen after my return to Toronto from Vancouver in 1946. We came from very different backgrounds. Earnest, frank, awkwardly gallant, four years younger than I, this ex-Maritimer, ex-law student, ex-Communist had settled in Toronto and was contributing columns to the Jewish press, nominally covering Jewish culture but by extension the whole local scene. His reviews of the New Play Society's initial season, that fall, alerted us to the arrival of a fresh critical voice hailing from outside the academic and journalistic mainstreams, and happily free of their respective vices: condescension and mateyness. It was my 1947 revival of Sean O'Casey's *Juno and the Paycock,* he claimed, that drove him to become a full-time critic. When CBC Radio sought a theatre reviewer for a new local arts series, I recommended him to Charles Jennings, then head of programming. Jennings returned a handwritten note in his trademark green ink, evasively questioning Cohen's "political and other ties." When I phoned to ask pointedly which ties he had in mind, Jennings waffled and promised to get back to me the following day — by which time he had approved the appointment and taken credit for the inspiration. For the next two decades Cohen and I ran a sort of vaudeville act, playing in turn each other's champion, rival, conscience, and scourge.

"His own experience," he went on about me in 1950, "should tell him that the Canadian public is more than eager to appreciate and support the efforts of its dramatic artists. The plays Mavor Moore has directed for the New Play Society have been the best patronized in that company's whole history. His comedy *Who's Who* drew more people into the Museum Theatre than any other of the original plays the NPS presented. (This writer, congenitally averse to superlatives, has not hesitated to describe him as the man who, by his work and influence, has done the most to raise Canadian theatre to a level of artistic excellence, our best regisseur, the only person to whom the word 'genius' can honestly be applied.)" Cohen finds Toronto playgoers not only "ready to support Canadian drama" but "disposed to show native playwrights a boundless tolerance," and praises them for "exercising a proper discretion" toward obvious failures.

As evidence, he cites the four-year history of the New Play Society:

> The Toronto public is not only anxious to give playwrights a chance; it shows the same partiality to the NPS itself. The figures contain proof. In the first year of operation, an NPS show ran two nights; in the second year three, in the third year seven. The NPS was able to expand in this fashion through the meritorious production of established dramas, experimental plays, and originals. Sometimes this audience persevered when the NPS reneged on its own standards. Audiences in Toronto unkind, bigoted, patronizing? Not at all. As the history of the NPS demonstrates they are loyal and, when need be, indulgent.

Mocking the idea that in 1950 Toronto had "an almost inexhaustible supply of artisans and creators whose lust for expression is thwarted by public hostility and indifference," Cohen bemoans the lack of designers, electricians, makeup artists, costumers, and "*competent* directors":

> I can think of no more than three who are reasonably proficient, and of only one — Mavor Moore — who understands that an acted play must have its own art content, separate and apart from that contained within the written play. Since Moore believes firmly in the humanities, he sees the theatre in its broad perspective, not as a commodity but as an influence, not as a glamorous means of employment, but as a superior social force.
>
> But . . . how much drama was the Toronto public offered in the past year [1950] that indicated the grandeur, the excitement, the humour, the wondrousness of the human mind in the process of creation and illumination? . . . I recall only one, [Moore's production of] *Heartbreak House*, which was dramatically and theatrically alive!"[1]

Half touched, half defensive, I replied to *The Critic*: "I was, if anything, a little generous; many Toronto citizens who regularly turn out in droves to see visiting theatrical celebrities from abroad stay away in droves when anything Canadian comes up. This leaves a small band indeed which we may excuse from the lecture."[2]

This exchange occurred less than four years after my return to Toronto from Vancouver, bursting, like Cohen, with great expectations. "Toronto," I had said, "is not a place but a time." What changed my mind? The Golden Age we were hoping for had not exactly been cancelled. At the very moment Cohen and I were facing off, a Royal Commission on National Development in the Arts, Letters, and Sciences, chaired by Vincent Massey, was preparing its heraldic report. The next three years saw the birth of Canadian television, the National Ballet of Canada, Le Théâtre du Nouveau Monde, the Canadian Opera Company, Les Grands Ballets Canadiens, the Stratford Shakespearean Festival, and many other lusty infants. Did my outburst spring from impatience at the extended pregnancy? Or was I, as my down-to-earth brother Peter maintained, kicking myself for having arrived the night before the party?

FOR ALL OF DORA MAVOR MOORE'S devoted years of preparation, the New Play Society was an improvisation. That the lecture hall in the Royal Ontario Museum had just become available as a public theatre was serendipity. That it was the only mid-city venue neither stigmatized by an amateur past nor already unionized by professional stagehands was coincidence. But she was pressing her luck when she immediately mailed out a brochure soliciting $10 subscriptions for six plays in the next three months without knowing what they were going to be.

Beyond opening with J. M. Synge's *The Playboy of the Western World* — to link the NPS in the public mind with Ireland's Abbey, the people's theatre she saw as a model for Canada — she had only a welter of possibilities, none of them Canadian. But even *The Playboy* was uncertain. The publisher's Toronto agent, a novice named Mona Coxwell whose specialty was helping by impedance, discovered after rehearsals began that all North American rights were tied up in a forthcoming Broadway revival. Permission to proceed was granted only after Andrew Allan gallantly flew to New York to argue that two nights in backwater Toronto was no threat to an all-star Broadway run. Confident that the Broadway production would sink itself with commercialism while hers in the defiant spirit of the Abbey would make history, DMM allowed none of this pother to interrupt rehearsals.

Through the immediate fog her objective was clear: a professional company versatile enough to perform anything — the classics, challenging works from the international repertory, and Canadian plays, when they came. They would come, she believed, only if there were companies capable of putting them on well. Defining "professional" and "Canadian" would have to wait. Had Aristotle not framed the laws of Greek theatre after the event? But to mount such a series, back-to-back, with only a month to organize plays, directors, performers, technical resources, and advance publicity called for ad-hockery of a high order.

In her circle of believers was an experienced Danish actress, Karen Glahn, who offered to direct Strindberg's *The Father* — not yet seen in Canada — as the second production. To close the series at Christmas she could revive one of the medieval Nativity plays she knew so well. *Lady Precious Stream*, the Chinese classic in English translation that she and I had seen in London, would tie in nicely with an exhibition of chinoiserie planned by the Royal Ontario Museum if she could borrow costumes from the Chinese community. I proposed Somerset Maugham's *The Circle*, to demonstrate that Canadian actors (especially with Jane Mallet in the lead) could trump American actors in English. DMM, similarly convinced that Scottish plays were more likely to find an audience in Toronto than in New York, wanted to include James Bridie's London hit, Mr. *Bolfry*, in which the Devil drops in on a Highland manse. That would give the NPS the cachet of a North American premiere in its inaugural season. Telegrams flew back and forth between Toronto and Glasgow, but for all Bridie's willingness Mr. *Bolfry*, like *The Playboy*, was locked into a Broadway option. (The flowering of Canadian drama in the next two decades owed much to the belief of British and U.S. literary agents that Canada was part of the United States.) At the last minute I suggested instead something all too aptly called *The Wind Is Ninety*.

This bill was announced, then immediately revoked. As *The Father* opened and I joined the fray as production manager, the succession was in disarray.

The hoped-for costumes from Chinatown for *Lady Precious Stream*, scheduled next, had not materialized. We had been upstaged by a professional Chinese troupe stranded in Toronto by the war, who rounded up every costume in town for their five-hour production of *Wang pao ch'mau* — which turned out to be the Chinese original of *Lady Precious Stream*. In desperation we invited the Chinese actors to accompany their costumes into the Museum Theatre and present their epic over two nights. I then made a virtue of necessity by announcing the event as part of "our plan to include in each series of plays a drama of another land, when feasible and practical in the original tongue." When Andrew Allan later offered to direct Eugene O'Neill's *Ah, Wilderness!*, following *The Circle*, he deftly rationalized the whole chain of flukes in a program note: "Having opened its first season with plays Irish, Swedish, Chinese, and English, the NPS continues quite suitably with an American play."

This juggling act, performed while I made a living from teaching and radio, was an experience so traumatic that 37 years later the memory of it caused me to explode with laughter during a solemn meeting in Ottawa. The assembled heads of the federal cultural agencies had just been told by a crisp assistant deputy minister of finance that we must each hew to "a five-year plan, with no ad-hockery!" When he took umbrage at my laugh, I quoted in self-defence the economist John Maynard Keynes: "The artist cannot be told his direction; he does not know it himself." "That," said the technocrat, his eyes narrowing along with his mind, "is what has got to change." He was soon elevated to the rank of deputy minister.

As far as the public knew, the launch had been a success. But inside, as soon as the NPS hit water, the cry was "All hands to the pump!" — starting with the family.

Before my arrival brother Francis had helped to rig and light the Museum Theatre stage. (After completing his interrupted education in engineering, Francis escaped to Montreal and another hotbed of ad-hockery — the aircraft industry.) Brother Peter, a major in the army he had joined at 17, was now demobilized, demoralized, and thus available as an overqualified stagehand. He was also our truck driver once he got his civilian driving licence — which was not until after the night he borrowed my car for a toot and bounced it off a telegraph pole. The police sergeant on duty turned out to be an old comrade-in-arms, who let him off with a sermon and strict orders to get a licence yesterday. As a dramatist, I was much struck by this proof of the power of coinci-dence. (Peter soon returned to the army, for which his stage manage-ment skills proved invaluable in several theatres of war.) Meantime the old homestead with its single bathroom and four bedrooms, two of them the size of closets, accommodated mother and three sons, daugh-ter-in-law Dilly — once more the costume maker — and whoever stayed overnight on the couch. Dilly and I moved out as soon as our furniture arrived from Vancouver and we found an apartment to put it in. This was only just in time; the house on Ridelle had become a reasonable fac-simile of Santa's workshop.

The extended family came from all quarters. Half the Village Players were backstage workers, well aware of the mission impossible expected of them. Electrician Jack Richardson, for example, was given $50 to build a switchboard for the Museum Theatre. Well-wishers with clerical skills, underemployed actors among them, attended to the paperwork; interning lawyers and tyro accountants kept us more or less legal. Everyone built sets, made props, distributed posters, and swept the stage. Word that the hive was humming soon spread to Montreal and Ottawa. Before long prodigal sons and daughters of Toronto began to trickle back from New York and London. When Mary Pickford's young nephew John Mantley arrived from Hollywood to find his roots, everyone could see that there was indeed a family tree.

They came to share in an experiment, but their agendas were far from alike. Some hoped for an art theatre, others a commercial theatre, a political theatre, or an avant-garde theatre. Some sought an apprentice-ship in acting, stage management, or teaching. Some were anticipating television. Most needed pocket money, which was all they got at first: $15 per production, rehearsals included, or sometimes $5 a night, the till permitting. Even this pittance was often in arrears, and I became expert at writing abject apologies laced with vows to mend our ways. How these diverse interests were to be held together on a continuing basis, let alone a five-year plan, was never discussed. There was too much to be done today.

Casts and crews had to be selected and persuaded to sign on, supplies purchased, letterhead printed, advertising space booked — all without any form of capital. Government grants and tax-deductible donations were unheard of. Corporate angels remained in the sky. For offices and set construction we had to cadge space from sympathetic small businesses. For rehearsals we leased a brightly lit hall from the School of Radiant Living, whose adherents covered the walls with invocations to Relax and Unwind on the Stairway to Heaven. This ambience was in marked contrast to our infernal grotto in the Royal Ontario Museum, reachable only through haunted galleries under 24-hour guard after the rest of the building was closed for the night. For months we were even refused permission to erect a modest sign outside to tell the public what was going on inside.

But it was precisely this crazy disparity between ends and means, I think, that bound our diverse enthusiasms together. Compared with the magnitude of the challenge, the slim resources of the challenger seemed absurd.

My mother was now almost 60. My feelings toward her, as colleague, vacillated daily between awe and exasperation. The source of both was her insistence on inspiration by example. From long experience we knew each other's strengths and weaknesses and divided the labour, regardless of title, with almost telepathic understanding. Yet whenever I or others close to her wavered in commitment, she took aim at the conscience as unerringly as Eros ever did at the heart. Her method was to throw herself into the breach. Did this curtain need hemming? She would attend to it. Was there no one to peddle brochures in the lobby? She would do it. People did things at her behest that they felt better for doing but afterward could hardly believe they had done. When DMM reached 85, Lister Sinclair said of her: "She taught us by showing, not by telling. She always showed us never to get angry or impatient, except with pessimism and a put-down; but with people who said things cannot be done, or were not worth doing, she showed us how to be very angry indeed."[3] Her irreverent sons, contributing to her meagre income, labelled this her Dora and Goliath Act. But her passion for human fulfillment coupled with her self-denial had an irresistible appeal to idealists. When the Village Players voted to form a professional company, the 22-year-old Donald Harron, still a struggling student, had been reluctant to go along. Yet within a month he agreed to play Christy Mahon in *The Playboy*, because (he told his fiancée) "Mrs. Moore is risking her frilly shirt on this venture and I can't let her down."[4]

If the pay, at first, was token, her dedication to professionalism was not. In her eyes being professional had to do with a pledge, not a wage. The Village Players had freely chosen to become initiates, and now she was providing the same free choice to others. The vow, once taken, must be respected regardless of the pay scale. She had been trained in a tough school: North American theatre before the advent of protective unions. I heard her once refuse to release from performance an actor whose father had died. "The only death that keeps you off the stage," she told him firmly, "is your own." She considered art less important than life, but one of life's most important justifications.

In the program for *Ah, Wilderness!* Andrew Allan explained why so many radio personalities of the day — Bernard Braden, Barbara Kelly, Jane Mallett, Tommy Tweed, Claire Murray, Budd Knapp, Ruth Springford, Lloyd Bochner — were ready to accept such uncompromising terms:

> Canadian radio drama, for its vitality and for the polish of its production, has been the admiration of American critics for several seasons. But the director of tonight's performance and several members of the cast he has brought with him believe firmly that no important work can be done in either radio or films unless it is based upon the legitimate theatre — performance by living actors before a live audience.

Yet the public was reluctant to admit Canadian theatre into the major league as readily as it had Canadian radio. When young Nathan Cohen made his critical debut reviewing *Ah, Wilderness!*, his ambivalence was explicit: "A brisk, professional affair that Broadway producers would have envied. It was the best-acted, best-directed amateur production we have ever seen in Toronto."[5] But this was the last time Cohen called the NPS amateur. Within four months he would speak of "that level which made the NPS a fine and splendid Canadian theatre repertory: professional in the best sense of the word."[6]

Other reviewers at first took refuge in the usual Canadian blend of praise and prudence: "made what may well be a contribution of durable value" or "its chief value is in the training of young players." Soon, however, came a note of rising surprise: "Its excellence was astounding" and "another of those surprisingly polished performances which, in the New Play Society's to-date short existence, have given it a remarkable prestige."[7] But the elder statesman of Toronto critics, *Saturday Night* editor B. K. Sandwell, was still wrestling with the paradox a year and a half later:

> The Little Theatre can command, in any place where there is radio production, a body of players who, while they have to perform in an amateur way, do so with professional skill and in a professional spirit. The New Play Society is one of the new type of Little Theatre organizations, though there is another contributing factor to its air of competent professionalism, in that a number of its members have had experience in playing to the armed forces in the last war. . . . The society has the enormous advantage of being able to fill the house and turn people away at practically every performance.[8]

We were well into our third year, receiving national coverage and the odd review in New York's *Variety*, before Sandwell worked his way out of his Little Theatre box to reach a delicate 50-50 compromise: "The performance was of a quality much superior to some of the touring companies stemming from Broadway, and equally comparable to a number of the better visiting productions."[9]

There was good reason for critical caution in the beginning when professionalism was a target more often missed than hit. Onstage, vigorous acting and obvious space limitations allowed us to get away with simple decor and basic technology; but in the office amateurism was rampant. We were all learning on the job, because there was nowhere else in the country to learn. With neither time to plan ahead nor money to hire expertise and proper equipment, the whole company was running on spontaneous combustion. When *The Coventry Nativity Play* opened on December 20, as the final production of that first 1946 season, we were all exhausted — as much from fumbling the can as from carrying it.

We awoke next morning expecting to read our obituary in the *Globe and Mail*. But critic Colin Sabiston, identifying himself as "a methodical atheist," recorded the event more like a Herald Angel: "Never in the history of Toronto's theatre has there been an evening of more concentrated beauty . . . . You will say: 'I have been to the theatre and have seen a miracle.'"[10] A more methodical atheist might have uncovered a more remarkable miracle.

Like crazed revellers writing their New Year's resolutions in blood lest they change their minds the next day, we had announced a second season of six plays, with the number of performances increased from two to three.

The truth was that the NPS was as unprepared for a second season as it had been for a first, and my own participation was increasingly problematic. In the months ahead I had commitments at the United Nations requiring periodic stays in New York. We had six weeks to line up plays, directors, and casts, having promised "one British, one American, one European, one classical revival, one foreign-language presentation, one 'free-choice' — to be Canadian when first-class plays are available."

For the foreign-language slot we had invited L'Equipe, the Montreal troupe directed by the meteoric Pierre Dagenais, to bring its production of Sartre's *Huis-Clos* — to mark the first time a francophone Quebec company had ever appeared in Toronto. But our only firm undertaking was to open with Bridie's *Mr. Bolfry*, the Broadway production having been postponed. In fact, Bridie himself had put a cork in it, strenuously objecting to the producer's plan to drain the Scotch out of his dialogue. We immediately saw a parallel with the self-determination of Canadian theatre.

O. H. Mavor/James Bridie had more than a familial interest in his cousin Dora's fragile venture. Three years earlier he and two friends (one a physician and one a dramatist, reflecting his dual personality) had founded the Glasgow Citizens' Theatre. The Citizens' basement auditorium in the old Royal Scottish Academy of Music was far more commodious than ours in the Royal Ontario Museum, and their operation — with Tyrone Guthrie among the directors — more ambitious. But the growing pains were similar. When I sent Bridie one of our flyers, he replied:

> I'm so ashamed, in the face of the latter, of our penny bazaar Citizens' Theatre printings that I won't send you any of them. . . . Our own outfit, with an empty till and a stupid and often hostile local press has managed to lift itself, mainly by pulling on its own bootstraps, into a position of some honour and glory. . . .[11]

He was, in fact, subsidizing the Citizens' with his lucrative West End comedies. And it was *Mr. Bolfry*, with Alistair Sim as the Reverend Mr. McCrimmon debating Raymond Lovell as the Devil, that had secured his reputation as a major British playwright. (Shaw sent him a postcard: "I was glad to know that if I had done nothing else for the drama I had at least made the production of such stunners as Bolfry possible.")[12]

Giving the North American premiere to Toronto was a gesture of solidarity.[13]

On the personal front I should have known what I was letting myself in for when I took on Bolfry. From playing the Devil on radio I had learned the exquisite thrill it held for a clergyman's son. But Bolfry was a more dangerous assignment: his adversary McCrimmon was a man of the cloth. I was about to do battle with my father, with my mother directing the proceedings. Bridie took refuge in theatrical advice:

> I don't know if there are any acting tips I could usefully give you. The high spot sermon by the Devil was considerably cut for the London version — I think the Ten Commandments came out — but it has always been played in full elsewhere & has managed to hold most audiences. I've never seen a satisfactory Devil. If we revive the play I think we'll go for another ego of the parson, i.e. He will look like McCrimmon in shiny caricature. . . .[14]

For McCrimmon we lured another veteran into the underpaid fold: Scots-born Frank Peddie, onetime British India hand now practising law to support his addiction to the stage. Peddie was older and shorter than I, with the stocky build and gnarled face of a boxer turned amiable in middle age; so we made Bolfry a caricature of McCrimmon's idealized youth, dressed in identical clerical black except for scarlet socks. We restored the Devil's Ten Commandments — a declaration of war on God's Ten — and on opening night I sailed through them so proudly that when the maid (Ruth Springford) cued me for the rest of the sermon ("What will happen if you win this War?"), I dried up. Turning to McCrimmon, I ad-libbed, "What do *you* think?" Peddie angrily returned the serve — "God has struck you dumb!" — and waited. I recovered only by summoning memories of other apocalyptic sermons from my childhood. But *The Star's* word-drunk theatre critic Augustus Bridle caught me at it: "If Mavor Moore's father, once curate of St. James here, could have heard his son in this play, he would have seen him brilliantly impersonate a legendary, spookish Mephisto-cleric. . . ."[15] How did Bridle guess my model? Could he tell I had not yet found the devil in myself?

I had presence of mind enough to write a note in the program forging a link between Toronto and Glasgow, "where works by Scottish dramatists may obtain a hearing, and where Scottish actors and actresses may make their own kind of contribution to the theatre of the world.

We of the New Play Society are working, with your help, toward a theatre of this kind for Canada." But I was soon hoist with my own parallel. When Fletcher Markle returned from New York to direct William Saroyan's *The Time of Your Life*, a Pulitzer Prize winner, we were immediately accused of abandoning Canada and selling out to Broadway.

The illustrious cast added weight to the charge that we were "going commercial." Radio's Lorne Greene, John Drainie, and Frank Willis joined us for the first time, as well as stage professionals Alex McKee and Robert Christie. ("There are no small stages," growled Markle, adapting Stanislavsky to our theatre. "There are only big actors.") But Saroyan had actually refused the Pulitzer Prize on the ground that commerce has no business patronizing art. Markle and I saw his unconventional hymn to underdogs as an invitation to be ourselves, not to get on the bandwagon. And in this regard Markle believed Canadian audiences had a thing or two to learn:

> The present day theatre is said to be suffering not from lack of audiences but from a lack of real theatre people. This is an American remark, about American theatre. . . . But here in Canada we seem to be caught in the truth of this statement in reverse. We have the actors and workers of the theatre . . . our actors are in the habit of acting. It is to be hoped that those who can make up our audiences will form the habit of coming to the theatre.[16]

Torontonians had long since formed a theatre-going habit: visiting imported productions at large roadhouses such as the Royal Alexandra. The existing audience, we now realized, would not easily be diverted from that habit. Canadian theatre was by definition alternative theatre, and we must develop an alternative audience.

We first tried the lure of the exotic. For the English play we proposed *This Way to the Tomb*, an avant-garde verse drama by Ronald Duncan with music by Benjamin Britten. (It succeeded only in prompting jokes about our buried theatre.) In the Russian slot I would stage Gogol's 1832 classic, *The Government Inspector*, as yet unperformed in Toronto. L'Equipe, plagued by illness, had bowed out as our "other language" attraction, but Les Compagnons de Saint-Laurent, a Quebec collective founded by the pioneering priest Emile Legault, had agreed to bring an evening of Molière — still exotic, in French, to Torontonians. ("We can make a mixture of our two cultures," Legault told the *Telegram*, "which will be particularly rich.")[17] The Canadian play was to be *The Man in the Blue Moon*, written and directed by Lister Sinclair, whose radio plays had already earned him, at 26, an international reputation.

The Government Inspector opened in April 1947, less than a week after Dilly produced our firstborn, Dorothea, initiating a family tradition of coincidental births and premieres that I too often used as an excuse for neglecting one or the other — in this case the play. Toronto's Russian language weekly resented our picture of life in the future Soviet Union, finding its "coarse buffoonery" particularly deplorable in a family with Russian connections such as the Mavors. Chauvinism, I concluded, must be as universal as the petty corruption satirized by Gogol. But I blamed some of the awkward cultural transition on the stiff American translation, for which we had paid an equally stiff royalty. The alternative British translations, however, were even more remote from both Russian and Canadian milieux.

Within the year, encouraged by Esse Ljungh, I wrote a radio version in Canadian English. It was criticized as "vulgar," so I knew I was on the right track. Had 19th-century British and American dramatists, faced with a temporary scarcity of native drama, hesitated to appropriate European hits? And what better text for Canadians than Gogol's "Don't blame the mirror if your face is cockeyed!" In due course I wrote *The Ottawa Man*, for which I transported Gogol from the steppes to the Prairies in the 1880s. The fit was elegant. I had stumbled across real historical parallels for the Russian's isolated town and paradoxical characters: a crooked mayor with a wanton wife, an unsanitary doctor, a "boughten" judge, a prying postman, a soused schoolteacher, even a sheriff nicknamed "Violet." What could be more quintessentially Canadian than to have them exposed by a down-at-heels English remittance man mistaken for an undercover Mountie?

When the NPS produced its first original Canadian play, however, I was, ironically, in New York. In manuscript form *The Man in the Blue Moon* had excited me. Lister Sinclair's fable about a death ray inventor's social responsibility, packed with youthful outrage at social and scientific orthodoxy, struck a note familiar in United Nations corridors. But when the piece was performed in Toronto, audiences and critics alike found it boring. Nathan Cohen praised the actors and saluted the NPS for "building a native Canadian drama movement," but deplored "the confusion of the theme and the manifest unfamiliarity of Mr. Sinclair with the stage medium." Then, to my astonishment, he accused *The Man in the Blue Moon* of a primal sin: "There is nothing Canadian about it, neither in content, characters nor atmosphere."[18]

Was Cohen another reductive nationalist? Must our writers be confined to quarters and barred from having world affairs? Then it occurred to me that Cohen might have a subtler purpose in mind: a preemptive strike against any implied link between being Canadian and being boring. A Canadian play might well be about bores, but it must never be boring; this boring play was not about bores, and was thus doubly un-Canadian. I was sensitive to the distinction at the time, having discovered that most of my U.N. colleagues assumed Canadians to be boring until proved otherwise, whereupon they were warmly embraced as exceptions to the rule.

The following fall, consequently, our choice of plays was markedly different. In the spring Cohen had complained that "of the five produced since January . . . only one, *Mr. Bolfry*, was really meritorious and even it was not the happiest of choices." He urged us to present "more well-established plays" and those "from the wealth of untapped treasures." Since his advice received telling support from our bank manager, we took it — unleashing *Charley's Aunt* and the fashionable *Amphitryon 38* (imported from the Montreal Repertory Theatre), along with Shakespeare, Barrie, and O'Casey. I undertook to direct *Macbeth* and *Juno and the Paycock* between trips south.

The point of doing *Macbeth* again (my third) was its acute relevance to world events: the deaths of Mussolini and Hitler, Stalin's purges, coups in Africa and Latin America. Without changing the time or place, I wanted to recapture the suspense implicit in the question: "*Can he get away with it?*" — surely felt as keenly by Scots in the 1040s as by us in the 1940s.[19] Our production made its point, according to the reviews, but only after a richly symbolic mishap on opening night: the Witches'cauldron exploded, enveloping the theatre in a mushroom-shaped cloud.

But revivals of Shakespeare Our Contemporary (as Jan Kott later called him) were not enough. The object lesson our theatre needed to learn from Shakespeare's was that "enterprises of great pith and moment" could be started by a dozen zealots in the face of competition from bearbaiting, cockfighting, public executions, and other primitive forms of television, if they believed in themselves. We had postponed the day of reckoning by believing, in print, that "more and more Canadian plays will become available as an outlet for them is provided; and we shall then have Canadians speaking to Canadians, in accents Canadian."[20] The Scottish connection, whether through the devil Bolfry or the demon Macbeth, had failed to make us see the light. It was the Irish *Juno and the Paycock* that turned the trick.

JOHN COULTER WAS the same age as my mother. Tall, spare of frame, his white hair and black eyebrows capping a passionate red face and searing eyes, this vital man had adopted Canada as a cause. Born in Belfast, he first encountered the Irish theatrical renaissance when he moved to Dublin at 26. It changed his life. He had seen his early plays produced there and in London, where he became known as an editor and radio dramatist before joining his Canadian wife in Toronto in 1936.

Coulter threw himself into the Canadian cultural scene, agitating for a national theatre while he continued to write plays about what he knew best: the Irish and the British. As an authority on the Abbey Theatre, he had been a valued champion of the NPS *Playboy of the Western World* and agreed to write a note for the *Juno* program. He turned the occasion into an emotional plea for a Canadian stage.

Irish theatre, Coulter said, arrived only when Synge and O'Casey dared to show Dublin audiences "their own mugs in their own Irish mirror."

> The moral for Canadians surely is: don't let any wild dog of a play-right [sic] who might feel like showing Canadian mugs in a Canadian mirror anywhere near a stage. The anguish and humilia-tion of having in our midst a living theatre of full stature might possibly follow.

Juno and the Paycock worked its catalytic magic again for us. O'Casey's play, wrote Nathan Cohen with a flourish, "has inspired the director, the cast and the crew of the New Play Society to a brilliant level of interpre-tation. . . . The entire production was provocative proof of what a true Canadian theatre can achieve. . . . The genius of dramatic art is begin-ning to flower on a Canadian stage, promising even better things to come."[21] The "better things," we both knew, could only be more plays holding our own mirror up to our own mugs. In an important sense the greater our triumph with an Irish play, the greater our own anguish and humiliation.[22]

After the success of *Juno*, excuses were no longer possible. The NPS was duty-bound to mount another season with at least one play as defi-antly Canadian as *Juno* was Irish. Yet none of the plays submitted seemed to us any more indigenous in content or style than *The Man in the Blue Moon*, which Cohen had dismissed as having nothing Canadian about it. To smoke out his criteria of citizenship, I sent him a draft of a stage play of my own, set in Muskoka. He replied in an article on the dearth of native playwrights, citing me as one of four exceptions:

> [Moore's] *Fox of Bay Street* . . . is still in script form and subject to revision. Even as it stands, however, it is a stage-wise affair . . . the play wrestles earnestly and affirmatively with questions which, if not inherently Canadian, are most certainly familiar to Canada. Mr. Moore's protagonist is a greedy and unprincipled Toronto financier whose repulsiveness is matched only by his determination to stay out in front in the rat race.[23]

Not "inherently" Canadian? My model was a millionaire summer cottager whose *toujours gaie* wife used to hold after-theatre parties for the John Holden Players in Bala. One night he boasted to me first of his chicanery on the stock market and then of his donations to the Canadian-born evangelist Aimee Semple McPherson, which he expected to balance his credit when he went into politics or the afterlife, whichever came first. Characters such as the Fox and McPherson seemed to me both Canadian and universal — were the adjectives mutually exclusive? — but obviously Cohen was looking for something more specific.

In November I read Hugh MacLennan's novel *Two Solitudes*, and coincidentally played, in the CBC *Stage* radio version, the Quebec priest who mediates between the francophone and anglophone families (a performance shamelessly modelled on Father Legault). If the *Two Solitudes* drama did not qualify as inherently Canadian, what could? We at once commissioned Hugh Kemp, who adapted *Two Solitudes* for radio, to write a stage version. An experienced Montreal dramatist, Kemp undertook to deliver it by the end of January for presentation in April. We announced it with a fanfare.

To accumulate money for the commission and for what was bound to be an expensive production, we announced an otherwise "safe" season, opening in January 1948 with Shaw's *Candida* — in which James Mavor Moore acted James Mavor Morell for the first and last time. We were in rehearsal for *Candida* when the letter arrived from Montreal, beginning "Dear Old Mavor":

I know of no other way to do this than by diving right in. After all my big speeches . . . I am now in great trouble with T.S. It's all in bits and pieces, and needs another full three weeks work. I haven't got the three weeks. Please let this be between us, Sir, but I am bankrupt. . . . I have to take a job and I have to do it right away. . . . I don't know where I'm going. Maybe back to the harlotry of an advertising agency. Maybe to Ottawa to punch it out in the Press Gallery. . . .

I know what this will do to you, and there isn't much sense in saying I'm sorry. It's another good hope gone west for all of us. I still hope to finish the play when my bank account and my nerve are under control. . . . I am sending you now a copy of the breakdown by incidents that I was working from. The rest is still too chaotic to read. Send me a note, even if it's filled with hatred.[24]

What I hated, I replied, was to see this venture go down the drain. With the cast and scene breakdown we could move ahead on the production if he would let us have the finished script in *six* weeks. Unwisely Kemp agreed to try. Unwisely we made no alternative plans. As *The Tempest* opened in the last week of February, no play had arrived and the playwright had disappeared. I put a note in the program about a "topical Canadian revue," but nothing was done because after *The Tempest*, I had to disappear to New York for a month, while Bob Christie staged *Uncle Harry*. We faced an opening night on April 1 with nothing even remotely Canadian to fill it.

Whether the April Fool's date had anything to do with it, I can't remember, but a small group met in hysterical conclave in mid-March to throw together a revue. Jane Mallett could do pieces from her Hart House *Town Tonics*; Peter Mews and Connie Vernon had songs and sketches from *The Army Show*; Don Harron had skits from college shows and an idea for a monologue by a sharp old farmer visiting "Th' Ex" (Toronto's annual fall Exhibition). Tommy Tweed's radio satire about labour relations had a song called "It'll Never Get Well If You Picket," and there were Lister Sinclair's lyrics for "We All Hate Toronto," both set to music by Lucio Agostini. A new British comic named Eric Christmas had arrived in town with a sackful of transmigratory material, and humorists from Pierre Berton to Len Peterson offered a helping hand. Emulating Mother (who had her doubts about the whole thing), I threw myself into the breach as director.

Still lacking a title, I appealed to Andrew Allan over a cup of coffee in the inauspicious CBC cafeteria:

AA: Has it any sort of shape?
MM: It's meant to be a review of the Canadian scene.
AA: R-E-V-U-E or R-E-V-I-E-W?
MM: I-E-W, I guess.
AA: Well, if it's a spring review, why not name it for the time in Canada when the snow melts and exposes the old galoshes and Christmas trees and iron bedsteads of winter? Why not call it *Spring Thaw?*

"I wish, now," wrote Allan, recalling the incident in his *Self-Portrait*, "I had asked for a royalty."[25] *Spring Thaw* '48 was a sensation. It was a misbegotten omnium gatherum of a show, derivative, gauche, and manic, but it was a sensation. "If laughter had been maintained at maximum intensity," the *Globe and Mail* reported, "the entire audience would have gone home with lockjaw."[26] What we had done, as accidentally as we had stumbled into the show, was to provide a whistle for a head of steam.

I must have known Canadians were bursting to laugh at themselves, since I pointed in the program to "the non-existence of Canadian national jokes" and to Gratien Gélinas as one who had "overcome the curse." But I never anticipated the enormity of our repressed urge to mock our institutions, public figures, political agenda, and local affairs. Several editions would come and go (as I did) before I appreciated the golden thread of self-satire running through our literature from "Sam Slick" through Stephen Leacock to Robertson Davies and W. O. Mitchell (whose novel *Who Has Seen the Wind* came out the same year as *Spring Thaw*). It was later still before I linked it to the older tradition of Native humour in the North and concluded that Canadians use jokes about their predicament as a survival technique.

It soon became clear, as well, that Canada, having few global responsibilities, was a perfect haven from which to mock the supercultures. This gave us a temporary advantage over the Americans, who had just elected Senator Joseph McCarthy.

The trail of successive *Thaws* will cross mine again. Indeed, it haunted me. Each year, actively involved or not, I quailed at the approach of spring. Outgrowing its "unabashedly short-sighted and provincial" origin, the annual review broke Canadian records in the fifties, went on national tours in the sixties, and after two decades became the longest-running annual topical revue in the world. It drew the attention of the international press and spawned material for the revues of London and New York. It subsidized the other work of the New Play Society, often threatening to swallow its parent whole. *Spring Thaw* had its detractors (including me, when I became a critic), and eventually petered out like a dying tenor after a series of spastic reprieves. But in the meantime it provided an unparalleled showcase for comedians, composers, writers, and directors on their way up (and too often out) — including, in addition to those mentioned, Lou Jacobi, Godfrey Ridout, Marian Grudeff, Rich Little, Stan Daniels, Brian Macdonald, Norman Jewison — and a vivid sampler of the Canadian condition.

But was that the condition I wished to stay in? Outside this frenetic hothouse was a world of opportunity. Before *Spring Thaw* erupted I received an invitation from Virginia Pettit and Catherine Huntington of the Provincetown Playhouse, Eugene O'Neill's launching pad, to direct their summer season.[27] I hemmed and hawed, since it would require leaving the United Nations in the lurch (this was the summer of the UNESCO Seminar on Teaching about the United Nations), and my absence from Toronto at the very time the NPS, after 24 plays in 19 months, would have to settle its future. The success of *Spring Thaw '48* settled it for us. We felt an obligation to mount a second edition in 1949 — and consequently a winterful of productions leading up to it, some of them Canadian. It was too late for me to leave.

That summer we approached a number of writers best known for their fiction or radio drama, including Harry Boyle, Andrew Allan, and the novelist Morley Callaghan. John Coulter, his eye at last on the Canadian scene, had begun work on his epic *Riel* but thought it beyond our limited production capability. Boyle, the CBC program executive whose stories of Ontario farm life charmed both readers and listeners, offered to write something but needed time. So did Allan, planning a whodunit about euthanasia. But Callaghan, I discovered, had an unproduced play in his desk drawer.

Morley Callaghan was then 43 and, to his chagrin and our shame, better known abroad than at home. His early novels and short stories had been highly regarded and widely published. A genial middleweight with a pugnacious streak (as his friend Ernest Hemingway knew to his cost), Callaghan had an abiding faith in the indomitability of the human spirit in a hostile world; but for close to a decade he had been in a literary slump. When I met him, he was living on gleanings from radio talk shows and a commission to write a history of the University of Toronto. At some gathering where he seemed particularly downcast, I asked if he had ever written a play. It was as if I had poked a wound; he confessed to a 10-year unrequited love affair with the theatre. "There's no reason you should know about it," he said with the hollow chuckle he had perfected with long practice. "Nothing came of it."

To Tell the Truth, written in 1938, had come tantalizingly close to Broadway production on three occasions. About a young Canadian optimist who transforms the lives of the habitués of a seedy Detroit diner, Callaghan's play had most recently been optioned and then dropped by the Theatre Guild. Its premise, they said, was too close to Saroyan's The Time of Your Life, written later but staged first. We could hardly miss the irony: Callaghan had been trying to sell his play in New York while we were presenting Saroyan's in Toronto. He agreed to let me direct it in January 1949, and set to work updating its political context.

In a program note I anticipated the obvious objection: "This play is not set in Canada. Whether or not 'Canadian' plays are made so because of their locale, is a question we leave open for angry discussion in the lobby. But it is a North-American play. . . ." Cohen, I thought, will leap on this rationale. Instead he lent it guarded support:

> [Canadians] want to be regarded as members of a mature state, accepted by societies elsewhere. The day in which we follow even the career of Olympic skating champion Barbara Ann Scott abroad shows that it's a common Canadian characteristic. . . . It's this motif, this quest for companionship which, in my opinion, makes To Tell the Truth a Canadian play.[28]

With its two dozen characters jammed onto the mini-stage of the Museum Theatre, To Tell the Truth was a test case for the NPS. It drew controversial reviews, full houses, and an invitation from general manager Ernest Rawley to move the entire production into the Royal Alexandra Theatre for an additional week — the first Canadian play with a Canadian cast in its 42-year-history. (That Rawley happened to be facing a dark week, otherwise, only did credit to his imagination.) We ended the week at the Royal Alexandra with a net profit of $114, which we split with the theatre.

Within days the following report appeared in the New York Times:

Headed for Broadway, possibly under the auspices of Cheryl Crawford [producer of *The Little Foxes*], is "To Tell the Truth," a play by Morley Callaghan, front-ranking Canadian novelist and short-story writer. . . . Present plans call for a fall production. "To Tell the Truth" was obtained for New York presentation under unusual circumstances. On Saturday John Yorke, Miss Crawford's business manager, flew to Toronto, where the play is being presented, to look it over, and he took an option within ten minutes after the final curtain. . . . The playwright is planning to incorporate "a few new ideas" in the play before it reaches the local boards. James Stewart and Margaret Sullavan may be approached for the leading roles.[29]

"To gain the world," I asked Callaghan the theologian, "do you *have* to lose your soul?" "No," Callaghan the continentalist said, "not when it's your own world."

With or without a Broadway imprimatur — and again none materialized — *To Tell the Truth* showed that Canadian drama (with Canadians doing the American accents, for a change) could hold its own on a main stage in Toronto. In Montreal, at the same time, Gratien Gélinas was making the same point with his first full-length play, *Tit-Coq*. The Toronto season ended with a second *Spring Thaw*, the revue modelled, however loosely, on Gélinas's *Fridolinons*. The two streams were beginning to converge.

Spring Thaw '49 proved so popular that it turned the annual into a perennial, and provided a secure financial base for the ambitious season the New Play Society now contemplated.

"IN ADDITION TO THEIR IMPRESSIVE LIST of Canadian plays," wrote Herbert Whittaker, newly arrived at the *Globe and Mail* from the Montreal *Gazette*, "the New Play Society is also harnessing a few dramatic Titans this season."[30] Around a permanent nucleus of six actors — Don Harron, Toby Robins, Lloyd Bochner, Pegi Brown, Robert and Margot Christie — we proposed to mount 10 productions at the Museum Theatre in 1949–50, four of which would be classics: *She Stoops to Conquer*, *Ghosts*, *Heartbreak House*, and *King Lear*. The other six, including *Spring Thaw*, would be Canadian. "No longer need we talk in 'ifs' and 'whens' about the Canadian Theatre," we boasted in the brochure. "The Canadian Theatre is here. Now it's up to everyone to support it."

Callaghan was revising a second play, *Going Home*, based on one of his early novels, and set, like *The Fox of Bay Street*, in Muskoka cottage country.

Harry Boyle was completing *The Inheritance* — family life on an Ontario farm — and Andrew Allan promised *Narrow Passage* for January. Coulter, seeing no other immediate prospect for his monumental *Riel*, offered it to us:

> It's an intolerable situation for me, to be living where there's an emerging theatre and myself not contributing to it in the one way I can contribute, i.e., as a playwright. . . . My own assurance is that [Riel] could fascinate an audience in the theatre. But I'm afraid this won't be tested till there are both the resources and the venturing spirit to tackle what is admittedly challenging and difficult.[31]

We told Coulter, with more guts than gumption, that we were willing to try. The other Canadian play, and the first up — the only one ready to go into rehearsal — was to be my own *Who's Who*.

Who's Who was a longer version of *I Know You*, the one-act comedy I wrote before going off to war in 1941. The short version began with a lawyer reading the will of an officer killed in battle, a former advertising executive. The reading reveals a split in the family: his daughter adored him, his son hated him, his wife despised his amorality, his lawyer finds him "only human." The argument escalates when kibitzers in the audience, claiming to know the real person on whom the fictional play is based, interrupt to support one side or other — and expands further when both the "Director" and the "Author" step onstage to dispute each other's interpretation of the script. At length the dead man materializes to announce that whatever he was in life, death has redeemed him. He is now a roving evangelist for human brotherhood — an "angel," he tells the audience, sent back to earth to put on morality plays like this.

On its opening night at the Arts and Letters Club, with the lieutenant governor in the audience, *I Know You* had caused a merry scandal. My first "plant" in the house was veteran actor Alex McKee, an unfamiliar face in town. As McKee made his angry way to the stage, the club president rose in alarm and was already muscling him out (to McKee's gleefully improvised protests) when "Director" Robert Christie strode on to assure him it was all part of the play. I was too fascinated to raise a finger. Afterward I realized I was onto a genuine Pirandello effect here, and in 1949 decided to enlarge the picture by having three of the debaters — the son, the director, and the kibitzer — stage their own versions of the advertiser's life, each in a totally different theatrical style. The result was *Who's Who*, which I directed myself.

I heard that *Who's Who* went well, that the cast was marvellous and the houses full. The Montreal *Standard* reported that it had "provocative and witty things to say about Canada"; Cohen called it "with all its failings . . . unquestionably the most important play so far produced by a Canadian"; Sandwell admitted he laughed a lot, although it was "not really a play."[32] But I never saw it. At the first performance I collapsed in pain, and at intermission was carted off to hospital with acute appendicitis. "No playwright," Harron told the press, "should ever have two openings in one night."

Eight days later, recuperating at home but determined to see the final night of the run, I got out of bed and started to dress. I was putting on my trousers when I felt two pounding jolts in my chest and just managed to yell to Dilly before passing out. I was rushed back to hospital with two errant clots in my right lung. I came to with a sense of déjà vu: had I not died once before and been brought back to life? The second time it was a young intern named Chisholm who sat up with me for three nights teaching me to breathe again.

When I was drowning, it was the past that flashed before me. This time, as heparin thinned my blood, it was the future — all mixed up with the play. In *Who's Who* I had not consciously written about my relationship with my father, nor about facing death myself. I believed I was tackling, at a comic remove, the question I saw as crucial in the immediate future: What happens to truth when everyone becomes a propagandist? But a propagandist was what I had become, working at the United Nations. No matter how lofty the cause, how could I go on being an apologist for anything but my own vision? If I got through this alive, I told myself, I would drop all these red herrings and pursue that vision. It was the least I could bequeath to my children.

Being Canadian, of course, I was far from sure what my vision was. Which of us could be sure without first discovering, by trial and error, what and where we were? A mirror had suddenly become essential. The theatre was now available to perform that function. Critics and audiences anatomized each of the new plays we produced that year, ransacking them for calling cards, clothing labels, blood type, condition of the teeth, pocket lint, and any other possible clues to national identity.

"For years," wrote Nathan Cohen, reviewing Harry Boyle's *The Inheritance*, "the favorite national pastime has been answering the question 'What is a Canadian? How do you distinguish him?' and so on." He went on to say:

> Mr. Boyle does not set out to answer any of these questions, but he does
> know rural Ontario and the people who live there, and that knowledge is
> manifest all the way through the play. . . . [He] does tell us what some
> average Canadians are like, and the amazing thing about them is that they
> are average, and are Canadian, and this gives the play a charm and authen-
> ticity that compensates for the awkward construction and drab plot.[33]

Was he damning the play with faint praise or praising Canadians with
faint damns?

Allan's *Narrow Passage* opened in January 1950, coincidentally with an
actual euthanasia/murder fracas in the United States. To many in the
audience he seemed like a clever cat having sport with an unwelcome
rat. Although set in Canada — Muskoka cottage country once again —
the play fitted neither their image of theatre nor their image of themselves. The *Star's* Jack Karr found it "not a pleasant piece of drama."
Cohen called it "unmitigated claptrap." Rose Macdonald in The *Telegram*
(where 10 years later I was to succeed her as drama critic) grieved: "The
Canadian play! We wait for it with hope undaunted if deferred."[34]

The problem was that by now anyone looking was looking for the
Great Canadian Play. Sandwiched between Goldsmith, Ibsen, Shaw, and
Shakespeare. It was close to a setup for the next candidate, Coulter's *Riel*.

With a cast of 35 and 15 scenes, *Riel* was as ambitious as its Prairie
protagonist, who twice took on the Canadian government and its "army
from the east." Earlier attempts to dramatize the life and death of the
Métis leader, in both French and English, had been naive. History books
of the time identified him, according to bias, as traitor or martyr.
Coulter was the first to recognize in Louis Riel not only an ambiguous
Canadian legend but a compendium of universal themes. For all his half-
breed local and psychological entanglements, Riel was the champion of
a small oppressed nation: a mythic archetype. The idealist betrayed by
guile, the thinker paralyzed by thinking, the odd man out, the victim of
a rigged trial, the lunatic hanged, the man who would play God. The
solution to the nationalist/internationalist dilemma, I felt, was exactly
this: a story at one and the same time ours and humanity's.

I wanted to direct the play, but my U.N. engagements made it awkward; with some logistical agility, however, I could get to enough
rehearsals to play the role of Riel, once John Drainie turned it down. We
needed Bob Christie for Sir John A. Macdonald (a role he made forever
his own). I thought it was high time our resident intellectual Don Harron

learned to direct; he had a sound knowledge of Canadian history, a grasp of the philosophical issues, and by now considerable experience onstage. In the event, Christie undertook not only Macdonald but also the technical aspects of the production, while Harron directed and played the provocateur Thomas Scott, with an Ulster accent stolen from Coulter. DMM, convinced that this time none could gainsay our dedication to the national cause, turned her energies to mobilizing the community.

As a melee, the final days of rehearsal rivalled the Battle of Batoche, Riel's Waterloo, in which my old regiment, the RRCs, had dubiously gained their colours. (A delayed train even caused me to miss the dress rehearsal; it was, Harron fumed, like rehearsing *Hamlet* without the Dane.) Our first night, February 17, 1950, was in several senses historic.

In the front row sat five bemedalled veterans of the 1885 march against the rebels, all over 80 and counting. One had met Riel, and two had known his lieutenant, Gabriel Dumont. Beyond them were rows of invited diplomats, professors, high school teachers, and history buffs; DMM had stacked the house. Our costumers and propmeisters had done their utmost to match the weapons, uniforms, clothes, and hair in the old prints and photographs, but terror ran through the ranks. Appearance aside, we would be caught out the moment we opened our mouths: our francophones were not francophone, our Natives were not native, and Louis Riel — already uncertain of his long speeches — was having a fish bone extracted from his throat half an hour before curtain time.

All but the diehards agreed Coulter had treated Riel with Jovian impartiality, but the diehards differed loudly as to whether the Métis leader had been whitewashed or blackwashed. Whittaker praised the effort needed to mount this "fascinating piece . . . especially impressive to Canadians who have seen their history only through clouds of dust." But Cohen attacked Coulter's appropriation of voice ("The real trouble with his one Canadian play, *Riel*, is that it has an Irish accent"), and Rose Macdonald deplored our bad taste in allowing the audience to see Riel hanged onstage. In later years I adapted Coulter's play for radio and for television, while he himself made other versions of the Riel story. But it was the NPS production of his first *Riel*, called "totally disastrous" by the author 25 years later,[35] that sparked the revival in Rieliana that swept across the country in the interval, inspiring, among other works, the opera *Louis Riel*.

Two weeks later — en route to Callaghan's *Going Home*, the next Canadian play — we opened an economy-sized *King Lear*. DMM was directing an unconventional text I had arranged, and discord reigned in more than Lear's kingdom. The first night garnered amazing reviews ("M. M. deeply moving as King Lear"), considering that I'd mimed my way through the dress rehearsal after searing my vocal cords with brandy on the train from New York. In the theatre ignorance is bliss. Don Harron, who played Edmund, swears that I also forged Shakespeare when a prop was missing:

> Where is the stool?
> Fool, fetch me yonder joint stool,
> And you and I shall jointly sit upon't.[36]

Plunging into Going Home before Lear was over, I felt I was extemporizing not only a few lines here and there, or even a whole show now and then, but my whole life.

"This is a notable service the New Play Society is contributing," Herbert Whittaker wrote in the Globe and Mail, "a chance for our playwrights to judge their own work as a play can only be judged — on the stage." The compliment came from the heart: I had persuaded Whittaker to design the set for Going Home, and he had understandable misgivings about squeezing a summer cottage, a dock, and a lake onto our tiny stage. When opening night came, he reviewed the production with exemplary detachment, calling the set "adequate" in light of the play's ambitious demands:

> Because the theme is bold and violent, because the conflict is strongly stated, and because it has unity . . . it is, of the new Canadian plays done by the enterprising New Play Society this season, the one which impresses as most likely material for Broadway. Indeed, there will be some who will say that it is better suited to Broadway's more sophisticated taste than to Toronto's more tender sensibilities.[37]

This theme was picked up by the reviewer for Variety, who thought that "with greater directional speed and some recasting, Going Home has fine Broadway possibilities."[38] But Cohen, who consigned Callaghan to the American mainstream, anyway, attacked the "thorough artistic paucity" of this portrait of a riven family:

> The play neither reveals an understanding of suffering or an ability to show the purgation of pity. All that it offers, apart from good intentions, is a collection of the shabbier ideas and symbols which currently proliferate in the American drama.[39]

Saturday Night's Mary Lowry Ross, a Callaghan champion, rose to the defence of what she called "probably the most controversial play that the NPS has ever put on":

> It has met with either extravagant praise or extravagant censure, and it is only fair to point out that much of the censure was based on a complete misunderstanding of the author's intention. *Going Home* was not intended to be presented or accepted as naturalistic drama.[40]

This was odd, because in concept and design the production was far from naturalistic, and because the playwright was closely involved in rehearsals. His change of mind about the proper approach occurred, in fact, on the opening night.

Since the house was filled, Callaghan and I spent the first act standing at the back. The performance was slow and (as Whittaker put it) "somewhat ragged." Now Callaghan, despite his pugnacity, was both a shrewd observer of his fellow humans and capable of deep hurt on their account. "What's wrong with them?" he whispered. "They're tired," I whispered back. "Overworked and underrehearsed." Then, just before intermission, a man rose noisily, pushed his way into the aisle, and stormed out, admitting a flare of light as he hit the door. Callaghan shot after him. Over the end of the first act I could hear raised voices outside. A moment later, as half the audience headed for the lobby, he appeared beside me, his fists clenched:

MC: I caught him getting his hat and coat.
MM: What did you say?
MC: I said, "Why are you leaving this beautiful play?"
MM: And what did he say?
MC: He said, "Because it's a pile of shit," and went.
MM: Did you offer him his money back?
MC: No, because he's right. The whole approach is wrong.

Callaghan, as indomitable as ever, immediately set out to revise *Going Home*. But no further word came from New York, and in any case it was too late to put revisions into the show. The houses were no more than half full. We were living on the advance sale for *Spring Thaw '50*, due to open in three weeks. It was our only hope.

The Royal Commission on National Development in the Arts, Letters, and Sciences, launched the year before with Vincent Massey in command, was under full sail. The commissioners were crisscrossing the nation to nose out signs of Canadian cultural life and to categorize the exotic forms it took. This time we were seeking a theme for *Spring Thaw* — some unifying framework to make it more "review" than "revue." The royal commission provided a perfect pattern. To open and close the show I composed a song for three commissioners, and in between we paraded the evidence before them.

With Bob Christie directing, I was able to spend more time seeking out and polishing original material. The main production number was Don Harron's "opera," *La Traviesti*, which simultaneously mocked Toronto suburban politics and our subservience to imported art forms. Among the other sacred cows scathed were "The Great Canadian Play" and "The Hollywood Version" — the picture of Canada being circulated by the U.S. networks while Ottawa and the CBC dithered about introducing Canadian television. Perhaps inevitably our show that year gave vent to the black frustration we felt at having to make our case to the obtuse politicians in this absurd way. Why waste time and money studying the obvious? Our performing arts were already subsidized — not by the government but by actors, singers, dancers, writers, musicians, and technicians. After 40 productions in four years we knew we could not keep it up, could only slide backward trying to mount masterpieces with 10 days' rehearsal, and new plays with no time for emendation. When was help coming?

Spring Thaw '50 had not yet ended — it ran for a record-breaking month — when I received a call from Fergus Mutrie, newly appointed director of CBC's nonexistent English-language television network. I knew and respected Mutrie, an intelligent former supervisor of farm broadcasts; and I knew the corporation had already been funded to test the TV waters, because my old boss Frank Willis had been sent abroad to see what the British and Australians were up to. Mutrie told me that pending the Massey Report the CBC had been ordered to proceed at once with the full-scale planning the report would soon recommend. His first step was to hire an engineering head and a programming head, and would I become the director of programs?

In a week I was due back at the United Nations, the scene of my limited experience in television, and requested that week to consider the offer. Before the time was up Mutrie phoned to ask for an urgent meeting. Acutely embarrassed, he entered my cramped office in our rehearsal hall on Avenue Road, without relinquishing his hat and coat, to announce that he was forced to withdraw the offer. The CBC board of governors had decided the position must go to an internal candidate.

The next day I set out by car — Dilly and the three-year-old Dorothea to follow later by train — for our sublet on Long Island, determined to leave my thankless, small-minded country behind for good. To hell with the Canadian theatre, to hell with the CBC, to hell with the bloody Royal Commission on National Development in the Arts, Letters, and Sciences! What other country would *need* to set up a royal commission to help it decide whether to develop or not!

Who cared about Canada? The world was my beat. In the past year Chiang Kai-shek had retreated to Formosa while on the mainland Mao Tse-tung proclaimed the People's Republic of China. Germany was split into two, Vietnam had achieved independence from France, and India had broken away from Britain. The Soviet Union had developed an atomic bomb, and George Orwell had just published *Nineteen eighty-four*. I plunged into work at the United Nations, pausing only to write and send off to *The Canadian Forum* the raspberry to my native theatre that goaded Nathan Cohen into replying.

If I was to abandon radio and theatre to go into television, I would go in at the top. The angry words were hardly out of my mouth when the opportunity arose.

Reverse the tape to an earlier visit to New York, in September 1949, when I was contemplating *Riel* for our NPS season. I run into John Coulter as we come out of a Broadway theatre. He has been corresponding with the producer Eddie Dowling about mounting *Riel* in America, but Dowling has now told him: "*Riel* should be a Canadian production. Open your play in Toronto. Pre-sell it. I'll bring in a few top critics to see it. I can sell it to Watts, Kerr, Chapman, Coleman, Taubman . . . New York is wide open."[41] In a word, Coulter will now let us do his play. And in this celebratory mood he invites me to accompany him to a party. The crowded affair is at the splendid Manhattan apartment of Worthington ("Tony") Miner, producer of *Studio One*, CBS television's flagship drama series. I fall into conversation about theatre with Jo Mielziner, the celebrated designer, and an enchanting actress who turns out to be Mrs. Miner. Then I fall into a heated argument about television with a short, stout, bald know-it-all — only to discover, after I tell him that whoever he is he's crazy, that this is Mr. Miner. Coulter and I leave shortly afterward.

Now fast-forward to May 1950. Sitting in my office at the United Nations, I receive a call from Tony Miner's secretary. Would I lunch with

Mr. Miner? I would. Grade A restaurant. After the pleasantries, the waiter sets down the soup. My spoon is halfway to my mouth. "I have looked into your track record," says Miner suddenly. "I want you to direct *Studio One*." I drop the spoon into my soup. Never wear the tie again. *Studio One* already has two directors, Franklin Shaffner and Paul Nickol; I am to be the third. (Later I learn Miner is about to drop Nickol.) I telephone Dilly and, in the best New York tradition, hire an agent to negotiate the salary.

Book Three

Mid-Century

Not to be cheered by praise,
not to be grieved by blame,
but thoroughly to know
one's own virtues or powers:
These are the characteristics
of an excellent man.

— ELEGANT SAYINGS
OF THE TIBETAN LAMAS

10

Into Television

MY ACQUAINTANCE with American television had begun a year earlier, in 1949, when Dilly and I drove down from Toronto, with baby Dorothea in the back seat, to an upper duplex on Long Island that I'd rented, sight unseen, for the summer. Determined to complete the journey that night, we crossed the Hudson River after midnight and had just entered a long stretch of unlit and unpopulated highway on the east bank when the foot brake failed. Using the hand brake, we made it past all the closed gas stations to our destination at about two in the morning, ready to collapse.

As we headed upstairs with our bags, we were greeted by sounds of bedlam from the room below: something smashing, furniture banging, people yelling.

> WOMAN: Kill him!
> MAN: Somebody stop him!
> WOMAN: Let me at the bastard!
> MAN: It's murder!
> WOMAN: Oh, my *gawd!* (*scream*)

We were about to call the police when the noise abruptly stopped. Was murder now being silently covered up? After four hours of not sleeping,

I arose to drive gingerly to the nearest service station, and thence to the United Nations at Lake Success. When I telephoned later, Dilly had solved the mystery. "Lucky we didn't call the police. He's a policeman. They were watching wrestling. They get into the spirit, she says, but turned it off when they heard us come in. We've got one, too."

Was this a bonus of the times or a time bomb? Three years of television in America had produced a fierce debate in the press. President Nathan Pusey of Harvard feared the arrival of a generation able only to "see with the eye's mind instead of the mind's eye." University of Chicago president Robert Hutchins waxed Gothic: "Under the impact of television, I can contemplate a time in America when people can neither read nor write, and will be no better than the lower forms of plant life." Psychiatrist Frederic Wertham claimed children were being led to "confuse violence with strength, low necklines with feminine ideals, sadism with sex and criminals with police." *New York Times* critic John Crosby reported the case of a small boy who, when informed that his grandfather had died, asked, "Who shot him?"[1]

In the trade, however, they were telling the story of the two academics discussing television at the faculty club:

PROF ONE: It's a disaster! Social life's gone down the drain, churches are empty, books are dying, families don't communicate, kids are being turned into thugs, schools can't cope — I tell you, civilization is on its way out!

PROF TWO: I know what you mean. We don't have a set, either.

Meantime the public bought sets as fast as the manufacturers could produce them, to watch — supposedly free — any programs the advertisers chose to transmit over the five highly competitive networks and scores of individual stations.

It was this Lowest Common Denominator market that the United Nations was attempting to infiltrate with its Highest Common Factor programs. In addition to radio programs, for the next two years, I was willingly pressed into service on public affairs television. (NBC eventually became so sensitive to accusations of mindlessness that it launched an internal campaign called "Operation Frontal Lobes" to inject "culture" into its "entertainment" schedule.)[2] When I worked at the United Nations in 1950, my radio documentary on atomic energy was to be followed by more television. Then North Korea invaded South Korea.

The United States suddenly found common cause with the United Nations, and the networks needed no further shots in the arm. Our modest Information Division was overnight transformed into a global communications centre.

But while General MacArthur and his combined U.SA.–U.N. force converged on Korea, I was engaged on three separate fronts, of which the Asian operation was only one. The second was the tempting offer from *Studio One*. The third opened up, unexpectedly, through a door I thought I had closed behind me.

Stuart Griffiths and I had gone to the University of Toronto at roughly the same time without our paths crossing. We first met at CBC International in Montreal, where he was, initially, head of press and information. But the title was misleading; he had turned the position into chief of staff to the director. To grasp the man's administrative genius — as I quickly learned — you had to get past appearances, because Stu Griffiths looked more like an enthusiastic chipmunk than an executive tiger.

His humble parents had given Griffiths both a social conscience and a determination to rise above their station, which is to say he was a socialist one week, a capitalist the next, and a workaholic all the time. Putting himself through college by repairing radio sets, he became a skilled technician, a shrewd businessman, and a scholar all at the same time. Now equipped with some French and German, he went abroad to study in 1938 — just in time to get himself arrested, in Munich, at an antifascist student rally where storm troopers smashed both of his feet with rifle butts. In due course this blessing rendered him unfit for military service, and after a brief stint in advertising, he joined CBC International. There he seized every opportunity to learn about production, bookkeeping, and staff relations — until soon he was the only person in that Tower of Babel able to talk to all ranks in their own argot.

Now, five years later, here I am at the United Nations when Griffiths telephones to say *he* is the internal candidate chosen to be program director for CBC Television.

I congratulate him. I congratulate them. I send our love to Alice and the two boys. I sympathize over the puny salary and mention my $500-a-week offer from CBS, which my new agent thinks she can jack up to $750.

SG: Shut up and listen. I may not take the job.

MM: But you must.

SG: I don't know anything about TV production. I've told them I'll take it only if you come as chief producer.

MM: The hell with them.

SG: We could work as a team.

MM: That would've been fun.

SG: You haven't signed anything down there yet?

MM: Forget it.

SG: I can't. My own decision depends on yours.

MM: That's blackmail.

SG: Of course. I'm serious.

The following morning I tell my agent to make a deal with CBS as soon as possible, at whatever salary they like. This only reveals my ignorance of the American way. Over the weekend, on the basis of some other contract just concluded, she has already raised the ante to $1,000 a week with a six-month guarantee. While this is under discussion, Griffiths phones again to make "a firm offer of $165 a week and a three-year contract with benefits." Dilly and I, seeing through Griffiths's tactics but also plagued by doubts about raising a family in New York, have a hilarious discussion of this arithmetic with its overtones of American risk-taking and Canadian prudence. I begin to look at the whole episode as high farce.

When CBS agrees to $1,000, my agent tells them that in view of a counteroffer from "another network" I am now worth $1,250. The moment CBS accepts this preposterous figure my psyche goes into reverse: the farce becomes *Faust*. On one side stands Mephisto offering me the earth to climb aboard his flashy bandwagon, while on the other the Angels promise self-sacrifice and the chance to design a better model. When I tell Tony Miner that Canada is winning, he makes a final offer of $1,500 that only confirms my suspicion. Knowing me better, Griffiths never budges from $165. The ratio, he points out, roughly reflects the difference in population.

At the end of July we left Lake Success and drove north to a rented cottage near Craigie Lea, Muskoka, for a fortnight's holiday. During the bargaining, I had been working 18-hour days compounding broadcasts from tapes coming out of the war in Korea, and felt as if I had been through it. When we stopped the car, I could not get out, and sat shaking uncontrollably for half an hour. I had no idea where I was.

"AMONG THE FADING VICTORIAN MANSIONS of Jarvis Street in Toronto," Pierre Berton wrote in *Maclean's* in May 1952, "there is a grey shingle barn of a building which once housed new immigrants to Canada. And here . . . the casual visitor might have encountered a chaotic scene." The article continues:

> In a space not much larger than an oversize living room six perform-ers, sweating under the glare of eighteen thousand watts of incandes-cent light, were going through a complicated twenty-minute routine . . . that no audience will ever see. Here, flanking a twisting mass of cables, were settings for seven scenes. . . . Through these paper-thin facades, jammed around the walls like pictures in an art gallery, probed the grey snouts of two television cameras moving silently on their rubber rollers. . . .

> Altogether there were seventeen [persons] in the control booth and on the studio floor, all working at once to keep six performers in front of the camera. In the background were other members of the Canadian Broadcasting Corporation's new television department — set design-ers, make-up artists, carpenters, costumers, executives — all caught up by the ravenous appetite of the most complicated entertainment me-dium yet devised.

> And on the sidelines, in a starched white shirt and bow tie, looking more like a scholar than an entertainer, stood an owlish young man with horn-rimmed spectacles and hardly any hair. . . .[3]

At that point we were four months from opening night in September, and it had taken us a year and a half to get there. The transmitter tower stretched its futuristic neck high above the seedy blocks around the CBC's Toronto base, technical equipment had been bought, staff trained, and program plans developed. But construction problems had delayed the two main television studios, as they had in Montreal, scheduled to go on the air at the same time. In the interim we used a makeshift studio in an old army hut behind the Georgian mansion, nicknamed the Kremlin, that housed the CBC's executive offices.

It was the set of blueprints for the proposed new buildings that had given me, on my arrival, the first hint of how far behind we were and how heavily encumbered by politics our progress was likely to be.

As this was my first experience with designs for a public edifice, I was deferential to the architects. I expressed only mild surprise that the project had reached such an advanced stage without advice from those who would have to work in it. We were assured this was the usual procedure at the Department of Public Works.

> MM: But why are the scene shops on the second floor?
> ARCH: To get them out of the way.
> MM: Then how do you get the stuff in and out of the studio?
> ARCH: Well, you hand it down.
> MM: And the materials coming in by truck?
> ARCH: You hand it up.
> MM: And where's the water supply?
> ARCH: Don't they use oil-based paints?
> MM: Not usually. Where's the nearest water?
> ARCH: Well, there's a john on the first floor . . .

I soon discovered that even relatively simple changes agreed upon by all in Toronto — Mutrie, Griffiths, our able technical director Reg Horton, and myself — had to be cleared through Montreal and then approved in Ottawa.

The explanation was as logical as it was Canadian. Ottawa, being the hub of government (if nothing else), was necessarily the site of CBC headquarters, since Montreal would not allow it to be in Toronto and Toronto would not allow it to be in Montreal. Since programming headquarters for all of the country except Quebec was necessarily in Toronto, engineering headquarters for all of it must be in Montreal. When television loomed, legislators nervous about giddy programmers naturally sought the advice of solid engineering types. Engineer Augustin Frigon, head of the French network and future CBC chairman, gave them the advice they wanted to hear: do not be "stampeded into premature action." (Frigon was a born bet hedger. Although well thatched, he wore a hat almost everywhere, and habitually greeted me with an alarmed "You 'ave no 'at?") From all of which it followed that the CBC's entry into television would be coordinated from Montreal by chief engineer Alphonse Ouimet.

A ranking pioneer in television technology and an early proponent of Canadian television, Ouimet had outstanding credentials. But like the Duke of Plaza Toro in *The Gondoliers*, he was leading his regiment from behind: Montreal was not the front line. American transmissions, received there through chronic "snow," were watched by few anglophones and fewer francophones. In Ottawa, where the bureaucrats roam, reception was nonexistent. It was along the southern borders of Ontario and British Columbia that Canadian set owners in the tens of thousands were aiming their aerials south and forming their viewing habits. In short, national television policy was being evolved in circles insulated from the daily impact of the U.S. commercial networks, and from the clamour elsewhere to get on the air with a Canadian alternative.

When Griffiths and I pleaded for staff and resources adequate to the challenge, we were told to reduce our horizons. Two hours a day were enough for CBC Television's debut in Toronto, because that was enough for Montreal. Stations in Vancouver, Windsor, Ottawa, Winnipeg, and Halifax would follow "if and when the resources are available." We were refused higher salary levels to entice back Canadians with television experience abroad, on the ground that our colleagues in Montreal, with few francophones to entice, did not "see this as a problem." When I reported that three of our best trainees — even before we went on the air — were being offered American jobs at triple their present pay, Ouimet shrugged charmingly and said, "Let them go!"

There was more to this, however, than institutional thrift or political rivalry.

Al Ouimet shared the Quebec credo that French culture, to survive in North America, must lift itself up by its own muscle. For this a creative plant was vital. Now luck, in the form of a double shield of language and poor reception, had given Quebec a priceless window of opportunity to build a television plant behind the lines. But Ouimet, although more gung-ho than Frigon, seemed incapable of grasping that this was a window denied to those parts of the country where U.S. stations were already in control of the air, with ground support from *Time*, *Reader's Digest*, and *TV Guide*. He also leaned toward the notion, especially common in Quebec, that the rest of Canada was a poor man's America in any case. Was the United States not where gifted *anglais* naturally went? *Que faire?* "Let them go" was less dismissive than philosophical. But in the unconfident corridors of Ottawa this defeatism was contagious, infecting too many anglophone politicians with terminal timidity just when they should have been contemplating bold and massive action.

Among beneficiaries of U.S. largesse, meantime, this cautious response only confirmed the national genius for missing the boat before it was launched. The day after Pierre Berton's article appeared in *Maclean's*, a woman reached me on the telephone:

CALLER: Why don't you just fire all those amateurs you have and let us watch Buffalo in peace?

MM: Wouldn't you like a Canadian alternative?

CALLER: What for? Americans are great entertainers, instinctively. Look at Hollywood.

MM: Ma'am, Hollywood is full of Canadians.

CALLER: They're *Americans!* Canadians will never make entertainers.

MM: Why not?

CALLER: Too many of us go to church.

Having accounted for our superior morality and our inferior entertainment in one stroke, she hung up on me. She had already hung up on the country.

For our first training program, nonetheless, we managed to find a few native talents to save, at least temporarily, from flight to godless America or wanton Europe. They came from film, theatre, vaudeville, radio, journalism, sports, visual arts and crafts, education, and related backgrounds. ("Let's not think of TV in terms of any other particular art," I wrote in the CBC *Times*. "It's a new one.")[4] Of the originals and their immediate successors, many stayed to shape Canadian television (Ross McLean, Norman Campbell, Robert Allen, Peggy Nairn, Joanne Hughes, Murray Chercover, Phyllis Duncan, Peter McDonald, Virginia Carson, Don Hudson), some went on to make their presence felt in British television (Sydney Newman, Gunnar Rugheimer, Griffiths himself), and others rose to glory in film (Norman Jewison, Arthur Hiller, Harry Rasky, Harvey Hart, Ted Kotcheff). For their teachers we hired Canadian specialists where available — O. C. Wilson and Oscar Burritt in film, for example — then imported outside help to repair the areas of ignorance.

Our master instructor was Rudy Bretz, the New York consultant and author (with Edward Stasheff) of *The Television Program: Its Writing, Direction, and Production*. To balance his emphasis on mechanics, we also brought in the American social analyst Gilbert Seldes, author of *The Seven Lively Arts*, the era's most cogent analysis of the medium and its audiences. Bretz and Seldes made a wondrously odd but complementary couple — one all lanky easygoing practicality, the other a hilariously testy Rumpelstiltskin, compulsively spinning golden theories for anyone in need of them by morning. It was Seldes who impishly named Canadian television's infancy "the Golden Age." NBC was "Tin," CBS was "Brass," and ABC was "Plastic."

The strategy Griffiths and I adopted to compete with the giant networks was to avoid, at least initially, the conventional categories — news, drama, comedy, public affairs, documentaries, sports, concerts, children's shows — and seek new configurations less likely to invite comparison. We called it "choosing our own weapons."

Instead of setting up separate departments we assigned directors and crews, on a rotating basis, to work with writers, technicians, and designers to develop fresh approaches and novel forms. This exercise was highly stimulating for those of us involved — I loved clambering over Maple Leaf Gardens to spy out camera angles for the classical drama known as hockey — but not easy to explain to viewers accustomed to pigeonholes labelled "entertainment," "sports," "information," "news," "education," "cartoons," and so on. To justify our departure from these conventional patterns, I pointed to the experience of American viewers:

> They have found to their horror that "educational" programs only convert the converted, while most of the public derives its learning and moral standards from what is innocuously labeled "entertainment." Children have developed a far greater taste for "adult" programs than for "education" no matter how nicely sugar-coated.
>
> We don't regard the two as mutually exclusive. . . . Every program that holds your attention educates you in some way — it may be down instead of up, but you get something from it. [Here followed the true story of a Japanese stripteaser who descended into the audience and was arrested on a charge of "excessive entertainment."] Likewise a program designed to educate will fail, no matter how educational in intent, unless the interest of the viewer is at the same time entertained. . . . The middle-ground — which we hope to explore — may be more fruitful than has been supposed.[5]

We mixed drama with panels; we mixed news with comedy; we mixed weather with puppets; we mixed documentary with cartoons; we mixed sports with dance; we mixed cooking with instrumental music. When I took a two-week break as consultant to an embryonic television station at the University of Iowa, I found a ready ear among the agriculturalists there for such experiments in crossbreeding. To them I suggested a quiz show to generate light instead of the usual heat; a panel would be asked to identify, through cartoon clues, the author and source of a famous dictum, and then to debate its validity. The concept later became the germ of CBC-TV's *Fighting Words*, to which Stuart Griffiths contributed the title, Harvey Hart the production, and Nathan Cohen the chairman's wit. Simulcast on radio, in due course, it ran for many years.

But long before we actually went on the air it became clear that any attempt to ignore American models in favour of our own would be interpreted in some quarters as inability to match them, and in others as abject failure to challenge them.

To begin with, the flexibility we sought made it difficult for sponsors — whose advertising spots were a necessary source of revenue — to identify a product with a familiar type of program. Griffiths and I took refuge in journalistic precedent. "They hope," Pierre Berton reported, "to be able to exert as much influence over sponsored programs as they have over sustaining ones, and it is quite likely that Canadian TV will follow the pattern of magazines and newspapers in which program material will be prepared by the CBC, just as editorial matter is prepared by editorial staffs — and the advertisers are handed it as a *fait accompli*."[6]

While commercial interests called this high-handed, others expected us to wield an even bigger stick. A Toronto school trustee named Cranham, unconsciously echoing the old New York anecdote about the two professors, showed a touching faith in our power to reverse the whole tide of television:

> Its development up to this point has been the greatest stumbling-block to education we've ever had. It gives the children bad eyes, makes them unable to sleep and unable to study, and I wouldn't permit it in the house. But I hope there will be a wonderful improvement once the CBC gets operating.[7]

Many of the general public believed they could have it both ways: a publicly owned network dedicated to uplift and unspotted by advertising, along with popular stations loaded with mercenary games and gamy mercenaries. But many intellectuals believed they could avoid television of any kind.

Thanks to Claude Bissell, the University of Toronto's farsighted vice president, Griffiths and I were invited to meet with Sidney Smith, the president, and a group of 60 senior academics to discuss the role of television in higher education. We were looking forward to a fruitful exchange, although the week before I'd had an unmistakable hint of trouble when I ran into my old philosophy teacher, Fulton Henry Anderson, outside the library:

FHA: (*amiably*) Well, Moore! And what are you up to these days?
MM: (*proudly*) I'm putting a television network on the air, sir.
FHA: (*gravely*) Oh, Moore, when are you going to quit fucking around!

The meeting in Simcoe Hall was more polite. Sidney Smith, a stuffed shirt when he addressed large audiences from behind a podium, chaired small gatherings with a dry urbanity I have aspired to ever since; but after his witty introduction, a show of hands revealed that none of the 60 academics present owned a television set and only five had ever seen a television program. This handicap failed to prevent one after another from rising to damn this "passing fad," most of them by comparing the worst of television (through hearsay) with the best of literature. When Bissell tactfully suggested the sophistry this trick involved, he was ignored. It was finally agreed that the president would install a set in his office for any sufficiently curious passersby.

As we approach airtime, the stakes rise and the tensions grow. In and out of the office we are pursued by opinion-mongers avid for platforms, publicity-seeking organizers of coming events, aggressive parents of undiscovered child prodigies. "I've got a girl does tricks with her eyes," says one mother. "She's a natural for TV." When I tell her we are not casting stunt performers yet, she adds, "Maybe I ought to take her to a doctor."

Groups on guard for their collective image visit us daily. A senior police officer argues that, because dramas may show police in an unflattering light, all shows involving police should be vetted by the force. Exeunt Gilbert and Sullivan, Sherlock Holmes, Mack Sennett, et cetera. A delegate from the Italian community asks us to avoid all reference to the Mafia and never to identify villains as Italian — although he would allow exceptions in the case of Iago or Lucrezia Borgia. A United Church official wants no on-screen drinking of alcoholic beverages, but retires gracefully when I ask if the rule should apply to the Last Supper. Not all such diplomatic negotiations end positively. My attempt to mount a religious program (generating light rather than heat, again) in which believers, heretics, and sceptics would present and defend their viewpoints, is blocked by the CBC's own Religious Advisory Council — the members of which are clearly more interested in closing ranks than opening minds.

For the programs now decided upon, money is scarce, equipment overextended, and staff overworked. One hot August dinnertime a month before opening night, at work in my second-floor office overlooking the base of the 260-foot transmitter tower, I become aware of a hubbub in the courtyard below. A crowd is gathering round the cage at the tower's base, jabbering, hooting, pointing upward. Before I can reach the door my phone rings. "Seems you're the senior guy on deck," says a policeman. Some guy has climbed the tower and is threatening to commit suicide, and what do I propose to do about it? Figuring that only one of our engineers would have a key to the tower, I phone Reg Horton at home. "Oh, God," says Horton, "I know who it's got to be. He's in trouble at home. I'll be right there soon's I can grab a priest. He's a Catholic."

By the time I get out there, the crowd is larger and uglier, its leaders trying to push past the lone policeman defending the unlocked gate of the cage to get at the spiral stairway inside. He tells me to take over while he runs for help. Spread-eagled across the entrance, like Harold Lloyd on a cowcatcher, I fend off jeering punks and grabbing drunks ("And who the hell are you, Charlie?") and use every rusty muscle I once developed in commando training to hang on with my hands while kicking with my feet. By the time the police return, the mob has taken up a chant to the lone figure above: "Jump, you yellow bastard, jump! Jump, you yellow bastard, jump!" while the poor fellow teeters on the edge of the small platform nearest the tower's tip and periodically yells, "Watch me!" Then he spots Reg Horton starting up the spiral stairway with the priest in tow and screams, "Beat it! Leave me alone!" As Horton and the priest get closer, he hesitates, retreats, starts to sob; they dicker inaudibly. A woman shouts, "Let him jump!" and others take up the refrain. Once the awkward three-man descent begins, there is relative quiet until a drunk loudly voices his disappointment — "Shit!" — and the crowd mutters its way back to the street.

What was I defending? And for whom, and against whom? And in the last resort did any of this matter?

Griffiths and I become convinced that despite the staff ceilings imposed from CBC-TV headquarters in Montreal, we cannot meet expectations without 20 additional key production positions, including floor managers and script assistants. We propose to Mutrie that we hire them on performers' "per occasion" contracts, which come out of a separate "talent" budget. Mutrie agrees to go along with this barefaced irregularity if Ernie Bushnell, now director general of programs, is fully informed. The three of us get on the line to Bushnell in Ottawa. Griffiths outlines the plan:

> BUSH: Hold everything. There's something wrong with this line.
> GRIFF: *We* can hear you.
> BUSH: Well, thank God for that.
> GRIFF: Do you go along with it?
> BUSH: Go along with what?
> GRIFF: With what we're trying to do.
> BUSH: I don't know what the hell you're trying to do, Griffiths.
> GRIFF: We just told you.
> BUSH: Okay, then. But remember, I didn't hear a goddamn word.

Later, when his connivance is discovered by the CBC's acting chairman, the officious Donald Manson, Bushnell is almost fired. But it is too late. We are already on the air, and the conniver is the hero of the hour.

The board of governors missed it.

Every minute of opening night, Monday, September 8, 1952, had been timed to the nearest second. After half an hour of preliminaries, the ceremonial debut (two days after Montreal's) was scheduled to begin at 8:00 p.m. with a live extravaganza before a studio audience. While other dignitaries were lodged in viewing rooms on the third floor, with Mutrie and Griffiths to guide them through the proceedings on monitors, CBC chairman Davidson Dunton and the board of governors, along with the federal minister responsible, J. J. McCann, were to occupy a block of seats among the audience in the studio. I was to receive them at the studio entrance inside the building at 7:30, brief them, and usher them to their places before the show commenced. When they had not arrived by 7:55, I gave orders for the double door to be closed, its NO ENTRY barrier dropped into place, and the red ON AIR sign switched on.

Two minutes later they bustle in to find the way barred and me — for the second time in a month — spread-eagled before the entrance like Horatius defending his bridge. The only one I know is Dunton, to whom I say, "I'm sorry." "So are we," says Dunton tactfully. "Dinner, I'm afraid. Can you sneak us in?" I say they will have to wait until we cut to the second studio when there will be a break. "Who the hell is *he*?" asks the Honourable Dr. J. J. McCann, a former dentist whose extracting skills have won him the jobs of minister of national revenue and (by the usual Canadian logic) minister responsible for the CBC. When Dunton introduces us, McCann inflates his chest and bumps mine. "And do you know who *we* are, Moore? We're your *baaahsses!*" Carried on a whiff of brandy, the word's sudden irony restores my sense of humour. "This broadcast is going out to a million Canadians, Dr. McCann," I find myself saying. "At this moment they're even more important than you are." To my great relief Dunton laughs and adds, "He's right. Let's go find a cup of coffee."

The night's performance, meantime, had already begun, after a fashion. At 7:30 p.m. our test pattern went on the air upside down. We recovered to present a three-puppet preview of the evening so offbeat that it almost made the gaffe look intentional. Then we had a stroke of good fortune. For our first newscast the infamous Boyd Gang of bank robbers, hiding out in a farm after a jailbreak, was recaptured in front of our mobile camera unit. In its first outing television news outshone the press.

At 8:00 p.m. came the extravaganza missed by the board of governors: a variety show featuring every available personality from sportswriter Ted Reeve to pianist Glenn Gould, followed by excerpts from several upcoming series, including Leacock's *Sunshine Sketches* (with young Timothy Findley as Peter Pupkin) and Ross McLean's prankish, innovative *Stop, Watch, and Listen*. Before the evening closed with a salute from Montreal we previewed our first full-length drama, *Call It a Day*, the domestic comedy I'd seen in wartime London and ever since wanted to reset in Canada. By the time it appeared in full two nights later, the accumulated tension of the openings was taking its toll in the studio. Halfway through *Call It a Day* (which was, of course, "live to air") one of the two cameramen fell off his mount in a dead faint. As his apprentice cable toter climbed bravely into the empty seat, director Peter McDonald earned immortality by extemporizing coverage on the remaining camera until the understudy collected himself, and then coolly guided him shot by shot through the rest of the play.

Canada's national symbol, I have often thought, should not be the beaver, but the carp. Of the three Toronto daily newspapers covering this opening night (all troubled by the spectre of losing advertising revenue to the new medium),[8] one merely acknowledged that the event had taken place. The second gleefully announced that Canadian television had bowed in backside foremost. The third was mock judicial:

"Canadian television was not triumphant in its opening. It was not really good. There was little worth sitting through and nothing you would want to endure a second time." *Canadian TV Guide*, a new offspring of the American publication, revealed the main source of this negativism, while for some odd reason excusing me from blame:

> The fact that Moore had been unable to pull together a series of hit shows for the CBC's television debut was no reflection upon either the man's abilities or his intentions. . . . If CBC television laid an egg in its opening week, then the fault rested squarely with the theory of government-monopolized television and its accompanying confusion — and not with the man who had tried to create order out of chaos.[9]

Happily our transmission reached across the border into Buffalo, the distribution point for most U.S. broadcasts received in southern Ontario. There the *Courier-Express*, untroubled by our national neuroses, took a different reading on the night's events:

> Three hours of unusual, interesting and highly professional entertainment . . . a pattern that could well be followed by the U.S. television industry. Observers in Eastern New York State say they are amazed at the professional skill demonstrated by CBLT. They recall to mind the early TV shows in the U.S.A., which were infinitely inferior. All in all, it looks as though Canadian talent is sure of a substantial U.S. audience.[10]

The question was whether Canadian talent was sure of a Canadian audience. The Canadian edition of *Time*, the U.S.-owned weekly advocate for the American system, did its utmost to spread alarm among the natives. *Time* claimed the CBC did only two kinds of programs: highbrow and awful. Any dance show emerged in *Time* as "ballet," any revue as "vaudeville," and any film as "old movies." The very week *Time* reported that TV manufacturers were "bitterly disappointed when no boom for sets developed," Toronto's *Telegram*, no friend of public broadcasting, reported "a boom that . . . whirled manfacturers' sales millions of dollars higher. . . . Set orders doubled."[11]

Although banished from our opening night, commercials were a necessary part of both systems — especially once the CBC abolished its unpopular $2.50 licence fee. To attract advertisers the CBC set up a commercial relations office. At the same time Griffiths and I were looking for inexpensive programming in the form of colourful local events for Syd Newman's Features and Outside Broadcasts unit to cover. On a Saturday morning in November, we knew, Eaton's Santa Claus Parade would wend its annual way through downtown Toronto to the delight of thousands lining the streets. "And possibly many more thousands," Griffiths added benevolently, "who'd like to watch it at home." Then he grinned, displaying his chipmunk incisors:

MM: Now wait. We'd have to get permission from Eaton's.
SG: Why? It's on the street — in the public domain.
MM: Maybe if we contributed something . . . for the kids?
SG: Are you crazy? It's worth a million in advertising.
MM: You mean, get them to trade the TV rights for the exposure.
SG: Oh, no. I mean, get them to sponsor it.
MM: But why would they if they know we'll carry it, anyway?
SG: Because if they don't, I'm going to sell ads to Simpsons.

When Eaton's told Griffiths to go to hell, he forthwith offered their annual parade to the rival chain, whose executives kicked themselves for not having thought of it first. Eaton's recalled Griffiths from hell and continued to sponsor the event for decades.

In addition to set owners who adjusted their aerials to catch our wavelength, our viewers included some who had waited for the advent of Canadian television before buying sets. But there were still the early birds with their aerials locked onto Buffalo. The first large-scale test of audience fidelity came on June 2, 1953, with the coronation of Queen Elizabeth II, a spectacle every network in North America was determined to be the first to show. In the presatellite era that meant being the first to fly the film negative across the Atlantic. NBC and CBS had leased large planes to take their lavish contingents to London, wait there, and return on cue; smaller and poorer ABC had chosen to buy our CBC coverage whenever we could provide it. We could afford only three people to cover the event, including Oscar Burritt as cameraman, and a small RCAF aircraft to get them there and back.

It was Griffiths who first thought of developing the exposed film on the plane. Reg Horton and Harold Wright came up with the hot processor. For the return flight, arrangements were made to refuel the plane in Gander, Newfoundland (still, as a hangover from the war, an American air base), for the trip to Dorval airport. At Dorval the film would be transferred to a helicopter, flown to the roof of the CBC building in Montreal, rushed into master control, and fed to the network.

On June 2 Bushnell was in Montreal on an open telephone line to Toronto, where Griffiths and I were following the events on radio while monitoring the three U.S. television networks via Buffalo. The race itself had become news. As the ceremonies in London drew to a close, we received word that the NBC plane had left Heathrow airport while our RCAF plane was preparing for takeoff; the CBS plane, for some reason, was delayed on the ground. Next we learned that ours was airborne. Within the hour we learned that the NBC craft had developed engine trouble over the Atlantic and was forced to return to London. We were ahead. Bushnell said he would drink to that.

Burritt telephoned us from Gander, the precious cans of developed film under his arm. Normally a gentle teddy bear of a man, he was almost unintelligible with rage. The base's American commanders (we finally grasped) had refuelled the plane but were refusing the Canadians permission to reboard — a clear case, claimed Burritt, of collusion with the U.S. networks. Bushnell, now fortified by more than one toast, was urging Burritt to get a U.S. official to come to the phone when Griffiths broke in:

GRIFFITHS: Oscar, how many of them are there?
BURRITT: Three.
GRIFFITHS: And how many of you are there?
BURRITT: Four.
GRIFFITHS: Then rush them.
BURRITT: (after a long pause) Okay. (he hangs up)
BUSHNELL: (appreciatively) Griffiths, you're a son of a bitch.
GRIFFITHS: I just don't think the Yanks want to lose that base.[12]

When the film reached Montreal, there was a further delay after it was discovered that in the excitement it had not been rewound, which gave NBC time to give up and buy our feed. CBS, its plane still in Britain, was reduced to showing strained interviews with uneasy auxiliaries awaiting its arrival in Boston. There was, then, this unique moment when the CBC signal, fed via Toronto to Buffalo and thence to both NBC and ABC, went out over all of North America. This victory meant nothing to the diehards, however. Audience surveys later showed that although the signals were of equal clarity, about a third of Ontario viewers watched the coronation of their own queen on a Buffalo station.

As Vancouver, Winnipeg, Windsor, Halifax, and Ottawa joined the network, the Canadian audience for Canadian television naturally increased. And once the *New York Times* had rendered judgement ("the shows are well done, the acting is generally good, and technically for the viewer they leave little room for improvement"), local critics tended to be more respectful ("CBC Theatre," the *Telegram*'s Ron Poulton said, "is the best live acting of any group appearing consistently on a North American screen").[13] But private station aspirants, unable to apply for licences until a CBC national network was in place, continued to paint public television as a disaster.[14] At the very moment several of our productions were winning prizes at the 1953 annual Ohio State Awards, in competition with the U.S. networks' nominees, one dogged Canadian columnist was calling the CBC "a presumptuous, empire-building group of bureaucrats who once and for all should be exposed for the professional incompetents that they are."[15]

As the debate over television policy grew more heated, and even greater reliance on revenue from advertising spots became probable, I was sent to London in February 1953 to make a close study of the commercial-free production methods of the BBC.

HUGH CARLETON-GREENE, head of external relations and consequently my host, was half a foot taller than I; but when we sat down, our bald pates and horn-rimmed glasses made us brothers with a common frame of reference. His eyes, in an otherwise usefully bland face, modulated as easily between mirth and murk as did the novels of his real brother, Graham Greene. He had been warmly commended to me by the CBC's alert London representative of the day, Andrew Cowan, and by my wartime BBC colleague Michel St-Denis.

Carleton-Greene's advice about keeping the hawkers at bay was to ignore the political wrangling and concentrate on making allies of the creative communities. Artists, scientists, writers, and teachers, he argued, are reluctant to be seen as sellouts (even when they are) and cringe when their works are decimated to accommodate plugs for potions and purges; they are therefore the natural friends of public broadcasting. I envied him the fidelity of successive British governments to full public ownership, the skills and training facilities available in London, and the maturity of the British entertainment unions. Neither of us foresaw the day when he would become director-general of a BBC in bitter competition with British commercial television.

I received a crash course in institutional dynamics. Program directors, department heads, producers, directors, authors' and actors' agents, filmmakers, publishers, and copyright lawyers bared their trade secrets. But I took soundings outside the BBC as well, lunching (the diary tells me) with J. B. Priestley, Wyndham Goldie, Sir Alexander Korda, Rose Lehmann, Duncan Ross and, at their Lincoln's Inn flat, Judith and Tyrone Guthrie, coping with last-minute crises afflicting the initial Stratford, Ontario, Shakespeare festival. Canadian expatriates Alexander Knox, Monica Mugan, Bernard Braden, and Barbara Kelly, all now well established in Britain, gave me insights into differences in national attitudes. Some Canadians who spoke to me were thinking of going home now that television and Stratford were there: Douglas Rain, Olga Landiak, Glenn Burns, and even Hamilton-born Robert Harris, a West End star mistakenly convinced that his fame had travelled to the land of his birth.

A month of interviews, rehearsals, demonstrations, and kinescopes later, I was invited to speak frankly to a selected group of BBC staff. My gratitude must have been obvious, and my high praise for most aspects of BBC administration and production methods was humbly received, but I raised a few eyebrows (accustomed, perhaps, to greater veneration) when I compared their camera work unfavourably to the American standard. And when I went so far as to criticize the drama department for presenting too many warmed-over classics and faded drawing room comedies, the meeting was hastily concluded with quips about my safe return to that citadel of civilization, Toronto. "Naughty, naughty," Carleton-Greene scolded, "but it needed saying." Ten years later my irreverent CBC colleague Sydney Newman, after making his mark in British commercial television with the first plays of Harold Pinter, Alun Owen, Angus Wilson, and the like, was appointed head of BBC drama with a mandate to revitalize it.

The most stimulating exchanges I recall, however, were with a gadfly no longer at the BBC: the novelist and futurist Norman Collins. Collins had taken up the cause of high-definition television, a technology that would allow superfine tape and big screens to replace films, cinemas, theatres, galleries, libraries, and other forms of mass communication. Too stylish a dresser to be taken seriously as a thinker and too avid a fortune hunter to pass as a humanitarian, Collins had a coherent if alarming vision of television as the web of the cosmos, in which entertainment would be a single all-embracing global enterprise, bypassing borders, nationalities, and languages, and subsuming such temporary expedients as religion and education. At the time I thought he was a charlatan; now I think he was a farsighted charlatan.

I returned to Canada convinced that the world needed more varieties of culture, not fewer, and that my own held considerable promise. I also found the national press (or as much as we had of one) now more supportive. The *Toronto Star Weekly*, for example:

> They have shown themselves able to tackle the most elaborate presentations, and in standard need bow to no-one. In drama particularly, CBLT has shone, doing everything from Othello to modern farce, and including the first plays of Shaw to be done in North America as well as some highly original plays by Canadian writers.

Griffiths and I were still determined to apply the newspapers' rule to our schedule, namely that if our programs must be subsidized by advertising, the sponsors must not dictate the contents. To abandon content to the marketplace would be to abandon the principle of public interest. I highly recommended Carleton-Greene's advice to strengthen our hand by involving the creative communities and encouraging more of them. We had hired a few masters, such as the Soviet refugee Nicholas Soloviev (one of Eisenstein's leading film designers) to demonstrate and pass on their skills. And, as production increased, we added more. But Canada lacked trained talent pools in several important areas, and we found that with the exception of the performers' association (ACRA, later ACTRA) we could not count on the existing unions to provide them.

Most Canadian entertainment unions, closely linked to "international" American bodies, were too enslaved to outmoded machines and antique rule books to welcome the chance to broaden their competence or increase their membership. The International Alliance of Theatrical and Stage Employees (IATSE), for example, made up mainly of film projectionists and a corporal's guard of legitimate theatre stagehands, regarded the new technology with a combination of suspicion and possessiveness — like old-time pirates into whose domain a ship from outer space had dropped. Canada's public broadcasting system, I wrote to a London friend, was caught between "radical capitalists on the right and reactionary unions on the left."

The Toronto local of the American Federation of Musicians was controlled, through sheer force of numbers, by part-time bandsmen. I knew its perpetual president, Walter Murdoch, as a brother officer and bandmaster of the Royal Regiment; but military music filled the only soft spot I ever found in Walter's heart. Taking his lead from the AF of M's "international" head office in Chicago and its corrupt president, Caesar Petrillo, he ceaselessly inveighed against all forms of recording — disc, tape, wire, film — as a lethal threat to live music.

CBC Radio had a long history of dedication to live music, and CBC-TV had shown a commitment to finding new ways of presenting music visually. We had no problem with the union on that score. But on the subject of taped and recorded background music Murdoch was adamant. One day Griffiths and I visited his office to reopen the matter. A grandfatherly figure, strikingly like Heinrich Himmler in appearance, Murdoch sat behind his desk in his herringbone suit and lectured us in an intense sotto voce on the evils of the tape machine, which he would never allow in his presence. While I listened, Griffiths was looking around, as if preternaturally bored. Suddenly he sprang forward and pulled open the top right-hand drawer of Murdoch's desk, exposing a hidden tape recorder. "Damn you!" Murdoch shouted several times as Griffiths expertly stripped it, gutted it, and broke it forever. "Now, Walter," he said, calmly returning to his chair, "let's discuss the merits of the tape recorder."

Our difficulties with commercial interests on one hand and unions on the other — not to mention the parliamentary caucuses' connections to both — were further complicated by the high political winds of the day.

The "20 years of treason" speech delivered by Senator Joseph McCarthy at the 1952 Republican convention, and the ensuing anti-Communist campaign waged by the U.S. Senate committee he chaired, had spilled across the border into Canada. Well-known figures in the entertainment world moved from the United States to Britain, and at the inquisition's height I would receive several phone calls a week from threatened (or merely outraged) American directors seeking work in Canada. After I explained our penurious working conditions, most had second thoughts, although we hired one, Ted Neeland of NBC, to codirect our main variety show for a few months. A number of freelance writers and performers from New York or Hollywood also moved to Toronto, including some expatriate Canadians — among them the satirist Reuben Ship, whose The Investigator was produced by Andrew Allan and made its way back into the United States as a recording to wreak vengeance on the senator.

At the same time the Canadian government, drawn into the storm by lightning in Ottawa (the notorious Gouzenko affair) as well as

Washington, began investigating the National Film Board, whose founder, John Grierson, had been fingered in both capitals. It was the CBC's turn next, and the investigators started at the International Service in Montreal, where the convicted spy Raymond Boyer once worked.

One day Bushnell — fully familiar with my wartime career in intelligence — summons me to his office in the Kremlin, locks the door, and comes straight to the point:

> BUSH: Is Griffiths a Communist?
>
> MM: If he is, Bush, I don't know when he does it. We've lived out of each other's pocket for nearly four years.
>
> BUSH: Was he *ever* a Communist?
>
> MM: He's always been quite open about being left wing as a student. Most of the bright ones were. Moles try to hide it.
>
> BUSH: What are his politics now?
>
> MM: I think he voted Liberal in the last election.
>
> BUSH: Hell, anybody can vote Liberal! What's he *committed* to?
>
> MM: Public broadcasting. If he didn't believe in what we're doing, I think he'd go out and become a millionaire.
>
> BUSH: That's what I think — and I'd hate to lose the son of a bitch!

Shortly afterward I was promoted from chief producer to assistant director of programs. And shortly after that Bushnell confided in me that CBC senior management, to fend off more drastic action on the part of the board of governors, was about to offer Griffiths a "less sensitive" position than that of director of programs. Bushnell was postponing the move as long as he could, but all three of us knew which way the wind was blowing.

To make matters worse, the imposition of political orthodoxy was accompanied by an internal drive to subject our creative confusion to the rigid methodology of conventional business.

In New York, where Wall Street and Broadway happily coexisted, I'd heard the story about Lou, the old vaudevillian whose banana barrow stood daily in front of the Chase Manhattan Bank. Observing Lou's hearty morning exchange with the bank's president, a reporter once asked Lou how such an odd pair came to be such good friends. "Easy," Lou replied. "I don't lend money and he don't peddle bananas." Some such understanding had been necessary to get Canadian television launched.

The CBC's assignment was to produce exciting television programs, not elegant management charts. But within every organization (I was beginning to learn), unless the true begetters are wary, the reins of power will be seized by cautious careerists whose reasons for being are the multiplication of rules and the complication of procedures. They are well named *auditors*, because they deal entirely with reports of what others *do*. Such reviews are essential in a democracy, but feasible only when based on appreciation of the process under review. Now that our irregular methods had produced a viable Canadian television system — speedily, inexpensively, and in the face of unequalled competition — regularity was poised to take over.

It had been discovered, for example, that while technicians were frequently idle between assignments, certain practices — with shocking illogicality! — encouraged overtime. Designers apparently wasted hours in the public library. Actors were seen to spend more time off the set than on. It never occurred to the overseers that mental activity craves idleness, that waiting for a cue is the corollary of taking it, or that some creative processes must be continued until completion because the configuration of factors cannot be reconstructed. As I recall, the memorandum that set off the loudest alarm in my mind was a proposal to force all script assistants — those dedicated right arms of the director, who nursed a production night and day through its natural span — to punch time clocks as they came in and out of the premises.

But were my own nights and days, as director of programs, to be filled with running nothing but such managerial obstacle courses? Already my chief producer's job had been triangulated; three divisional heads now stood between me and the productions I used to take such an active hand in. And while I was waging the paper war instigated by commissars and apparatchiks, my creative skills were rusting away.

I had not acted for four years. The last piece of original writing, composing, and directing I had done was *The Best of All Possible Worlds* for CBC Radio in 1952. For the two years before CBC-TV went on the air I had concentrated on training other directors, and since then I'd had little time to direct anything but the traffic. I worked spasmodically on a musical comedy version of Stephen Leacock's *Sunshine Sketches of a Little Town* even as we adapted it for a television drama series; but I did it on stolen time. As head of production, I was my own lone substitute, pinch-hitting when others already more experienced than I were ill or away. I achieved notoriety of a sort while directing *The Big Revue*, when a visiting hypnotist put compere Peter Mews to sleep for the rest of the show and knocked out enough susceptible viewers to persuade the authorities to ban hypnotic acts from television forever after. My other contributions — adapting and producing CBC-TV's first Canadian play, Callaghan's *To Tell the Truth*, and later my own *The Ottawa Man* and Robertson Davies's timely *Fortune, My Foe* — made less of a sensation. But they were all exceptions to the rule.

In my new capacity I found myself functioning increasingly as a combination of fixer and hustler: fixing kinks inside the organization and hustling for audiences outside. The situation was uncomfortably reminiscent of my days as a wartime propagandist. ("On, bacons, on!") In fact, it was an incident connected with one of my audience-building stratagems that made me most sharply aware of my irrelevance.

Live television was a one-time-only affair; viewers' interest had to be seized in advance. Until we had stars luminous enough to draw that kind of attention, we needed to woo Canadian viewers with foreign stars in their eyes — the only brand most of them recognized. To this end I shamed Sir Cedric Hardwicke, over lunch in New York and the objections of his American agent, into putting his knighthood to honourable use for Canada, as he had during the war. For half his usual fee he agreed to host our principal drama series, titled (without a hint of irony) *General Motors Presents*. The stratagem worked. Hardwicke charmed both audiences and critics, telling all who would listen, including the *Globe and Mail*'s Herbert Whittaker, that "the CBC achieve[s] a higher standard than most of the American shows with far less chaos and panic."[16] But the incident I now relate was a by-product of his presence.

Sir Cedric (as I knew when I approached him) was particularly vulnerable to my appeal at that moment. Having divorced his first wife, Pixie, who needed no title to identify her as a lady, he had recently married an ambitious American starlet clearly more interested in the knighthood than the knight. The new Lady Hardwicke had been blotting the escutcheon. She accompanied him to Toronto for the first program, playing the role of prize nuisance while he worked liked the dedicated professional he was. To keep her out of the way during the dress rehearsal I was detailed to take this bauble to dinner, simply because I was the senior supernumerary available. As she recited her litany of complaints about geriatric husbands and the trials of the rich and lonely, I suddenly realized I had stopped tuning her out and was, in fact, drinking in every word she said: I was making mental notes for a character in a play.

It was at that precise moment I knew, once again, that I was in the wrong place.

Griffiths and I, both now 35, had done what we set out to do. Less than four years after starting from scratch in 1950, Canada had become the world's second largest producer of live television programs. "In Canada, because we have come lately into the field," I wrote in an early CBC-TV manifesto, "we have a rare chance to build anew, a rare chance to do something freshly Canadian."[17] We had been able to seize that chance only by taking a direct and active hand in the building. Today it was clear that if Griffiths were moved over (or possibly out) and I stayed to climb the ladder of the CBC hierarchy, I would be stuck behind a desk for the rest of my life.

This prospect turned me pale on the night I was invited to address the annual alumni dinner of my old high school, UTS. Each of my contemporaries, I could see, had firmly cast himself in a life role and adopted the appropriate makeup and costume. There was Z, the earnest tennis-playing Greek scholar (barely adequate at either), now a black-suited dog-collared clergyman with a fixed seraphic smile and blond hair as carefully curled as an angel's. There was Y, the class cynic, who had gone into banking and now boasted striped pants, a gold chain over his tumorous vest, rimless glasses, and sparse hair combed sideways over the top. There was X, the football hero, who had blossomed into a construction tycoon — everything in blossom from his nose and his beringed fingers to his shirt and his belly. There was W, the promising mathematician turned reporter, his tousled beard vying with stained tie, mismatched tweed jacket, and bags, to make absolutely sure no one could miss his scorn for convention. There was V, onetime skirt chaser and pinup connoisseur, shrunk to the propriety of grey flannel suit, school tie, and plucked eyebrows. I looked for (and missed) U, a close and brilliant friend, the son of married physicians, who had thrown away a scholarship on full-time gambling and was dressed, when last seen, in a dank tanktop and sockless sneakers; he would never have come. Then I realized, with a shock, that I myself had on the approved navy blazer and pressed slacks with white shirt, medium-starched, and — my only concession to exhibitionism — a bow tie. ("Mavor," Pierre Berton once quoted an anonymous friend, "would dearly love to wear a cape. He'd like to be a Bohemian, in the true sense.")

But how to escape such a fate? What were my options? I had burned my bridges to CBS in New York and insulted my hosts in the drama department of the BBC in London. In any case, Dilly and I had no wish to move. "I am," I had boasted to my fellow alumni at the UTS dinner, "among the first generation of Canadians to make a living here in the theatrical arts — at least to settle down with a house and family."[18] To make a living: if not in television, then in what?

My visits to New York and London had taught me that our most serious lack in Canada was a professional plant of sufficient breadth and depth to support the whole spectrum of performing arts. "Everyone is born an amateur," I told the columnist Alex Barris, "the question is: how fast can we learn?" If we want to contribute to the international scene, we must create "a situation where trading back and forth replaces one-way traffic."[19] This lesson was never more keenly driven home than when the first artistic director of the Edinburgh International Festival, Ian Hunter, gave a speech in Toronto soliciting Canadian participation. He had devoted considerable thought to the matter, Hunter said, and would like Canada to send over her Mounted Police to perform their incomparable musical ride. I was not the only one present to object to being represented by a company of horses, no matter how talented. But Hunter silenced us by asking what other Canadian attraction his international clientele would pay to see?

I should go back, I convinced myself, to what I first set out to be before world events and other bright beacons lured me off the path: a playwright, director, and producer. But this time I would proceed in a logical order. The first necessary step was one I had somehow skipped: to apprentice myself to a master director.

"I should not let the month go by," Alan Sangster wrote in the March 1954 *Canadian Forum*, "without at least a brief reference to the departure from the Corporation's television staff of one of the most able and gifted figures ever to serve the CBC in any capacity. Mavor Moore who has been, from the beginning, chief producer of television at Toronto, has resigned in order to return to the freelance field and will be seen during the summer as an actor in the Shakespearean Company at Stratford. One cannot be too caught up over his departure, however, for this is the third time that Mr. Moore has left the Corporation's fold and each time, after an interval, has bobbed up again, not like a bad penny but like a bright new one."

In case I felt any temptation to let the praise turn my head, the day after I left (for the third and last time) CBC management installed the dreaded time clocks for script assistants that I had kept at bay. And in due course Stuart Griffiths accepted the "less sensitive" post of supervisor of commercial relations, where his matchless executive talents could be safely exercised negotiating advertising rates with Imperial Oil, Labatt's, Lever Brothers, and other altruists.

11

Stratford to Mariposa

"I'VE GOT THIS GUY HERE. Could I bring him to see you? He'd like to come up to Canada to act, and he's a great admirer of yours."[1] The caller was a journalist with Maclean Hunter named Tom Patterson, whom I did not know; the time was April 1952, six months before CBC-TV was due to go on the air, and I was wary of red herrings with a line of flatter. But Pierre Berton had just interviewed me for his *Maclean's* article and I somehow connected the two.

If Hugh Carleton-Greene had the misfortune to look like me only taller, Tom Patterson looked like me only shorter: bald pate, horn-rimmed glasses, bow tie. His companion was a young New England academic enamoured of Canadian radio, whose presence became incidental as soon as Patterson explained, with the apologetic air that was to prove so effective on so many, what had brought them together. The American had heard a radio item about Patterson's dream: a Shakespearean festival in his hometown, the minor Ontario railway junction wistfully named Stratford. I knew nothing of this scheme, but one aspect of it caught my ear at once. Patterson was talking not of a half-amateur rent-a-production, but of a major effort to steal a march on the American competition — paralleling Andrew Allan's aim in radio and now ours at CBC Television. His optimism, however, seemed based on blissful ignorance of the odds. He had tried unsuccessfully to interest Laurence Olivier or some other out-of-reach star, when what he needed first was not an actor but an animator. Not Hercules but Zeus. I sent him to someone better acquainted with theatrical Olympians than I: my mother.

DMM's acquaintance with Tyrone Guthrie had begun in 1931 when he first came to Montreal to produce some of our earliest radio dramas, armed with an introduction from her cousin James Bridie. I knew him (as he knew me) only through my performance in his radio play *The Flowers Are Not for You to Pick.* In 1945, while I was still working in Vancouver, she made a significant reference to him in a letter:

> Incidentally, I heard that Tyrone Guthrie is expected in Montreal soon . . .
> I also heard through another source that Guthrie had written to the Arts &
> Letters [Club] offering to put on a production of Peer Gynt in Toronto —
> which offer had been declined. Such things make me mad.[2]

Guthrie, according to his biographer James Forsyth, had received a letter from his fellow Ulsterman John Coulter in Toronto, heralding a national theatre movement in Canada and inviting him to join it. Guthrie thereupon offered, if matters progressed, to come to Canada "at cost of transportation and maintenance only." For the opening attraction he was prepared to bring over his production of *Peer Gynt* with Ralph Richardson — the same one I had seen in wartime London the previous year.[3]

None of this (let alone much else about the theatre) was known to Tom Patterson when he sought DMM's advice in 1952. What had made her mad in 1945 was neither Guthrie's oversize offer nor its inevitable refusal, but wasting his interest in Canada on the chimerical notion of a National Theatre sprung fully armed from the brow of the Arts and Letters Club. By 1952 the climate had changed. The New Play Society and groups in other parts of the country had emerged to prove — with plays such as Coulter's *Riel* and Gélinas's *Tit-Coq* — that Canadian theatre had come of age. Guthrie had been kept informed of these developments by Coulter, by Brenda and Robertson Davies, who had worked with him at the Old Vic, and by his old crony Rupert Caplan in Montreal. So that when Tom Patterson dropped in on Dora Mavor Moore with his home-made bomb, she inevitably made what Arthur Koestler would call a bisociation. Guthrie was not only a possibility; he was *the* possibility.

By coincidence (that mother of twins) John Coulter was at the moment in London seeking Guthrie's interest in a West End production of *Riel.* DMM cabled him for help in reaching the director (thus engaging

Coulter's support) and followed the cable with a letter to be passed on. Guthrie replied, as she had reason to hope, that he was "most interested in the project, if it offers fresh possibilities for an advance in Shakespearean production."[4] All this was prelude to Tom Patterson's phone call, from DMM's office in Toronto to Annagh-ma-Kerrig in Ireland, in which a shot in the dark struck a willing target.

The story of the Stratford adventure has been told often. Here you will find only that part of it on which my own story sheds some light, and vice versa.

"IT REMINDS ME of my mother's house," said the giant as he stepped/stooped into our 135-year-old log house in July 1952. Unable to afford a hotel for his guest, Patterson had asked Mother to put Guthrie up overnight before the next day's drive to Stratford, and hoped he wouldn't mind. (He felt so much at home that he dried the dishes that night and often thereafter.) I first met him as he extricated himself like an unfolding giraffe from Patterson's Volkswagen, which brought them from the airport. The evening was hot, and we sat on the verandah, fanning ourselves with assorted brochures: Guthrie, DMM, Tom Patterson, and his wife, Robin; Harry Showalter, chairman of the Stratford committee, and his wife, Madeleine, who had driven from Stratford; Robert and Margot Christie, who had acted under Guthrie at the Old Vic; Andrew Allan; Dilly and I.

Seven years later, in a column for the *Telegram*, I fleshed out my notes of Guthrie's comments after he had quizzed Showalter and Patterson about the proposed festival, and the rest of us about the state of Canadian theatre:

> Since the whole advantage of the scheme, as he saw it, lay in starting with a clean slate, we should make everything from scratch: theatre, scenery, costumes. . . . Yes, we should certainly harness the current wave of activity in Canadian theatre and television, its actors, musicians, and so on. But we would have to bring in a few high-priced technical experts, and we must certainly have an expensive star or two for box-office. Then we could hardly start with fewer than two plays. . . .

> "You are going to need," he said blandly, "quite a lot of money." We allowed that money could be found — within limits. "Not good enough," he replied. "We simply cannot run out of change for Little Miss Muffett's tuffet the day before we open. Once we've decided what it's all going to cost we must get it in the bank first. And you'd

better face the fact that you're going to lose most of it, and may very well end up in debtors' prison."

There was a long pause. Then he put a simple question to us. "Is it making money you're interested in?". . . Harry Showalter, a bluff, transparently honest chemist and smalltown businessman, said gently but firmly: "We want to put on the finest productions of Shakespeare in the world." "Good," replied Guthrie with a warm smile, "because otherwise I should have gone home at once." . . . "The main thing," he kept saying, "is that we mustn't lower our sights." It dawned on us that already he had slipped into the use of "we" . . .[5]

After his return from Stratford with the board's signal to proceed, I brought him into the CBC Television plant to see our operation and to meet design, costume, and construction staff. Between his trips with Patterson to see performances in various theatres, I played him transcriptions of CBC Radio dramas to let him hear the voices of Canadian actors, on which he made notes. Among them was *The Best of All Possible Worlds*, my musical version of Voltaire's *Candide*, which became a source of lively debate when Guthrie, soon afterward, was invited to stage the Leonard Bernstein/Lillian Hellman *Candide* on Broadway.

When talk arose of performing the initial season in a tent, I steered Guthrie and Patterson to *Melody Fair*, an American summer stock outfit performing condensed Broadway musicals, with imported leads and Canadian supporting casts, in a large tent on the Canadian National Exhibition grounds. Having set up *Melody Fair*'s local auditions, I had few illusions about its standards but respected the expertise of the old hands running it: conductor Arthur Lief and director Leighton Brill. (Brill, a white-maned veteran of a dozen companies and almost as many wives, was pure New York flint. "Honey," he once told a posing soprano, "I'm gonna hafta cut off either your right arm or your left breast.") Guthrie sat quietly through both acts, then walked around outside, examining the tent from every angle. Once inside the car he said simply, "The tent's the thing."

When I saw the Guthries in London the following spring, he asked if I were interested in joining the enterprise. I said I was committed to television, which was in a critical phase, and thought I might be of more help on the outside. When Cecil Clarke of the Old Vic arrived in Canada as production manager, with his marvellous prop-maker wife Jacqueline Cundall and the ace costume-cutter Ray Diffen, CBC staff assisted them in finding equipment, making contacts, shopping, and acquiring help.[6]

Once rehearsals began I would slip down to Stratford whenever possible to watch the master at work. More than half the company were New Play Society alumni, and Louis Applebaum, who had scored some of my U.N. shows, was the musical director. Guthrie's clear vision of where he was going, and the alternating currents of delight and sarcasm with which he moulded the actors' ways of getting there, were a revelation. At an early dress rehearsal of *All's Well That Ends Well*, he mounted the stage to sort out a courtly dance that had fallen apart. For the courtiers he had imported a bevy of enthusiastic amateurs from nearby London, Ontario, who dissolved with laughter at their own gaucheries. As he strode past them on his way to the orchestra niche to hand Applebaum a note, Guthrie gave them a whiplash framed in a dazzling smile. "Fun, isn't it!" This, I told myself — watching approvingly from the sidelines — was the tough professionalism we needed.

When the triumphant 1953 opening ensured the festival's continuation, Robertson Davies, Andrew Allan, and I were added to the board of directors. Mother was made a patron, giving her honour without access, which vexed her. ("I am not a patron. I am a doer.") But suspicion of imperial Toronto is a Canadian condition. She was too close to "Tony" Guthrie; the use of the NPS office as an unofficial Toronto base, and of its workshops for auditions and costume-making, had exaggerated Toronto's importance in the scheme of things. No matter that she had used her influence freely in the cause, that in the final pinch it was she who had initiated the last-minute pledge from an anonymous patron (Vincent Massey) that had allowed the festival to go on, or that her later offers of winter jobs to Clarke and some of the actors were well meant. It was all read by some as ambition to forge a link between her Toronto operation and Stratford's. So patron it was. Briefly, because the following year she declined all formal connection, and settled thereafter into the more acceptable role of Mother Carey.

My appointment to the board, on the other hand, like that of Andrew Allan, had more to do with expectation than reward. The CBC — our constituency — was seen not as a local rival but as a valuable national ally in the coming expansion which, at that moment, led not east to Toronto but west to Alberta.

"Did you talk with Tony about his ideas for the West?" Stratford businessman Alf Bell, the board's vice president, asked me in a letter written shortly after the opening. "They have inspired us and we have had an official talk with Dr. Ned Corbett and invited some of the people responsible for the Banff School to come down and see what we are doing in the hope that they will take on a similar venture there. This would give us the chance of running six weeks at Stratford and moving the Company west for a run of several weeks, thus cutting our overall costs and making it a truly National venture."

The convivial home of Alf Bell and his architect wife Dama, at which I often stayed, was the festival's unofficial information exchange. More business was conducted in their garden than at the Stratford Chamber of Commerce. This latest letter was to prepare me for the next board meeting:

> We have had preliminary discussions with Tony before he left and he is willing to come back next year but suggests that we appoint Cecil Clarke as Director of the Festival and Tony would direct one play. . . . I gather his idea is to build Cecil and ultimately create a year-round job for him in Canada. . . .
>
> Our biggest problem, and one where I feel you can be of immense help, is our General Management. Without being coy, I'm sure you are aware that Tom Patterson, while largely responsible for this venture, is not good at administration. This has caused a great deal of heartache on the part of the board and it is obvious that [it] cannot continue in the future. We must have a strong administrator capable of creating an organization to carry on the work. . . . Everyone is most impressed with Cecil Clarke's ability but he wants to stay away from administration and develop from the artistic side. . . . Also we must find some name for Tom, because it is important to have him associated with the Festival if at all possible. This might be on a part time basis and ultimately rather honorary. . . . A permanent building is also a must . . . but this will have to wait until finances permit.
>
> This will give you some of the problems that must face the Board shortly. We know that this has gone over this year because of fortuitous circumstances and probably because we were too ignorant of the problems but the future must be properly organized. . . . Here is where you can help and I hope you will be forceful and positive in your recommendations and opinions. It's been a help to even write this down and we'll look forward to your visit. Hope Dilly is progressing as planned and in good order.[7]

The last reference is to the imminent arrival of Rosalind, our second daughter, which occurred on November 2, 1953. Mother and child returned from hospital just in time to catch the televised Eaton's Parade that was almost sponsored by Simpsons. The timing also made Rosalind a charter citizen of Metropolitan Toronto, the coalition of 13 municipalities that turned Toronto into Canada's largest city. This arrant imperialism was scoffed at in Montreal, but duly noted in nearby Stratford.

The Patterson "problem," traceable to Tom's justifiable exhaustion as much as his inexperience, seemed to me soluble if he were kept in the cabinet but given another portfolio — relieved of managerial detail and positioned to do what he did best: generate ideas, explore the future, and personify the festival's Canadian initiative. I submitted to the board an organizational chart, with (from my U.N. vocabulary?) a governing troika consisting of an artistic director (Clarke), a director of planning (Patterson), and a comptroller (TBA). This was implemented in September.

There was general agreement that the comptroller, in accordance with Guthrie's aim to make the project progressively Canadian, should be someone conversant with Canadian practice. Clarke, Alf Bell wrote, was willing to "assist and advise on the administration if, as looks possible, we have to get someone not too conversant with theatre. . . . We should move as quickly as possible . . . since decisions for next year must be made soon."[8] When I could find no one with appropriate experience willing to leave a long-term haven to leap into outer space (I even tried to talk Griffiths into it), we turned to the University of Toronto to see if they would release an experienced administrator on temporary leave. The trail led to Roy Loken, comptroller of the Royal Conservatory of Music, an institution long connected with the performing arts, who moved into position almost at once.

Just before Christmas 1953, Guthrie again approached me about joining the company.

"The readiness is all," Hamlet says. It was only a week since I had begun to question my future in television. To persuade Alec Guinness to star in the first season, Guthrie had urged him "to take part in a pioneering venture of a gallant and unselfish kind, a venture which, if successful, might have lasting and important results." Planning to make this second season his last, he urged on me the similarly gallant and unselfish gesture of making the venture Canadian. Eager to make it so, but unsure of how I might best contribute, I thought I would leave it to him. Here, after all, was a great actor-director-playwright-producer, like myself still active in radio-stage-film-television, giving me the chance of a lifetime to learn his recipe.

We discussed what I might do. He spoke of setting up a training program in which I might be one of the directors, but thought that in view of my experience, acting would be the most immediately useful talent. By the time I asked Dilly, who was game enough but concerned about the considerable drop in salary and about what might happen at summer's end, the mental die was cast. I telegraphed Guthrie a single word: YES. A letter came back offering me roles in all three plays: Baptista in *The Taming of the Shrew*, the Chorus Leader in *Oedipus Rex* (both directed by Guthrie), and Escalus in *Measure for Measure* (directed by Clarke). I replied that I would accept any roles he cast me in, but given a choice would prefer it if all three were not old men, and was Petruchio cast yet, and what about the directing job?

Before any answer came I received a phone call from Herbert Whittaker, who was obviously either clairvoyant or well connected. His column in the *Globe and Mail* the next day contained an item headed A CANADIAN STAR:

> Mavor Moore is likely to become the Stratford Shakespearean Festival's first Canadian star. The present [assistant] director of programs for CBC television has been offered an important role in next year's festival and is said to be considering quitting TV to go back to the stage.
>
> Mr. Moore would not reveal what part he had been offered but it is pretty certain to be that of Petruchio in *The Taming of the Shrew*. This is the play in which the British star, James Mason, will not be playing, and when he was here Monday, Cecil Clarke stressed the intention of Dr. Tyrone Guthrie, who is directing it, to make this play an almost completely Canadian effort. As yet, however, Mr. Moore says he has signed no contracts and, indeed, has not discussed his retirement from TV with CBC officials. . . .[9]

In due course the letter arrived from Guthrie, inviting me to play Petruchio in *The Shrew* and confirming that I would direct in the training program. I gave three months' notice to Mutrie and Bushnell, who were — considering they read it first in the newspapers — benevolence itself. I signed the Stratford contract as presented.

Then I went into training. With diet and exercise I went from 185 to 145 pounds. I returned to the Royal Conservatory — where John Drainie and I had once studied voice under Guthrie's own tutor, the visiting Bertie Scott — to take singing lessons from the reigning maestro, Ernesto Vinci. As an exercise in production, I presented on CBC Radio my musical adaptation of Stephen Leacock's *Sunshine Sketches of a Little Town*, on this occasion called *The Hero of Mariposa*, with Jackie Rae directing and arrangements by Howard Cable. ("Fast-moving and hilarious," said *Variety*, "it should have a hearing here.")[10] To work the rust out of my stage muscles, I used the month between leaving the CBC and joining Stratford to direct and act in *Spring Thaw '54*, which included, along with the return of Jane Mallett, a send-up of Stratford's *Richard III*.

Finally I hid out for a week in New York, borrowing the vacant Greenwich Village apartment of Vincent Tovell (now at the United Nations), to concentrate on the three plays. There the only rival for my attention was the television coverage of Senator McCarthy's comeuppance at the hands of an upright New England lawyer — a plot much indebted to *Measure for Measure*. After reviewing all the commentaries on *The Shrew*, I learned Petruchio's lines by rote, carefully avoiding any particular interpretation since I had no clue as to Guthrie's approach. Acting for so long under my own direction or my mother's, I knew, had led to self-indulgence. I made up my mind to do what I was told. I would be putty in the master's hands.

IT WOULD BE PLEASANT to write, now, that when the time came Dilly and I rented a pleasant bungalow in Stratford for the summer and drove the family down there in our top-laden Austin Mini, but that would be dull stuff. The reality was more romantic. Back in commando form, my armour polished, my lance sharpened, I leaped onto my white steed and rode forth to join yet another crusade.

Had I learned nothing from reading *Don Quixote?* Even before leaving Toronto I realized, from the geyser of gossip that erupts when a theatre company assembles, that, like Cervantes's cavalier, I had seriously miscalculated my coordinates. "When I changed status from Member of the Board to Hired Hand," I wrote to Loken, "I was particularly anxious not to behave like a privileged person . . . but I am wondering now if perhaps I am leaning backwards perilously far. In spite of the fact that I shall be just about the hardest-worked member of the entire company this summer, I discover that my salary is exceeded not only by some of the other Canadians but in some cases by those doing only two of the plays." Having signed a contract, I would not reopen the question of salary, but wanted to raise the matter of credit — not covered in the contract, I had assumed, because we would all be treated equally.

> When the brochure for the [Training] Course came out, I was a little surprised to find my name at the very end of those mentioned, when I have in fact taught many of those who preceded me. And when I saw the brochure for the Festival itself and noticed that not only were performers other than the star [James Mason] capitalized, but I was listed even further down the line, I was a shade put out.[11]

The reply came not from Loken — who was already on his way to becoming the first casualty of that confused season — but from Cecil Clarke, who was destined, although he knew nothing of it then, to be the last:

> Your letter . . . has disturbed me because I feel that it is not justified, if the objects of the Festival are to be borne in mind. Taking the question of salary first, it is not my business, but I would have thought that you were guilty of being somewhat soft in your bargaining and I feel that it is entirely your own fault and should not be blamed on this organization, if you have now found out that others are getting more than you. They argued about their offers and won.
>
> About "billing." There may be many other Canadian actors who feel the same way about this as yourself . . . I know that it must be hard on many of you to see Douglas Campbell and Frances Hyland featured, but it is laid down in their contracts and that is that. . . . I do not know how to end this because I am very distressed that we have our first case of "billingitis."[12]

And he signed his full name and rank.

That my bargaining was "soft," I fired back, "should have prompted a friendly word of regret rather than an adjuration to bear in mind 'the objects of the Festival.' The trouble would appear to be that I bore them too much in mind. I confess I had become accustomed to thinking of

221

the Festival in terms of contribution, and not as an enemy over whom one 'wins.'" I went on:

> In any case, I only raised the matter because I felt . . . that it represents an inequality which might in some part be redeemed by credit. But it appears I am as much at fault for arguing about this as I was for not arguing about money. And you do me the further injustice of suggesting that I have asked for "star" billing. I have not, Cecil, nor would I presume to do so . . . I completely endorse the principle of company unity. My complaint is that you do not seem to be honoring this principle yourself. . . .

> If the company is to be treated as a unit, you will find me one of the supporters of the cause most ready to submerge himself in it. . . . If not, you will understand a reluctance on my part to be found as simple about credits as I apparently was about fees.[13]

In return I received a handwritten letter addressed to "My dear Mavor" and signed "Cecil," pleading mutual misunderstanding. No "ranking" was intended and he was "indeed sorry if we give the contrary impression." As for "the salary business":

> I do believe most strongly that, in [the Festival's] present position, no actor should feel under any obligation to make sacrifices for the cause. The sooner everyone appreciates that actors are not beings who do things for love, the better for the profession. . . . Enough of all that, but do realize that if you feel strongly about salary matters, I will do something about it. . . . See you soon — no hard feelings — & above all, many good thoughts from us all for a brilliant success.[14]

Hell, had I felt strongly about "salary matters" I would not have been in Canada in the first place nor joined the Stratford Festival in the second. My motive, if it needed saying, was the very same sense of obligation Clarke believed "no actor should feel." And the half-truth that actors do not "do things for love" would have killed the budding Canadian theatre that made the festival feasible. At the same time I could not help noticing the irony of my position. Here, in all its glory, was the tough professionalism I had worked toward for so long — without, obviously, expecting it to be used on me. When I assured

Clarke I was not angling for a change in salary, he did "something about it" by equalizing the load instead: before the start of rehearsals I was relieved, without discussion, of my third role as Chorus Leader in *Oedipus Rex*.

But this was only a preliminary bout. The main mismatch was yet to come.

The Guthries were our neighbours in Stratford that summer; their garden backed onto ours. We could chat over the fence and occasionally visit each other. Judith was charming and Tony accessible. The strange thing was that although we talked about many things during the first few days, *The Shrew* was not one of them. I was given no hint of Guthrie's conception of the play or the characters, let alone a production plan or a look at the designs; not a whisper of a fantastical cowboy romp in mixed accents, or what Robertson Davies called, after the event, "a wild improvisation — an extravaganza — to charm and delight the audience without consideration for time or place."[15] All will be made clear, I told myself, at the read-through.

There was no read-through. Without a word of introduction, he had Petruchio and Katherina (Barbara Chilcott, equally mystified) mount the stage, book in hand, and improvise moves for their violent opening encounter. Ten minutes into the rehearsal he stopped us with one of his famous handclaps and said to me, "It's obvious you can't play him in the big style. Let's try a timid man."

Unaware of having played him in any style at all, I could only conclude that whatever Guthrie wanted I had failed to provide. Disappointed in his hope for a bullyboy, I thought, he's settling for second-best. I'd give him a bullyboy if he wanted one, and I said, "I'm just waiting to find out what you want." But the more I asked for guidance the more he asked me to try something else, as if each attempt were wider of the mark than the last. After three or four days of this, the putty turned to jelly.

For two weeks I tumbled and slithered about in a brilliant imitation of an untrained seal lost in a circus. Then my long and almost unbroken record of improbable theatrical accidents came to the rescue of all concerned. In a burst of enthusiasm (the only resource I had left), I tripped on the edge of the thrust stage and impaled myself on a metal trash can in the gulley. When I returned from hospital two hours later with both cracked ribs heavily taped, I attempted to continue the rehearsal where I had left off — about to execute an arm's-length swing twice around a pillar that would fling me into a grand stance in centre stage. Instead, to general merriment, it flung me onto my butt, writhing in pain, shame and, finally, defeat.

Suspending the rehearsal, Guthrie and Clarke took me up into the back seats.

> TG: I'm afraid this means you must give it up.
>
> MM: I don't think I ever had it, Tony, whatever it was you wanted.
>
> TG: Our best hope was your energy, and this has torn it.
>
> CC: We'll release you from the contract and pay you in full.
>
> MM: Why? There's still Measure and the training course . . . Escalus is arthritic, and I can cope with the directing.
>
> TG: (eye-checking with Clarke) Right. We'll carry on, then. Sorry about the ribs and all that. Let us drive you home.

On the way home I shared the back seat of the car with Bill Needles (who, it emerged, had already been told to stand by to replace me, after Don Harron, out of loyalty, had refused) and sat in burning silence while Guthrie, in front, discussed the parameters of the role he had neglected to discuss with me. Something about Harold Lloyd.

The most impressive thing about my elder Escalus in Measure for Measure was the way I modelled Tanya Moiseiwitsch's costume. But my dereliction was less noticeable here because the production as a whole was in serious trouble. Cecil Clarke's move from production manager to director was not working; the cast grew rebellious and Guthrie was forced to take over the final rehearsals. The season had therefore scarcely opened when Clarke, still the festival's artistic director, became its third casualty. From then on we were fellow walking wounded, and beneath our mutual civility there was an unspoken bond. We shared in a fateful experiment.

The share that mattered most to me was directing Philip Massinger's A New Way to Pay Old Debts with the apprentices in the training program. The classes were held in an old school nearby, free of the tensions of the tent, where I could apply the principles of human geometry I had absorbed from Guthrie but had been unable, for lack of a governing focus, to apply to myself. Everything else, every day, was like a hair shirt. Although my family was a haven, the mortification was driven home (literally) every time out-of-town friends dropped in — the Bissells or the Greenes, or Broadway producers Bob Whitehead and Roger Stevens — requiring a recitation of the decline and fall before Dilly could change the subject to refreshments.

What rankled was less the collapsed pride than the overwhelming sense of failure: mission unaccomplished. I had failed my family, failed the Mavors, failed my generation, failed the country. While former boardmates were kind and the old NPS gang (the Harrons, the Bochners, the Christies, the Hayeses, Peter Mews, Toby Robins) were supportive, most of the company sent me to Coventry — avoided me in the cafeteria, moved discussions out of my hearing, crossed the street when I appeared — whether out of embarrassment or animosity I could not tell. The sleepless depression of pariahdom was a new experience, and in my nightmares I conjured up the poor devil who tried to commit suicide from the CBC-TV transmission tower — except that this time instead of being at the bottom I was at the top, like a circus high diver cowering on his pinnacle while the crowd below kept yelling, "Jump, you yellow bastard, jump!"

"The train," I wrote afterward to Guthrie, "had been gathering a good deal of momentum over the last few years, and the derailment was a serious one, though fortunately not fatal."[16] In time we sorted it out; like Alphonse and Gaston, each was waiting for the other to make the first move. He asked me back to Stratford in 1956 (I did not go), and we contemplated other projects together, as we shall see. My saving grace in Stratford that summer, however, was James Mason.

James and Pamela Mason had a daughter, Portland, the same age as our six-year-old Tedde. The families became friends partly so the two girls could be thrown together. I use the verb advisedly, as Portland was a violent child given to smashing toys with an abandon that delighted her up-to-date parents. Tedde was her frequent accomplice in demolishing cardboard cutout movie sets that the Masons imported from California, which may have coloured her view of Hollywood for life. Portland's mother Pamela, an intercontinental missile born and bred in the world of film, hated everything about the festival, Stratford, and Canada: the old house they were in, the small-town inertia, the omnipresent churches, the fetid liquor stores, James's long rehearsal hours, and finally James himself for dragging her there. She believed his sentimental return to the theatre, for which she blamed Guthrie, was making a fool of him. ("I'm leaving," she announced backstage halfway through the first night of *Measure for Measure*, her voice carrying over the top of our adjacent dressing rooms. "I've had all of this I can take.") And James, like me, was having directorial problems, with Clarke in *Measure* and Guthrie in *Oedipus*. ("Don't you realize," Guthrie scolded him publicly, "that you're pulling the chain before you've done the job?") But through all vexations, marital and extramarital, he maintained a droll detachment about the course of his life that made a mockery of my self-pity. "It's nothing but a fucking bump," he said. "Have a drink and get on with it."

The premise was faulty, but the advice exactly right. There must be a better way, I told myself, of making Canadian theatre work. The popular musical perhaps — the glory of the modern stage. The trick was going to be to find a model of our own, neither Gilbert and Sullivan nor Rodgers and Hammerstein. Something was in the air. Halifax had recently seen *Bonanza!* by Chet Lambertson and Jim Richardson, and Vancouver's Theatre Under the Stars had mounted *Timber!* by Dolores Claman, David Savage, and Doug Nixon. A television version of my radio musical *The Hero of Mariposa*, retitled *Sunshine Town*, was already in the hands of CBC producer Norman Campbell.

With time on my hands I now devoted the remainder of the summer to writing a full-length version of the Leacock musical for the stage. It would require a cast of 40 actors, singers, and dancers, a full orchestra, period costumes, and sets designed to accommodate a locomotive entering the station, the burning of the Anglican Church, the sinking of the *Mariposa Belle*, and the 1911 federal election. "In the fall," the *Stratford Beacon-Herald* reported, "he hopes to produce *Sunshine Town* at the Royal Alexandra Theatre in Toronto."[17] On what, I had no idea.

MY CONNECTIONS WITH THE THEATRE, during my four years with CBC Television, had not been entirely severed. *Spring Thaw '50* was intended to be my swan song with the New Play Society. When it closed, DMM abandoned the Museum Theatre, hoping to find an alternative space to share with Murray and Donald Davis's Straw Hat Players. Neither space nor alliance materialized; and when she tried to reengage the Museum Theatre, she found the prime periods booked by a rival professional group, the new Jupiter Theatre. Without a venue for the winter, she presented only a Christmas pantomime at the Royal Alexandra, which despite its popularity lost money.[18] She was able to book the Museum Theatre again for *Spring Thaw '51*, her only means of recouping the loss, so I took time out from television to stage it. That done, I once more retired.

The following March she was again able to get into the Museum Theatre, presenting Shaw's *Arms and the Man* to favourable reviews but insufficient receipts — and again I felt obliged to take on *Spring Thaw '52* to balance the books. With the beloved Jane Mallett still the star, it generated enough profit for a single production that winter: an elaborate *Peter Pan* at the Eaton Auditorium, with Toby Robins as a flying Peter. (Robins, who adored her, often told how DMM handed her the script in the receiving line at her wedding to Bill Freedman, with instructions to study it during her honeymoon.) *Peter Pan* made a profit of more than $5,000, leading me to believe I was safely off the hook for *Spring Thaw '53* and all its heirs and assigns.

But DMM, after a difference of opinion with Jane Mallett (about what, neither would say), had built the annual review around a relative unknown: an English-born musical parodist named Anna Russell who had come to roost in Toronto. Already established on the touring club circuit, Russell had stayed at Dora's house while learning how to play the bagpipes — a proof of friendship she never forgot. She performed *How to Play the Bagpipes* and her operatic mishmash *Potted Met* at a money-raising concert for Dora's charitable Zonta Club. ("You don't need any stage-hands or union help," she says Dora told her, "so you are cheap to produce.")[19] The audience roared, so DMM engaged her for *Spring Thaw '53* and imported New York director James Light to stage it. Overcome by culture shock, Light promptly drank himself into oblivion ("A lesser Light," cracked Russell), and I was once more pressed into service. By chance the Metropolitan Opera Company was in town, and on the recommendation of some of his singers the Met's Canadian-born general manager Edward Johnson came to see what all the laughter was about. After that Russell's career soon went into orbit ("if that is the word," as she might say), but she left me well prepared to face my own operatic career, when the time came, without breaking down or breaking up.

Spring Thaw '53 was the most profitable yet. Its success permitted the New Play Society, now back in the Museum Theatre for the winter, to plan a full season starting in the fall. But that year the competition, like Toronto itself, had multiplied.

Jupiter Theatre, employing many of the same performers and with fine plays by Lister Sinclair and Ted Allan to its credit, had booked productions into the larger Ryerson Institute auditorium and the Royal Alexandra itself. And on the heels of Stratford's triumphant debut, the Davis brothers converted an uptown cinema, the Crest (with modest backstage areas left over from vaudeville days), into a legitimate house for a season commencing in January 1954. Challenged by Stratford's design and technical prowess, all three companies sought a higher level of visual polish. And their program policies, give or take an ideological nuance, were remarkably similar: the classics when affordable, new British or European plays when available, an American attraction when advisable, and a Canadian work when admissible.

Nathan Cohen, surveying the 1953 scene from his CBC microphone, saluted all this activity: "This is the year when the Canadian theatre achieved public recognition. And to this biased observer that's a development to be shouted jubilantly from the rooftops!" But in the same broadcast (possibly influenced by the failure of his own play *Blue Is for Mourning*, produced by Jupiter the previous year), he showed a disenchantment surprisingly reminiscent of *The Canadian Forum* article for which he had lambasted me four years earlier:

> In Canada, the arts matter only to a tiny minority. They continue to be . . . a rickety part of a shaky superstructure, maintained by a dedicated few, and recognized, mostly with passivity, by a somewhat larger group eager to prove that they are not entirely absorbed in material pursuits. . . .
>
> As a matter of fact, the pressures against the arts ever becoming creative in English-speaking Canada are quite formidable: our whole way of life shows that. We are psychologically married to the principles of caution and conciliation. Extremism and originality form no part of our character.[20]

Canada will have no lasting art, he said, "until we develop artists with a clear or significant vision of Canada and Canadian life, and the stamina, the will power to express and keep on expressing it." The message was designed partly to rebuke the imploding Jupiter, partly to warn the fledgling Crest, and partly to stiffen the resolve of Dora Mavor Moore.

The winter of 1953–54 had begun promisingly. Determined to lead off with a Canadian (and, at that time, feminist) statement, DMM persuaded the novelist Mazo de la Roche to give her the rights to *The Mistress of Jalna*, an unproduced sequel to her widely acclaimed *Whiteoaks*. To star in it she lured home her friend Catherine Proctor, a Canadian-born actress with a distinguished Broadway record. Despite these grand auspices, however, *The Mistress of Jalna* was a flop — perhaps because DMM entrusted its direction to Basil Langton, who among other failings was both British and male. Moreover none of the playwrights that followed — Christopher Fry, Mary Haley Bell, Herbert and Eleanor Farjeon,

Molnar, and Molière — was either Canadian or profitable. As April approached, the NPS had lost a total of $18,500.

This debt placed a heavy burden on *Spring Thaw '54*, the one I staged before reporting to Stratford. With Jane Mallett back, joined by a new comedian named Dave Broadfoot, it ran for five weeks — a long-run record for English-speaking Canada. But its profit was not enough to erase the deficit, nor its Canadian content enough to outweigh the numerous imports. By summer anyone could see that the society for producing new Canadian works, which only five years ago had boldly mounted six of them in one season and lived to tell the tale, was as compromised as it was broke.

My mother was now 66, and visibly tiring. The movement she had started seemed to have moved beyond her. She cancelled all plans for a 1954–55 season, relinquished the Museum Theatre, and sent me a copy of the report she delivered, as managing director, to the New Play Society's board:

> I would like to express my deepest regrets for having run the organization into debt. It has really knocked the stuffing out of me. . . . I would like to assure the board that if I could raise the money myself I would do so. As tangible proof I have taken no salary since November and have put into the New Play Society one thousand dollars on loan. My son Francis has underwritten the two-thousand-dollar overdraft at the Bank. I am . . . loath to put such a burden as this on a board composed of professional people.[21]

She thanked the stalwart president, Margaret Hyndman, Q.C., and the dedicated treasurer, James Kearns, C.A., for their patience and tolerance toward "one who must have been, at times, exceedingly trying," and turned her attention to the NPS school and the touring Mental Health plays she was developing with the backing of the Zonta Club. With no government granting bodies yet in place to appeal to, the volunteer board members (not a moneybags among them) were quietly approaching a few corporations and foundations with a view to giving the New Play Society a debt-free burial — but without much hope.

It was in the midst of these last rites that I landed back in Toronto, talking about raising $50,000 to produce an elaborate and untried musical comedy, to be followed with a full season in an as yet unspecified theatre, devoted entirely to original Canadian plays and musicals not yet in hand. Caught between the devil and the deep, the NPS appointed me director of productions. It was not the first time DMM opted, when she was down, to give the devil his due.

WHILE RAISING A FORTUNE, naturally, I must make a living. I plunge into the familiar acting market, only to find the demand for fallen idols particularly slow. Radio drama, still presided over by Allan, Willis, and Ljungh, now complemented by Kay Stevenson and Lola Thomson, is a lifesaver. And I soon become a regular panelist on the weekly quiz *Now I Ask You*, hosted by the bushy-eyed and bright-tailed journalist J. B. (Hamish) McGeachy. My fellow regulars are Morley Callaghan, foreign correspondent James M. Minifie, and a mysterious cosmopolite (ex-novelist, ex-circus tout, ex-boxer, ex-gigolo, ex-navy commander) then calling himself James Bannerman. But television, I find, is a different story.

Some of the directors so recently in my charge discover, to their distress, that they have no suitable role at the moment, or only the odd cameo that I would surely find beneath me. (In fact, very little is beneath me, except commercials.) The nadir is reached when producer Silvio Narizzano, a tangled talent whom I nursed through a protracted apprenticeship, sends me a one-hour script containing a 10-second shot of a bald man sitting at a bar . . . "if you would care to do it." Fortunately other former colleagues rally round, and David Greene — not one of the originals but a roving English actor dragooned into directing when I needed someone classically trained — restores my confidence by hiring me for such a variety of roles that the wig department keeps a separate box marked "Mavor's."

An important test, for me, is playing Judge Brack in Ibsen's *Hedda Gabler* with a cast of leading Stratford Festival actors, headed by Barbara Chilcott (my erstwhile Katherina) as Hedda, and Bill Needles as her husband Tesman. My nervousness gives the cool Brack a human core, for once, and we work splendidly together. When Pat Pierce writes in the *Montreal Herald* that "Mavor Moore has now joined that very select group whose name on a TV cast is automatic insurance of an excellent performance,"[22] I feel sufficiently vindicated to adopt a new rule of thumb regarding my acting fee: I will work for as little as anybody provided nobody is paid more.

The money, after all, is destined for a worthy cause: the Canadian musical.

The January 3, 1955, *Time* reported "an ambitious new television program aimed not only for [CBC Radio] *Wednesday Night's* rarified audience, but for a slice of the middlebrow music-and-drama fans as well":

> For *Scope*'s debut, Toronto's jack-of-all-entertainment Mavor Moore condensed Stephen Leacock's *Sunshine Sketches of a Little Town* into a 90-minute musical comedy of life in the fictional village of Mariposa. To stage *Sunshine Town*, producer Norman Campbell used 17 sets, manoeuvred his young cast of 32 with a properly lighthearted approach . . .

The timing was no accident. Immediately after returning to Toronto — with no capital whatever — I had tentatively booked the Royal Alexandra Theatre for two weeks, starting January 10, and Her Majesty's (last of the old Edwardian roadhouses) in Montreal for the following week. Then, to give the production a trial run before coming into Toronto, I booked the Grand Theatre in London for final rehearsals and an out-of-town opening on January 6. The *Scope* production — the first musical on CBC Television — would give *Sunshine Town* national publicity just before its London premiere, and more: royalties for me and for Howard Cable's musical arrangements, costumes and orchestra parts for later rental, and a cast with songs and dances already in their heads. It also meant extra income for the leading players Norman Campbell and I had settled on, as we had on the CBC's Jack McCullough for designer and the renowned team of Alan and Blanche Lund for choreographers. Unable to provide contracts, I could only ask them to "stand by" for the theatre tour after the television show.

My boyhood friend John Hayes, the Stratford Festival's able stage director, had agreed to join the enterprise as general manager, as soon as we could start paying him. Now neck-deep in promises, I could no longer postpone raising capital.

"For some time now many of us have wished that Canada might be represented in the world by creative exports commensurate with our material goods," I wrote to a list of prospects in Toronto, London, and Montreal, where Stephen Leacock had taught at McGill for 33 years. "The New Play Society, which has already made a solid contribution by producing . . . more Canadian shows than anyone else, is embarking on a new and exciting venture: in future all its production facilities will be dedicated only to the works of Canadian writers and composers." After describing *Sunshine Town* ("beloved Canadian classic . . . carefully chosen to arouse the broadest possible public interest"), I made the financial pitch:

> Since the NPS is a non-profit, tax-exempt organization, money for this challenging enterprise can only be raised in two ways: donations, or loans. To get the present plans under way, only fifteen thousand is needed, some of which has already been found. [I neglected to say that the latter consisted of a loan of $2,500 from my father-in-law, and that much more than $15,000 would be needed once we were "under way."]
>
> I am asking those who might be interested in sharing in the venture if they will lend me — personally — a sum (earmarked for "Sunshine Town") at an agreeable rate of interest for a period of six months.[23]

I was appealing over the heads of the usual cultural suspects (welcome as they were) to those unaccustomed to thinking of theatre as an investment, a tourist lure, or an exportable product; and to those likely to swallow art only in the syrup of entertainment. I lion-hunted in the financial pages, and then sought introductions from any intermediaries I could think of: schoolmates, teachers, army pals, parents of talented children, lawyers, dentists, artists married into wealth, and anyone with a link to Stephen Leacock, including his surviving brother George, the electrical engineer, who wore a perpetual fedora with holes in it and big boots that he propped on the desk to make sure you knew which Leacock you were dealing with. George (who always claimed Stephen stole those stories from him) gave me $100 and five other names — "All richer than I am, because of Stephen."

Broadway shows have long had the advantage of dunning audiences in advance with recordings and sheet music, so that they enter the theatre humming the hits. So I persuade BMI Canada to publish three of the numbers, and the Lou Snider Trio to record them. Armed with these, I make the rounds. You haven't read Leacock's book? I'll get Jack McClelland to send one right over! Concerned about our track record? Spring Thaw has made a profit for seven years running! Doubtful that we have the talent? Look at the Stratford Festival! Just made a donation to Stratford? Show your faith in private enterprise! Long-term prospects? Well, there's England, New York . . .

With such un-Canadian salesmanship the borrowed capital accumulates, but in amounts severely limited by congenital caution. "We're short a millionaire or two," I tell Hamish McGeachy one day after a broadcast of Now I Ask You. His jovial face falling into rich creases of thought, McGeachy says, "Have you talked to Jimmy Rattray?" I have never heard of him; his name is not in the papers.

As a young and illiterate prospector, Rattray had struck the richest gold mine in Ontario. Never married, he had withdrawn increasingly from business and now lived, tended by a succession of comely nurses, on a secluded lakeshore estate. At one end he kept a stable of horses and at the other a guest house for an even more exotic recluse, the Grand Duchess Olga, only surviving sister of Nicholas, Tsar of All the Russias. Fiercely tight with his millions, he had been known to back occasional feats of daring, such as swimmer Marilyn Bell's epic crossing of Lake Ontario, after which the beneficiary would join his small circle of friends. "He's lonely," said Hamish's wife Cynthia, "and he likes kids." "We're going on Sunday," said Hamish. "Why not bring the family?" By chance our seven-year-old Tedde had recently fallen in love with horses, and she and old Jimmy hit it off at once. After tea, during which I said my piece, he took me into his study. "Look," he said, "I don't give a shit about the theatre. People and horses are more interesting. I think you're nuts, but interesting. We've had a good time, and I want you to come again. Would $5,000 help?"

The rehearsals were hysterical, and not only on account of the absurdly short rehearsal period for a new work. Free to talk and sing in the familial accents, old character hands like Christie, McKee, Paul Kligman, Beth Amos, Drew Thompson, and young singers like Robert Goulet and Jacqueline Smith — not to mention the crew — were continually breaking up at moments of self-discovery. Here were no Democrats or Republicans but solid Liberals or Conservatives (with Dean Drone's brother Edward running on an independent platform suspiciously like the CCF's), and not a single elected judge — only old Pepperleigh, appointed by the Crown, which is to say by God.

In the staging, the Lunds and I look for a relaxed style to fit Leacock's deadpan humour, not at all the conventional Broadway zip and flash. The sets are modelled on soft-hued Edwardian flip-up postcards. No show-off arias or end-of-number plaudits interrupt the action; high spirits are natural; the finale, like Leacock's, is gently wry.[24] The music (in critic Chester Duncan's description of the radio version), is "not a poor Canadian imitation of a Broadway musical" but "just itself." It is left to the only American in the company, conductor Arthur Lief of *Melody Fair* (by now immune to Canadian excuses) to call the parade to attention and keep the troops in line.

Without Lief's discipline in the pit and stage manager Grania Mortimer's cool head backstage, *Sunshine Town* might not have survived its Thursday, January 7, 1955, opening night. The local union orchestra and stage crew were oversize, overscale, and therefore underrehearsed. The technical effects were amazing only in that they sometimes worked. But the audience was on our side when they faltered, and the *London Free Press* was able to report the improbable: "Mavor Moore has a hit on his hands — audiences have a treat in store."[25] Only John Hayes and I knew, that night, that we might not open in Toronto on the following Monday.

Ernest Rawley of the Royal Alexandra has demanded his two weeks' rental in advance. By now we have used up all my borrowed capital and are living on ticket sales. Hayes generously cashes in some personal bonds, but we are still $5,000 short, with the banks closing for the weekend. So I spend Friday, the only day we have to doctor the show, racing around London trying to raise cash. I reach two of my early backers, lawyer Joe Jeffery and surgeon Charles Isard, who between them lend me an extra $2,500. As I thank Isard, I ask desperately if he has an approachable friend. "Try Doug Weldon, London Life." From the nearest phone booth I call Weldon (later my precursor as chairman of the Canada Council) and talk my way past his secretary. "Sorry," he says, "I'm leaving for Europe in 15 minutes." "I'll be there in five," I say and hang up. But there is no taxi in sight. Running several blocks, I step into Weldon's office as he is donning his overcoat:

WELDON: My God, I thought I'd got rid of you.
MM: Here's my card, Mr. Weldon.
WELDON: What do you want?
MM: Twenty-five hundred dollars.
WELDON: And Jeffery and Isard are in on it?
MM: Yes.
WELDON: Okay. (*handing me a cheque*) So long. (*goes*)

The whole thing is straight out of Leacock's Whirlwind Campaign to save Mariposa's Church of England Church, in my first act.

In Toronto, where DMM once more showed her mettle by hawking songs in the lobby, business was brisk — despite a first night I described in a letter as "Amateur Night in Hog's Hollow." The musicians' union, attempting to force Rawley into a new long-term theatre contract, had chosen our opening night to strike; Rawley countered by telling them

Mavor Moore would conduct from a piano in the pit. Taken in by this fairy tale, the union yielded, and after a sketchy rehearsal the curtain rose. What saved us was the row among the critics. On one side were Robertson Davies ("a very Canadian show, handsomely presented"), the Star's Jack Karr ("bright and cheerful"), and Canadian Press ("catchy tunes, clever lyrics, bright, light comedy and brilliant choreography").[26] On the other was the Telegram, with two separate reviews blasting our failure to come up with a Broadway hit — both of them promptly disavowed by the managing editor.[27] The Globe and Mail's Whittaker, risking self-parody, came down on both sides: "Sunshine Town may seem a little quiet, even markedly homegrown, but there is no denying that it has its own qualities of endearment."[28]

The full measure of the rift became evident on our last night when I was handed a copy of a telegram sent by the Toronto Women's Press Club to their Montreal branch:

> THE CLUB HAS FALLEN IN LOVE WITH THE WHOLE HAPPY PRODUCTION OF MAVOR MOORE'S SUNSHINE TOWN. COMING YOUR WAY FOR ITS OPENING THIS MONDAY. AFTER A TWO WEEKS SUCCESS IN TORONTO. THE PRESENTATION IS A WONDERFUL PIECE OF LAUGHTER BEAUTIFULLY MOUNTED AND ACTED. AND WE THINK EVERY MONTREALER WILL FALL IN LOVE WITH IT TOO. WE'D BE GRATEFUL IF YOU WILL ALL INTRODUCE YOURSELVES IN PERSON TO OUR NEW MUSICAL FAVORITE AND MAKE A BIT OF A FUSS OVER IT IN PUBLIC AND IN PRIVATE AND BY WORD OF MOUTH.

Despite such exceptional (and irregular?) support, the response in Montreal was the reverse of Toronto's: the critics united in praise while audiences stayed away. "The first Canadian musical comedy of any stature," the Montreal Star's Walter O'Hearn said. "Better fun than the productions of South Pacific or Oklahoma which played here."[30] From Toronto? his readers asked. Incredible! Novelist Hugh MacLennan wrote letters to the editor blasting the "Canadian-colonial" mindset of his fellow citizens, swearing that in his book "Pajama Game couldn't hold a candle to Sunshine Town."[31] The London Free Press reported that "Montreal critics were so incensed by lack of English population support of Sunshine Town that one . . . wrote: 'The one right you have in the theatre is to stay away. But why practice it on this splendid show?'"[32]

It was too late to stay for an answer. In a frantic effort to survive we returned to Toronto for a week ("by popular demand"), and then back to London, to close with a whimper where we had started with a bang five weeks before. When it was all added up, the production had cost not $50,000 but $75,000, and I owed $30,000 — $10,000 in out-standing accounts and $20,000 in personal loans.

On the morning I awoke to the gravity of my situation, about six o'clock, I was sitting in my pajamas on the edge of the bed when I became aware that Dilly had awakened, too. I turned to her and said, "Well, I started with nothing and I'll start with nothing again" — and methodically began to get dressed. I knew exactly what I had to do. It never occurred to me, at the time, to ask why it was that only six months earlier I had been plunged into a black depression by a con-tretemps over a summer job, while now, faced with financial ruin, I felt an equanimity bordering on euphoria.

12

The Five-ring Circus

THE AVENUE THEATRE had no stage. A plain box-frame cinema next to a vacant lot on Eglinton Avenue near Avenue Road, an area being smartened up, it had only the bare essentials: an entrance lobby, washrooms, tiny offices, raked seats and a screen two yards from the back wall. Its sole recommendation for use as a live theatre was that it was due to be torn down and was up for rent in the meantime.

While *Sunshine Town* was out on tour, DMM had gone into real estate. She was looking for a new site for her NPS School, and a new theatre. Reverting to its natural bent, the Museum Theatre was now a thing of the past. She was determined not to allow the losses from *Sunshine Town* to sink the rest of our plan: a theatre devoted to our own works. If anything, she thought, the experience had underlined its urgency: "Our great problem," she told her steadfast board, "was getting enough people to believe in a Canadian production which was wholly Canadian. When are we going to wake up to our own potential power? I hope before the remainder of our talented young people have left for greener pastures of appreciation and opportunity."[1]

An entire season of Canadian works had never been attempted. But where were we to find the means? "In effect," I reported to the board, "I shall have to take on myself the responsibility of paying off the loans out of income."[2] Each *Sunshine Town* creditor was approached and asked to wait; some reduced the debt; a generous few wiped it out. By writing, acting, and directing in Toronto and New York, with journalism added, I was confident I could repay the remainder within a year. There would be a fifth ring to the circus, because the NPS had its own debts, and only one way to meet them: *Spring Thaw '55*. DMM and I agreed that the Avenue Theatre had possibilities.

And so, for topical satire, had the year 1955.

Winston Churchill was replaced by Anthony Eden, a more inviting target. The United States–Canada DEW line, recently strung across the north, made Canadian sovereignty moot and the Natives justifiably restless. President Eisenhower's secretary of state, John Foster Dulles, was practising "brinksmanship" in Europe and Asia (abetted by the CIA, run by his brother Allen), while next door in Central and South America the generals played musical chairs with guns. The Warsaw Pact, an East European chorus conducted by the Soviet Union, found harmony elusive as the Malenkov–Bulganin–Khrushchev Trio jostled for the podium. Rock and roll seeped from the underground, and Disneyland was built on top.

All of this was grist for *Spring Thaw's* mill, but we had never taken *Spring Thaw* seriously. To DMM it had always been little more than a happy bonus, a lark by and for a younger generation. She would do anything to promote the show, yet she often felt left out and sometimes embarrassed by it. Politics and current events were not among her main concerns, and she often suspected that in-jokes were slipped by her. When I was at hand, she trusted my judgement. But despite my keen interest in national and global affairs, the truth was that I myself had considered *Spring Thaw* a sort of end-of-season blowout, a chance to play the fool while making money to subsidize weightier fare. Events now conspired to show that both of us had underestimated the hardy perennial.

After *Sunshine Town* ended in February 1955, I went to New York to see about a summer job at the United Nations. Back in the international whirl I was once again stirred to indignation by its gravity and to laughter by its absurdity, as I had been five years earlier when I found an outlet in *The Best of All Possible Worlds*. My notebook bulged with ideas for sketches far outside the Toronto scene. But friends among the transplanted Canadians in New York — Bob Whitehead, Hume Cronyn, Jessica Tandy, Dan Petrie (who tried to get *Sunshine Town* on the *U.S. Steel Hour*) — thought I was missing a bet. In post-McCarthy America, they said, political satire was still an endangered species. Pointing to the impact of CBC's *The Investigator* on McCarthy's downfall, and to the success of Wayne and Shuster's literate lampoons on *The Ed Sullivan Show*, they argued that for the serious satirist, at the moment, Canada was a better vantage point than America.

To date *Spring Thaw* had been deliberately parochial, on the premise that those who are not themselves will always be less than those who are. But I was beginning to see that with sufficient purchase on our own roots we could confidently reach out and tackle the follies of a wider world. If we were to enlarge *Spring Thaw*'s range and sharpen its presentation, it might become a model, an incubator of satirical material for other stage revues, for radio, television, and film, in Canada and abroad.[3] (In due course *Spring Thaw* alumni such as Stan Daniels, Rich Little, Alan Manings, Peppiat and Aylesworth would become pillars of *Laugh-In*, *Saturday Night Live*, and other outspoken U.S. television programs and films of the era.) There was too little lead time to turn *Spring Thaw* '55 into such a model, but we could make a start.

On my return I approached stockbroker Percy Gardiner, Helen's father, and got $500 as a deposit on a lease for the Avenue. We built a thrust stage over the first dozen rows of seats and barely adequate dressing rooms, with a single toilet, in the vertical space behind the screen. Simultaneously we opened a box office and sold tickets for a show not yet written, composed, or cast. What might follow it was even less certain.

Rehearsal time was so short before the April 27 opening that we had to divide the labour and coordinate the structure carefully. Choreographer Gladys Forrester, pianist Marian Grudeff, and composer Ray Jessel joined the team, and Bob Christie shared the direction to allow me more time to edit and assemble the bits and pieces. With Jane Mallett attending to social affairs and Dave Broadfoot minding the politics, we set out to rectify the shocking lack of Canadian content in the programs of the National Ballet and the Mendelssohn Choir. *Beaver Lake* ("the first truly Canadian ballet") was a northern fish hunt danced entirely on snowshoes[4] to a set of variations on the world's best-known Canadian song, "The World Is Waiting for the Sunrise." For the Choir, we commissioned a contemporary oratorio from composer Godfrey Ridout. With the finale of Ridout's "Handel Home Owners with Care," a fugal feud between developers and conservationists over Rosedale's forested ravine, we pioneered a way of ending such confrontations that has been universally copied: declare an intermission and clear the stage.

Spring Thaw '55 ran for a record seven weeks and paid many bills (my loans excluded). In my report to the board I stressed the "stringent penny-pinching rules . . . put into operation at the start," and the "extra profits . . . squeezed out of every possible source, such as the [soft] drink and ice-cream bars." In noting that "the NPS is the only theatrical organization in eastern Canada which functioned all this winter in cooperation with ALL the entertainment unions," I attributed the leniency of the musicians' and stagehands' demands to guilt over their treatment of *Sunshine Town*. We ended up with $2,500 and a choice of future courses: "One is to become as active as possible, the other to do as little as possible and concentrate on a production of *Spring Thaw* in 1956." I was clearly mutating from artist to entrepreneur.

For some reason I also included in that report my plainest manifesto yet, urging all and sundry to emulate American enterprise, not its products:

> I do not believe for a moment that the theatre (any more than any other means of expression and communication) is necessarily "a good thing." It depends entirely on what use it is put to. I have never seen . . . any point in trying to convince people to come to a theatre — merely on the grounds that it is a social activity — to see there something they can see better done on television, the films, or even in another theatre. In . . . Toronto we now have excellent facilities for seeing the best that Hollywood, Broadway, London, Rome and Paris can produce, besides the fruits of our own television. WHAT WE DO NOT HAVE THE OPPORTUNITY OF SEEING IS A CANADIAN REPRESENTATION OF CANADIAN LIFE. . . .

> A fresh start is made . . . by building on what we have here . . . with vigour and honesty, not with borrowed polish. American poetry got nowhere until Whitman dared to ignore (not adopt) the polished techniques of the rest of the world. American music is filled with forgotten pieces by forgotten composers who learned their European lessons, and sneered at Gershwin, who didn't. . . .

> Our aim . . . must be to leap over the conventions of the time in Britain and America into the future. . . . We should use [our theatre] to put on Canadian plays which will start Toronto, then Canada, then the world arguing and talking. We will never do it by making bad carbon copies of what is already growing dated in London and New York.

"We can do it, without breaking our necks," I concluded with a revealing non sequitur, "if the winter's bill of fare is judiciously planned to include other activities of another kind for which we rent out the theatre but do not tax our production resources."[5]

The board took the option of lying fallow for a year. We found groups willing to rent the Avenue for commercial runs of Broadway successes, while we prepared for a revitalized *Spring Thaw* '56 and a full winter of Canadian attractions to follow. DMM set up her school in new quarters and, like Finnegan of song, "beginnegan." Dilly and I went to Stratford to see Lorne Greene make his Stratford Festival debut as Brutus in *Julius Caesar* before dividing forces: she and the girls went off to the Faessler cottage in Muskoka while I headed for New York and a salary.

STRATFORD, CONNECTICUT, HAD MISSED the boat. Before Tom Patterson dreamed his dream the New York Theatre Guild's Lawrence Langner had dreamed of a monument to the Bard on the banks of the Housatonic. Ontario's Stratford beat him to it with a tent. But Langner persisted, and in July 1955 opened his theatre with another *Julius Caesar*, also directed by a Briton, Douglas Seale, and starring two Canadian expatriates: Raymond Massey as Brutus and young Christopher Plummer as Mark Antony. As the closest Canadian spy, I attended the glittering opening night incognito.

After 10 splendid minutes of Roman panoply, the evening came progressively unstuck. The theatre was fashionably functional, but the stage was a compromise between Edwardian proscenium and contemporary apron that figuratively fell between two stools. The figurative became real in the dramatic quarrel scene when Massey, as uncertain of his moves as he was of his lines, sat angrily on a three-legged stool that beat him to the floor. From that point on no recovery was possible. By intermission, the time chosen by Langner to read messages of congratulation from Winston Churchill and half the Anglo-American establishment, about a third of the audience had departed. Langner plowed on, randomly mispronouncing names, and finally invited onstage "the English ambassador," who strode sonsily up in a kilt and Prince Charlie jacket to make it "pairfectly clear" that he was the British ambassador. He got the biggest hand of the night. I telegraphed Alf Bell in Stratford, Ontario: "WHAT CONN CANT CAN CAN."

Within a week I saw a third production of *Julius Caesar*, an American television version directed for the *U.S. Steel Hour* by the Canadian Dan Petrie. I thought it the finest of the three and wrote Petrie to tell him so.

241

Two days later he rose at dawn to fetch his *New York Times*, only to find his *Caesar* murdered in print. He dressed and went directly to the office of the series' producer. The producer had not yet arrived, but already pinned on his desk blotter by some eager rival lay the murderous clipping. Petrie retreated to his own office to prepare a resignation, read my letter, and decided to fight back. "All this intrigue," he said on the phone. "It's like ancient Rome, eh?"

"Come to the United Nations," I replied. "I'll show you ancient Rome."

EVEN LESTER AND MARYON PEARSON had seen *Spring Thaw*. I found it unnerving, while working on such grave matters as technical assistance to African farmers, to be greeted with a laugh every time I met our secretary of state for external affairs in the corridors or the Press Club. (When he became prime minister and I his television coach, there was always the risk that he would slip into the old *Thaw* mode and ruin his carefully rehearsed sobriety. Still later, when his government became the butt of *Pearson's Pets* and other *Thaw* sallies, he took them in his stride; but she was not amused.) It was not the first time I noticed that others had difficulty deciding which cap I had on at a given moment: the fool's cap, the skull cap, or the black cap.

When I first saw Mike Pearson in action, I thought he was a visiting professor caught at high altitude without knowing which airs to put on. At the United Nations, where diplomats seldom write their own speeches and depart from the text with caution or regret, Pearson's informality made him the pet of the media. When diplomats extemporize, newspapers drop, sleepers awake, earphones sing, and pencils cock. Will something slip out? Will we hear, for once, what the messenger thinks and not the echo of instructions? Pearson's reputation owed much to his mastery of the conversational equivalent of exhibition canoeing. Disarmed by his earnestness and by that incurably unheroic voice, observers failed to notice that while the current boiled and bubbled his craft hardly moved. The illusion of progress was almost perfect. He would inflate an issue with the air of candour, while saying nothing his listeners didn't already know but were flattered to hear confirmed by an insider. Pearson was no dissembler; he had simply perfected a method of keeping secrets by giving away truisms. This feat gained him such respect among his fellow diplomats that when he took a stand on the Suez Canal dispute in 1956, his plan was at once widely accepted as the product of independent meditation uncontaminated by platitude. Like that of Ralph Bunche before him, it was a technique worthy of the Nobel Peace Prize. But even though I saw what he was doing at the time, or thought I did, I failed to foresee that one day he would use it on me.

A more immediate catalyst in my life, among the acquaintances struck that summer, was George Ivan Smith, an Australian broadcasting pioneer on a fast track to the upper echelons. (G. I. Smith became a valued adviser to Secretary-General Dag Hammarskjöld, accompanying him on many of his world travels.) Armed with imagination, energy, and purpose, he and his wife Mary were out to embrace as much of life as time and fortune allowed or they could get away with. I spent an occasional weekend at the family farm near Lake Success, a retreat always enlivened with some combination of their five children (two of his and three of hers), where the activity was contagious and the talk riotous. Domestic affairs and sheer nonsense had equal time with world affairs. As he listened to George's "'Stryne" in full flight one day, his young son Tony (attending a New York school) said, "Dad, you towack funny!" So we dropped everything to have a contest to see who talked funniest. My Canadian won easily. But one Saturday night the guest was abruptly inducted into the family.

The oldest daughter, Penelope, whom I had not met, was late for dinner. In her early twenties, she arrived in a whirl of Titian curls, eyes gleaming in a pale face, pursued by demons. Her conversation was as incandescent as her appearance, and she seemed able and willing to talk about anything, including the demons. At 16, she unhesitatingly confided, she had been raped by a thug in Central Park, and her world had turned into close-ups and flashbacks. (Thereafter periodically anorexic and alcoholic, shedding partners, including John Osborne and Kenneth Tynan, along the way, Penelope Gilliatt rose to be one of the world's most influential film critics. "You met her on the one night she came to our farm," her father wrote me shortly before he died in 1993, "and typically at 7:00 a.m. the next day, Sunday, remembered she wanted to be at a New York theatre, for which I put her on the bus. The story of her life; always she arrives anywhere with departure in her head compulsively.") For me her story connected with a different compulsion, and it caught me by surprise.

I suppose a first encounter with the actuality of rape, in those suppressed days, would have made any man examine his assumptions about men. Since I was past shock at what men were capable of — look at

Hitler; look at my father; look at me! — it forced me to revise my assumptions about women. I had been raised by a strong mother, with the help of a series of sturdy housekeepers, each several cuts above the deadbeat she had married. Inspired in my youth by more than one invincible great-aunt and powerful female teacher, I was now blessed with a staunch wife and two daughters already promising to be more forceful than strictly necessary. It seemed to me self-evident that the generality of women were tougher and steadier than men. But if I was right, what good did it do them in the face of such random brutality? And if I was wrong, what terrible dangers they must face every day! Worse still: was I really 36 years old and only now asking these questions?

As usual, I dramatized the internal debate. For CBC-TV I wrote a veiled account of my crossed-purposes episode with Guthrie at Stratford, with the actor now a woman and the play *As You Like It* — in which Rosalind (a role associated with my mother) disguises herself as a man to avoid violation in the forest of Arden. Adapting *The Best of All Possible Worlds* from radio to stage (as *The Optimist*, Voltaire's subtitle for *Candide*), I elaborated the role of the highwayman Cacambo, already changed from male to female, into a woman dressed as a man so she could travel with the naive Candide and save them both from assault. Once back in Toronto I agreed, for a brave new theatre in Chatham, to direct Shaw's *Pygmalion*, which I now saw as a tale of attempted intellectual rape: the weak, over-mothered Higgins tries to make Eliza his "creature," but Eliza turns the tables and becomes the master (mother?) of her male "creator." To make the point, I used as narrator the overmothered Shaw himself.[6]

The question was inescapable: was I dramatizing these deep waters, or was I adrift in them?

That winter I necessarily put all such introspection aside as I plunged into another whirlwind campaign to restore my bank balance — writing new plays for radio and television, adapting old plays, recycling my old scripts. My hope that *Spring Thaw* would become an incubator of material for others bore fruit when Harvey Hart proposed a satirical year-end retrospective, *The Best of '55*, for CBC Television. Supplementing the old with the new (including a sharp Len Peterson travesty of the festival syndrome, wherein Paris, Ontario, tries its hand at an annual Folies-Bergère), Hart and I solicited sketches and songs from across the country, building a network of writers for the future.

And all the while, the unsinkable DMM and I were plotting a 1956–57 year of Canadiana at the Avenue Theatre.

The plans for *Spring Thaw* '56 included a five-city tryout tour before the Toronto premiere. The critics noted the additional polish of the performances and the decor, the costumes of Suzanne Mess, and the "consistently high level" of the material as it ranged from tomfoolery to pointed caricature, although they seldom agreed which was which. We had recruited new writers and composers, including Lyn Howard and Stan Daniels, and a new head of publicity: the truehearted and incorruptible sportswriter Trent Frayne. Herbert Whittaker said: "*Spring Thaw* does the incredible in '56 — it tops its own reputation."[7] But no reviewer (in the absence of Nathan Cohen) seemed to grasp the dimensions of the transformation.

This version of *Spring Thaw* was the first year of the Formula. After all the experimentation, I had a clear sense of what I wanted: a commedia dell'arte troupe of precisely four women and five men, all able to act, sing, and dance, whatever their primary skill. With time to audition properly, Alan Lund (the now and forever choreographer), musical director Marian Grudeff, and I cast the tightly knit company with great care: a principal comedienne (Barbara Hamilton), a soubrette (Diana Laumer), a dancer (Sheila Billing), a female singer (Margot Mackinnon), a principal comedian (Dave Broadfoot), two character singers-comedians (Paul Kligman, Andrew MacMillan), a male singer (Robert Goulet), and a "fifth business" (Peter Mews). We were obviously assembling the nucleus of a permanent year-round company, although that, too, went unnoticed.

The pattern of the show was equally precise, filling two hours and 20 minutes, including one 15-minute intermission, the first half lasting 70 minutes and the second 55. With enough material now being submitted to allow rigorous selection, we were able to commission additional works on neglected topics, following a design instead of depending on last-minute assembly. The more intellectually demanding material was put in the first half and the horseplay in the second, since I had found that a thinking audience appreciates being allowed to relax while a relaxed audience resents being made to think. We set each section in place in order of its importance in the dramatic scheme. First, the act 1 finale (to send them into the lobby exhilarated); next, a physically energetic production at the apex of act 2 (to push laughter to the limit); third, the act 2 opener (to rekindle the fire); fourth, a substantial sketch halfway through act 1 (on a major target); fifth, the opening number (insolent). If all of these met the test, almost anything worked as a closing number. The rest was filler — often, as in any collage, the hardest to get right.

The set, costumes, and properties must dance — with as much flexibility and speed as the performers — while providing a unifying design. Locale had to be changed with the flip of a symbol. Since versatility is made a point of, each actor must be instantly recognizable (by hair colour or other trademark) throughout the various roles. The formal principles followed most closely were those of music: contrasts in mood, tempo, volume, and style, and alternation between frivolity and cutting edge, hope and outrage, frank laughter and punctured dignity. The objective was to leave no customer unsatisfied or unchallenged for long, so that everyone would enjoy at least half the show and consider it a bargain. Success was measured by how often any two critics' lists of the best/worst items in the show cancelled each other out.

This emphasis on control and structure, I knew, was bucking the trend toward collective improvisation beginning to emerge from counterculture comedy groups such as Chicago's Second City. But Dionysus always needs Apollo to kick around. And in addition to my colleagues' welcome insistence on discipline, at this stage of the game in Canada, I had begun to notice that it reflected a deep psychological need of my own: to reduce the chaotic outer world to a pattern I could cope with, and to bring order and symmetry to my fragmented inner world. Overreaching, overworked, overdrawn, I was holding myself together with an armature of aesthetic discipline.

And the formula was working, for the moment, on both fronts. By the end of its record three-month run, *Spring Thaw* '56 had erased all the debts of the New Play Society, including the outstanding loans from my mother and myself, and provided enough capital for us to open in September with a full winter program.

The windfall also brought me time to deliver some necessary but unremunerative broadsides.

For the summer issue of the *University of Toronto Quarterly* I wrote an essay on the new nationalism in the Canadian theatre, deliberately choosing that in-house organ to dissect the "internationalism" of the academic establishment. When France sent La Comédie Française to Montreal and Toronto, I noted, the gesture was hailed as an example of internationalism, while the return visit of Le Théatre du Nouveau Monde to Paris was seen as an exercise in nationalism. A neat verbal ploy was concealed here, like the anthropologists' insistence that big powers have "civilizations" while lesser societies have "cultures." Art may be *supranational*, but *internationalism* in art requires both nations and something to move between them. If instead of producing something of our own we merely adopt forms developed by others, I argued, we would "deservedly end up with a carbon copy of someone else's personality, recognizably Canadian only in its weakness." My ending was blunt:

> What matters in the long run is not that we are Canadian, but that *because* we are Canadian we have an unparalleled opportunity to contribute something new and vital to a world that . . . expects it of us. If we miss the chance, our face in history should be not only blank but red.

In the same vein I addressed the 25th national Couchiching Conference in Geneva Park, Ontario, on "The Impact of Television in Canada." The target this time was the head-in-the-sand business crowd that believed us immune to cultural invasion. The Winnipeg industrialist Thor Hansen, for example, had said: "Culture is something you cannot buy, something you cannot import, something you cannot learn or produce at will. . . . Culture is something that evolves out of the simple, enduring elements of everyday life . . ." This invited a debunking:

> Mr. Hanson and I cannot have had access to the same history books. Does he seriously believe that we are *not* subject to influences other than "the simple, enduring elements" of our own local everyday life? Has he never met a Canadian Indian and asked him what happened to his folk arts and crafts (let alone his religion)? Do Africans acquire a taste for motion pictures by some sort of internal combustion? Does he really believe the youngsters of today learn their folk-songs from crooning mothers when even the mothers get theirs from billion-dollar recording industries?

Then I took on the optimists who believed television could simply be kept out of sight:

> We may as well face the fact that we have invented a medium that *succeeds* in holding the mirror up to Nature. Young people are now going to get an increasingly broader, clearer, and honester impression of what their elders are like, and what their ideals undergo in practice.[8]

247

The *Optimist* was an appropriate title with which to open the New Play Society season in September 1956. Written at the United Nations (with irony intended) as *The Best of All Possible Worlds*, it had first been produced on CBC Radio in 1953 and enthusiastically reviewed in Variety as well as Canada. I drafted a stage version during the next year, only to learn that composer Leonard Bernstein was working on a musical *Candide*, to a libretto adapted from Voltaire by Lillian Hellman, for Broadway the following season. Had someone shown Bernstein the *Variety* review?

Tyrone Guthrie, who had heard a recording of *The Best of All Possible Worlds* before being invited to stage *Candide* in New York, discussed the two treatments with me in some detail. The approaches were quite different: mine a chamber operetta, Bernstein's an elaborate opera buffa. I used Voltaire as narrator and in various cameo roles throughout; he did not appear in Hellman's libretto.[9] I made a major scene out of Candide's visit to El Dorado; Guthrie thought "the city of gold" best left to the imagination. I dispensed with the Old Lady (Bernstein's best elaboration) and instead changed the highwayman Cacambo, dispensed with by Hellman, into a woman. Hellman's realistic version used a huge cast; I turned the story into a nightmare for Cunegonde and Candide by having 11 people they knew at home appear as all the characters in their odyssey. But still, my ace was looking at a very high trump.

In view of all my pontifications about indigenous theatre, furthermore, *The Optimist* barely qualified as an opening production for an all-Canadian season. There were only three things Canadian about it: my words and music, the pertinence of Voltaire's parable to my wildly optimistic fellow citizens, and the fact that I stole it first. It would have been more appropriate to open with Don Harron's dramatization of Earle Birney's picaresque war novel *Turvey*, but that would not be ready until December. We decided that valour was the better part of discretion and went ahead.

We were confident that we had a strong team: the select *Spring Thaw* corps augmented by leading singers from the Canadian Opera Company, including Alan Crofoot, Ernest Adams, and Alexander Gray. Robert Goulet had his first leading role as Candide (after which Thunder-ten-Tronckh turned out to be within driving distance of Camelot). Gladys Forrester shared the direction with me; the set was by Richard Knowles, the costumes by Suzanne Mess, on her way to becoming one of North America's premier designers; and Howard Cable's arrangements were conducted by Mario Bernardi — the future maestro grande's first appearance in the pit.

The Optimist was rewarded with laughter, friendly reviews, and an extended run of eight weeks. (It closed a month before *Candide* opened on Broadway — not, in its first incarnation, successfully. "My direction," Guthrie wrote, "skipped along with the effortless grace of a freight-train heavy-laden on a steep gradient.")[10] But much of our audiences' evident pleasure came from disregarding the message. When Voltaire (Drew Thompson) dryly pointed out that both factions in the local war had God on their side, he drew a chuckle. When he went on to read the casualty list, the audience fell about with laughter:

> The discharge of cannon you heard neatly laid flat about six thousand heroes on each side; the musket bullets then swept away — out of the best of all possible worlds — nine or ten thousand scoundrels that infected its surface. The bayonet was next the cause of the effect of death in another five thousand; all in all, about thirty thousand heroes went to their reward. So that the prayers were eminently successful.

I was becoming used to the fact that people had difficulty seeing past my smile to my teeth. (I remembered how *Gulliver's Travels* had been defanged for children.) After the radio version, my excruciatingly banal love duet ("Perfectly lovely! Simply divine! You are so perfect I wish you were mine!") was called by the *Star's* Gordon Sinclair "as catching a ballad as ever came from the piano of a Cole Porter, Noel Coward or the great Gershwin." After seeing the stage version, Herbert Whittaker wrote: "Lovers of the happy musical must be assured that it is a most cheerful kind of pessimism that Candide acquires, and that the satire Mr. Moore distilled from Voltaire is of the most cheerful brand."[11] I was ready to dismiss Canada as a land of optimists blinder than Candide, when I read Martin Stone in the Communist *Canadian Tribune:*

> The Optimist . . . dissects society with a sharp scalpel. It is witty, intelligent, adult and it has considerable application to our own day. One puzzling post-script: why did none of the critics from the three Toronto dailies mention the point of the play? Do they, with Pangloss, consider ours the best of all possible worlds?[12]

For the weeks following *The Optimist* DMM and I had agreed to lease the theatre to an independent production of a new work, *Three Rings for Michelle,* by the Canadian playwright Patricia Joudry. This fitted into our plans both philosophically and practically, giving us a break before our Christmas attraction, *Holiday Party,* an innovative musical happening for families, with pianist David Ouchterlony and singer Bill White, and designed to arouse interest in the wealth of Canadian choral music.

An exotic specimen of *auctor Canadensis,* the glamorous Joudry arrived in Toronto from Montreal in the early 1940s with an impressive record in a tough medium — situation comedies. In addition to her Canadian credits she had scripted *The Aldrich Family* for NBC Radio in New York. In 1953 Andrew Allan presented her sensitive play about teenagers, *Teach Me How to Cry,* on CBC Radio. Staged in New York in 1955, it was called "one of the best plays of the season" and went on to be filmed as *The Restless Years.*[13] *The Sand Castle,* a satire of psychoanalysis, went from CBC-TV to the Margo Jones Theatre in Dallas. *Three Rings for Michelle,* on the explosive topic of fundamentalist religion, therefore came with both artistic and commercial pedigrees. But the play, the direction, the reviews, and the empty houses proved equally murky. Its backers lost their investment, and Joudry and her husband moved to England. There, despite promising overtures, she became best known for a series of post-obit plays by George Bernard Shaw, dictated to her from his spectral desk on the Twelfth Plane. These ghostwritten works have regrettably devalued her own.

But *Three Rings for Michelle* gave both me and DMM time for other ventures.

CBC Times, October 21–27, 1956. TV Documentaries — a Bold New Series:

> CBC-TV's boldest venture to date in the documentary field will be launched at 10:00 p.m. on October 23 after many months of planning. It will be a one-hour program called *Explorations* and, in the words of planner Eric Koch, will explore our society, our origins and the physical world around us.
>
> *Explorations* will make use of many different television techniques — dramas, film documentaries, discussions — to present subjects from science, law, history, industry, labour, education and society in general. The host will be Mavor Moore . . .

I was also writing a good many scripts. Two years earlier, while composing *Sunshine Town,* I had visited Orillia, Leacock's model for his fictional Mariposa. A concerned friend drove me to the writer's famous summer house on Brewery Bay, left to his son Stephen Junior, who apparently seldom used it. The place was in disrepair, abandoned to weeds and weather. My driver, fully intending to shock me further, led me to the half-open back door, allowing entry through a filthy kitchen, its sink piled high with old dirty dishes and verdigrised cutlery, into a billiard room where a once fine table was collapsing under a pool of water from an overhead leak. The library, its bookcases faced with grilles, seemed intact. But in the study soiled clothes spilled from a closet, and the desk was strewn with unfinished letters blotched with long-dry ink from a broken fountain pen. Typed manuscripts lay on the floor. Bullet holes were clearly visible in the living room's vaulted ceiling. Although my grandfather had known Leacock well (they were fellow economists), I knew nothing about the family's domestic affairs. Rumours about young Stephen's wild parties had not reached me, nor word of a plan brewing among the writer's admirers to purchase the house and restore it as a Leacock memorial. But what kind of son, I thought, would allow this to happen to his father's memory? Then an afterthought hit me like a returning boomerang: what kind of *father!*

In Orillia, whose citizens Leacock had disguised only thinly in *Sunshine Sketches*, people were sensitive about stolen identities. When I later wrote a play called *The Well*, about the disillusioned offspring of a black humorist, my models were said to be the Leacocks, *père et fils*, and I had to issue a denial in the *Packet and Times*. Stephen Junior pronounced the idea "far-fetched."[14] The truth was that the visit to Brewery Bay had given me — thrust on me — an idea for a play, not about the Leacocks but about my father and myself. A son acts out, in real life, the hell his father cynically exploited in his sermons, *because the son alone takes them seriously.* Soon afterward I was hospitalized in New York with an illness diagnosed as nephritis, an often fatal kidney disease. Transferred to a Toronto hospital, I lay for a week obsessed by my atrophied relationship with the father I now appeared to be in danger of predeceasing! I then sat up and for three weeks filled a notebook with a strange half-factual document: a dying moralizer's letter to his estranged son, rationalizing his misspent life on the ground that life itself is immoral. The letter is deposited with a lawyer, to be delivered after the father's death, thus giving him the last word. The exercise banished the nephritis symptoms, and in due course yielded the play called first *The Well*, then *The Son*. In it the son, taking the father's confession as gospel, creates his own hell until, of course, his last-minute rescue by a strong woman.

While the Joudry play occupied the Avenue in November 1956, this play about my own inner space was presented first on radio, and then on television — at the same time as I was hosting *Explorations*, which was all about "the physical world around us." Only Nathan Cohen, then CBC-TV's drama editor, asked me if the two were not inversely related. In both productions of *The Son*, the father was played by Andrew Allan (a father figure), and the son by young William Shatner, who promptly carried the tape with him to Los Angeles and took off for outer space.[15]

During the same weeks of early December 1956, my mother (who had never driven a car since her early dustup with the Model T) embarked on one of her periodic missions requiring my help as chauffeur. She was mounting a Nativity play with the mental patients of the Ontario Hospital in Whitby, an hour's drive east of Toronto. A social worker named Doris Holliday, familiar with DMM's long-standing interest in mental health and her skill at "bringing people out of themselves," had persuaded the superintendent, Dr. Donald Fletcher, to try an unconventional experiment.

The Virgin Mary, as I recall, was a schizophrenic. Joseph, who had to carry a heavy staff, was a murderer. The First Shepherd, who "lights" the onstage fire, was an arsonist. A woman gospel reader, when rehearsals began, had spoken to no one in two years. The cast and crew of 48, and the choir, were all patients. The single performance took place before approximately 700 fellow patients and friends.

"I know nothing about psychiatry," DMM afterward reported to the provincial minister of health. "I am only a teacher of art. I can only treat those taking part as I would a group of students." Having worked out the text and music with the Jewish, Catholic, and Protestant padres, she tackled the other elements:

> We wanted all this experience to be a "home project," so with advice and some designs from outside . . . we were able to carry out in home surroundings the entire construction, painting and erection of a very fine set; the dyeing and making of costumes; and the erection of (borrowed) stage lighting. . . . The program cover design in linocut was also done by a patient.
>
> It was a rewarding experience for me as we came nearer and nearer to the great night and I became familar with these people, and was greeted with huge smiles, whereas near indifference, for the most part, had

been the attitude at our first meeting. Then when the night arrived, there was no confusion, all was orderly, and each of the 48 players was anxious not to let the play down. There was no prompting — none was needed. In the still tableaux, the actors were so still that I held the tableaux 30 seconds longer than I could have done with a normal cast. . . .

What remedial effect or permanency this experiment has achieved for those taking part, it is not for me to presume to voice an opinion, but I am convinced that the dramatic form of expression, with all its attendant artistic activities, could develop possibilities under proper and experienced guidance.[16]

Dr. Fletcher came to the same conclusion in his medical report:

It reaches every class of patient and can be used in every degree of illness. . . . [I]t is almost unbelievable how willing, even anxious, all patients are to take part. It is effective. A high percentage of those taking part are out earning a living and the rest, almost without exception, are obviously making a better adjustment than before.

I think the secret is that Drama takes them into a legitimate land of make-believe which they can share with others, and thus get a limited harmony with their own environment, which can then be easily extended as the fantasy (or play) life blends into the workaday world. The staff get a new outlook which has been reflected in the care of all patients.[17]

The experiment was repeated once, at Easter, but Fletcher died within the year and the government discontinued its support. One of the few miracles I have ever witnessed, it also prepared me for an experience with a fictional mental hospital, in the months ahead, that almost destroyed my own "limited harmony."

While the holy day was being reenacted at Whitby, we had Holiday Party running at the Avenue, and Turvey, Don Harron's adaptation of Earle Birney's army novel, rehearsing in a downtown warehouse. Turvey, with Bob Christie directing Douglas Rain in the title role, opened in mid-January with half the character actors in town crammed into the narrowest dressing rooms in the country, doubling madly between scenes by switching rank, unit badges, and division flashes on their uniforms, thanks to patches of the newly invented Velcro. I could not help thinking what a brilliant technique it would have been for confusing the enemy in wartime.

But while engaged in these frantic frontline manoeuvres I was also concerned with the grand strategy emerging from headquarters in Ottawa. The Canada Council had just been formed. When I wrote about its advent in the January 1957 issue of *Canadian Commentator*, I could hardly foresee that 22 years later I would be in charge of its policy-making.

> It is ironic that federal support for the arts was finally brought in handsomely by the back door after having been so long refused entrance at the front. . . . As recently as this spring, government spokesmen were temporizing on the recommendations in this area of the [1951] Massey Report, blandly enumerating stumbling-blocks which everyone recognized as footling. Whence the dawn?
>
> Happily four separate problems have come to a head at about the same time: the increasing urgency of the university crisis, the necessity of supporting such successful ambassadors abroad as our Stratford and National Ballet companies, the desire of the government to re-establish its concern . . . at home, and the existence of a considerable surplus. . . . Presumably the interest on the principal will be distributed in the form of grants to organizations, individuals and groups. . . . But if this is the simple and obvious course, it is also the lamest.
>
> This is a country in a hurry. Its cultural pattern — when it holds still long enough for one to catch a glimpse — is in a state of precipitation. In this flux landmarks arise and are swept away, movements spring up and as suddenly dry up. . . .
>
> The real danger is that the "safe" way will be taken — that grants will be made only to elder and respectable institutions and individuals so rigidly traditional that they repress the genuinely fresh impulses among us that will eventually count. This danger will be multiplied a thousand-fold if — as is far from improbable — the Canada Council itself is composed of sterling citizens as notable for their thickheadedness about the creative process as for their hardheadedness in politics and business. . . . We need a council made up not of cautious pillars of society but of shrewd gamblers.

It is conceivable that I wrote those words knowing that the New Play Society, insofar as government grants were concerned, had backed itself into a peculiar corner. While chartered as a nonprofit organization, and highly eligible for public support for its money-losing contributions to Canadian drama, it had succeeded in subsidizing itself — with a single annual bonanza, from which its producers were not permitted to profit. Meanwhile DMM was running a theatre school (not eligible) on a shoe-string, and I was still paying off debts by taking on every job I could find, including that of "cultural editor" of the new monthly, *Canadian Commentator*.

Despite their healthy runs, every production in our Canadian season at the Avenue Theatre, to that point, had lost money. Once more, only a gamble could save us. We opened *Spring Thaw '57* on March 1, a month earlier than usual, with almost the same team and cast as the previous year. We had the formula down pat by this time, and it worked like a charm.

Among the spellbound was Brooks Atkinson, the principal drama critic of the *New York Times*:

> *Spring Thaw* is a satirical review mainly concerned with Toronto topics. It is written with skill and humour and briskly acted by nine amusing performers and singers. It is civilized without being egregiously clever and it has a fresher score than those to which Broadway has turned its tin ear this season.
>
> Although all of *Spring Thaw* is entertaining, the Bopster's version of *Hamlet*, called "Something Cool in Denmark" [by Don Harron] is particularly witty. For the spacious rhythms of Shakespeare is substituted the curt, contemptuous argot of the bopster. When Hamlet stabs Polonius, for instance, Queen Gertrude gets to the point much more directly and laconically. "You goofed," she says.
>
> Nobody goofed in any department of *Spring Thaw '57*.[18]

Opening a week after *Turvey* closed, the show had been a tremendous effort for all concerned, and more than ever a strain on my domestic life. Dilly was six months pregnant, yet even while at home I was catching up on past-deadline writing chores. I was also due to begin rehearsals for a television drama: an adaptation of Chekhov's short story *Ward Six*, directed by Harvey Hart. *Ward Six* tells of a Russian psychiatrist who establishes such an extraordinary rapport with a patient in his mental hospital that he cures the patient (played here by the American actor Jack Klugman) at the expense of his own sanity and ends up trading places with him. During the rehearsal period, a number of developments conspired to put me dangerously close to the doctor's shoes.

The first was that Atkinson's review had sparked speculation about taking *Spring Thaw* on a national tour, possibly even to New York. Certainly if we were to hold such a talented team together we would have to keep them busy. The second was that Tyrone Guthrie had expressed an interest in staging *Turvey* in London, if suitably revised, and in looking at *Sunshine Town* for the same purpose. The third was that Lorne Greene, in demand as an actor in New York and Hollywood, thought he could keep one foot in Canada by becoming active as a producer; he and I discussed forming a company (for which he undertook to raise the money) to take *Spring Thaw* across Canada, then to Britain, then to New York, as a first step in a larger plan. But it was the fourth complication that turned rehearsals for *Ward Six* into a nightmare.

Whether or not she was frustrated at having so little to do with the efficiently running *Spring Thaw*, or resented my exploration of its exploitation, my mother began to give notes to the cast and crew, in my absence, contradicting my directions. One night I arrived before the show to find one such argument in progress and told her to leave the theatre. It was an echo of my first altercation with a producer, long ago at CBC Radio, when I ordered George Taggart out of the studio, saying, "One of us is leaving," knowing he knew I was the one who had to stay. DMM stood her ground like a lioness for about 30 seconds and then walked out.

We did not speak again for two years.

I survived *Ward Six*, thanks to the patience of Harvey Hart and the sensitive partnering of Jack Klugman, only to catch myself in a whirl — too disorganized to be called a series — of completely irrational acts. I would write dozens of letters to the editor and not mail them; shout obscenities to myself as I walked down empty streets; fall asleep at noon and spring to life at midnight; and go on long, fast drives after phoning Dilly to tell her, absurdly, not to worry. During meetings and rehearsals, my mind would dart chaotically from topic to topic, while my hand, insisting on the imposition of order, drew three-dimensional structures on any paper within reach. One moment I seemed to be at the top of my form, the next without any form at all. Our longtime family doctor, Jim Gillespie, had me subjected to a thorough physical examination, and then sent me to a psychiatrist.

James Grant was noted in the profession for his bluntness. It was said that when he was in general practice a woman once called at midnight to say that her child had not had a bowel movement all day. "Madam," replied Grant, "neither have I," and went back to bed. When we met, it took him about half an hour to reach a diagnosis. "You, sir," he said, "are a manic-depressive. Like every artist I've ever come across, you also have obsessive-compulsive tendencies. You have a guilt complex, you have a mother problem, and I expect they're related." "I thought I had a father problem." "That's his problem. Yours is your mother. I don't know how the hell you've lasted this long without going berserk." "Neither do I," I said. "Tell me more."[19]

I must be careful not to oversimplify complexity. Manic-depressive psychosis is an intricate and contentious illness about which much more is known today than when I was diagnosed in 1957.[20] Characterized by alternating periods of elation, gloom, and normalcy, it follows a cycle dictated by the body's chemistry that is unrelated to the events of real life. I found this the hardest factor to grasp: that on one day I could receive a million dollars and still feel glum, and on another be arrested and feel great. Now also established as genetic, the disease has various degrees of seriousness, and different therapies work better in some cases than others. In 1957 there was still vigorous debate between the champions of psychoanalysis and the believers in drug therapy, of whom James Grant was one. At our next meeting he suggested I keep a daily record of my moods for a month; if the changes proved to be cyclical, he would put me on a course of levelling medication for nine months. Meantime I was to drop everything and go away for two weeks.

How does one explain to physicians that one cannot stop working and still pay one's bills? I did what seemed the next best thing: hoping the trip would pay for itself, I decided to fly to London to explore the possibility of British productions of Turvey and my own musicals. To alleviate my parental guilt, I suggested to Dilly that I take 10-year-old Tedde with me; in return for sight-seeing she was to do our washing in the hotel room. Leaving Spring Thaw in the hands of my colleagues, I set out for London with Tedde within three days.

Despite the generous assistance of various friends, especially Bernie and Barbara Braden, my advances were coolly received. James Bridie/ O. H. Mavor was no longer alive to give advice. A London production of Bernstein's Candide was already a possibility. The Optimist was doomed either way: if Candide worked in London, my Voltaire was dead; if Candide flopped (again), Voltaire was dead. The barrier was no longer condescension toward the colonials; Stratford's reputation, the success of the Australian Summer of the 17th Doll, and the West End appearance of the Crest Theatre's The Glass Cage, written for the Davis family by J. B. Priestley, had changed all that. Indeed London-based Canadians were being scolded for not turning out, as the Aussies had done, to support the home team. The recipe needed was a configuration of timeliness, public demand, a producer, and a theatre. *The Optimist* had none of these.

Through the Bradens I got the script and recording of *Sunshine Town* to Hugh "Binky" Beaumont of H. M. Tennant, the most powerful producer in London, who recommended it to theatre owner Prince Littler. (A high?) Later I wrote to Braden: "Beaumont tried to engage Prince Littler's interest but Littler had none to be engaged."[21] (A low?) Tyrone Guthrie, who had earlier expressed enthusiasm for staging *Turvey* in London if Harron's revisions were to his liking, was directing at Stratford-upon-Avon. I took him a copy of *Sunshine Town*, and he replied: "I think it is very charming; I loved it; but I do think it needs quite a lot of work. . . . If you are interested, I have views about several possible lines of approach; and I don't doubt that you have several more! . . . Can we meet?"[22] (A conditional high?) Above all he encouraged Lorne Greene and me to form a company as a vehicle for such works.

There was one encounter so mixed in its effect I found it impossible to rate in the log. I took young Dorothea-known-as-Tedde to meet her namesake, her Great-Great-Aunt Dorothea, still confined to her automated bed in Frognal Gardens. Lady Butterworth was now 79 and tired of life. The astonishing beauty and vivacity that had lasted into her sixties had thickened and slackened; her hands had become puffy and useless. Flashes of fire and glee still lit up her eyes, but between flashes all was closed and dark. When I told her of the situation with Mother, she said, "How sad for Dora. How lucky for you." Then she burst into a raucous laugh that died with a dismissive sigh. She eyed Tedde appreciatively for some minutes before speaking:

DOLLY: Why don't you call yourself Dolly, like me?

TEDDE: Because I don't think of myself as a Dolly.

DOLLY: Neither did I.

TEDDE: Then why did you call yourself that?

DOLLY: I didn't. *They* did. And I hated it.

TEDDE: Then why didn't you change it?

DOLLY: I did, several times. But then I rather got to like it. I called my daughter "Thea," so we wouldn't get mixed up. Your "Tedde" — is that from the "thea" part?

TEDDE: I suppose so.

DOLLY: You'll change it. Many times. In the end it doesn't matter. What's more important is what you are. And then what you do. What are you going to do?

After our return events moved swiftly, as did the corresponding notations in my daily log. Lorne Greene and I incorporated our company and set up a one-room office, right next to that of Canadian Actors' Equity, in a corner of the old Jarvis Street mansion where Vincent and Raymond Massey grew up. I worked on budgets while he raised $50,000 in promises on the telephone. Then he took off for Los Angeles while I announced the formation of Lorne Greene and Mavor Moore Productions, Limited, at a May 30 press conference attended by the *Globe's* Herbert Whittaker:

> After consultation with Dr. Guthrie, Mavor Moore, recently returned from England, reports that . . . if [Turvey] were to be redirected it would go to the West End under the joint auspices of Mr. Moore and Lorne Greene. Mr. Greene and Mr. Moore have other West End plans, too. . . . [But] he has nothing to report . . . until after consultation with Mr. Greene, who is due back from filming in Hollywood next week. . . . The immediate Greene-Moore plan involves a Canadian tour and West End showing of *Spring Thaw*.[23]

Once back in Toronto, Lorne wanted to proceed immediately with a trans-Canada tour. He raised another $25,000 in promises, and then returned to Hollywood for "an important audition." On June 12 *Spring Thaw '57* celebrated its 105th performance, breaking the existing long-run record, and looked good for another month. With plans almost complete for the tour (but none of the capital actually in hand), I signed winter contracts with three of the crucial performers — Barbara Hamilton, Dave Broadfoot, and Robert Goulet — and started negotiating with the others.

On June 25, 1957, Dilly and I, with the help of Dr. Gillespie, welcomed a third daughter, Marili, named after Charles Faessler's sister in Switzerland. What a world she was coming into! Sputnik One had just launched the space age; the first computer language was upon us; Jack Kerouac's *On the Road* hailed the beat generation. To cope with all this, what had we provided her with? What price nature and what price nurture? To what extent are we free to invent ourselves and to what extent the slaves of biochemistry? The graph in my psycho-log was beginning to look like the humps of Ogopogo. What would Marili's graph be like, or become?

Soon after that Lorne returns to town, comes into our office, plunks his large frame into the chair on his side of our desk without removing his trench coat, presents me with a pair of black-and-gold Comedy and

Tragedy cuff links in a box marked HOLLYWOOD, and asks, "Mavor, how do you tell your best friend you're a shit?" He has just signed a long-term contract to star in *Bonanza* and must leave at once.

Since no money has yet flowed from the outstanding promises, he offers to pay the outstanding bills. But there is the matter of the contracts . . . and the tentative bookings . . . and everything else. I drive directly to Jim Gillespie's medical office and wait until he can see me. I ask about the results of the tests. "I could give you the fancy names for what showed up," he says, "and you may even have some of them. But they're all stress related. You have a simple choice, laddy. Either you stop what you're doing, all of it, at once, or your wife can use the money to buy you a beautiful coffin. When's your next appointment with Jim Grant?" "July 10." "That gives you a week to sort out what you have to. Then you're going to do what he says."

The manic-depressive waves were indeed systematic and predictable, with little perceptible relation to the ups and downs of the real events just described. Events long past, such as Dr. Blatz's insistence that I not marry my first love, made sense for the first time. I started on medication immediately. The tour was cancelled. With the consent of those concerned, the three contracts were voided. I resigned from the New Play Society, leaving its future (bolstered by the profits from *Spring Thaw '57*) in the hands of DMM and the board. Then, as I wrote to Bernie Braden, "Dilly and I distributed the kids between camp and kind friends and took off on a holiday."

We had no sooner returned than I received a call from my old mentor John Holden, back in Toronto to direct Agatha Christie's *Witness for the Prosecution* at the Crest. I had not acted onstage since my debacle at Stratford. I had never worked at the Crest, simply because I thought it would be disloyal to the NPS. "Now that you're free," Holden said, "isn't it time you did both?" It was something pleasant and regular, I thought, helpful to the medicinal process, and once running would give me time at home during the day. When it opened in mid-September, *Witness for the Prosecution* became a critical and popular success for the theatre, for Holden, and for me. But I could hardly help noting that my professional career was back where it started 20 years earlier in Bala: acting for John Holden in a pretested British hit, in an English accent and even, this time, in an English barrister's periwig.

And once again I had not the faintest idea of where I might be going afterward — except that the "I" would be a stranger.

Book Four

Both Sides of the Fence

Decay is inherent in all component things:
Work out your salvation with diligence.

— LAST WORDS OF THE BUDDHA

13

The Critic

For some time past — perhaps as an instinctive way of maintaining my balance by natural rather than chemical means — I had been acting as a double agent.

I worked in the theatre yet wrote theatrical criticism; I worked in public broadcasting yet attacked CBC policy; I earned money from commercial television while reviling advertising; I produced films for the United Nations and essays critical of U.N. actions; I was an entrepreneur who sat on union executives and a nationalist when our achievements contributed to internationalism. Far from interfering with this balancing act, the little red pills designed to stabilize my manic-depressive swings joined forces with it. Staying on an even keel sometimes means being prepared to rush from one side of the boat to the other at short notice.

For example, after appearing in that ingenious but improbable trial drama *Witness for the Prosecution*, I felt obliged to compensate by acting in Ted Kotcheff's television re-creation of a real Soviet trial, in which freedom of speech stood accused. It proved less popular than Agatha Christie. With John Diefenbaker's new Progressive Conservative government in power some CBC brass were so fearful of political trouble, and some viewers so avid to see left-wing bias in anything Russian, pro or con, that I wrote a piece for *Maclean's* ("Who's High-Pressuring the

CBC?"), blaming both internal cowardice and public hypocrisy. While most Canadians resent government pressure on the CBC, I noted,

> paradoxically, citizens seek political interference as a first recourse when they personally or collectively object to a program or have something to promote. Recently a New Brunswick M.P., in the course of attacking the television panel "Fighting Words" [in which I also took part] confessed in the House of Commons that he based his criticisms on complaints from constituents — to him, not to the CBC! . . . Add together all the lobbies representing groups which dislike seeing themselves or their jobs in any but the most virtuous light and you have a formidable array of self-righteousness.[1]

This caveat about self-serving lobbies was prophetic, but, in fact, I had just helped to form one. Theatre people from across the country, responding to a call from the Paris-based International Theatre Institute, met at Stratford in August 1957 to found a Canadian Theatre Centre and elected me to chair it.[2] (This was a perfect example of the misfit in my psyche between event and mood: I was convinced the honour was a charitable gesture to a loser.) Then when the new Canada Council held a public meeting in Kingston, I shamelessly used the CTC position to lobby on behalf of Canadian theatre.

Nor did I hesitate to try a triple play, as long as it helped to balance the scales. When CBC-TV launched its Folio series in April 1958, I guest-directed my comedy The Ottawa Man, followed it with an article on why I stole Gogol's plot and set it in Canada, and a month later boldly presented the stage version at the Crest as a "Canadian play." ("In this historical comedy," Bob McStay wrote in Variety, borrowing freely from my article, "Moore has stripped fact from historical fiction and hilariously upset the establishment of what national holiday orators describe as 'the founding of a great nation.'")[3] Three hours after the curtain fell on the first performance, the whole juggling act was crowned by the birth, on cue, of Charlotte Moore, whose mother had had the foresight to invite Dr. Gillespie to accompany her to the earlier of the two premieres.

But was my elation traceable to the occasion or to a blip in the psychosis? Why did I plunge, if only for a moment, into the primal rue that my fourth daughter was not a son,[4] then vault into euphoria at the thought of siring four such women, then shrink in shame at my parental deficiencies? Recovery would clearly take time.

I was soon off again, in search of income, to produce a new film series for the United Nations. And, for a double agent, world events that fall were rich with material for *Canadian Commentator* columns. Khrushchev, de Gaulle, and Pope John XXIII had all come into power, and the European Common Market had arrived, along with the United Arab Republic and the Hula Hoop. But since my fellow columnists included pundits Robert Mackenzie, Ann Francis, John Bird, Willson Woodside, and James M. Minifie, it behooved me to be diplomatic about choice of subject matter. I would not, for example, have quizzed Sidney Smith, the Diefenbaker government's new secretary of state for external affairs, about foreign policy, even though I had known him well as president of the University of Toronto and as another devotee of *Spring Thaw*. (He used to send me charming fan letters, apparently an early-morning indulgence.) Instead I contrasted the demeanour of the 61-year-old Smith with that of Pearson:

> Mr. Sidney Smith is being understandably cautious. . . . When the unguarded slip is so avidly anticipated, when obscure rules are invoked to trip, when one-upmanship may consist of . . . a casual enquiry after the health of an alphabetic Organization of which one may never have heard, a man of Mr. Smith's dignity does well to tread warily. Banana peels litter the place.
>
> But . . . taking the odd misstep is less dangerous in the long run than taking no steps at all, which may be interpreted as inability to walk. [Mr. Smith] is, when relaxed, a man of wisdom, wit, charm and intellectual honesty — qualities sorely needed among our leaders, and qualities readily appreciated here if they are allowed to shine. We can only hope that very soon he will feel secure enough to relax, be himself and join in the game Mr. Pearson played so well, if differently.[5]

But this report only hinted at a human tragedy. When I first caught Smith's eye in the Press Club, he excused himself from the knot of grandees around him to cross the room and give me a hug. He was gabbling happily away about old times when we both became aware of two grim young presences, impeccably dressed, on either side of him. He paled, his smile dropped, his voice petered out, and he said lamely, "Well, be seeing you, Mavor." And they led him away. A few days later I passed a U.N. radio studio where Smith sat alone, reading a statement into the microphone. The same two apparatchiks were in the booth, giving him instructions over the intercom. They had him correct a phrase, and then another, and then a third. He was trembling, not with rage but with impotence. He stumbled slightly on a date. They made him do it again, and again, and again. I walked on, remembering the mad Lear's "great image of authority: a dog's obey'd in office." In less than a year Sidney Smith was dead.

Toronto *Telegram*, interview with George Brimmell, October 18, 1958:

> . . . Moore, who has been able to get home only weekends from New York for the past few months to see his wife and four daughters, was in rehearsal for his [CBC-TV] play, *The Man Who Caught Bullets*. . . . Right now he is producing a series for the U.N. Entitled *Dateline U.N.*, the documentaries will go on a network of top U.S. television stations, about sixty in all, and possibly on the CBC. Moore wrote the first three programs in the 26-week series himself . . ."

In addition to the columns for *Canadian Commentator* I covered the waterfront in two chapters, those on Theatre (English) and Radio/Television, of *The Arts in Canada: A Stock-taking at Mid-Century*, edited by Malcolm Ross — writing up the very history in which I had been so actively involved.[6]

One of my mentors in the art of working both sides of the fence, Toronto drama critic Herbert Whittaker, happened to be in New York that fall as guest reviewer for the *Herald Tribune*. The *Tribune's* regular critic, Walter Kerr, had taken leave of absence, having found it hard to maintain his critical detachment while deeply involved in a Broadway-bound musical named *Goldilocks*. Whittaker, on the other hand, had never allowed his position as critic to interfere with his career as designer and director. In Canada this dual allegiance frequently forced him to resort to double entendres to veil his participation in the deed under scrutiny. But once in New York and relieved of his veils, he had become a regular Salomé in his demands, day after day delivering the most cogent criticism in town. Many observers expected him to become the *Tribune's* permanent critic. But *Goldilocks* failed, Kerr retreated to the higher ground of criticism, and Herbert Whittaker was back at the *Globe and Mail* by the time I returned to Toronto in November.

Our mutual friend Nathan Cohen, meanwhile, had managed a balancing act of a different sort. While acting as story editor for CBC-TV's drama department — where he encouraged, among others, the prolific

Arthur Hailey — he continued his regular critical programs on radio and acted as moderator of his own weekly drama series, *Cohen's Choice*. At about the same time as I visited England, he had also become a once-a-week columnist for the Toronto *Telegram* (where veteran Rose Macdonald was still the drama critic), with a broad mandate for commentary on cultural affairs. Cohen's cleft stick was having to solicit, as an editor, plays from writers he had offended as a critic. His rationale for doing both jobs at once was that he applied equally rigorous standards to each.

Toronto's third (and largest) daily, the *Star*, had as theatre critic a newsman of wide experience, Jack Karr, whose judgement was highly valued for its freedom from any contingent ambition to direct, design, edit, produce, or appear in theatre, television, radio, film, or any other medium. Karr's sole allegiance was to journalism which, in a world of double agents, proved to be his undoing.

All this was to change in the space of a single month, during which I came to the conclusion that all my activity was leading nowhere.

That November I was invited to deliver a sermon to the First Unitarian Congregation in Toronto, to which Dilly and I had belonged since our marriage. To me it was the least objectionable of the established churches, generous enough to accommodate a religious pluralist. I had returned from New York in a melancholy state aggravated by bronchitis, loneliness, and poverty, and was reaching out for bearings as one does for chair-tops when moving about in the dark. Using as my text Thomas Traherne's "One star made infinite would all exclude," I argued that all religions claiming exclusive access to divine truth and its approaches (e.g., "rigorous standards") cancelled each other out, although there was no shortage of claimants. "The richness of human life, as of the universe, lies in its variety, and we ought less to be sending missionaries than exchanging them." At the same time, I said, the common notion that because there were many different makes of furnaces we could do without heat in winter was sheer folly. Learning from each other, we must continue to reinvent furnaces, religions, society, ourselves.

It was now winter, literal and figurative, and I had no time to lose in reinventing myself. We did not want — could not afford — to move to New York, yet aside from Robert Weaver's proposal for a year-end radio revue (*Young Moore's Almanac*), there were only spasmodic prospects of work in Toronto. After Lorne Greene's departure, I had truncated the company name to Mavor Moore Productions, but the corporation had no capital and nothing to produce. And what could be worse, I asked myself, for the extended course of medication I had embarked on than the volatile life of a freelance, which depended on starting hares I was in no condition to pursue? What I needed, according to Dr. Grant, was something I had not had since leaving the CBC: a steady job.

That was when I received the call from the *Telegram*.

John Bassett was an impressive pirate king (then 43, four years older than I, and several inches taller), thoroughly at home in his patrician skin, expensive suit, and business throne. We had not met, but did so in the knowledge that each knew quite a bit about the other. Since purchasing the *Telegram* in 1952, he said, he had been gradually reshaping its departments and had now arrived at the arts. Was I interested in becoming its theatre critic? I split the question into two: did I want to be a full-time critic, and if so on what terms? The first, Bassett said, only I could answer; the second we could discuss. I would find it hard to separate theatre from musicals, opera, dance. Then do all four, he told me. I felt his readers should know more about what was happening across Canada, and Canadians needed to know more about world theatre. Okay, he agreed, some travelling. What about Rose Macdonald? No problem. Nathan Cohen? No problem. Their assignments, he insisted, would be different. I begged 24 hours to think it over.

Dilly and I sought the advice of our closest journalist friend, Pierre Berton, then at the *Star*. Berton asked why, if I had decided to become a critic, I would want to work for that rag. "Because it asked me," I replied. "Let me think about it," said he. "I'll get back to you in half an hour." Fifteen minutes later he asked me, "How'd you like to come and work at the *Star*? Higher pay, bigger audience." I said I could hardly do that when it was John Bassett who had suggested the whole idea. "It's up to you," said Berton. "Make enough demands and he'll bow out of the bidding." I returned to Bassett, who agreed to the only extra demands I could think of: freedom to do television, an annual trip across Canada, two weeks in Europe and two in New York every year, and first-class plane fare. I immediately informed Berton, who said, "Well, let's see what happens!" The *Telegram* announced my appointment on December 5, 1958.

The following day Cohen was offered the posts of drama critic and entertainment editor at the *Star*, with all the perks I had initiated, and resigned forthwith from the *Telegram*. Events at the *Star* moved so swiftly that Jack Karr, the reigning critic, learned of Cohen's appointment from a remark overheard in an elevator. Whittaker, who had for years financed an annual European trip out of his own pocket, asked the *Globe and Mail* for a reappraisal of his contract. War had commenced.

FEATURES EDITOR ERNEST BARTLETT, who in some naval connection had acquired the title of captain, was my instructor. He seemed to live at the newspaper, tucked away in an office that might have sat for an illustration by Arthur Rackham, the painter of gnomes' lairs and Old Curiosity Shops. No one ever saw Bart eat there (although sandwich ends occasionally peeked from sections of newsprint), but the sign that you were accepted was an invitation, anytime after midnight, to share a nip of his inexhaustible supply of Pernod. While mastering every trick of his trade he remained attached to its highest principles, such as that *very* must never be used to modify a participle. Even now habit forces me to say I was very much honoured to know him.

Bart and his seniors Burt Richardson and Doug MacFarlane, along with Frank Tumpane, Clyde Gilmour, and other old hands, had much to teach me about newspapers in very short order. Some courses, such as Communal Consumption of Beer, I failed miserably. But others, such as Starting with a Barrage, I picked up quickly.

"Critics are called many names," I began, "but here is one who dislikes being called a critic. . . . You never hear of a Sports Critic or a Business Critic or a Women's Critic on a newspaper; they're all Columnists or even Writers." Denying possession of the Ten Commandments of Art, I proclaimed my pluralism in the first of the columns I carefully called "About the Theatre":

> It is my observation that faults may be found in everything, depending on your point of view. The best bathtub makes a mighty poor boat. . . . Wagner's *Liebestod* is not ideal for square-dancing. Bull-fighting leaves something to be desired from the bull's point of view. Those who like the same things do not always agree on the reason. One of the most trenchant dramatic criticisms I ever heard came from a matron emerging from T. S. Eliot's verse play *The Cocktail Party: "Wasn't it marvellous? — you'd hardly know it was poetry!"*. . .
>
> We are the richer for our differences. "Why should we refuse to admit the infinite complexity, the innumerable windows through which the soul may view the astonishing landscape?" — as the philosopher [Macneile Dixon] said . . .
>
> So my New Year's resolution for 1959 is to be busier opening than closing windows; to be more diligent in acquainting you with alternative interests than in decrying those you may have; to provide you not with absolute standards but with standards of comparison, so you may have plenty of evidence on which to base your own judgment.

> We are all human, and I may fall off the wagon. I confess to a weakness for invective; I'll try to control it. Other times I feel vastly well disposed to practically everyone. I'll try to control that too — but not right now.[7]

In hindsight what strikes me about this column is not my predictable dislike of absolutes but my confessing to a manic-depressive problem in the last paragraph. While probably unconscious, it clearly implies concern about its effect on my judgement.

In my second column I continued the barrage, proposing the translation of Shakespeare into modern English. Anticipating the outcry, I had asked Middle English scholar Charles Dunn to render a speech from *Hamlet* into the vernacular (to show how much of Shakespeare's meaning playgoers unwittingly missed), and arranged with Ted Reeve, our beloved sports editor and bardophile, to write a stinging reply so we could get a debate going between the sports and entertainment sections.[8] From the highbrow I turned to the lowbrow. The tatty Casino Theatre on Queen Street, sometime home to every top banana and bottom drawer in burlesque, was due for demolition in the Civic Square facelift. There I went to pay my last respects to the closing stripper and the closing theatre in a joint epitaph: "All bad things must come to an end, and she finally came to hers."[9] Some editor solicitous of our family readership changed "bad" to "good," and I had to point out that in this case good made bad worse.

I praised the Montreal scene ("the most vigorous and advanced theatre in Canada") at Toronto's expense, and predicted that Toronto's coming O'Keefe Centre would be "all-purpose, suitable for no purpose." The Stratford Festival was faulted for ignoring Canadian talent, and a *Telegram* editorial rebuked for defending the festival. I called the National Ballet's sets "antediluvian" and engaged in a debate with Celia Franca over British hegemony at the National Ballet School. ("I want everyone concerned to note where the school is: in Canada, North America.") Of *Spring Thaw '59*, which my intrepid mother had mounted in yet another theatre, team-directed by my old colleagues, I wrote that it was too much like the ones I had done: "What *Spring Thaw* needs more than anything else, dare I say it, is to forget its past and get on with it."

All of this was designed to prod artists and audiences into thinking of alternatives to accepted wisdom. But unfortunately I had scooped myself with an article in the *Canadian Commentator*, written before my first

Telegram columns but not published until after they appeared, assaulting the root assumptions of dogmatic criticism.[10]

The *Star*'s Cohen wasted no time in picking up the gauntlet:

> Since your columnist has frequently noted what ails other critics, it is only fair Mr. Moore should retaliate. . . . [He] ticks off this corner as an old-fashioned absolutist and avers that the true critic will want all kinds of play to flourish. He will encourage a diversity of entertainments, or favour a temple with many chambers of many sizes. . . .
>
> Comparing respective attitudes, Mr. Moore sees himself as a horticulturalist who cherishes orchids "precisely because of their pre-eminence among other flowers, not among weeds." By contrast, your columnist emerges as a weed-killer who looks out on a "flat and depressing cultural swampland, relieved here and there by a free-standing sunflower." . . .
>
> As for the claim that this corner is a dogmatic, who believes that he alone understands what is truth and beauty, this corner admits to holding strong convictions, because drama and theatre are things worth feeling strongly about. This may rub against the grain of moderation in criticism which Mr. Moore so admires, now. [I had said nothing about moderation.] But let him reflect. In his own experience, was it not when he had strong convictions about the kind of theatre we need here in Canada that he himself made his most influential and exciting contribution?
>
> True, there is room in the theatre for all types of plays, and all types of critics. To this corner, though . . . bricks put together by passion and with the highest standards of workmanship build the most solid foundation.[11]

His claim to intimacy with the "highest standards," however, was precisely the issue on which we differed. The rest, such as putting my "strong convictions" in the past tense, was his way of regretting that I had deserted the theatre to write about it. He preferred me on the other side of the fence.

"Criticism," Oscar Wilde cracked, "is the only civilized form of autobiography." I went into the profession knowing, from earlier sorties, that it involved revealing one's own strengths and weaknesses. George Jean Nathan, the terror of Broadway in the 1920s, went further;

he firmly believed in exhibiting them. "All criticism," he wrote, "is at bottom, an effort on the part of its practitioner to show off himself and his art at the expense of the artist and the art which he criticizes. . . . The great critics are those who, recognizing the intrinstic, permanent and indeclinable egotism of the critical art, make no senseless effort to conceal it."[12] To me, painfully aware that the self (so easily modified by chance and chemistry) was anything but "intrinsic, permanent and indeclinable," this was a dishonest and dangerous fallacy.

If indeed the critic is a fellow artist, subject to the same pressures, arousals, fantasies, common colds, and lousy coffee as poets, musicians, painters, and dancers, then to elevate his or her own mind-set, frozen in time, to the level of universal and eternal verity is nothing less than a giant fraud. My curiosity extended — as it had back in the days of my graduate studies in semantics and my first job with the Holden Players — to the motivations and habits of critics, audiences, and artists (including myself), to their conventions and the relations between them. We were on a mutual voyage of discovery, and such things as eternal verities and highest standards, if there were any, would emerge at the end, not the beginning, of the voyage.

On the day after Cohen's column was published I flew to Dublin, then to London and Paris, to continue my education and share it with my readers.

I learned more about the Abbey Theatre from joining director Ria Mooney and her cast in the pub afterward than I did from watching the evening's two plays, the one in English sold out, the legally mandated afterpiece in Irish performed for six of us. Mooney, familiar as the ingenue in the Abbey's Toronto visits, had in her maturity followed Yeats's spiritualist bent far around the corner: we welcomed the golden dawn with a candle-lit invocation to the ghost of Synge, much as Pat Joudry had summoned Shaw from the beyond to write more plays. Synge refused to cooperate. In London I discovered two strong Irish actors, Patrick McGoohan and Peter O'Toole ("A walking erection," I called him, but censored myself), whose presence in the English capital, along with other Irish stars, explained much about the theatre in Dublin. Just as seeing Stuart Griffiths as program director of Britain's Granada TV said much about Canadian television.

In London, too, I caught Peter Finch's debut in Peter Shaffer's first hit, Five Finger Exercise, and, in Bournemouth, John Osborne's first failure, The World of Paul Slickey ("Angry young man demoted to peevish boy"). A

Taste of Honey at Stratford East gave me a taste of Joan Littlewood's collective methods, and a visit to Pitlochry in Scotland taught me a rule about festivals without a focus ("The slighter the play, the greater the audience"). A confusing all-star *Othello* was at Stratford-upon-Avon, with each star, from Paul Robeson down, playing in a different accent.[13] At the same time London hosted an international festival that featured an unforgettable Shakespeare entry in a single unfamiliar language: a Zulu *Macbeth* — with running translation through individual earphone — that unaffectedly demonstrated the importance to the play of ritual, both royal and magical. This production greatly influenced my own later *Macbeth* at the Crest Theatre.

"In Paris," I wrote, "we can find the best of three theatres: the past, the present, and the future." The past was represented by Jean-Louis Barrault's catherine-wheel staging of Jacques Offenbach's *La Vie Parisienne*; the present by Jean Anouilh's wicked *L'Hurluberlu*, in which a pompous general, looking faintly like de Gaulle, decides to straighten out the country; and the future by Eugene Ionesco's double bill, *The Bald Soprano* and *The Lesson*, still running in a pocket theatre on the Left Bank. ("Immediacy, audience reaction, irrationality . . . Ionesco has succeeded in uniting the three main threads of the modern theatre in one strand.")[14]

In Paris another international festival was in progress: plays, operas, and ballets from 18 countries. Among them was a *Julius Caesar* from Bochum, Germany, which — with Caesar made up as Hitler and the conspirators as Göring, Goebbels, Himmler, and the rest — made Shakespeare's play a study in internecine nationalism. The only touch of colour amid the black-and-white sets and costumes, at first, was the red of Caesar's cape. During the play, spots of red multiplied, detail by detail, until at the end the stage was covered in red blankets. The symbolism had an unexpected meaning for me. Although taking my red pills daily, I had given little thought to the cumulative effect of their gradual spread through my system, blanketing my highs and lows, leaving me free, it now seemed, to respond not to a compulsive mood but to the events I was witnessing, such as this.

It was therefore with a renewed sense of confidence that I returned to Toronto and on May 25 went to Maple Leaf Gardens to review an opera in Italian:

> The Metropolitan Opera came to town last night and tripped over *Tosca*. It made an awful mess. . . . Let me give you a short list of blunders which I consider unforgivable in so senior a company.

273

On Tosca's first entrance into the church she complains to her lover, the painter Cavaradossi: "Why did you lock the door?" But he didn't — he didn't even unlock it to let her in. What she was yowling about outside I don't know; she could have come in anytime. Having entered, she makes a fuss about a "blonde" whose portrait Cavaradossi is painting into his mural. This is odd, because this Tosca is a blonde herself. No wigs available? . . . [After listing more problems with doors, windows, coiffeured choirboys, and miraculous torture — "Not a stain or a rip on his white shirt, not a button or a cuff undone" — I came to the performers.]

Let us not hedge: Miss Eleanor Steber is too fat to perform this role. When she falls to her knees we hear it, and fear she will be unable to rise again. When she fights off the advances of Scarpia, it seems too likely that she will win. When she is called upon, at the end, to jump from the parapet, catastrophe is only averted by allowing her to move first behind a sympathetic piece of scenery . . .

This kind of inadequate, sloppy, preposterous production, coming from so pretentious a source, is unfair to opera, unfair to an audience, and unfair to the Rotary Club which sponsors these visits. I look forward to better things during the week, for they could hardly be worse.[15]

That I complimented the second night's *Carmen* ("marvellous, vigorous, assured"), or the final *Madama Butterfly* ("permitted the Met to rescue from ignominy a week that threatened to strain our love affair") did nothing to help — *Variety* had picked up my candid comments about Steber and spread them, headlined, all over the United States. I received threats from members of the company. The Rotary Club tried, unsuccesfully, to get me fired. Then my comments on the set for *Pagliacci* were circulated: "One gets tired of supposedly solid walls which flutter with each passing villager, of skies with permanent folds, of upper windows which serve no purpose, of improbable laundry lines . . ." In a word, my reputation as a critic was made.

I stayed with the *Telegram* for almost two years. During that time, the cure for my biochemical imbalance was sufficiently successful that I have never again been subjected to the systematic mood swings that for so long plagued my life and the lives of those close to me. I have, however, remained in some ways an obsessive-compulsive character. The path traversed is evident from the daily columns I wrote in those two years, which show an increasing evenness of temper, but also an obsessive interest in the variety of connections between the art, the observer, and the point of view.

Now this is not the task of the conventional journalistic critic, which Susan Sontag once described as "handing out grades to works of art." For grading one needs a firm mind-set and the cocksureness to measure everything by it.

Time and again, as I reread after 30 years the columns written in Canada or abroad, I see myself assessing my own mind-set, vis-à-vis those of the artist, of other immediate observers, and of the times. The task is not to grade the work of art but to identify its possibilities. Beauty, in my book, is neither a light in the eye of the beholder nor the glow emanating from the object, but the quality of the transaction between the two — in mathematical terms, a dimension or function. Like a clothesline, it only operates when attached at both ends. We must entertain the possibilities inherent in differing approaches to art.

The Spectator, London, "Ballet: The First Classics," by Clive Barnes, March 31, 1961:

> The other day a Canadian man of the theatre, Mr. Mavor Moore, spoke his mind about the Royal Ballet. On a Toronto radio programme he deplored the company's "artistic homosexuality." *Quelle délicatesse!* But it seems that, despite his queer turn of phrase, Mr. Moore was apparently concerned with the company's alleged abandonment of dramatic values and concentration on decor. His point is at once defensible and debatable. . . .

Three years later Susan Sontag, in her famous essay on "camp," used the phrase "homosexual aestheticism" to the same end. My point was that the early ballet classics, with their resolutely heterosexual plots, should either be convincingly presented as such or frankly reconstructed to express alternative relationships — or, better still, replaced by new works reflecting the varieties of human relations. I thought that all classics, the products of earlier times, earlier mores, should be extended the same courtesy. The issue (which involves racial, religious, and cultural as well as sexual stereotypes, and audiences as well as performers) has since become commonplace.

The Telegram, "Mavor Moore About the Theatre," University Alumnae Coach House, January 27, 1960:

> If James Reaney continues to write plays, as he must, *The Killdeer* is likely to become an historic event. . . . His signal triumph is that he has succeeded in doing for Canadian character and speech what John Synge did for the Irish. He has taken a regional dialect (south-western Ontario), fed it through his own highly personal imagination, and produced a flexible, full-bodied idiom which no human being ever spoke before but which all of us recognize at once. In brief, from our somewhat raw and sweet Canadian wine, someone has at last distilled an Aqua Vitae . . . *The Killdeer* may very well mark the turning point in our theatre and our dramatic literature: the day we stop copying and begin creating.

While working as a critic, moreover, I was doing my utmost to be part of that creative process. Since I was reviewing only what was on the stage, I persuaded myself, writing and performing for radio or television involved no conflict of interest. With John Drainie, Ruth Springford, and Diana Maddox I was a regular on John Reeves's weekly radio anthology *Four's Company*. In television I was active as both actor and writer, adapting many stage plays such as Arthur Miller's *The Crucible* — often working one day with someone encountered in the theatre the next. I was also writing essays for the *Manchester Guardian* and other journals, and light verses for *Maclean's* on the trades and professions, including criticism:

> The critic is the public's friend.
> From lofty summits we descend
> To answer the eternal question:
> Is it Art or Indigestion?

> Without our taste (the keenest known)
> You would be forced to use your own;
> And it takes years to learn the knack
> Of finding hay in a needle-stack.[16]

Such extracurricular activities allowed me, at last, to pay off my remaining debts from *Sunshine Town*. But thereafter I felt increasingly limited by the demands of my nightly reviewing schedule. And the frustration of being so often an observer instead of a participant reawakened echoes of my war career, when I was cast so often in the role of cheerleader for those doing the dirty work. One directly conflicting interest, in fact, proved irresistible. One of my duties at the *Telegram* was to review productions of the Canadian Opera Company, which I always did in envy of those involved with its mighty form of collective art.

The COC's director-general, Herman Geiger-Torel, a refugee from Hitler's Vienna, looked like a Wagnerian troglodyte spruced up for a meeting in Valhalla. The ferocity of his frown in the first incarnation was dispelled by the radiance of his smile in the second. A former stage assistant to the great director Max Reinhardt, he had fled to South America and for years made a living in the leather business and any nearby opera house. He was brought to Canada by his old friend Nicholas Goldschmidt, who needed a stage director to train students and mount productions at the new Opera School of the University of Toronto's Faculty of Music, and eventually succeeded Goldschmidt as head of the professional Canadian Opera Company that grew out of it. My CBC colleague Franz Kraemer persuaded Torel to pioneer opera on television; and DMM, at my suggestion, engaged him to stage the *Cinderella* she presented at Eaton Auditorium in 1953. He had also been of great help to me when I was assembling casts for *Sunshine Town* and *The Optimist*.

He had few illusions about the level he was brought in to raise, but a shining confidence in making the young exceed their reach. This he achieved by cajoling and hammering his charges in a florid mixture of English, German, Italian, French, and Spanish that frequently raided one another for help. He knew the business as well as the show side of show business, and at once befriended anyone prepared to join him in lighting firecrackers under the apathetic. In the summer of 1959 Torel knowingly piqued my curiosity by asking, without further explanation, if I would be around in September and October. For what?

His COC season at the Royal Alexandra was to open with Prokofiev's fantastical comic opera *The Love for Three Oranges*, and Jean Gascon was to direct. Gascon, invited to stage *Othello* at Stratford, was now hedging; Torel needed a standby. The day Gascon withdrew Torel handed me the score:

MM: But, Herman, I've never directed an opera before.
HGT: You are going to direct an opera now.
MM: I don't think my timetable will allow it.
HGT: I will allow it. What's a timetable! It is to fix.
MM: I'll have to review it for the paper.
HG: So? For once you will know what you talk about!

The Love for Three Oranges opened on October 13, 1959. Side by side on the amusement page of the *Telegram* next day were George Kidd's musical review, and a piece by me safely discussing the difference between staging operas and plays. With Ettore Mazzoleni as conductor, an ingenious set by Murray Laufer, outrageous costumes by Marie Day, and a cast almost every member of which rose to later prominence, the unfamiliar work was the unexpected highlight of the year. But for me the highlight was the chance to work with Torel as he insisted, joked, badgered, raged, and sank pleading to his knees, all the time chewing on the cigar that separated him, by design, from the singers. From him I learned all I know about staging opera, including the cigar, which I abandoned, as a gesture of deep respect, after his death.

I was to stage four more operas for the COC in the next four years: *A Night in Venice, Orpheus in the Underworld* (with Torel), *The Bartered Bride*, and *Don Giovanni*. Each of them was a master class with Torel. In a dress rehearsal for the *Don* a visiting diva was misbehaving when Torel suddenly appeared in the aisle beside me and whispered fiercely, "Lose your temper!" "I'm not mad enough yet," I whispered back. "Lose it before *she* does," said Torel, almost exploding with the effort to keep his voice down, "or you're a dead goose!" I followed his advice and have never since hesitated to lose my temper when the moment, not my humour, demanded it. I have found the technique especially effective with children and committees.

Having finessed my first opera, I could hardly resist the call when Murray and Donald Davis at the Crest invited me to direct *Macbeth* with Powys Thomas and Charmion King. The strong cast included John Vernon, Amelia Hall, Bill Needles, and (as First Witch) a recent alumna of the National Theatre School later known as Martha Henry. It would be my fourth production of the play, but it was only now, after the Zulu version had prompted me to further studies in historical witchcraft, that I felt I had a grasp of it.

The witches in Shakespeare's play are young countrywomen of the old pagan religion, out to earn an honest penny fortune-telling (in dreadlock masks) for their betters. They lie in wait for the homecoming General Macbeth, who reads his own ambition into their simple benedictions; his sceptical companion Banquo mocks them and scares them off. They are later scolded by their head priestess, Hecate, for exceeding their limited powers of divination; and to make recompense, the four women — when most of Macbeth's other adversaries have fled the

country — take it on themselves to hex him to death. In modern par-
lance the witches in this play are the good guys — and it seemed to me
time they were given their due.

Declining to review this unorthodox production myself, I sent my
deputy at the *Telegram*, Ron Evans, who had the self-possession to criticize
it severely. Herbert Whittaker at the *Globe and Mail* and, in Nathan Cohen's
absence, the *Star's* alternate critic, were less than spellbound. But when
Cohen returned to town, he gave the production an extraordinary review:

> . . . an at once simple and daring solution of the play's most trouble-
> some feature. . . . By treating the weird sisters as real people, director
> Moore is able to turn them into an ironic, integral and continuing strand
> of the plot. They cease to be a theatrical embarrassment and structural
> nuisance. . . . A *Macbeth* without apology, and with meaning. Simple,
> unforced, freshly thought-out, it is an important artistic achievement.[17]

Perhaps it was his way of urging me to get back into the theatre.

Less than a year later it happened. In the fall of 1960 two successive
columns from Stratford (which showed no interest whatever in my
Macbeth) demonstrated that I could no longer stretch myself in so many
divergent directions. The first was a report on the third annual meeting
of the Canadian Theatre Centre. As its first chair, I had been intimately
connected with the movement to found a national theatre school. I was,
that is to say, reporting as a supposedly impartial journalist on a movement in which I had a direct and passionate stake:

> The subject of most excitement and comment at yesterday's meeting is
> the new National Theatre School, scheduled to open in Montreal this
> November. . . . Applications have already been received from more
> prospective students than the school will be able to accommodate. . . .
> An outstanding staff has been lined up. . . . Many ideas emerged from
> the frank discussions which suggest that at long last our theatre has
> found a national voice which can be heard from coast to coast.[18]

Was this honest reportage or propaganda for a personal cause?

And was I, on the other hand, all too ready to disparage causes I felt
left out of? Two days later I reported on the first two Canadian plays to
be presented at the Stratford Festival: John Gray's *The Teacher* and Fred
Euringer's *Blind Man's Bluff*. Staged at the smaller Avon Theatre, they were

runners-up to the unworthy winner of a contest for "best Canadian play," *To the Canvas Barricade,* by Donald Jack, due on the main stage the following year. Gray's work I found "genuine and unhackneyed" if "still amorphous"; Euringer's I found "as corny a piece of imitative claptrap as I have ever seen." This was "grading" with a vengeance. But instead of admitting it, I denigrated the whole enterprise, saying I could not understand "this contradictory selection by a panel including such knowledgeable playwrights as Peter Ustinov and William Inge, and producer Robert Whitehead, except on the grounds of charitable condescension toward the still infantile Canadian theatre."[19]

Either I had to remain an external observer, committing myself to a dogmatic judgemental grid, or I had to be a part of the creative process — that is, to do and make things others could later judge according to their own grid. If the latter, I could try to write and produce dramatic works designed to save us in future from such "charitable condescension" and, in a more general way, help to organize the development of the arts in Canada as part of the world community.

One other incident, out of the blue, played a role in my decision.

I had not lost track of my mother, even though we had not been in touch. She continued to train actors at her school and to tour the province with her effective plays, sponsored by the Zonta Club, promoting mental health. I reviewed the *Spring Thaws* she produced in 1958 and 1959, and the one in 1960, when she leased the title to the group behind *My Fur Lady,* the McGill University revue staged by Brian Macdonald that had toured across Canada. I covered a brave "Director's Stage" studio series she had mounted, with Herbert Whittaker, George McCowan, and Leon Major as the directors. (It generated a battle with the actors' union that led — too late to be of use to her — to a separate contract for nonprofit productions in small theatres.) But the New Play Society as such was moribund. With the recent sale of the old building in which she rented premises for the school, she was in danger of losing everything she had worked for.

"Is the NPS finished?" Nathan Cohen asked in his June 2, 1960, column in the *Star*:

> On at least five other occasions that I can recall, Mrs. Dora Mavor Moore, with resources of spirit, courage, resilience, faith and determination the rest of us can't even imagine, has pulled the NPS through crises which common sense declared were incurable. Somehow, I believe we have not heard the end of the NPS.[20]

A month later Tyrone Guthrie, in Ireland, heard of her misfortunes and wrote:

> . . . a) to sympathize with you in what is — temporarily — a grievous position; b) to *encourage*. I feel sure that, given a bit of time, your many friends and sincere admirers will get the thing onto its feet again. Phoenix-like, you will rise . . . etc., etc. But — far more important than that (tho' that is important too) no temporary reversal of fortune can alter the fact that you, almost single-handed, kept a lamp burning in the temple for *many years*. . . .

> Even if your life's work may, to a myopic view, appear just now to be in ruins, these ruins have been productive of more of what is significant in Canada of the theatre we both "believe in" passionately. Also what look like ruins one moment become foundations of the next.[21]

Where my mother was concerned, I had always, I suppose, seen myself in the roles my father had failed to play: supporter and provider. Yet in the last two years, aside from sending her monthly cheques that she kept but refused to cash, and notes on Christmas and her birthday that she refused to acknowledge, I had done nothing. Then one afternoon I received a phone call from her devoted secretary, Emma Benson, tearful but firm: "Mavor, your mother is down at the School. The movers left an hour ago. She is standing alone in the middle of the studio, with everything gone but a few scraps of old scenery. She has been standing there for an hour without moving. She is 72 years old. You must go to her."

DMM took in my arrival with a glance. There was a long silence as I looked about. "How about a cup of tea?" I asked. "I'd like that," she said. "I think they've left the kettle." And we picked up from where we had left off, as if there had been no interval in the eternal conversation, begun in my childhood, about where to go from here.

The plan I had formed on the way down was to raise enough money to buy the New Play Society's one remaining asset, the rights to the title *Spring Thaw*, so that she might have enough capital to carry on somewhere else. Then — although I quailed at the prospect — I would raise as much again to revive it in 1961, at the Crest, hoping to recover both investments.

One of my last columns for the *Telegram* was a testament to my decision to abandon criticism as a full-time career. The new O'Keefe Centre made its debut with the world premiere of *Camelot*, starring Richard Burton, Julie Andrews (whom I had once escorted to the United Nations), and my protégé Robert Goulet as Lancelot. After watching the three-and-a-half-hour opening night, I wrote an open letter to director Moss Hart:

> While I wish you all the luck in the world, and cannot imagine a doctor more worthy of our confidence, the operation required to put a skeleton into the body after birth would tax the powers of old Merlyn himself. I'm heartily glad it's your problem and not mine. And lacking the temerity to instruct so learned a master in what will or will not go on Broadway, I can only tell you what occurred to me in seat H21 in the O'Keefe Centre.[22]

I then made a number of specific and practical suggestions for cuts, revisions, additions, cast changes, and the like — some of which, I heard, actually got as far as being discussed.

"That man," Julie Andrews told Bob Goulet, "is on the wrong side of the footlights."

14

Art and Politics

UNTIL THE AGE OF 40 I had avoided connection with any political party. I prided myself on my independence, considering the extremists foolish and the occupants of the middle of the road alike in their opportunism. This was not from lack of concern or interest. I voted, when the time came, for the worthiest candidate in my riding, regardless of party, on the theory that a party composed of the largest number of worthies would make the wisest decisions for the country. I followed the scene both at home and at the United Nations, watching the ward heelers and the wheeler-dealers with equal interest, but chiefly as characters in a play I would write someday. Politics at every level seemed to me a theatre in which conjurors of interchangeable stripes manipulated the public through its own gullibility.

"We live in a propagandist's paradise," I wrote in a 1957 *Maclean's* article on the Big Lie, as popularized by Hitler and Stalin and now eagerly adopted by industrial societies under the guise of many Little Lies. "Ours is the proud age of the scientific method . . . but it is also — alas! — the age of Bridey Murphy and falsies. Of course, it is not the first time we have been blessed with phony books and phony glands; but if our splendid new inventions are to be used to perpetuate demonstrable error, if freedom for the many means only the opportunity to duplicate the past follies of the few, we had best stop boasting of our 'advanced' civilization. . . . 'Giving the public what it wants' is for some people the highest form of public service. Does this mean that to flatter the public is a greater service than to tell it the truth? . . . What will happen to a generation that really believes the flattery? We are doing our best to find out." I blamed both the puppeteers and their puppets in the arts and communications media.

Tracing the link between sponsors and artists to its origin in religion, I saw the Protestant Reformation ("ascribable to a bungled public relations job on the part of the Roman Catholics") as the historical turning point. "The arts were banished from many European churches on the truthful grounds that they appealed to the senses. . . . Freed from the obligation of being apologists for a particular theology, the artists ran for help to the state or the nobility, undertaking in return for payment to make them even more noble in the eyes of posterity." In our day, I noted, aristocrats have largely been replaced by distillers ("the sale of spirit repaid in things of the spirit").[1]

It was this roundhouse style of attack — accusing politicians, business, churches, artists, and communicators of conspiracy in a fraud, while I remained detached — that allowed me to lash out in all directions in the early *Spring Thaws*. But by 1961, when I again picked up the reins of that annual revue, my attitude toward political involvement had changed. Although I have never, to this day, become a member of any party, I came to see that political celibacy in the age of mass media was naive. Action on behalf of positive forces was urgent if we were not to lose what we had so recently gained. If everyone had kept their hands unsullied we would not have the CBC, the National Film Board, the Canada Council, the National Theatre School, and all the other institutions now in place. I would judge parties, I decided, on their support of cultural initiatives, and support the supporters. This could not be counted as "single issue" politics, I argued, because it was all-embracing: no culture, no country.

John Diefenbaker's Progressive Conservative government, reelected in 1958, had bungled the test. Although his party had created public broadcasting in Canada and some caucus members still understood its role in conserving the nation, Diefenbaker promptly introduced a new Broadcasting Act to accommodate private broadcasters — which meant more U.S. programs even before the public network had outlets across the nation. The new Board of Broadcast Governors, heavy with patronage appointments, proceeded to license private stations in places not yet covered by the CBC (despite the government's assurances to the contrary), and was about to award second licences in eight major cities. In 1959 — with Castro's Communists taking over Cuba, Nixon and Khrushchev exchanging visits, and the Soviets shooting pictures of the other side of the moon — everything, it seemed, including art, science and technology, was being politicized.

When CBC producers in Montreal go on strike to establish their authority over program content and casting, an essentially local jurisdictional skirmish threatens to ignite two national powder kegs: unionization of the federal civil service and Quebec independentism. Fearful that the insubordination may spread, the government sees a chance to intervene when CBC president Alphonse Ouimet has a heart attack and his beset pinch hitter, vice president Ernest Bushnell (who speaks no French), later resigns. Against Ouimet's advice the Cabinet replaces Bushnell with a compliant plodder, the equally Frenchless W. E. S. Briggs. This appointment, widely interpreted as a shortening of the traditional arm's-length relationship between government and crown corporation, fans the fire — as I discover when I visit Montreal to join a McGill University forum on "English–French Relations in Canada." The other participants are literary scholar Malcolm Ross, historian Michel Brunet, and my former International Service colleague René Lévesque, now one of the strike leaders and on the verge of a political career. Lévesque turns the occasion into a polemic on freedom from uncomprehending federal authority — using as his prime illustration the fact that the discussion was being held in English. I leave persuaded that if everyone disdains political involvement now, there may soon be no Canada to become involved in.

Stuart Griffiths, meantime, has returned from Britain, with a sizable stake from Granada Television to buy into Canada and a mind to teach the CBC a lesson. He forms Upper Canada Broadcasting, a group seeking the licence for Toronto's second station, which he easily persuades me to join, along with Sir Ernest MacMillan, Tom Patterson, Wayne and Shuster, architect Anthony Adamson (a visionary with impeccable Conservative ties), and enough well-heeled shareholders to take the financial gamble. My contribution is a program schedule. But doubt about our chances of getting a licence arises when stories circulate that the application has been fixed — one of the sources, and one of the alleged fixers, being another of the nine applicants, my former *Telegram* boss John Bassett. (Federal cabinet minister George Hees later boasts publicly that he was "very helpful to [Bassett] in getting his licence.") Bassett's quondam program director Ray Purdy, sent back to Canada from Britain by Roy Thomson, a Bassett ally, tells me Thomson instructed him to "draw up the best goddamn schedule you can, then we'll talk about what we'll *really* do." Purdy is soon out of a job.

The general cynicism is so thick that no surprise attends our loss of the bid, and no one sees fit to seek redress. This debacle reinforces my resolve to wade more deeply into politics, while keeping my head above water with income from television and theatre.

By February 1961, it amazes me to report, I am being compared by the *Star's* Blaik Kirby to an octopus, with "tentacles in everything":

> Moore insists, "I am fundamentally lazy." Despite his lazy ways, he's been seen recently as:
> • Star of *The Eye-Opener Man* . . . telecast last weekend.
> • Panelist on *Front Page Challenge* and *Live a Borrowed Life.*
> • Co-director of *Orpheus in the Underworld,* the Canadian Opera presentation which will be seen here on Monday . . .
> • Star of *King Lear* at the Crest.
>
> Right now he's writing a 90-minute televersion of *The Man Born to Be King,* to be shown by CBC at Easter. He's doing [several] one-hour radio plays (he'll also act in all of them) for broadcast this summer on *Four's Company.* He's also involved in dramas for the *First Person* and *Festival '61* TV series. This fall he'll again direct one of the Canadian Opera Company's productions.
>
> He is one of the leading lights behind the forthcoming quarterly *Theatre Canada;* is on the board of directors of the National Theatre School, and an editor of the opinion magazine *Canadian Commentator.* . . . He's chairman of the performing arts section of the Canadian Conference of the Arts, to be held in May. . . . And, of course, he is owner, producer, director, composer and lyricist of *Spring Thaw.* . . which rolls into Toronto this year on March 31.[2]

Kirby is unaware that I am also visiting Ottawa regularly to hold talks on cultural policy with the Liberals' former secretary of state, Jack Pickersgill.

With one exception, Kirby's is a list of endangered species. Before the year is out both *Canadian Commentator* and *Theatre Canada* will cease publication. And the CBC, the Crest, the Canadian Opera Company, the Canadian Conference of the Arts, and the National Theatre School are the natural prey of a government that sees culture as a commodity.

Three months after the opening of the National Theatre School I receive a letter from its director Jean Gascon, warning that it may not have enough funds to get through the first year. (Within three years it will be hailed by the leading U.S. theatre journal as the best on the continent.) At my home we hold an emergency meeting of Ontario board members, headed by the vigorous Pauline McGibbon. A national campaign is soon launched under the patronage of Vincent Massey himself. But the campaign is barely over when I find myself writing unofficially to Peter Dwyer, the associate director of the Canada Council, "to explore the possibility of an *advance* from the Council in respect of its next grant. I don't particularly like the idea of asking officially, yet . . . nor do I like the idea of mortgaging our future. But the immediate crisis is so serious that unless we weather it there may be no future to mortgage."[3] The Canada Council — now chaired by onetime *Sunshine Town* backer Douglas Weldon (who took the job, he tells me, because "I thought it would be the least demanding of several Dief offered me the morning after the election") — is itself at political risk.

The exception — the only free-standing, self-supporting item on Kirby's list — is the upstart *Spring Thaw*. Little wonder that it now becomes more political than ever.

I WRITE OF THESE EVENTS, 30-odd years later, in the light of a recent fashion to dismiss *Spring Thaw* as "undemanding evenings of gentle balladry, parochial humour and theatrical in-jokes"[4] — possibly on the supposition that that is what the antiquated audiences of the time laughed at. The harbinger of this disparagement may have been a 1980 article, bereft of research, in the *Toronto Star:*

> Toronto reviewers spewed venom every spring, competing for soul-destroying adjectives while vainly seeking logic for the show's success. It was collegiate humour, they yelped. Its satirical swipes were delivered with feather dusters; it was the great Canadian joke. . . .[5]

Compare the actual reviews for 1961, in Toronto or anywhere else: "The most pointed and sustained satire on current Canadian affairs it has ever been our luck to see" . . . "It has bite, thrust, punch" . . . "A deadly weapon against the smug and silly sides of Canadian life" . . . "Rapidly becoming one of the few major safety valves of our society" . . . "Every barbed shaft hit its target with uncanny accuracy" . . . "Slaughtered as many sacred cows as it could in a 2½ hour massacre" . . . "The trade [Broadway] is missing a similar bet . . . such hard-hitting, penetrating comment might be a sensation in New York." One critic quantified the poll for posterity, had posterity cared to check: "rewarded by rave notices by 99% of the daily news critics" — and chastised the remaining one percent: "It would appear Mr. Cohen had an axe to grind."[6]

Or perhaps indigestion. One of the items snubbed by Cohen was *Togetherness*, an ecumenical quartet for Roman Catholic cardinal, Anglican archbishop, United Church moderator, and Greek Orthodox patriarch, who distance themselves (in Alan Lund's subtle staging) as they sing in harmony. *Togetherness* went on to create a scandal in both New York and London. On Broadway it helped to sell Leonard Sillman's *New Faces of 1962* by being pronounced sacrilegious.[7] In London it appeared in the Canadian revue *Clap Hands* and, as reported by the Montreal *Gazette*, "caused quite a rumpus":

> The BBC-TV daily magazine program *Tonight* decided to add a footnote to a religious gathering held in Trafalgar Square, by getting the cast of *Clap Hands* into the studio to render *Togetherness*, Mavor Moore's satirical ditty. . . . The protests and phone calls to the BBC, and the press, and from the pulpits, rivalled the uproar caused the other day when . . . *That Was the Week That Was* assessed the various religions as it might be done by a consumer's guide.[8]

"Moore's song," the report continued, "might never have got on the air had it not been for the lifting, this week, of their ban on references to religion, royalty, politicians and sex, in light entertainment." The rule changer at the BBC was its new director-general, my old friend Hugh Carleton-Greene.

Had we mocked God, queens, governor generals, prime ministers, and assorted high dignitaries long before this, only to be labelled a "feather duster"?

Among other subjects *Spring Thaw '62* tackled separatism. The sketch *Le Dernier Cri* from that year was singled out by Montreal's leading critic. Jean Béraud of *La Presse*, when we brought *Spring Thaw* to Quebec two years later ("The spirit of Toronto blows across Montreal — it is a revelation!") to play in Gratien Gélinas's Théâtre de la Comédie Canadienne:

Westmount is besieged; the whole town is occupied. The Westmounter hopelessly implores: "What are you going to do with us?" And the Separatist replies: "Don't fight us, join us!" And then he lists, from one end of the country to the other, those who would join the movement until finally the whole Confederation is reconstituted! . . . A simple solution, but it makes you think, doesn't it? It is astonishing to note how this digest of seventeen annual revues still has a grip on the here and now.[9]

But even in the months preceding *Thaw '62* the line between art and actuality was one I seemed to be crossing with alarming regularity.

In January, while nightly playing Julius Caesar in Shaw's *Caesar and Cleopatra* at the Crest Theatre (Leon Major's production, with Toby Robins as a wondrously credible girl-empress), I found myself in the company of politicians during the day, as well. A federal election was at hand, and all parties had suddenly developed a keen interest in the cultural vote — or at least an appreciation of its image-making power. John Robarts, Ontario's new Tory premier — a statesman as honest as Shaw's Roman, if not as tough — was encouraging the arts in ways that put the federal Tories to shame. (Caesar: "We must respect literature, Ruffio.") Robarts hosted a series of lunches for artists, respecting art even on the occasion when Dennis Burton, the celebrated garter-belt painter, having fortified himself with martinis before lunch, dropped his face into the soup and left it there. Ignoring the spectre at the feast, Robarts broached for the first time his plan for an Ontario Arts Council.

Robert Winters, the most Caesarian of the Liberal leaders, understood that the arts were labour-intensive, growing industries. (He showed tangible proof of his confidence by investing in *Spring Thaw*.) The Liberal candidate in my riding was Mitchell Sharp, soon to join the handful of piano-playing finance ministers known to history. Sharp recognized the importance of developing a creative base in Canada if we were to compete abroad, a stance that permitted me to support his party while adhering to the principle of voting for the worthiest candidate in my riding.

As soon as *Caesar and Cleopatra* ended, I found myself in Ottawa coaching Mike Pearson, then leader of the Official Opposition, in how to perform on television. Pearson had a slight lisp that was often remarked upon — it would not have served Caesar well — but his diplomatic training had left him with a more serious handicap: he tended to agree with the last person who spoke to him. At our first session I was delighted at his progress; at our second I realized others had been at him in the meantime. And so it went until I realized he could never relax and be himself before the camera, as I remembered his doing before small gatherings at the United Nations. Deliberating between alternative advice, he became deliberate in his delivery.

When we filmed a series of interviews for the campaign, with me as questioner, his adroit political adviser Tom Kent insisted on my giving Pearson the questions in advance. Clutching my last vestige of independence, I insisted on spontaneity. We compromised: I agreed to provide Pearson with a list of the areas to be covered. But even this was fatal to his spontaneity. In prior conversation I had asked him what he thought of third parties; he chuckled and said, "They always come in third." Not true, but at least human. When I asked him in the filmed interview, he delivered a lecture in political science:

> In politics I think the best way of operating is through a two-party system, one party emphasizing change and reform and the other party emphasizing conservation. As far as minority parties are concerned, especially minority parties which have a narrow occupational base — I don't think that's the best way for democracy to operate, because you might well have a minority party of that type frustrating the desire of the people for change by allowing a government which the majority of the people disapproves of, to continue as a minority government.[10]

The message conveyed by this, whatever its merit, was one of guile. He was trying to pin the tail on the Conservatives, who in fact went on to win the 1962 election with a minority. But when that government failed and the Liberals won the 1963 election with a minority, Pearson found himself in the donkey's position.

In Toronto, meanwhile, John Bassett was running for the Progressive Conservatives in the 1962 election, in the polyglot riding of Spadina. Still burning from the fixed licence affair, I offered to speak out for the Ontario Liberals and was asked to introduce their candidate in Orillia, whom I did not know. I was aghast when I met the man, as may be inferred from the report in the *Toronto Star*:

> Mr. Moore last night said he was politically independent. He has voted CCF and in the last election voted Conservative because "the Liberals were tired and needed a rest. I thought it was time for a change but we jumped from the frying pan into the fire. . . ."[11]

I was even more aghast when I attended a party for Liberal candidates in Toronto and met Bassett's rival in Spadina, lawyer Perry Ryan. A sacrificial goat, I guessed. In another room, however, Ryan's organizer, the veteran Bill Campbell, was complaining through his teeth to a group of party heavyweights: "If you sons of bitches would only come into Spadina and give me a hand, I could get this idiot elected." He did.

FROM THE ART OF POLITICS, I found, it was a short leap to the politics of art. The fact was that the arts in Canada had grown in a single decade on a scale unmatched in any other time or country. The Canada Council, established in 1957 and already the mainstay of a still-expanding complex from Atlantic to Pacific, was both cause and victim of its own success. In addition to existing institutions, new arts spaces and companies were springing up in every city worthy of the name, and looking to government for subsidy. The Canadian Players, for example, was started with private backing after the 1953 Stratford Festival by Tom Patterson and Douglas Campbell to take Shakespeare and other classics into towns across Canada and the United States; but within four years it was seeking a Canada Council subsidy. Calgary and Edmonton had vast new jubilee auditoriums. Vancouver, where Nicholas Goldschmidt held an ambitious annual International Festival, had the large Queen Elizabeth Theatre and (by 1961) the smaller Playhouse. There was a strong movement to revive professional theatre in Halifax. In Winnipeg the fiercely Canadian immigrant John Hirsch and local accountant Tom Hendry had founded the Manitoba Theatre Centre, and watched it become, with council assistance, a model of community theatre for the continent.

Hirsch had understandable dreams of glory. When I invited him to the Canadian Conference of the Arts in May 1961, he replied:

> Last week I visited Edmonton on the invitation of the local theatre groups there. It seems they would like to start a Theatre Centre, fashioned after our own. This is exactly the kind of development I am hoping for all across the country. . . . I heard very good things about your King Lear. What are your plans for the future?[12]

I wished I could have told him. Matters were moving so quickly that every night we went to bed expecting the Future to arrive in the morning. At the conference in May, attended by arts activists from east and west, there was talk of using the nation's centennial, six years hence, as a motive to build a chain of arts centres across the improbable country, linking its fragmented population in a way previously possible only by telephone, radio, and television. But were such enterprises the responsibility of national, regional, or municipal government — or of none? In the master plan known as the British North America Act, the Fathers of Confederation had neglected to mention the arts or communications, while in the 1960s many of their successors saw them as purely commercial in nature. Such excuses allowed the Conservative government in Ottawa to ignore their importance, while the government of Quebec saw them as means to fortify Québécois identity.

Apart from the overextended Canada Council, there was little federal machinery to deal with the logistics of the museum system, national schools of the arts, or nationally touring bodies such as the Canadian Players, which by 1962 was almost bankrupt. In June 1962 the council's astute art director, Peter Dwyer, sought my views about the Players' future in the light of so much competing regional theatre activity. "I feel," I replied, "that where a local operation is of demonstrably high standard, as in Winnipeg, occasionally in Vancouver, and in the future perhaps in Halifax, the important bonus which a [regional] tour can bring to the local centre outweighs other benefits to be derived from the use of a national company. But until adequate coverage can be given from such centres as Winnipeg, there is a genuine need for some organization to fill the bill. This organization is presently and uniquely the Canadian Players."[13]

The next two months made me even more acutely aware of the need for national action. I spent the summer in Vancouver, where Leon Major was restaging his Crest Theatre *Caesar and Cleopatra* at the Vancouver Playhouse with a distinguished West Coast cast. Dilly and I rented a cottage on the West Vancouver mountainside overlooking Burrard Inlet and brought the three younger children — Rosalind aged eight, Marili, five, and Charlotte, four. Tedde, 14, stayed behind at Camp Tanamakoon in Muskoka. (She was a rare third-generation camper. Her grandmother Dora had started its dramatic arts program; her Uncle Fran built and equipped its open-air theatre; now Tedde was performing in it — to be followed, in due course, by her daughter Suzanna Shebib, whose . . . but I fantasize.) The rest of us spent an idyllic summer in Vancouver, with Dad going off every evening to take part in political theatre. But there was no escaping the politics of Canadian theatre.

Like their fellow professionals in Toronto and elsewhere, Vancouver actors, designers, and technicians needed a production base with regular seasons to keep them busy and keep them there. Drawn into discussions about a permanent company for the new Playhouse, I made the acquaintance of its leading proponents, including banker Alec Walton, brother of the English composer Sir William. After my return to Toronto, I wrote Walton a letter that catches the heady nationalism of the day:

> I called Dwyer the day I got back and found that he was in Newfoundland for a meeting of the Canada Council, from which he returned only this morning. . . . Meanwhile Leon Major has been in touch with Halifax and found their plans marvellously far advanced for the opening of their theatre [Neptune] in the summer of '63.
>
> As you will remember, the suggestion was thrown up during our lively and fruitful discussion that a national foundation might be formed to act as an umbrella for the various projects concerned. The one existing foundation of this kind is the Canadian Players . . . with an already impressive board of governors, ranging from one coast to the other. . . . By coincidence, the Canadian Players Executive Committee held a meeting this week designed to introduce a "crash program" of improvement and expansion, the upshot of which was an approach to me to become its Executive Producer. . . .
>
> This morning I talked at some length to Dwyer in Ottawa. He is most excited with the way the pieces of the jigsaw are falling into place, and thinks that we must ride the crest of the wave apparent on every hand. The best date for a meeting would seem to be Sunday, September 9; Dwyer is here for other meetings, Major will have returned from Halifax with the story there, and by then I shall have had time to clarify the situation with Canadian Players. Will it now be possible for you to send someone from Vancouver to attend? I shall also get in touch with Hirsch in Winnipeg, with a view to his attending.
>
> Let me know your thoughts on all this. I really do feel that something of enormous importance to the country can be midwifed here and now, if we attend the birth with skill and determination.[14]

When I informed Montreal's Guy Beaulne, the new chair of the Canadian Theatre Centre, of the plan "to establish a national organization of regional theatres" with the Canadian Players Foundation as the instrument, he cited the growing resentment in Quebec over Toronto's arrogation of names such as the Canadian Opera Company, the National Ballet

Company, and various "Canadian" associations. But opposition also arose from Hirsch, who naturally saw the universe unfolding more suitably from Winnipeg. I arranged three productions for the Canadian Players that winter, reduced the company's debt, and quit — convinced that its role could only decline as that of the regional theatres grew.

After a tour of southern Ontario, Spring Thaw '63 opened at the Royal Alexandra to tepid reviews, prompted by the mad success of an overture to which the unusually serious show proved anticlimactic. There was, in those days, a bylaw requiring the playing of the national anthem at all public performances. I had Lucio Agostini arrange a compound of "God Save the Queen" and "O Canada" in different keys. The audience, caught standing, was variously outraged or jubilant. Immediately after the first night, director Leon Major left for Halifax to launch the first season of Neptune Theatre. I was to join him later to direct two of the plays and appear as Undershaft, the arms magnate, in Shaw's Major Barbara, the opening production.

I had no premonition whatever that Undershaft would be my swan song as a stage actor. But between the two events John Hirsch and I had a collision 3,000 miles away.

Both of us were hired to direct at the annual Vancouver International Festival, where artistic director Nicholas Goldschmidt had been succeeded by Dino Yannopoulos of the Metropolitan Opera. Each year the festival was dedicated to a different country. It was the turn of British culture to be saluted that year. Yannopoulos, unfamiliar with Canadian resources, brought his own production team from New York. The young Mike Nichols also came to direct a stage play for the first time: The Importance of Being Earnest. In addition to casting Earnest for Nichols, I was to stage a revival of the old English musical Florodora ("Tell me, pretty maiden . . .") in the large Queen Elizabeth Theatre and mount a West Coast Spring Thaw in the small Playhouse, with Vancouver-born Dave Broadfoot heading a local cast. Yannopoulos himself would direct those two celebrated British operas, Verdi's Macbeth and Nikolai's The Merry Wives of Windsor, as well as Shaw's Saint Joan — for all of which the stars were imported from Broadway and Hollywood. Hirsch was to stage J. M. Barrie's Peter Pan, with Heath Lamberts. Spring Thaw was, so to speak, the token Canadian content. ("Canada's culture is not strong," Eric Nicol jibed in The Province, "but it is extraordinarily absorbent.")

Mike Nichols, who could wring amusement from watching people come to terms with his fake hair and eyelashes (he was otherwise hairless), had a keen eye for human foibles. He sneaked into a rehearsal of *Florodora* at which I introduced a crescent moon that moved with the lovers (two vain Broadway singers foisted on me by Yannopoulos), and hid behind a rear seat, suppressing his hysterical laughter lest he betray to these egoists how they were being upstaged. But the rest of Yannopoulos's team was working less for the festival than for Yannopoulos. When it came to lighting *Florodora*, which needed all the help it could get, I was told every lamp had been set for the operas and none could be altered. Hirsch, arriving later than I, was forewarned and raised an effective fuss. But it paled beside the fuss I raised when I learned that despite the festival's huge deficit Hirsch was being paid for one production nearly twice what I had accepted for two and a half. It was a repetition of the Stratford caper. From then on, despite our considerable mutual respect, Hirsch considered me soft and I considered him sharp.

Nor were matters helped by the sequel. Immediately after the first night of *Florodora* I departed for Toronto, en route to Halifax, leaving the West Coast *Spring Thaw* playing to full houses in the smaller Playhouse. As the Festival progressed, attendance dwindled at every one of the elaborate attractions in the larger Queen Elizabeth Theatre until, for the final week, the management cancelled them all and moved in frugal little *Spring Thaw*, which continued to sell out. This lopsided victory for the home team was neither nationally noted nor universally approved.

THE DAY I ARRIVED in Halifax, after crossing the country, marked the start of my higher education in the politics of boards. In later years I would draw a compound portrait of the Balanced Theatre Board:

> X would not remain on the board unless Y was booted off it. If either went, another Catholic would have to be found. Z, running for some political seat or other, was mainly interested in photo opportunities. B wanted to vet the plays (think of the children), while C thought they should challenge convention, and D didn't give a damn about the plays so long as they made money. H, an academic, regarded all theatre as a natural opportunity for the exercise of his own art form: criticism. K simply adored giving parties. The Mayor was onside, but that meant the Publisher was against it. The provincial cabinet was split, but prepared to back it as a tourist magnet, which the opposition could hardly paint as wasting taxes on art. N was having an affair with Q, and P was clearly there as a mole for the feds.[15]

I had previously dealt with boards of various sorts in Toronto, and sat on others. But the Toronto boards I knew were usually small and composed of diligent supporters such as Charles Tisdall, the piano-playing public relations magus who accompanied the first *Spring Thaws* and stayed on to become president of the New Play Society in its day of adversity. Doubtless the membership of such boards included social climbers, but timeservers and tyrants soon found themselves at the wrong address. The founding board at Stratford was a stripped-down band of the faithful, dedicated to a vision and to the man who would implement it for them. The nascent Vancouver Playhouse board was bonded by the western oxygen of venture into the unknown.

But moving directly to the East Coast from the West (as they were then), I at once noticed three general differences: the greater antiquity of the buildings, the pervasive smell of older fish, and a striking antithesis in drinking habits. At parties in Vancouver the heavier drinkers became comic extroverts, doing imitations or jumping into the nearest pool with their clothes on; in Halifax they descended into gloomy Celtic introspection or broke into arguments. The reason, I concluded, had less to do with the local waters than with history.

If Vancouver was giving birth, Halifax in 1963 was on the verge of a rebirth. A full two centuries earlier, this vital Atlantic port and military base boasted Canada's first newspaper and first resident professional theatre. By the mid 1800s, when Sam Cunard ran his shipping company from there, it reached a prosperous golden age graced by four universities. The devastating harbour explosion of 1917, the biggest man-made blast before Hiroshima, had levelled its prospects along with its buildings; and not until the Second World War did the city begin a comeback. Like all ports, it had a populace both sophisticated and hard-bitten — a marriage of convenience that in this case bred a politics of cynicism. The universities, all of them sprung from church roots, had not yet succeeded in enlightening the resident racists; natives and the numerous blacks took even less part in social life than they did in parvenu Toronto, and the first Jewish judge had been appointed to the bench just before I arrived. This did not mean he was welcome at the golf or social clubs.

I came early to find summer quarters for the family (Tedde, now 16, was to be a wardrobe assistant), and to meet prospective cast members. Artistic director Leon Major greeted me in the office already set up in the old film/vaudeville house at Argyle and Sackville streets, now renamed the Neptune Theatre, and still in the turmoil of renovation. But also in turmoil was the board of the Neptune Theatre Foundation, as it tried to accumulate social, intellectual, financial, and political clout.

Its steadfast chairman, Arthur Murphy, was (like James Bridie) a surgeon-turned-playwright who moved easily in all four circles. But this avidity for influence had a price. Leon and Judith Major were Jewish, connected to Halifax through Judith's father, Robert Strand, an ebullient U.S.-born publicist who was one of the project's first advocates — and now, as Neptune's publicist, one of its beneficiaries. It was Strand who had suggested Leon (along with Tom Patterson and Toronto playwright Jack Gray, now the theatre's writer-in-residence) to write the report that led to Neptune's founding. Renovations were supervised by resident designer Les Lawrence, also of Toronto. Long before rehearsals began for *Major Barbara,* therefore, the 30-year-old Major — as two disaffected patrons of the arts hastened to inform me — had committed half the sins in the Decalogue: he was self-recommended, appointed through nepotism, a consorter with Americans, an importer of cronies from Upper Canada, a Shavian socialist, and Jewish. But would I care to join them for dinner at the golf club?

During the summer, however, this sociopolitical theatre was driven into the wings by the sure hand of surgeon Murphy (who had achieved fame as a scriptwriter for U.S. television's *Medic* series), and by the dedicated company Major had assembled from Halifax and points west. As in Toronto and Vancouver, CBC Halifax had generated a corps of polished performers, such as the versatile Joan Gregson and David Brown, eager for more stage activity. CBC Television was employing carpenters and lighting technicians, musical talent was all around, and the crucial Nova Scotia College of Art was preparing designers and crafters for new challenges. In brief, despite the manoeuvring at board level, the creative critical mass proved more potent than the political clucking that accompanied it.

The echo, which I heard as I walked along Barrington Street, came from one of my documentaries: *There may be obstructions, local prejudices may arise, disputes may occur, local jealousies may intervene, but it matters not — the wheel is now revolving and we are only the fly on the wheel . . .* It was Upper Canada's John A. Macdonald, stopping in Halifax on his way to a meeting of colonial leaders in Charlottetown to discuss the confederation that took place three years later.

FRANK MACKINNON, a deceptively Rotarian, cigar-smoking political scientist, was then principal of Prince of Wales, a junior college in Charlottetown. My exact contemporary, he always wore spectacles, although one could have sworn he had eyes in the back of his head, and occasionally hearing aids that allowed him to pretend he was deaf. After long study, MacKinnon had developed a novel theory about boards.

In 1950 he had presented a brief to the Massey Commission proposing a national memorial to the Fathers of Confederation. Tiny Prince Edward Island (population then 105,000) seemed like an unlikely site, especially since it had opted out at the time of Confederation and joined only after the event; MacKinnon pointed out that Prince Edward Island already attracted four times its population in summer, but official approval was denied. He kept quietly at it, however, eventually extracting a promise from the premier of Prince Edward Island (obviously convinced the project would never fly) to provide a site, fund the maintenance, and "keep politics out of it."[16] By 1958 MacKinnon had privately assembled a compact board of 16 members from all the provinces. He then flattered Prime Minister Diefenbaker into making a commitment (which the PM did not take seriously enough to share with his officials) of "$2,800,000 on condition the provinces pledge the other half." This was considered impossible, since it had never been done. Of the 10 provincial governments of the day, four were Conservative, three Liberal, two Social Credit, and one socialist. MacKinnon and his cohorts began at the coasts and worked their way inland, kiting as they went — telling each premier that his neighbours were in, and vice versa — and finally confronted the prime minister with his bond and a done deed. MacKinnon personally collected the first installment from Diefenbaker just before his Progressive Conservative Cabinet fell apart, precipitating a federal election. All this was achieved, and probably only achievable, with no government studies, no public committees, and no publicity until agreements had been signed.

By a stroke of luck the old potato warehouse beside the provincial Legislature where the Fathers once met had burned down (there were those ready to swear MacKinnon had a hand in it); and after an architectural competition (wangled by MacKinnon out of the Canada Council), excavation began in the winter of 1963. In July, as I played the equally pragmatic Undershaft at Neptune, the cornerstone was laid by the new prime minister, Lester B. Pearson, with naval guns booming in the harbour. The picture in the Halifax newspaper the next day was all I knew about the Confederation Centre when I got a call from Frank MacKinnon: Would I come to the island for a day's fishing?

I was the fish. "We had noted," MacKinnon wrote in a later memoir, "how much trouble had occurred in some other new enterprises when the first administrators had been political appointees or artistic people with high profiles but inadequate abilities. We enquired about possibilities at a time of acute shortage of cultural administrators in Canada, and decided not to have a competition but to aim for the best. Only one person was interviewed even though we were told 'You'll never get him.'"[17]

The unorthodox two-way interview consists of a drive around the island's magnificent beaches with retired navy commander Ken Birtwistle, in charge of the island's 1964 centennial preparations, a splendid lobster lunch, and an informal meeting with the local executive committee. To this point nothing has been said about a job. I am shown a model of the building, with its handsome theatre, art gallery, museum, memorial hall, and library, and listen to MacKinnon outline the centre's aim: "To blend the idea of a national memorial with the local interests of the island and the wishes of the large numbers of tourists, while avoiding the limitations of localism . . . to implement the advantages of a public trust while avoiding political identities and patronage . . . to encourage the flourishing of the arts as valuable national and local assets while fostering artistic and financial responsibility." "Very impressive," I say, thinking that only a Canadian would believe it feasible.

Then comes the quiet, precise lure. "We were hoping," says MacKinnon, "you might tell us how to go about it." *The same homespun bait that caught Guthrie at Stratford!* Waffling between awe and anticipation, I look around the room and see only steadfastness: Alan Holman, of the loyal department store dynasty; Frank Storey, furniture retailer, Lieut. Col. (ret.), Army Signals; Loy Duffy, dentist; Florence Matheson, teacher, national president of the Women's Institute; Philip Matheson, farmer, provincial Cabinet member; Mac Putnam, surgeon; Father Adrien "Bubbles" Arsenault, poet-priest, Canada Council member; Charles Scott, canny Ottawa lawyer; and MacKinnon.

> MM: Well (*suddenly aware I have adopted Guthrie's quizzical tone*), it seems to me that a memorial to the birth of the country should be used to do new things.
>
> FM: (*after a drag on his mangled cigar*) Such as?
>
> MM: I don't know yet. But a memorial to the Fathers should also be fun, because there was a lot of celebrating.
>
> FM: That's what we think. (*drag*) How'd you like to do it for us?
>
> MM: Do what?
>
> FM: Run the place. (*another drag*) And our centennial next year.

I ask to see what there is of the building — only, as yet, the foundations. Donning hard hats, we negotiate our way through the incipient library, gallery, and great hall onto the block of concrete that will support the stage. I look out over the concentric rows where the seats will fit, rising toward the back, filled only with promise. I glance back at my silent hosts, who with their partners across the country have brought the improbable project this far. I can say nothing. Early the following morning, before I leave for Halifax to talk it over with Dilly, MacKinnon and I go fishing in the silent lake by his home.

MM to Eva Langbord, CBC casting director, Toronto, August 14, 1963:

> I have taken on the job of Director for the [P.E.I.] Centennial in 1964. It will mean spending a good deal of the year in Charlottetown. I shall be returning to Toronto on Sept. 5th [to direct Don Giovanni] and expect to be there until about mid-October. I shall then be in Charlottetown for the rest of October and all of November; back in Toronto from December 1st until January 1st; in Vancouver for the rest of January and all of February [launching The Best of Spring Thaw on a national tour and staging Julius Caesar for the Playhouse] and then back once more to Charlottetown, more or less permanently until mid-September. . . . I would love to do two or three shows during the year, if anything comes up at these times.

The final, operative sentence reflects the $17,500 bank debt bequeathed me by Spring Thaw '63. Nineteen sixty-four promises to be a hectic year for the Moores.

WE WERE, AFTER ALL, in the sixties, and teenage Tedde was beginning to display the decade's characteristic anomie. The Berlin Wall, that immense symbol of rupture, was now complete. John Glenn had been in orbit, John Kennedy assassinated, and John Profumo disgraced. Martin Luther King was on the march, a hotline linked White House and Kremlin, Timothy Leary was dropping acid, and Tedde Moore was threatening to drop out of school. (All our children went to public schools, partly because their father visited on them his aversion to private schools.) Dilly and I decided that since I was to spend so much time in Charlottetown, Tedde should come with me and attend Prince of Wales College as a boarder. For two months she hated it, as she made amply clear, since the other students gave short shrift to her Upper Canadian airs; and then (or so she said) she began to appreciate being brought down to the island's good red earth. By July 1964, when her mother and sisters joined us in a seaside cottage, she had passed her 17th birthday and all understanding. A year later . . . but wait.

Meantime I was focusing on macro-matters — the construction and staffing of the centre, and two centennial celebrations, one for the 1964 meeting of the Fathers in Charlottetown, and a preliminary run for the national event in 1967. My first step was to engage the best and earthiest publicity director in the country, Mary Jolliffe, because we had no time to lose in getting the word out, both on and off the island.

The timetable for the building was extremely tight. Before I arrived in October 1963 the board had made two firm commitments: to host the 1964 Dominion Drama Festival in the theatre in May (nine months away), and to host a royal visit in October when the queen would open the whole centre. Early television traumas had taught me something about construction, but this time, as the centre's director-general, I was called upon to take a direct hand in it. And the hand needed the dexterity of a U.N. diplomat. We were working with a national foundation chaired in Calgary (by oilman and philanthropist Eric Harvie), an architect from Quebec (the innovative Dimitri Dimakopoulos), a general contractor from Ontario, suppliers from New Brunswick and Nova Scotia, stage-rigging experts from Britain, and a famous acoustical engineer from New York (George Isenhower) — all the while aiming to please 11 governments, including a P.E.I. Cabinet sensitive to local resentment of interlopers "from away."

Organizing the provincial celebrations, mind you, opened my eyes to the resources on hand. Just as Cecil Clarke discovered a theatrical bootmaker in Toronto for the Stratford Festival, I discovered a former head wig dresser of the Royal Opera House on a Queens County farm. But ideas and skills turned out to be plentiful among those who had always lived there, starting with the First Peoples. With the invaluable Ken Birtwistle I traversed the island, visiting towns, hamlets, and reservations to talk with local enthusiasts. History buffs in the navy collaborated with the native Micmacs to restage the arrival of the Europeans on the north shore. Groups and individuals came forward with proposals for craft and other exhibitions, books, choral events, concerts, artworks, and plays of striking proficiency as well as enthusiasm — belying the cynics who said a Charlottetown arts centre was a contradiction in terms. What began as a reminder of a past political event turned into a celebration of present cultural vitality. That is the proper measure of political deeds.

Simultaneously we laid plans for a June-to-September celebration of national prowess in the arts more ambitious than any yet attempted anywhere. Since it constituted a relatively inexpensive dry run for the country-wide centennial to come, the federal government provided a supporting grant. The main subsidy, however, came from the artists themselves, who responded as if to a call to arms.

At this remove I cannot believe we did it, let alone recount how. The staff was minimal and with few exceptions inexperienced. From Vancouver I brought the skillful young stage manager of the West Coast *Spring Thaw*, Robert Dubberley, promoting him to production manager. Andis Celms, a bilingual dynamo, was hired as technical director, and designer/director Ronald Irving, a Maritimer, as theatre coordinator. Once *Spring Thaw* arrived, I retained its accomplished musical director, John Fenwick, and involved all the trained skills available locally; we had to be teachers as well as practitioners. I put the industrious Dubberley in charge of program arrangements during my frequent absences in the preceding winter.

On New Year's Eve, 1963, I wrote to the shareholders of Mavor Moore Productions:

> I leave for Vancouver tomorrow to commence rehearsals for the national tour of *The Best of Spring Thaw*. . . . We have the strongest cast in years, tried and true material, and the fine reputation we established at Vancouver last spring to go on. . . . The tour will cover 41 towns and cities and nearly 10,000 miles — a unique venture in our theatrical history. . . .[18]

My plan is for *The Best of Spring Thaw* to conclude its grand tour at the Confederation Centre in June to open the summer gala. This to be followed by the musical *Irma La Douce*, as staged for the Vancouver Festival by Jean and Gabriel Gascon of the Théâtre du Nouveau Monde; setting a North American precedent, the show will close on one coast on Saturday, fly (scenery and all) across the continent on Sunday, and open on the other coast on Monday. Next, the premiere of Don Owen's film *Nobody Waved Goodbye* and another NFB feature, *The Drylanders*, starring Frances Hyland. After that the Royal Winnipeg Ballet in Canadian works . . . the Canadian Opera Company's *Die Fledermaus* with the Halifax Symphony . . . the Toronto Children's Theatre in *Sleeping Beauty* . . . Neptune Theatre in Tommy Tweed's comedy about the first prime minister, *John A. Beats the Devil* . . . Don Messer and His Islanders . . . *Wayne and Shuster in Charlottetown* (their first stage appearance since *The Army Show*). And on Sundays a concert series: Léopold Simoneau and Pierrette Alarie, Lois

Marshall, Glenn Gould, Maureen Forrester, Jon Vickers, Oscar Peterson, the Baroque Trio, the P.E.I. Centennial Choir, the National Youth Orchestra . . .

The art gallery and museum, meanwhile, were to spring fully armed from the fertile brow of Moncrieff Williamson, whom I recruited while in Vancouver in the same direct fashion as MacKinnon had recruited me. All the advice we received pointed to this Scots-born globe-trotter, another veteran of wartime intelligence, onetime director of the eclectic Glenbow Museum in Calgary, and now mastermind of the Art Gallery of Greater Victoria, British Columbia, where I found him. Within a few months the enthusiastic Crieff would corral five private collections of vintage Canadian art; organize the first retrospective of Prince Edward Island's celebrated portraitist of the Fathers of Confederation, Robert Harris (1849–1919); mount an exhibition of historical objects, mostly from local sources; and assemble, through his personal contacts, a show of contemporary Canadian works by an unheard-of method: "permanent loan" from painters and sculptors across the country.

But before all this happens we must be ready to host the finals of the amateur Dominion Drama Festival in May, with the prime minister and other dignitaries in attendance.

As DDF Day approaches, the starting contestants fear they will be penalized for having to break in our equipment. The stage is indeed held together by pink string and sealing wax, but it works. In the auditorium, however, acoustical engineer George Isenhower, a giant physically and professionally, is having grave difficulty with the push-button cantilevered panels he has invented for the side walls; they are locked in their extended position, cutting off the side seat sections, and will not budge. On the eve of the opening I retire to my room in the Charlottetown Hotel at about one in the morning, leaving Isenhower to wrestle with his baffles. An hour later I am awakened by DDF revellers in the adjacent room. After a fruitless call to the front desk, I don a dressing gown, prop my door open, knock on theirs, and icily suggest they choose between a party tonight and a festival tomorrow. They agree to pipe down, but my return to my room is anticipated by one of the female revellers, who offers to help me get back to sleep. I say something rude but effective about amateurs. At six in the morning the phone rings; George Isenhower is in the lobby and wants to come up. Unshaven, clearly exhausted from working through the night, big George, the world expert, flops into the armchair and says, "Mavor, the goddamn things don't work." We go to the theatre and pin them back against the walls forever.

I throw the carpet layers out of the theatre two minutes before the audience is admitted, and join the committee of blithe smiles welcoming the prime minister, the lieutenant governor, the premier, and their wives at the door.

Aside from the night Glenn Gould's piano arrives without Glenn Gould, the summer goes more smoothly than we have any right to expect. Wayne and Shuster, at the height of their fame on *The Ed Sullivan Show*, capture the mood in their theme song: "They all sat down in Charlottetown, and built themselves a land!" When they emerge from the stage door on opening night, they are greeted by a throng of admirers fronted by two urchins reconvulsed with laughter at the sight of them. "Youse guys," says one, "are so comical it ain't funny!" In our euphoria we do not dream that a quarter century later another group of politicians sitting down in Charlottetown to rebuild the land will elicit a similar response across the country.

During July and August, the bank clearance figures on the island increased by 25 percent over previous years. This index of retail activity, a measure of the centre's economic spinoff, did more than the events themselves to convince sceptics that culture was not entirely marginal. The national media, however, paid little heed to either artistic or financial success. It was the late-in-the-day presence of Royalty that drew attention.

Frank MacKinnon was a devout monarchist, believing, as a political scientist, in the separation of pomp and power. Half the troubles in the United States, said MacKinnon, were caused by having a president who embodied both, wasting his time shaking hands and making speeches when he should be running the country. I was by now a confirmed republican, but one clearly in the position of a visitor in Rome invited to put on a spectacle for the emperor. I was also genuinely curious about the rituals of monarchy. With that in mind I proposed the first Royal Command Performance in Canadian history, but the palace, perhaps fearing the worst, insisted we drop the "Command." So I and Alan Lund, a veteran of two such events in London, substituted "Variety" and set about enlisting talent prepared to show up for expenses and glory.

Lorne Greene, the patriarch of the Ponderosa, fetching up to $50,000 an appearance these days, is invited to be master of ceremonies. I am cashing in an old IOU; he knows it and accepts without mentioning money. Gratien Gélinas, the father of modern Quebec theatre, consents to do a scene from his play *Tit-Coq*. (Whether the Royals' French

encompasses *joual* nobody seems to know.) The now renowned Anna
Russell has met Her Majesty before and is delighted to renew the
acquaintance. "I collect queens," she says. Dave Broadfoot will appear as
the stout-headed Renfrew of the Mounties. Almost all those invited agree
to come except the popular Quebec chanteuse Monique Leyrac. When I
phone her from Gélinas's office in Montreal, in French, she is gracious
but firm. "For you, Monsieur Mavor Moore, I would come, but not for
her." *Que dire?* I am the one politicizing art.

A royal fanfare has been commissioned from Louis Applebaum.
When the night arrives and the audience is seated, my last duty before
ushering in the royal party gathered in the upper lobby is to call backstage to the stage manager to cue the trumpeters to enter. It is one of the
rare occasions attended by both governor general and prime minister, as
well as the lieutenant governor, the premier, and other dignitaries and
spouses, including mine. Tails have come out of mothballs, long gloves
out of tissue paper, and jewellery out of profits. Orders are the order of
the day. The queen's dress is elaborate, the duke's uniform well tailored,
but the erect, silver-haired Vaniers — he in an earned general's uniform,
she in a classic white gown — seem more royal than the Royals. Protocol
straitlaces everything together until, report has it, I break all the rules by
cheerfully dashing up to Her Majesty and saying, "Well, are we all set?"
"All set!" she says, equally cheerfully, and away we go.

Robertson Davies's "Charlottetown Prologue," read by Lorne Greene,
is like nothing she has ever heard. Verses of welcome to crown and audience are followed by:

> Tomorrow for certain the Press will raise a stench
> If every second word I say now isn't French.

> And perhaps that is right
>   When you come to consider
> Her Majesty's Norman forbears
>   Spoke French on Sundays;
> The Hanoverians spoke German,
>   The Stuarts spoke Gaelic in church
> While the Tudors spoke Welsh —
>   And Irish on alternate Mondays.
> And of course here in Canada
>   We not only speak French,

> But a lot of Ukrainian, some Dutch,
>   Ojibway, Cree and Algonquin,
> Italian galore: and Eskimo
>   (Not quite so much)
> An English *patois* of sorts —
>   Surprisingly good Portuguese,
> Some Yiddish, and by all reports
> It's allowed to swear oaths in Chinese
>   In our magistrates' courts . . .[19]

After which, to general astonishment, Pop Cartwright breaks into the limpid French of Davies's coauthor, poet Robert Finch, until rescued by Gratien Gélinas.

There is a song in the show from a musical version of *Anne of Green Gables* recently seen on CBC Television, with words by Donald Harron and music by Norman Campbell. As we make our way backstage to meet the cast and crew, Queen Elizabeth confesses how much she has always loved Lucy Maud Montgomery's novel, which was her introduction to Prince Edward Island. "When," she asks, "are you going to present the whole play?" "Next year, ma'am. We plan to have a whole festival of Canadian shows." "Oh, really!" she says, managing to sound not only unsurprised but keenly interested. "Well, jolly good luck!" Desperately changing the subject, I ask how she copes with the time changes when travelling between continents. "It's really quite simple," she replies, as warmly as if she were sharing a recipe. "I always keep my watch on British time."

I think of my father, born in a mean row house in Sheffield, and check my own watch.

15

A Hundred Years Old

"CHARLOTTETOWN SOUNDS GREAT, but that's just the appetizer," said the fervent grey flannel suit at the Arts and Letters Club lunch. "Pearson has to pull the country together in a hurry, and the centennial's the way to do it. We need you here."

I cannot remember when I first met Arthur Gelber. Growing up, I knew of the family: the four sons and one daughter of a courtly, well-to-do wool merchant and his wife, who had quietly broken the barrier against Jewish students at Upper Canada College and Havergal, the girls' school. The youngest, tall, lordly Sholome, had been John Terrace's chum at high school. Like Arthur, he was an ardent amateur actor, but after I miscast him as a tough cop in *The Time of Your Life* at the New Play Society, he wisely abandoned the acting profession for Wall Street. I next met Marvin, art collector and sometime Liberal MP, at the United Nations. I recall being introduced in Ottawa to the vital Sylva, one of the rare senior female mandarins, and meeting on Bloor Street the oldest of the brothers, Lionel, Rhodes scholar, roving historian, and world strategist, who would occasionally return to Toronto in his black homburg and velvet lapels like some exotic homing eagle. But Arthur, the closest to my age and the only one with a family of his own, seemed simply to be there, as if I had always known him.

Being there, when needed, was Arthur Gelber's art form. He dutifully went into the family business instead of theatre or university; but finding that a well-spent hour or two a day at his office produced enough income for comfort, and that his wife Esther shared his enthusiasms, he decided when still a young man to devote his lifetime to building a more significant place for the arts in the community. Believing them to be an essential path to civilization (which like charity begins at home), he began to ally himself with existing initiatives and to launch others, often behind the scenes, or doing the spadework for figureheads. At once businessman, artist manqué, patron, and card-carrying Liberal, Gelber invented a new full-time unpaid profession: forging links between culture, commerce, and government.

But to implement any cultural policy the new Liberal minority government in Ottawa depended on support from other parties. The centennial's charm as an instrument for both cultural animation and national bonding lay in its multipartisan appeal. It was a card-carrying Tory, Anthony Adamson, town planner, heritage buff, skipper of our unsuccessful bid for a TV licence, who earlier prodded Mavor Moore Productions into forming a subsidiary called Legendrama to re-create history with sound-and-light spectacles at Dundurn Castle and other Ontario sites. ("The last time I came to Dundurn," one visitor told the *Hamilton Spectator*, "was to see a two-headed calf. What an improvement this is!")[1] At the same time many of the liveliest talents writing, broadcasting, painting, and filmmaking were radicals for whom the centennial was an opportunity to revise the past and seize the future. Thus the Gelbers and Adamsons of the world found themselves making common cause with a wide range of political and cultural interests. It was an unusual alliance, generated by a rare set of circumstances, and thus transient. ("What goes up must come down," as the valet remarks to his boss in *The Ottawa Man*, "but it's very nice in the meantime.")

In the months leading up to the P.E.I. centennial in 1964, I was increasingly drawn into governmental preparations for the countrywide event in 1967. As rumour had predicted, Maurice Lamontagne, Pearson's intellectual secretary of state, invited the provinces and cities to join in building a chain of centennial halls across the land, tossing in a year-long crisscrossing festival of attractions to go into them. ("These halls," Lamontagne said, "are going to play in the cultural field . . . as positive a role as that played in the economic field by the railways built by our great-grandfathers." He had no premonition of what would happen to the railways.)[2] I soon found myself sitting on an advisory committee for a National Arts Centre in Ottawa, talking with Arthur Gelber about another for Toronto, and co-chairing, with Roland Michener and Hector Boivin (the mayor of Granby), the overall National Conference on the Centennial of Confederation. Note the delicate casting: Michener the Alberta-born Conservative, Boivin the Quebec Liberal, and an independent from Ontario with one foot in the Atlantic.

The minutes of a meeting in Stratford, of the future National Arts Centre's advisory committee for theatre, make a splendid illustration of the politics of art, as distinct from the art of politics. The cast: Jean Gascon (in the chair), associate director, Stratford Festival; John Hirsch, Manitoba Theatre Centre; Michael Langham, Stratford's artistic director; and Leon Major of Halifax's Neptune and myself. (Absentees include the only woman member, Yvette Brind'Amour of Le Rideau Vert.) Nicholas Goldschmidt, now organizer of performing arts activities for the Centennial Commission, is sitting in, along with Hamilton Southam, the project's coordinator, who has just outlined his plan for a resident theatre company:

> **Mr. Southam:** It was for decision whether the sort of theatre organization he had in mind [the centre itself to be responsible only for efficient management but funded sufficiently to subsidize a tenant company] should be organized in Ottawa from scratch, or whether some existing theatre organization . . . could be persuaded to develop their activities further in the Ottawa context.

> **Mr. Langham:** If the Ottawa company were to rise to the occasion in 1967, it should be formed and set to work long before . . . [and] he doubted whether the present atmosphere in Ottawa was propitious, or Ottawa's present artistic resources adequate. . . . In his view the organization should be set up in Toronto to begin with . . . on the understanding that it would move lock, stock and barrel to Ottawa when the Centre opened in 1967.

> **Mr. Goldschmidt:** Strong reservations about this. . . . Once an organization had been set up in one city, with the strong community backing that would be necessary, it would be well nigh impossible to move it to another city, and certainly very bad from the public relations point of view.

> **Mr. Hirsch:** The Federal Government should be aware that a special subsidy for the Ottawa company would be acceptable only if increased subsidies were made available to existing theatre companies elsewhere. . . .

Mr. Moore: [Are you proposing] an exchange of visits, with the Ottawa company playing another city at the same time as that city's company was appearing at the Centre in Ottawa?

Mr. Southam: There was no thought that the Ottawa company should ever compete with other companies.

Mr. Major: While the larger theatre companies might be developed in the Ottawa/Toronto/Montreal triangle, the needs of the regional theatres in Halifax, Winnipeg and Vancouver, for example, should not be overlooked, nor the particular contribution they could make to professional theatre. . . .

Mr. Gascon: Urged that a small professional theatre company be started in Ottawa as soon as possible. The present lack of theatre facilities in Ottawa might mean that its Ottawa season would have to be short, and it would have to play more in Toronto and Montreal until the Centre was built. . . .

The consensus . . . was in favour of Mr. Langham's suggestion that . . . there would from the outset be three full-time professional companies, two English-language and one French-language, for the three cities; the first of the English-language companies would be the existing Stratford festival company, which would establish a winter base in Montreal; the second English-language company would be a new one to be formed in Toronto, which would move to Ottawa on completion of the Centre. . . .[3]

This Stratford-über-Alles song bore no more relation to needs across the country than Hitler's Lebensraum to those of Europe in 1939. "There are," I wrote to Southam, "two challenges which I think we as a nation must at once take up: the production of Canadian plays (without which our 'theatre' is a mockery) and — not unrelated — the production of Canadian feature films. . . . If we are to have a 'national' company, let it be one that performs Canadian plays."[4] I went on to propose a resident touring company so different from available models that competition would be unthinkable and international fame assured: a bilingual company able to perform both new plays and classics in either of the two global tongues.[5] We could have done it. But the argument continued to be over "Who's in charge?" instead of "What must be done?"

I was perforce learning to be more bilingual myself. At the inaugural meeting of the National Conference on the Centennial, in Ottawa, I made my first impromptu speech in French. It came on the spur of the moment, as I realized that my fellow anglophones were avoiding the risk, run every day by our francophone colleagues, of making fools of themselves in a second language. My punishment was to be made permanent chair of the Standing Committee on Cultural Affairs, which first met in Charlottetown two weeks before the Dominion Drama Festival hit town. An extract from the minutes, dealing with "the Canadian content of the proposed Canadian Festival of the Performing Arts," will suggest the scale on which, suddenly, we had all to work:

> The realistic approach, according to Mr. [Don] Jamieson . . . conditioned by the necessity to fill our arts centres, makes it mandatory to think in terms of international troupes as well. The World Exhibition Corporation in Montreal [Expo 67] is inviting performing groups from various countries of the world. And in many instances, according to the Chairman, these foreign groups of performers will only come to Canada to perform at the World's Fair if they can be guaranteed other bookings.[6]

I was able to speak with authority on the Expo 67 situation because I had just been approached to produce its international theatre festival. Committed to Charlottetown, I could not accept. But shortly thereafter I was drafted as theatre consultant to the fair's Canadian Pavilion.

These early affinities were the prelude to an affair with the centennial that was to last until long after the fine frenzy passed, and to take some surprising turns. To begin with, on my return to Toronto the publisher of *Maclean's*, Floyd Chalmers, invited me to lunch and a Cuban cigar.

I had first heard of Chalmers, in none too complimentary terms, from my Uncle Smoot, the soldier, who had him as a lowly batman in the First World War; but then Smoot never understood how a batman of his could ever have made it to tycoon. A high school dropout who went to work at 16, Chalmers ended up as chancellor of York University. Beginning as a journalist, he became executive vice president of the *Financial Post* at 27, and in short order president of the whole Maclean Hunter publishing empire. Taking part of his pay in stock options, he amassed a fortune, for which he and his perceptive wife Jean found a better use than what he called "high living." While Gelber took on the Canadian Conference of the Arts, the National Ballet, the Ontario Arts Council, and the Art Gallery of Ontario, the elder Chalmers attended to the Canadian Opera Company, the Toronto Symphony, and the Stratford Festival.

He is an august and impenitent 65, 20 years my senior, and before lunch known to me only as a personage. After ordering the food, he comes to the point without small talk, as if anticipating the long interval before its arrival:

FC: I want to commission an opera for the COC for the centennial.

MM: Great idea.

FC: Geiger-Torel tells me you should write the libretto.

MM: I've never written an opera.

FC: He says it's time you did.

MM: He always says that. You need a composer first.

FC: He says the toughest part is finding a story that'll work.

MM: He may be right. I've had to rewrite some librettos.

FC: What about an original one?

MM: (firmly) I don't have time.

FC: On a Canadian subject.

MM: (all ears) Oh.

FC: Any ideas?

MM: Sure. Louis Riel.

FC: You have any composers in mind?

MM: Sure. Harry Somers.

The Ping-Pong is precise because I have only recently dismissed thoughts of the Riel story as the basis for a musical for Charlottetown.

After working with John Coulter's *Riel* in the theatre and adapting it for radio and television, I wondered why, for all its high dramatic skill, it lacked the incandescence to serve as a metaphor for Canada.[7] Riel became another of my obsessions. I read everything available on him, including Joseph Kinsey Howard's evocative novel *Strange Empire*. The clue finally appeared in historian A. R. M. Lower's description of the conflict as "Canada's great leitmotif"[8]: only an operatic treatment could do justice to the soaring theme. Conversely Somers's earlier one-act opera *The Fool*, to a libretto by Michael Fram, had revealed a soaring dramatic tension in the orchestra pit far more exciting than the narrative unfolding on the stage. I longed to marry Riel and Somers, but foresaw that the offspring would fit neither Charlottetown's budget nor its merry image. And I had, before my host spoke up, no other prospect in sight.

Chalmers was a history addict as well as an opera fan. Although he had missed Coulter's play, he had read *Strange Empire* and other Riel material; and despite a self-declared taste for vintage music, he had been impressed with Somers's *The Fool*. I had to fly to Ottawa that evening, but we agreed to meet with Torel when I was next in town. At the airport I happened to cross paths with Somers, but could only say in haste that I hoped to have something exciting to tell him when I got back. Did I actually promise Chalmers that I would have an outline ready by Christmas?

To meet all of these obligations I had to make radical changes to the rhythm of my life — not for the first time. At school my day had been governed by school hours and after-school work; the army taught me to rise at five and quit when I had the chance; broadcasting's crazy hours were dictated by variable pressure; acting in theatre meant a methodical evening timetable, while acting in films meant showing up at dawn; reviewing imposed a night schedule, with bed at 2:00 or 3:00 a.m. and brunch for breakfast. A nine-to-five job seemed to me highly irregular. But now I had to be in the office when others expected to find me there, take my briefcase home like any budding executive, read documents until I fell asleep, and comfort myself that a change was as good as a rest. Weekends were spent writing, and half the rest of my time in airports.

And not only airports. Our sound-and-light company, Legendrama, of which Dilly is secretary, depends heavily on technology developed by Philips of Eindhoven, the European *son et lumière* experts. In December 1963 we travel to France and Italy to study Philips's installations at the Bastille, the Colosseum, and other venerable sites. Since Philips is also illuminating the closed Sistine Chapel, we are allowed access to Michelangelo's mighty vision of creation, incredible in several senses. ("Where," asks psychologist Phyllis Chesley sternly, "is that male god's mother?") Soon afterward the Department of External Affairs sends me to Britain for a weekend — which strikes me as the height of profligacy — to advise on Canada's participation in a Commonwealth Arts Festival planned for London, Cardiff, and Glasgow. Going through the file in Canada House, in the room that had been my wartime office, I am plunged back into psychological warfare mode — and in an epiphany see the Commonwealth for what it is: a brilliant propaganda stroke. Not above using it for Canadian ends, I recommend sending, among other contributions, Le Théâtre du Nouveau Monde in Jacques Languirand's *Klondike* and the Royal Winnipeg Ballet in one of Brian Macdonald's Canadian works. My nominations bring cries of indignation from the

Stratford (Ontario) Festival and the National Ballet Company, but I see no point in sending coals to Newcastle.

During those frantic months I was not the only one thrust overnight into unfamiliar ten-league boots. The Canada Council's Peter Dwyer, for all his quick grasp of the Canadian cultural scene, was a former British spy-master. The National Arts Centre, designed to elevate Ottawa from company town to capital city, was fostered by a dedicated diplomat, Hamilton Southam, and programmed (at first) by a former assistant general manager of the Metropolitan Opera, Henry Wrong. The head of entertainment pro-gramming at Montreal's Expo 67 was a onetime publicist, Gordon Hilker, whose stint as general manager of the Vancouver International Festival had been as contentious as it was brief. The commissioner general of the Canadian Pavilion was a genial (until crossed) federal bureaucrat named H. Leslie Brown, innocent of show business, whose main concern was to keep the chain of command kinkless. I had the distinct impression that each of us was being promoted to brigadier on the battlefield.

Could we handle it? Even if they wanted to celebrate, did Canadians know how? (At the end of Expo 67 publicity director Yves Jasmin was asked what had been his most difficult task. He replied, "Convincing Canadians that it would happen.") A question being asked in editorials across Canada, in those days, was: "Do we have the talent?" or "Where's the expertise?" I decided the best way to find out was to make some-thing happen in the one place I could.

WHEN THE FATHERS OF CONFEDERATION met in Charlottetown in 1864, they spent only about a third of their time in meetings, the other two-thirds merrymaking. The formula produced Canada. In their memory, there-fore, we planned a merry festival ("of Music and Laughter," Johnny Wayne suggested), hoping that Charlottetown would also become famous for giving birth to Canadian shows.

In our innocent enthusiasm we had not imagined how difficult it would be to put together an entire program of Canadiana.

MM to Donald Harron, Los Angeles, October 1964:

> MY PLANS FOR CHARLOTTETOWN FESTIVAL 65 NOW ACCEPTED AND AM ANXIOUS
> GET YOU WORKING IMMEDIATELY ON STAGE VERSION OF ANNE. CAMPBELL ADVISES
> POSSIBLE PROBLEM WITH RIGHTS TO BOOK SINCE ORIGINAL HAS BEEN SOLD TO NEW
> YORK PUBLISHERS. AM INVESTIGATING . . . BUT SUGGEST WE GO AHEAD MEANTIME.
> COULDST ADVISE WHEN TIME MIGHT PERMIT YOUR WRITING.[9]

The Journal Pioneer, Charlottetown, January 1965:

> The summer festival will feature four shows . . . *Laugh with Leacock*,
> with John Drainie, and a musical version of the Lucy Maude
> Montgomery novel *Anne of Green Gables* . . . which is being written now.
> This show will be directed by Alan Lund with sets and costumes
> designed by Murray Laufer and Marie Day. The other two shows are
> the 1965 version of *Spring Thaw*, now on its cross-country tour, and a
> new version of *Wayne & Shuster in Charlottetown*. . . . After the festival
> winds up here *Wayne & Shuster in Charlottetown* will be taken on a six-
> week cross-country tour. . . .

**MM to Jack McClelland, McClelland and Stewart, publishers. Re:
Request for "token" performing rights to *Laugh with Leacock*:**

> I appreciate your despair that I am "up to my old tricks again" —
> namely trying to do too much on too little. But just so you get the pic-
> ture, my total budget for the Charlottetown Festival is less than the
> Canada Council is giving the Stratford Festival to meet *part* of its deficit.
> The only reason I am doing it, once again, is that this is the first time I
> have found a bunch of guys in charge of one of these festivals pre-
> pared to stick their necks out on behalf of something Canadian.[10]

Peter Dwyer, Canada Council, to MM, September 10, 1965:

> Now with regard to [your application for a grant from] the Theatre Arts
> Development Program. . . . When one is setting up something of this
> kind on a national scale you have to take pretty broad strokes to get it
> started and be prepared to adjust as it is worked out. One of the broad
> strokes was that festivals should not be included for the time being,
> because (for your private information only) we wish to avoid including
> the festivals in Vancouver and Montreal for reasons which may splinter
> your mind. ([Handwritten in the margin] I dictated "spring to," but I
> am not sure that my secretary's version may not be more vigorous.)

I was confident that even at this late date a grant would come, because
— as I assured the courageous board and island politicians who shared
the suspense — the Canada Council had never been more firmly seized
by its fundamentals. The grant came.

We were, however, out on an equally long limb artistically. Despite efforts to brace the summer with well-known national assets, from Montgomery and Leacock to Wayne and Shuster, we had no completed script or score for three of the four shows, let alone copyright permission to proceed with *Anne* and *Laugh with Leacock*. (In fact, the respective publishers were sceptical that we would have any impact whatever on their sales.) Meantime, with rehearsals scheduled to begin early in June, we had to carry on with casting, designing, and building the productions.

The missives flying back and forth tell their own story.

Don Harron to MM, Toronto, April 7, 1965:

ARRIVING TORONTO MAY 13 HAVE FINISHED FIRST HALF OF SCRIPT. WILL SEND IT AIRMAIL TOMORROW. HAVE SENT CAMPBELL THREE LETTERS CONTAINING LYRICS. NO REPLY: WHY? [Norman Campbell was chained to his piano.]

Don Harron to MM, May 13:

FILMING FORCES ME REMAIN UNTIL MAY 27 SEE YOU THEN.

MM to Don Harron, May 15:

SYMPATHISE WITH CAUSES KEEPING YOU THERE BUT DELAY SPELLS DISASTER FOR US SINCE ALREADY BEHIND SCHEDULE ON SETS SCORING ARRANGING ETC. CAMPBELL LUND MEETING HERE TOMORROW MORNING DISCUSS PROBLEMS AND WILL WRITE OR PHONE MONDAY.

MM to Bob Dubberley, Charlottetown, May 27. Re: Anne Shirley [for whom we needed an experienced singer-actress who could pass for 12; we found Texas-born soprano Jamie Ray at the Opera School]:

Am most distressed about the delay in getting out the publicity about Anne . . . caused by Miss Ray's delay in getting a suitable picture to us. She begged me to let her get it taken in Texas. . . . The picture was a fortnight getting here and proved to be utterly unsuitable. It made her look like a decayed southern belle with an overgrowth of facial hair. I wired her at once to get another taken, simple and young and clear.

Pat Patterson, Charlottetown Festival PR head, to MM, Toronto, June 10:

We are dying to know what Anne of Green Gables looks like. The *Atlantic Advocate* wants it, the press of three countries are screaming for it, and if you could arrange a shot of her in costume so much the better.

Graham Spicer, stage manager, Toronto, to Props, Charlottetown, June 21:

Bottle of dye is for appearance only. The raspberry cordial is to be drunk.

Bob Dubberley to MM, Toronto, July 9:

RE LOST SCENERY. SHIPPED TO BILL HALL CONVENTION PALACE CNE INSTEAD OF BOB HALL HORSE PALACE. COULDST CHECK CNE AUTHORITIES RE DELIVERY TO OTHER DOOR.

Spring Thaw '65 — the 18th, and my last — arrived on cue to form the core of the festival company. "The longest-running annual review in the world" may have made its most durable contribution in the form of the team, so adept as co-workers, that it bequeathed to Charlottetown. Alan Lund, turning director with *Anne of Green Gables*, was more than a superlative choreographer with a rare common touch; he was a master of visual effects and a superb teacher. John Fenwick's range as a musician was phenomenal: scholar, composer, arranger, conductor, pianist, vocal coach, equally at home in classical and popular idioms. Most of our technical crew, moreover, had been on the road with the review, and our wardrobe mistress was *Thaw*'s veteran Mary Shaw. What they all needed — like their eager colleagues on the island — was room to grow.

Only an acting company drilling together for years could have prepared two new musicals in one month while performing a third, and added a fourth while performing the first three. Barbara Hamilton (the first Marilla), Dave Broadfoot (costar of *Laugh with Leacock*), Peter Mews (the first Matthew), Dean Regan (Gilbert Blythe), Liane Marshall (Miss Stacey), Jack Duffy (Mr. Phillips), Marylyn Stuart (Diana), Gayle Lepine (Josie), Richard Braun (Stationmaster), and dancer Shirley Milliner were all with *Spring Thaw* '65. The technical crew heads came with the tour. Paul Kligman, Drew Thompson, Diane Stapley, and Tom Harvey were alumni of previous *Thaws*. The orchestra for everything was the *Spring Thaw* quartet: Fenwick and Jack Bristowe on pianos, John Collins on trumpet, and Ray Reilly on percussion. Many had worked with Wayne and Shuster on television.

Drainie, who had not been onstage for seven years, had assembled the Leacock show as a last labour of love; he was gravely ill with cancer, which claimed him a year later. "Never a man of natural eloquence," Bronwyn Drainie wrote, "my father used Leacock's words and humour to express the thing he felt most deeply: the loss and alienation of modern man's spirit through consumerism and a naive faith in science."[11] He told nobody, not even the director (me), and gave no hint of weakness during rehearsals or in performance, where he controlled the audience like a relaxed master puppeteer. Months later, after I knew, he muttered some excuse about not wanting to pee on the Fathers' parade. It was a black joke, siting the malignancy.

If the Charlottetown Festival had done nothing but give this extraordinary actor an occasion to personify the country's most extraordinary humorist, it would have justified its existence. But as it happened, the whole summer's gamble bore out one of Leacock's most famous aphorisms: "I am a great believer in luck, and I find the harder I work the more I have of it."

The comic art of Johnny Wayne and Frank Shuster was recognized in the United States, Britain, and Europe (where it won global awards) as having a stamp of its own. To Canadians hooked on American comics, of course, this departure was uncalled for. Unlike the Bob Hopes and Milton Berles, Wayne and Shuster wrote their own material, which stood somewhere south of satire and north of slapstick, equidistant from stateliness and crudity. The lasting effect of their international success was to nudge the popular image of Canadians from drab to motley, opening the way for others to change it further. This they did by capitalizing on their off-centre Canadian perspective while applying the most exacting world standards to their craft.

Their creative method was akin to karate. Intellectually alert, physically fit, married to vital women, the team (Shuster happily surviving as I write) were blessed with the comic lenses without which many thoughtful clowns become misanthropists. They made great company. But when writing or rehearsing, they sparred with deadly seriousness, punctuated by bursts of mutual laughter as a pass worked. Wayne, the more Gothic and dynamic, would attack his partner with a ferocity amazing to those unfamiliar with their ways, until Shuster, with cool head and steady hand, rose to the occasion and they would implode in a laughing embrace. In brief, they worked on each other until the sketch worked and then removed every trace of labour.

"For weeks now," writes Nathan Cohen in the *Toronto Star* in mid-August, "word has been filtering back to Toronto and the rest of the country of a show in the Charlottetown Festival which is an unqualified hit. . . . The stories tell of capacity audiences and standing ovations." The *New York Times* announces that "Anne Shirley has just made a triumphant return to her native land." A Japanese producer, "knowing how with deep and lasting love this original book is read all over in Japan," inquires about obtaining the rights for Tokyo.[12] On August 21 the unpredictable Cohen writes a column from Charlottetown that shames the Canada Council into action:

> Small towns are best for arts festivals — especially if they are hard to get to, have no cultural tradition whatever, and are administered by artistic directors with bees in their bonnets — Bayreuth, Salzburg, Spoletto, Cannes, Tanglewood, Stratford . . .
>
> [T]o Mr. Moore the Charlottetown invitation was a chance to put to the test his particular dream — the mounting of a program that would be all-Canadian in material and content. It was easy enough for the board of directors to endorse that approach last year, when the federal government defrayed the expense of bringing . . . performing groups from all across the country. But it showed enlightenment on their part, and a fine courage for Mr. Moore, to stick to the all-Canadian policy this summer, when the festival was on its own economically. . . .
>
> The exciting news is that the response has surpassed the hope. . . . For the first time in the national experience, a program has been assembled using Canadian performers and strictly Canadian material which is thoroughly professional in production standard and which has received genuine public acceptance. . . .
>
> In its first independent season the Charlottetown Festival has become a major focus for the theatre arts in Canada. The rest of the country must look to it for example and inspiration. . . . Although it may never have the same impact in international terms, and perhaps would never have come about without it, for Canada itself the Charlottetown Festival is already of greater value than the one in Stratford. Stratford gives work to Canadian actors and technicians. Charlottetown is giving them that and a spirit, an honest-to-goodness, distinctive identity. . . .
>
> Truly, truly, something wonderful has happened in Charlottetown.[13]

If critics must hand out grades, this one was welcome.

Whether the rest of the country was ready for the news was another question. The Canadian Chamber of Commerce first agreed to sponsor the national tour of *Wayne and Shuster in Charlottetown* as a harbinger of the 1967 centennial, putting up guarantees in the major centres. But not all branches would come aboard and at the last moment the deal collapsed. Unwilling to saddle the centre with the gamble or the high cost of cancelling it, I threw Mavor Moore Productions into the breach.

The tour opens in Montreal, and despite the lack of advance publicity, the response is warm and continues to be. But as we proceed it becomes clear that arousing public interest in the coming 100th birthday is uphill work. At every stop the indefatigable stars, making themselves freely available for interviews, are asked by a suspicious press, "Why are you still in Canada?" Their replies — to the effect that they are Canadian, like living here, prefer sending their offspring to school here, and are freer to experiment on CBC Television — do little to mollify the cynics, who cannot bring themselves to credit such incorruptible patriotism. Then just before our arrival in Edmonton a journalist there pens a scurrilous attack on the pair — accuses them of returning home because they have flopped in America, reverting to theatre because they have failed on television, and speaking at charity events as a publicity stunt. Since they turned down international dates to make the tour for a fraction of their regular fee (and in deference to our cash flow have deferred collecting even that), they reach Edmonton in a towering rage. At the opening night party Johnny Wayne, surrounded by prominent Edmontonians with propitiatory drinks in their hands, proceeds to flay the entire city with such dark brilliance that the victims stay rooted, mesmerized by their own scathing.

In Vancouver we end the tour with a hearty reception that makes up for everything except the $15,000 I have lost.

A short time later I find myself in Ottawa with Frank MacKinnon, lunching with Finance Minister Walter Gordon to seek basic funding for the maintenance of the Confederation Centre building. "Why come to me," asks Gordon, "when you have one of the richest men in the country as chairman of your board?" The same generous Eric Harvie, I tell him, has just covered most of my loss on the tour, since Revenue Canada disallowed it as a legitimate business expense on the ground that theatre is no different from horse racing! In any case, MacKinnon adds, surely no private citizen should be expected to perpetually subsidize a national shrine. "Okay," says Gordon, "I guess we'll have to. But, Jesus, just the building, eh!"

I marvelled how far I had travelled from DMM's belief in two boards and a passion. We had, according to Nathan Cohen, "performed an economic wonder. . . . Seldom has the dollar been stretched so far or used so well. Mr. Moore has proved that it's not how much money you get but the way that you use it that really matters." What we proved was that to sustain a festival of large-scale original musicals we had to rely on the missionary zeal of our performers, and on finding new works with instant box office appeal — an oxymoron.

Fortunately we had rough-weather friends. The historic Halifax Symphony, from which we drew many of our musicians in the second year, was deeply in debt, as was the New Brunswick Symphony. With the backing of the Canada Council we helped to meld the two into the Atlantic Orchestra, ensuring it a summer engagement in Charlottetown. In 1966 we repeated *Anne*; turned the Birney-Harron *Turvey* into a musical, with a delicious World War II score by Norman Campbell; and revived *The Ottawa Man* with Don Harron and another Canadian star eager to lend her support to the Festival — Kate Reid. In 1967, along with *Anne*, we presented Pierre Berton's Klondike musical *Paradise Hill*, a gold rush that (like the original) ruthlessly exposed a lack of preparation among the prospectors. The third production was an essential risk: something from Quebec.

Prince Edward Island has its own francophone community, and Festival appearances by fiddler Jean Carignan, folksinger Félix Leclerc, and the folk dance troupe *Les feux-follets* had succeeded in attracting tourists from Quebec. Gratien Gélinas then invited me to translate his 1966 hit *Hier les enfants dansaient*, the first play to deal with the rise of separatism. We agreed to premiere the English version[14] at Charlottetown the following summer, with the bilingual Montreal cast, including Gélinas' and his wife Huguette Oligny as the federalist parents of the young revolutionary, played by Gélinas's son Yves. We would direct it together. Since he had staged the original, the collaboration would be a test of our long friendship and a reenactment, in its way, of the national theme.

The initial rehearsals are awkward as the actors naturally turn to the actor-playwright onstage for guidance. Out front, I, too, defer to his intent. Then one day, just as I sense an odd-man-out crisis, Gélinas parries a colleague's appeal. "Don't ask me, ask him — he's the director!" From then on I belong to the team. "At last, at long last," writes Cohen in the *Toronto Star*, "a play that deals forthrightly with the central fact of the Canadian conscience . . . a play which disturbs, unsettles and amuses and vaults to an extraordinary level of political insight." But equally interesting is the drama no critic covers: two generations of sensitive, politically alert Quebec actors settled in the bosom of a mainly anglophone theatre family, performing a work that exposes the raw nerve of divided loyalties. The goodwill is evident in the event itself; but all of us become aware of how little time we have to get to know each other better. "For my divided house," the father prepares to tell his anglophone audience in the last line of the play, "will not go down without shaking yours to its very foundation."

Yesterday the Children Were Dancing was the last play I would direct for 20 years. Guthrie, who left Stratford after three seasons, once told me that no artistic director should stay longer, for the sake of the enterprise. For the festival I later wrote the librettos for *Johnny Belinda* and *Fauntleroy*; but the Charlottetown experience had shifted my interest to what an arts centre could do for a community — and this was most evident in the winter when I was elsewhere. The art gallery could not accommodate all the young people wanting classes; a full-time dance teacher had to be imported; public library lending rose threefold, and to children sixfold; one of the largest film societies in the country sprang up. Islander Frank Storey had already succeeded me as general manager of Confederation Centre. I passed the festival reins to Alan Lund and concentrated on other centennial affairs, many already under way.

BEHIND ITS MASK OF STULTIFIED PROPRIETY Toronto had undergone a metamorphosis. The city's reputation for successfully fusing greed and sanctimony had not prepared the rest of Canada for the metropolis that emerged in the mid-1960s.

Hogtown on the Don, people elsewhere used to say, could only grow exponentially stodgier as it grew bigger. The subway, the arterial roads, the ships coming and going through the now open St. Lawrence Seaway, the lofty banks and head offices, even the striking new City Hall in the shape of an upended oyster on the edge of a skating rink — these were the expectable accoutrements of commercial gigantism. And while everyone knew that the University of Toronto was Canada's largest, like the museum and the library system, and that English-language publishing and broadcasting were centred here, this hegemony was attributed more to Upper Canadian arrogance than real superiority. But . . . poetry readings in pubs, theatres in gussied-up garages, chamber music in old churches, folksingers in holes-in-the-wall, and great jazz in spaghetti joints? Slum houses restored to Victorian charm? "Honest Ed" Mirvish's brilliantly humble emporium with attached village? More small art galleries than Los Angeles and Chicago combined? Hippie love-ins in Yorkville pads, a block from Bloor Street with its haute couture designs on the future? *Toronto?*

"Something powerful and new is stirring in Canada," U.S. architect Edgar Kaufmann, Jr., wrote in 1967, "a new turn in how to think about buildings as human implements and poetic human expressions. One big idea is that the unit of architecture is no longer an individual building, but a whole milieu."[15]

It was exactly such a big idea that Arthur Gelber broached to me as early as 1962, brandishing a Toronto Planning Board report that said:

> Toronto lacks a focal point, a centre of gravity, for the expression of its arts. The proposed development will serve as an important element in the artistic and cultural fabric not only of the immediate region but of the province and, indeed, of the nation itself.[16]

When Maurice Lamontagne and his provincial counterparts then announced centennial grants to municipalities to erect buildings for cultural purposes, a Toronto Arts Foundation (TAF) was created to establish Metropolitan Toronto's most pressing needs. After eliminating renovations and other ineligible proposals, and commissioning an independent management study, the TAF recommended a medium-sized theatre, a small concert/lecture hall, and a workshop facility.[17] But Metro Toronto chairman William Allen, a petty finagler whose name survives aptly on a stunted expressway, saw an opportunity to get separate grants for each of the amalgamated boroughs. If the city of Toronto wanted an arts centre, Toronto could build it alone.

A campaign for private funding was launched, but by May 1964 the project was facing more than financial odds. In Charlottetown I read about it in the *Toronto Star*:

> Toronto's proposed St. Lawrence Centre for the Arts isn't even on the drawing board but it's providing a public show. However, the show is displaying an art never dreamed of for the centre — political infighting. Protagonists are [Toronto] Mayor Philip Givens, defender of culture for the common man, and Controller [Allan] Lamport, who says the common man would rather have cash.
>
> Once moving serenely . . . along as everybody's favorite centennial project, the centre has become a political pot-boiler. The reason isn't hard to find. Controller Lamport would like to be mayor. The centre looks like a good issue.[18]

Lamport was a renegade Upper Canada College old boy turned dema-
gogue, playing to a constituency he called "the lunch-bucket crowd." He
was said to take good care of his friends and relatives while abandoning
his principles, and to keep reporters in his debt while staying sober himself. Lamportisms ("If someone stabs me in the back, I want him to look
me in the eye!" or "We have theatre seats coming out of our ears!") have
been collected in anthologies of the absurd; but they were regarded by
his followers as models of plain speaking. When a group of us appeared
before the city's board of control on behalf of the arts centre, Lamport
unwittingly put the issue squarely: "It's all very well for these people to
have imaginary ideas, but we don't have the money to have imagination!"

It was Gelber, by now chair of the TAF board of management, who
talked me into becoming the future St. Lawrence Centre's general director. This was not difficult. The time was October 1965, following the
first Charlottetown Festival, and I already had a notion of what might be
done with such a community dynamo. I said I would take the job for
four years until the place was up and running. Recalling CBC Television,
however, I was concerned about what the architects had done before me.

Gordon S. Adamson and Associates, known for their solid traditional
schools and public buildings, were right at home with a commission for
a monument. But this monument was to be a place of entertainment and
enlightenment. At our first meeting I complained of the forbidding exte-
rior, which I thought would serve nicely for a post office, or possibly a
jail. "Tell me what you have in mind,"Adamson said. For half an hour I
talked about playfulness and involvement, using as examples the
Stratford theatre, the New York Museum of Modern Art, and the like. At
the end Adamson nodded gravely and said, "I'm not quite sure what you
mean." I believed him.

Not all of Toronto was ready for the stimulating fare we had in mind
for the centre. There were skirmishes to be fought.

Toronto *Globe and Mail*, November 29, 1965:

> Mavor Moore, the [general] director of Toronto's projected St.
> Lawrence Centre for the Arts, yesterday assailed the court ruling that
> paintings shown by an art gallery run by Dorothy Cameron are
> obscene. Mr. Moore, speaking at a service of the First Unitarian
> Congregation . . . said, "It's a terribly dangerous principle, that our
> minds and senses should be confined to what he, the magistrate, calls
> the middle ground. . . .

"The second most curious rule he invoked was that some of the actions depicted would be liable to charges of gross indecency. If you rule out *representations* of indecency and crimes like murder, it becomes utterly absurd. . . . The Bible has about the grossest crimes in the catalogue. . . .

Delivering sermons is becoming a habit, and I begin to see myself looking daily more like my father as I remember him in the pulpit. What I should have been doing was not preaching but praying.

Toronto Star, April 30, 1966:

The 859-seat theatre and 750-seat concert hall of the St. Lawrence Centre for the Arts will be ready for use late in 1967, it was announced yesterday. Approved last week by the Toronto Arts Foundation, the project will become a reality through a federal and provincial centennial grant of $1,300,000, a grant from the City of Toronto of $2,350,000, and $2,300,000 in public subscription money, part of which ($1,700,000) has already been raised. . . . The remainder of the project, an arts facilities building, will be built . . . when further funds become available.

As political roadblocks continue to be thrown up, I write an article for *Maclean's*, which they publish under the title "Mavor Moore's War on the Yahoo Establishment." There I stand beside a massive new overpass, holding a poster for the national centennial's *Festival Canada*, above the byline "Mavor Moore ponders a cultural wasteland." I thought it odd that a society would spend $15 million on a cloverleaf yet wrangle over spending a third of that for an arts centre — as if a road were more important than what lay at the end of it. Alderman Fred Beavis, pinked by Toronto's purchase of a Henry Moore sculpture for the civic square, had said, "How much longer are we going to have this art and culture stuffed down our throats? And I do mean that." "Longer and harder, Mr. Beavis," I say in the article, "and I do mean that. . . . The creative artists of Canada are fed to the teeth with being trotted out as prize exhibits whenever anyone wishes to boast about the nation's achievements and returned to the scullery between receptions." My hardly revolutionary argument, supported by hard evidence, was that culture was no frill but both a necessity and an investment opportunity.[19]

In November 1966, six weeks before the centennial year is about to commence, Mayor Givens reports to City Council that the completion date will be extended to the end of 1968 ("nearly all centennial projects across the country have encountered some delay"). He also reveals our program plans:

> The eventual operation of the Theatre will involve a resident repertory company "committed to freshness, to vigour, to our country in our time" — and to bringing the public the most pertinent attractions being mounted by other Toronto and Canadian companies. The Town Hall will actively program public affairs, serious music, popular entertainment, and other community services such as film societies, ethnic societies, religious groups and many others.[20]

To this already ambitious agenda is added a Universities Committee for the St. Lawrence Centre, to be chaired by University of Toronto president Claude Bissell. (Beset by student violence on the campus, the great humanist characteristically finds time to support a positive alternative.) His eminent committee undertakes to "guide the Centre in an experiment in total environment unique in the world":

> The aim of this project will be to keep a complete documentary record of the Centre's activity from its inception, to co-ordinate activity in all the arts, and to make the SLC a centre for scientific and technological experiment in the creative and communicative processes.[21]

What echoes of the dreams of a young philosopher! What a consummation of the thought of Brett, Innis, McLuhan, Penfield, Frye! What a chance to weave together all the threads of my life, and make sense of it! And what a setup for a pratfall!

From this height there is nowhere to go but down, even if the fall can be softened. Givens loses the next election to William Dennison, who after a campaign in which his sympathy wavers, turns out to be a firm supporter of the St. Lawrence Centre. But after months of trilevel political, financial, and bureaucratic adventures, including the time my lawyer was all set to sue Lamport for slander, the centre seems less certain than ever. Other enterprises call.

If we are to have a supply of Canadian films to show at the St. Lawrence Centre, or anywhere else, we need many more of them. Kurt Swinton, one-time backer of the *Canadian Commentator*, has moved to England as managing director of one of J. Arthur Rank's film companies. In October 1965 he writes: "I am more than anxious to discuss with you the possibility of an

Anglo-Canadian film venture, involving also possibly an operation in Europe." Our go-between in London is my daughter Tedde, 17, following in her grandmother's footsteps at the Royal Academy of Dramatic Art. At the bottom of Swinton's letter she scrawls: "Where the hell is my money? I miss you awfully." Amid all these grand schemes I am having cash flow problems.

I write the topical lyrics for Dinah Christie to sing on *This Hour Has Seven Days*, CBC Television's popular weekly bow to impiety. When management reaches over the head of producer Doug Leiterman to fire anchorman Laurier LaPierre for weeping on the air, the ensuing fracas threatens to topple CBC chairman Alphonse Ouimet, who wants to retire, anyway. At its height I receive a summons to Ottawa to dine with Secretary of State Judy LaMarsh, whom I have met once in Toronto in connection with the St. Lawrence Centre. Arriving punctually at her House of Commons office, I am asked to wait. Five minutes later the inner sanctum door bursts open and the ample LaMarsh, with sudden familiarity, says, "Come on in, Mavor, I've got a friend of yours in here." Honest Al Ouimet occupies a deep leather chair, his face as sunken as his body. After pouring herself and me a Scotch, LaMarsh puts her feet up on the desk:

JL: Mavor, what are we going to do about all the queers at the CBC?
MM: (*after a fortifying sip*) What are you going to do about the CBC?
AO: (*icily, as he rises*) I have been asking the same question. You may have better luck. (*exit with a mocking bow to LaMarsh.*)

LaMarsh is less interested in sexuality than in gauging reaction to shock. It is her favourite tactic. She wants to discuss Ouimet's successor as CBC chairman, and asks my opinion of Stuart Griffiths, now running private station CJOH for Ernie Bushnell in Ottawa. A practical visionary, I tell her, by far the best equipped person for the job; and we rehash the old discredited Commie charges. Am I interested? No; the chairmanship is a political job; get Griffiths. Over dinner we discuss other nominees, of whom only *This Hour*'s Patrick Watson and CTV's Murray Chercover know anything at all about broadcasting.[22] The government should introduce its new broadcasting act, I argue, before choosing who is to implement it; if the executive vice presidency — the operational post — is given sufficient clout, I would consider that.[23]

At the Chateau Laurier that night I run into Robert Winters, who introduces me to visiting Premier Joey Smallwood of Newfoundland. Ten days later Smallwood calls me from St. John's, shouting as if the telephone were an impedance: "Look, we're building this gaahd daamn Arts and Culture Centre. I hear you did a hell of a job in Charlottetown. Will you come over and tell us what the hell to do with this one!"

On arrival in St. John's, after surviving my introduction to screech, I am given a crash course in Newfie ambivalence: culture is both worshipped and pissed on. ("Every effort must be made to involve all sections of the community," my report will say, "and not only those with an existing taste for 'the arts.' No taste can be formed for something one does not come in contact with; a lass who comes to Watusi may wind up looking at Whistler.")[24] But money is scarce and a second centre is still to be built at Corner Brook. I query a seeming extravagance: a huge double door halfway up the back wall of the stage with no apparent access or purpose. "Ah, well," says my guide, "it's for the opening ceremony. We'll put a catwalk in behind so that on the night the premier can come through the door and down a big stairway with a red carpet." Before leaving I ask a trustworthy friend whether Smallwood is crooked. "The question is not *whether*," he replies evenly, "but *how*. Joey is creative."

The question of what is to occupy the theatre of the Canadian Pavilion at Expo 67 is equally problematic. Many producers are eager to show their wares there, but an end-to-end series of in-and-out shows would break the budget and fragment the audience. With only four months to go before the opening, I seek a clarification from commissioner general Les Brown:

MM: How will the audiences break down? What percentage do you figure will speak English and what percentage French?

LB: Fifty-fifty.

MM: What? With all the American tourists?

LB: Fifty-fifty.

MM: Surely more like seventy-five-twenty-five.

LB: That's what I said — fifty-fifty.

Faced with this categorical fiction, I recommend an attraction that will circumvent language: Les *feux-follets*, the fine Quebec folk dance troupe that Alan Lund and I once helped to reorganize after extensive tours had exhausted the original amateurs. The group now performs dances from across the country. (After Expo 67, Les *feux-follets* will have trouble obtaining funding in the face of another categorical fiction: its work is judged too polished to be folk art and too folksy to be dance art.)

The National Arts Centre in Ottawa was also claiming my attention. Board chairman Lawrence Frieman consulted me about its administrative structure, with a view to my becoming director-general. On January 31, 1967, I replied:

> The executive head of any organization is put in a difficult and weakening position if those normally under his control are appointed by (and have direct access to) the Board. . . . The various elements must work together under the director general in the implementation of an integrated policy. . . .
>
> To achieve the object of making an international as well as a national mark, we must carefully choose our own weapons. . . . Doing better what no-one else can do as well also applies to the orchestra. I do not believe Ottawa could or should compete with the great symphonic ensembles. . . . It could and should develop a reputation for an orchestra of its own kind, [fulfilling] its responsibility to give recognition to Canadian expression.
>
> I am not herein defining my own conditions; I have been trying to define the structure that I think will work best. . . . My own position [otherwise occupied] is still as stated. . . .

The Honourable Judy LaMarsh, rumour had it, was able to get unanimous approval for the National Arts Centre in the House of Commons, after Lamontagne the intellectual had failed, because she was a slob and what was okay with Judy was okay with the other slobs. The Slob was a false face that she relished because it notarized her. For LaMarsh to travel incognito, with her spectacular hats and loud horn-rimmed glasses, was a contradiction in terms; yet just before Expo 67 opened she made an unofficial visit, for which I was requisitioned to show her quietly around. We travel in a go-cart, alighting at various stops where she could show surprise at being spotted, discussing the NAC, the NFB, the St. Lawrence Centre, and the CBC (on all of which she is very well informed) between exhibits. She tells me Pearson is not prepared to stickhandle Griffiths past the right wing of the Cabinet; the PM and she have had a row, and he has taken the appointments out of her hands. But she must field the rumours, including the one that she is about to resign and take the job herself.

By late spring the press is onto the government's short list for the CBC like a terrier to a root. I have seen the PM. Jules Léger, our ambassador to France, who has won respect for his handling of the separatist issue with de Gaulle, is the one Pearson now has in mind for chairman, with me as executive vice president. On July 20 there is a leak in the *Ottawa Journal* to this effect, which I am forced to dismiss as "speculation"[25] since arrangements have already been made for me to meet Léger privately in Ottawa, and each of us has already been briefed on the impending legislation. On July 23 Léger and I meet for three hours in the Chateau Laurier and find we agree on the important matters. The next day, in Montreal, de Gaulle delivers his famous *"Vive le Québec libre!"* speech; Léger tells Pearson he cannot now abandon his embassy without appearing to do so deliberately, and returns to Paris. Pearson asks me to hang on and say nothing while he finds another francophone for chairman. I feel obliged to take Arthur Gelber into my confidence.

Then came months with no communication except periodic phone calls from the prime minister, without secretarial intervention ("Mavor? Mike Pearson here!"). At first the calls come every couple of weeks, at home, at night, to say he is working on it and will let me know "next week." This is more than he tells his secretary of state.

MM to the Right Honourable Lester B. Pearson, October 23, 1967 (confidential):

> Some months ago, you very kindly asked for my confidential comments on the draft legislation concerning broadcasting, and I was most happy to comply. Now that the new bill has been made public, I hope you will forgive my temerity in offering further comments. . . .
>
> I speak not as a candidate for any of the heart attack-inducing positions within the CBC but plainly and simply as one who has spent a lifetime in broadcasting. . . .
>
> The bill stipulates a board of directors for the Corporation of fourteen — none of whom, by law, can be connected with broadcasting in any way. I understood from our discussions that the presidency would likely go to a public figure whose qualifications in the field of communications might be regarded as secondary. This means a hierarchy of fifteen amateurs, which leaves, as the only possibility open to a professional, the executive vice-presidency. . . . But I see a still worse danger arising . . . the possibility that even the executive vice-president may not be drawn from the ranks of the professionals. . . .

I have encountered a curious philosophy among many public servants in Ottawa . . . that if you put a good administrator in charge of anything, he can easily hire those with ideas. Exactly the reverse, in my experience, is the case: put the one with ideas at the top and he can hire administrators a dime a dozen to implement them. . . . Until and unless [someone] with programming ideas and the experience to implement them is appointed to head the CBC, it will continue to be a sick body — if for no other reason than that the most experienced of administrators, lacking . . . ideas and knowhow, is at the mercy of those who have them.

After that the phone calls came once a month.

ON ANOTHER FRONT the centennial year was going well. In November I wrote Frank Storey in Charlottetown:

I have just received the figures for the *Anne of Green Gables* national tour. It did an average of 93.5% across the country — the highest attendance mark run up by any theatrical attraction in the whole of the Centennial year, beating the Stratford Festival, the Nat'l Theatre of Gt. Britain and everything else! In Toronto, we achieved a new high in the 60-year history of the Royal Alex for a Canadian show, topping last season's record-breaking engagement of [Don Harron's] *Spring Thaw '67*.

While *Anne of Green Gables* was crossing the country, *Louis Riel* was at the O'Keefe Centre.

Backtrack. My outline of *Louis Riel* was approved in January 1965. A month later I notified Floyd Chalmers, with a copy to Geiger-Torel, that "I have done three full scenes, torn them apart with Harry [Somers], and revised them. At this point it is terribly important that the pattern set now satisfies us, because it is in the same vein that the writing will have to continue."[26] The sketch is approved. The first draft of the full libretto, in English and my apology for French, is in Somers's hands by May 1. In June Chalmers (now president of the Stratford Festival) sends the libretto to Guthrie, who expresses interest in staging it in the fall of 1967. On June 2, 1965, Guthrie writes me from the theatre named after him in Minneapolis:

> I've just read (very quickly and once) the Riel piece. A quick reaction: in general a *noble* piece of work. Makes its point without preachment, without sentimentality. Some reservations: too much narrative. . . . Too little opportunity for chorus. . . . Too few set pieces. . . . I don't understand . . . the end; and anyway I think all that is rather fussy and corny (the possibility of an eleventh hour reprieve). We know Riel was hanged; we're all ashamed about it; give him a fine dignified death scene (Father forgive them for they know not etc.) and leave it at that!
>
> I am thrilled that there might be a possibility of working with you again.

Somers and I proceed, often by correspondence between Toronto, Charlottetown, and Montreal, where the Quebec playwright Jacques Languirand is improving my French scenes.[27] In March 1966 I send a revised script to Guthrie in Ireland, who returns a three-page commentary:

> I think the Church scene pretty confused and stagily unstageworthy. . . . Indian braves stalking in, in a mass of fur, feather and fin, gets one into an altogether other, and rather boringly picturesque, department. . . . The trial will be a bugger to stage but I think it's a v.v.g. solution of its problems — who wants to hear all those witnesses taking the oath and so on?[28]

In April 1967 Guthrie comes to Toronto and works through the piece with Somers and me. "However," I write Chalmers, "I had a feeling from his comments in the car as we drove over to Harry's that he had already made up his mind that it would be impractical for him to tackle it." He is too busy in the interim.

> He feels . . . the director of a new work simply cannot be left out of the consultations during the formative period. We are naturally disappointed but not downcast: we have had the advantage of his detailed comments and advice, and we shall now have, with Leon Major, the advantage of a Canadian with devoted historical insight to carry out the project.[29]

In July, when Murray Laufer's inventive sets and Marie Day's authentic costumes are well under way and the chorus is already rehearsing under conductor Victor Feldbrill, I notify Torel that Somers and I, in the interest of brevity, have cut one entire scene and half of another. ("I regret any inconvenience or unnecessary expense these cuts cost — but better now than later.")[30] In the interest of all concerned I stay a mile away from rehearsals, not appearing until the *sitzprobe*, when singers and orchestra first meet. Torel has mounted this extravaganza without a try-out or even a workshop; his faith in his team, and ours in him and each other, is as high as the risk.

The *Telegram*'s George Kidd caught the atmosphere after the first performance on Saturday, September 23:

> When the curtain had fallen for the last time the usually orderly atmosphere backstage went completely mad and the corridors, generally ample in their space, were not nearly big enough to contain the excited well-wishers and the sound of their voices as they soared upward into unidentifiable chaos. It was impossible to get near the dressing-rooms for at least half an hour. . . . Mr. and Mrs. Floyd S. Chalmers and their son and daughter were all in different parts of the backstage area, unable to make contact with each other. . . . It wasn't a question of how you could leave but just how you could fight your way to an exit.[31]

The next day the grades were handed out. "*Louis Riel* rolled into public view like a mighty cannon dead on target" (Winters, *Telegram*). "A howling success" (Kraglund, *Globe and Mail*). "There are not many occasions which feel historic as they are happening, but the world premiere of *Louis Riel* was undoubtedly one of them" (Franklin, *Montreal Star*). "We were all aware in the audience that we had been present at an electrifying event" (Arnold Edinborough, CHFI). "A total theatrical experience, swift, moving, pungent . . . constantly interesting, even to a non-Canadian" (Ericson, *New York Times*).[32] At Expo 67 and in a later appearance at Washington, D.C., as Canada's contribution to the U.S. Bicentennial, the COC production was received with the same acclaim, whatever the usual caveats and complaints. "A most provocative, skillful and often inspired creation . . . the first opera of importance to come from a Canadian composer" (MacLean, *Montreal Star*). "The English–French libretto . . . is written and constructed with a master's hand. The music reveals a technician versed in orchestration, a subtle colorist, a composer never short of melodic ideas" (Thériault, *Le Devoir*). "The music is one of the most imaginative and powerful scores to have been written in this century. The libretto . . . is a masterpiece" (Wendell Musgrave, *Washington Star*).[33]

Reviews of the 1969 CBC Television version maintained that it was even better than the stage version. The historic Washington performance, recorded by the CBC, was later published by Centrediscs. But the fittingly Canadian ending to the story is that since then no other opera company in the country has produced it. Certainly not the National Arts Centre. It left so little trace that by 1979, when I appeared in Ottawa before the Task Force on Canadian Unity, its learned co-chair Jean-Luc Pépin asked me, "Why don't you, for example, write something about Louis Riel?"

THE TENDERS FOR CONSTRUCTION of the St. Lawrence Centre for the Arts had come in far over budget. Allan Lamport pronounced the project dead. So did many journalists ("Moore himself sort of went down with the St-Lawrence-Centre-for-the-Arts bust.")[34] In September 1967, just after the opening of *Louis Riel*, out of sheer cussedness Gelber and I concocted a resurrection. The centre's two auditoriums would be compacted onto one site instead of two, allowing it to be built for the budget in hand. The Toronto Arts Foundation, inspirited by the $10 and $20 donations still coming in and the maxim that half a loaf is better than none, took up the cause again. Against the advice of his finance commissioner, Mayor Dennison lent the plan his support, calling it "the only worthwhile centennial project we could sponsor" at this late date; and LaMarsh offered further federal funds if and when the city applied. If all went well, we could begin construction in April 1968 — or possibly June, and open in 1969 . . . or possibly 1970. But the infighting in City Council degenerated, with the sympathetic female controllers, Margaret Campbell and June Marks, now targeted by Lamport and Beavis.

With both the centre and the CBC on indefinite hold, I began to think that it was my 100th birthday, and that I had no time to lose.

I started a monthly column on the arts for *Maclean's*. I commuted to Ottawa for Stuart Griffiths's TV station to host *Crossfire*, the panel show on everything under the sun — graced, among other marathon talkers, by Mayor Charlotte Whitton, who knew everything and insisted on saying most of it. For Charlottetown I wrote the book and lyrics for *Johnny Belinda*. I went back and forth to the National Theatre School in Montreal. I travelled to international theatre conferences in Budapest, Bucharest, and Istanbul, where I embroiled our ambassador, my old friend Klaus Goldschlag, in promoting an East-West Festival of the Arts. For the Department of External Affairs I lectured to cultural attachés-in-training. For the Ontario Arts Council I ran the Ontario Theatre Study, which developed the world's first profile of arts audiences.[35] When Floyd Chalmers offered me the job of general manager of the Stratford Festival, I said I would accept only if it carried responsibility for the whole operation, such as Geiger-Torel had at the COC. ("I can see one little difficulty arising," Chalmers replied. "We have already appointed Jean Gascon as executive artistic director. We did not take the precaution of presenting him with a flow chart of authority. . . .")[36] I continued to write for radio, act in films, and make rousing luncheon speeches for backsliders.

"How and why does he keep up the frantic pace?" Don Rubin asked in the *Toronto Star*. "The question is impossible for him to answer. One comment he does make, though, is that 'the only thing men have never been able to do is nothing.'"[37] The reply was disingenuous. I knew perfectly well what lay behind the frantic pace: for more than a year I had been running as fast as I could from myself.

I had left home. My marriage of 23 years and four children had ended in divorce, fulfilling the pattern of what I saw as repeated failure to live up to my responsibilities. It was not a case of financial neglect, although I had now and then taken unconscionable risks for the sake of some grand scheme or other. And it was far from a question of lack of concern; I believed that the only hope for young people in the modern world, facing a future more accelerated and less tractable than any before, was to develop their own resources — which meant being forced to study the options and make their own choices. But the more I wanted to do for them the more I was rent by the knowledge that I was too seldom there to practise what I preached — the very fault for which I blamed my own father. However imperfectly, I loved my family; the one I had grown to hate was me.

This was not the nadir of a recurrent manic-depressive cycle, although it was not the first time I believed I had let everyone down; it was the arc of a lifetime. The constant reinvention, I convinced myself, was proof that the article had been defective all along. As early as 1963, in an unguarded moment, I had told a columnist who asked what was my "most paradoxical quality" that I had *always* lived "stretched between a desire to be a responsible member of society and to run away from it all and do what I want — be a Bohemian, perhaps." I was not alone in that human condition. But when the interviewer wanted to know "the chink in my armor," I also said, "I find it difficult to be ruthless."[38]

A decade later, when I asked a wise psychiatrist how I could have brought myself to leave my children — whatever the motive — he answered with another question: "What was the most hurtful thing ever done to you as a child?" I said it was my father leaving the family, but surely, I added, that would make it impossible for me to do the same. "Not at all," he said, "if you're trying to prove yourself as ruthless as your father."

It was then, and not until then, that I saw my adolescence, with its instant judgements and high colours, its simplifications and rationalizations, as the incubator of a dreadful misapprehension. Why should my father have accepted my hostile image of him? He did not leave home; like Candide, he was kicked out! Had he not suffered this indignity, he might never have gone on to become a pillar of the U.S. Episcopalian Church and editor in chief of its influential Forward Movement Publications, receiving, when he retired at 75, praise for "an aplomb, a true sophistication, and above all, a sense of humor" attributable to "a beautiful sense of values" and "an understanding heart."[39] Whatever self-image he managed to construct out of his life's materials, he had obviously come to terms with it — which was more than I had. As for my mother, she certainly did not wait upon my image of her, or anyone else's; she knew exactly who she was. It was only I who made a habit of accepting any decent role life offered me — without ever learning to accept myself. By the time I realized this, 10 years after I had left home, it was too late to do anything except make what amends I could.

At that moment my misapprehension of myself was hopelessly entangled with apprehension about the nation and the world. Canada's centennial seemed more of a coda than a prelude, and 1967 was also the year of the Six Day War in the Middle East, North African famines, South African riots, Mao's Cultural Revolution, and the long, hot racial summer in the United States. Yet here I was again frittering life away on the sidelines. In an article for *Maclean's* I spelt it out:

> When I was young, the disturbing thought was that what I did, as a Canadian, would never really matter — and I suppose that, in a sense, I succumbed to the happy mediocrity of domestic laughter by joining it. Now time is running out, for me and my country. Neither this century nor the next will belong to a people that lives in a perpetually irresponsible adolescence, whose finest boast is that it can laugh at its own mortification and turn humiliation into humility.[40]

It was a far cry from Charlottetown's merry festivities.

As if to mark the end of an era, in December 1967 Prime Minister Pearson announced his resignation, and a leadership convention in April to choose a successor. As the new year began, I heard he had quit trying to find a francophone for CBC chairman and had settled on a short list of three anglophones, the nominee being expected to draft a Quebec running mate. The phone calls stopped. Then came the baptism: George Davidson, secretary of the Treasury Board, was named president (a new title), with Laurent Picard, associate director of Montreal's L'Ecole des Hautes Etudes Commerciales, as executive vice president. Pearson had done exactly what I and a thousand others had advised him against: appointed two administrators, both from outside the industry. In due course he sent me a warm note commending my patience, adding that one day he would "reveal the mystery," which lay, I subsequently learned from Vancouver publisher Stuart Keate, in the confidential short list. It was headed by Keate, who declined; Davidson was second, and accepted; the third was myself, the broadcaster who never wanted to be president in the first place.[41]

What I saw at the time, within and without, was missed opportunity — my own career, the St. Lawrence Centre, the National Arts Centre, the Stratford Festival, Anglo-Canadian Films, the CBC, television in general, the whole country. Without doubt the view was solipsistic. But if it was not given to me to do much about the institutions, I could at least once more reinvent myself.

Toronto Star, "Theatre," by Nathan Cohen, May 28, 1968:

> Double congratulations to Mavor Moore. He married literary historian Phyllis Grosskurth on Sunday, and on Monday the City Council finally gave the go-ahead signal for the building of the St. Lawrence Centre. Moore's faith in the project and his perseverance with it . . . is the kind of heroic saga . . .

The St. Lawrence Centre for the Arts had an official birth in the final week of December 1969 so that the city could say it was only two years overdue.[42] In fact, a tragicomedy of construction holdups and equipment stammers delayed the theatre opening until the end of February 1970: three years late, seven years after its conception, two years beyond the four I had signed on for, and at least six months premature. I had resigned before this happened. But I stayed on through the disastrous debut (made more so by the ambition that preceded it), and left to my close colleague Leon Major, the theatre director who succeeded me as general director, the task of regrouping for another assault on Parnassus.

The previous May I had been given an honorary doctorate by York University, the young but flourishing institution that boasted Ontario's first

Faculty of Fine Arts. There I met the theatre department's Joseph Green, who as a newly arrived American sought advice on the local scene. By January 1970 we were discussing possible faculty recruits to teach theatre history, when he said matter-of-factly, "I don't suppose you'd be interested."

Without hesitation I found myself replying, spurred by what aggravation I cannot remember, "Yes, I would." Thus I became an academic.

"He is, after all," Sid Adilman of the *Toronto Star* pointed out sympathetically, "50 years old" — implying that I was ready for the sort of pasture popularly supposed to exist at universities. In fact, I had only reached a watershed, ending one life, public and private, and beginning another equally challenging.

The academic was by no means the last of my disguises, nor did I abandon the others. But here the present chronicle of my first 50 years must end. What lies ahead, both intimating the new and consummating the old, I have sketched in a closing chapter.

16

Coda

THIS METAMORPHOSIS REQUIRED not only a reinvention but a reeducation. I had read much but never systematically; marked up many books but seldom taken notes; taught frequently, but not since Crescent School been responsible for young lives. On such novel subjects as Canadian theatre history (there was only one usable text, and that in French: Jean Béraud's *Three Hundred Years of Quebec Theatre*.) I had to undertake primary research. I soon moved from theatre courses to interdisciplinary and multimedia programs, and eventually to graduate courses for the English department in Shakespeare, Shaw, and modern drama. Probably the only full professor in the country teaching graduate English with a mere B.A. as his only earned degree, I had to do more homework than my students.

The times required me to reach out to both dropouts and sit-ins. When my first playwriting class was given a short exercise in dialogue, one youth objected. "Hey, man, dialogue is, y' know, like, I mean, *nowhere*." My suggestion that he write an action scenario instead clearly puzzled him. "Yeah. But. Like. That's, y' know, *words*." I suggested he try a course in music or dance notation. He dropped out. But I also wrote an essay on "The Decline of Words in Drama."[1]

To the period 1970–72 also belongs my series of one-act plays exploring the interaction of three different perspectives on reality: what is said, what appears to be happening, and what the audience does. I was returning to my never quite abandoned university thesis. The better to fathom the relationship between figure, ground, and observer, I wrote each in three variations, for stage, radio, and television; and in one form or another, thanks to the intervention of the great London literary agent Emmanuel (Jimmy) Wax, the plays found an audience in Britain and the United States and in translation in Germany, Italy, and India.[2] In 1975 I was elected founding chair of the Guild of Canadian Playwrights.

In 1973, as a useful bridge between the arts and academia, I was appointed a member of the Canada Council, which then still embraced both the art and scholarship. When the Trudeau government decided, against the unanimous advice of the council, to form a separate Social Sciences and Humanities Research Council, I found myself once again embroiled in national politics as seen from Ottawa. Although an admirer of Trudeau — I had first met him in 1968 at a congenial Sussex Drive dinner for artists[3] — I had been publicly critical of the vagueness of the "democratization" policy announced by his then secretary of state, Gérard Pelletier, who was sufficiently pinked to respond with a long personal and confidential defence — written, he wrote, "while listening through my left ear to the speakers at the Constitutional Conference." I was thus already known as a conscientious objector.

I was also angry at the government's continued use of political patronage, rather than familiarity with the issues, in making Privy Council appointments to the cultural boards. When a later secretary of state, John Roberts, asked me to chair the Canada Council in 1979, I declined, even though it was the first time the post had been offered to a professional artist. Four months later he repeated the request, showing me the alternatives he was faced with if I refused. They were all people whose chief qualification was political. I agreed to take the job on condition that all future nominees to the board would be informally subject to the chair's approval. Although Trudeau agreed, and was as good as his word, the arrangement did not sit well with the Clerk of the Privy Council, Michael Pitfield, who fancied the palm of his hand as the locus of all power to appoint. Supported by York University, I chaired the Canada Council from 1979 to 1983, with results I leave to the historians to grade.

In 1978 the remarkable Phyllis Grosskurth and I had been amicably divorced. Two years later I married Alexandra Browning, a distinguished opera singer recently returned to Canada from Britain. I continued teaching at York until the spring of 1984 when I quit (becoming professor emeritus) to devote more time to writing.

When Maureen Forrester was asked to succeed me at the Canada Council, she was expected to resign as national president of Les jeunesses musicales and head of the arts advisory committee of the Canada–Israel Cultural Foundation, so I agreed to switch jobs with her. I also became a board member of the Center for Inter-American Studies in New York, and a director of the Canadian Music Centre. But I had hardly settled into this new path when yet another turn appeared. ("Still around the corner there may wait," Tolkien says, "a new road or a secret gate.")

Denis Harvey, then managing editor of the *Toronto Star*, invited me to write a weekly column on cultural affairs in general — an innovative idea at the time. While I was considering the offer, Harvey and the *Star* abruptly parted company. Two weeks later I received a similar overture from *Globe and Mail* editor Dic Doyle, which I accepted immediately lest it meet the same fate. A week later Doyle was kicked upstairs all the way to the Senate — but not before he had seen to his will. Within weeks Alexandra was offered a teaching post at the University of British Columbia, her alma mater; and since the *Globe and Mail* was agreeable to my writing from Vancouver, we moved there. I thought I would get more writing done out of the eye of the storm.

But in Vancouver I soon found myself involved in Expo 86, for which I hosted the World Conference on the Arts, Business, and Politics. I joined the original board of the British Columbia Science Centre, keeping in touch with Ottawa as a member of the advisory committee to the National Museum of Science and Technology. I joined Vancouver's vital Race Relations Committee, chaired UBC's advisory committee on continuing education, and helped to plan the Whistler School for Business and the Arts. On a dare from Carousel Theatre's Elizabeth Ball, I wrote and composed a musical version (my third adaptation) of Dickens's *A Christmas Carol*, which has travelled across the country. In 1990 Alexandra and I were invited to join the faculty of the University of Victoria, British Columbia, where we now live, kept alert by our teenage daughter Jessica.

In my final column for the *Globe and Mail*, on March 4, 1989 — five years after my first, and only days before my 70th birthday — I tackled "the issue that looms largest, from my perspective, as we approach the next century." It was not the clash of armies or corporations, but the clash of cultures. Pandemic throughout the globe, this clash had a special meaning for Canadians:

Canada was founded on the assumption that common interests made possible the federation of two different societies. The waves of immigration after the Second World War led most Canadians to the comfortable hypothesis that an even larger number of peoples could get along together as individuals, if only religion, language, heritage arts and other incidental baggage were subordinated to common interests such as the public school system and the Gross National Product.

Later a serious error was discovered in this hypothesis: it turns out that we define our individuality in terms of all the things we had been asked to consider irrelevant. Outflanked by numbers, bicultural policy gave way to multiculturalism. If multiculturalism works in Canada we shall have given the world a useful model. [But multiculturalism] presupposes a respect for cultural opportunity in general. If the Canadian mainstream (however defined) cannot be maintained as an alternative to the American, what chance have the alternatives to the alternative? What price multiculture if culture fails?

Canada has repeatedly been brought close to entropy by tunnel-visioned leaders, in and out of government, mistakenly imposing their economic and political mind-set on issues that require cultural solutions. Each time we have escaped by a narrow margin, yet one wide enough to allow the rising generation a ray of hope and the fallen a measure of immortality.

My friend, ally, and worthiest adversary Nathan Cohen died at 47 in 1971 while undergoing heart surgery. His achievement was acknowledged by his peers throughout the English-speaking world.[4] Yet in one of those Canadian ironies he would have relished, when a doctoral student of mine at York University elected to write his thesis on Cohen, the proposal split the English department, the nays maintaining that Cohen was unworthy of such attention. The ayes barely won.

In Ireland, two months later, the giant heart of Tyrone Guthrie failed him at the age of 70. Andrew Allan, his final years a victory of intelligence over alcoholism, lasted until his 65th birthday in 1974. The world's foremost master of radio drama made a gracious exit as a supporting actor and occasional essayist.

Ernest Bushnell, the same age as the century, died gently in 1987. He was soon followed by Stuart Griffiths, 20 years his junior, felled by a massive heart attack. After being rejected for the CBC presidency as too left-wing, Griffiths turned Bushnell's Ottawa television station into a model of public-spirited capitalism. On the back lot he built a hand-crafted yacht, which he sailed, on his retirement, to the West Indies. From there he explored both coasts of North America, periodically returning to Canada to give advice on broadcasting policy to governments too obtuse to follow it.

My father died in 1968 at the age of 83, long since retired from the church that had been his life. We had never reopened relations, and I regretted it. My brothers attended to the obsequies in Cincinnati. The Episcopalian elders were not aware that he and my mother had never been divorced, and Peter took it on himself to demand a widow's pension for Mother. They obliged. As she opened the first cheque, the widow wryly observed: "He's more use now than he was before."

Peter himself finally fell victim to his war wounds in 1973, at the age of 51, when a heart operation was ruled out on account of the surrounding scar tissue. To the end he retained his mordant sense of humour. The surgeon who tried to save him was the same one who had attended him once after battle. "He knows his way in," Pete said, "but can he find his fucking way out?"

I am told that one of the worst of psychological traumas is to be predeceased by one's offspring, and Peter's death weighed heavily on my mother. But obeying his injunction to "soldier on," she continued teaching and crusading until her late eighties. She followed my activities closely and supportively. A month after I received my first honorary degree from York, she received her first, from the Western College for Women in Oxford, Ohio. Only after this American honour did the University of Toronto see fit to grant a degree, 66 years late, to its failed undergraduate. In the same year a tribute to her was mounted at the St. Lawrence Centre, at which the charter of the New Play Society, every penny of its lingering debts paid off, was cancelled.[5] By then she had moved into a small apartment, leaving Francis and his family in the house on Ridelle, with its Indian marking tree and ancient memories. She kicked up her heels until a broken hip laid her flat at 88, then moved back into the old house to be nursed by my kind sister-in-law Helen until she died in bed two years later.

Floating in and out of reality, she once said to me, "Well, I'm going to take a walk now." "Dearie," I said, "where do you think you're going?" With a wicked grin she pointed up. One of her last acts was to sign, shakily, a document allowing her name to be used for the annual Toronto Theatre Awards, known ever afterward as the Doras.

Her older brother Jim had died earlier, and the younger Wilfrid did not long survive her, ending his days in a military hospital among his old comrades-in-arms. My own brother Francis died in 1987, after retiring from a second career as a high school teacher of science, math, and civics, during which he trained many a stage technician.

But the living, as always, must have the last word.

Phyllis Grosskurth, who was told she had terminal cancer a dozen years ago, is completing her fifth book since then. Darwina Faessler Moore still resides in Toronto, where we see each other now and again with the guarded warmth of old friends who shared a good part of their lives. Since I had so little to do with it, I shall refrain from boasting of our children's exploits. But I may say that Tedde has moved from theatre to film, presented me with my oldest granddaughter Zoë, now 21, and with filmmaker Don Shebib's help produced both Suzanna and Noah — all three of whom are obviously well equipped to write their own damn books someday. Rosalind, an artist, has had a career as checkered as her father's, most recently as stage designer, gourmet cook, couturier, teacher, and office manager of the Canadian Opera Company. Marili, who graduated from the University of British Columbia in botany, is currently computerizing collections of all sorts at the Royal Ontario Museum. Charlotte, who studied theatre at York University, acts, sings, and dances all over the place. She recently disturbed the peace by winning a Dora for her performance in The Rocky Horror Show, an eventuality unforeseen by her grandmother.

Having finished these memoirs, I can now get back to writing plays. Thirty-five years ago I raised a rumpus over the contemptuous entry on Canada in the 1957 Oxford Companion to the Theatre — "probably no more amateur than were the first plays of medieval Europe." We had changed all that. In 1989 the publishers atoned by bringing out an Oxford Companion to the Canadian Theatre, in which theatre historian Rota Herzberg Lister calls attention to "Moore's dramaturgical preoccupation with the elusiveness of identity and the unpredictability of public and private interactions."

Where on earth could she have got such an idea?

Notes

MM = Mavor Moore
MMY = Mavor Moore Papers, York University Archives
DMM = Dora Mavor Moore
DMMT = Dora Mavor Moore Papers, Thomas Fisher Library, University of Toronto

CHAPTER 1: PRELUDE

1. See James Mavor Moore, "Why 'James Mavor' Morell?" *The Shaw Review* 23.2 (May 1980).
2. James Mavor, *An Economic History of Russia*, 2 vols. (London: J. M. Dent and Sons, 1914).
3. Mavor, *My Windows on the Street of the World*, vol. 1 (New York: E. P. Dutton, 1924) 311.
4. Mavor, "Hasty Judgments" (monthly log sent home to Scotland), September 1, 1892. James Mavor Collection, Thomas Fisher Library, University of Toronto.

CHAPTER 2: KID STUFF

1. Roy Mitchell, *Creative Theatre* (Westwood, NJ: Kindle Press, 1969).

CHAPTER 3: IN ALL DIRECTIONS

1. In 1935 she wrote to Gibson's father: "I wish I were in a position to write something encouraging. . . . To quote Dr. Mitchell, with whom I had a long talk, 'William would be worth helping if he would only help himself.' Indeed this 'slipping' has been more a blow to me than I would like to admit for he brought a great deal of brightness into our little household." Quoted by Paula Sperdakos, University of Toronto, in her unpublished thesis on DMM, DMMT, Box 62.
2. MM, *Pandora's Box*, juvenilia, MMY.
3. F. J. Moore, letter to MM, March 25, 1946, MMY.

CHAPTER 4: AWAKENING

1. MM Diary, March 1936–37, MMY.
2. Margaret Hayes's son John became a lifelong friend and made a distinguished contribution to the professionalization of Canadian theatre.
3. DMM, letter to Mrs. Derry, July 5, 1936, DMMT, Box 158.

4. Ronald Mavor, *Dr. Mavor and Mr. Bridie* (Edinburgh: Canongate Publishing and the National Library of Scotland, 1988).

5. H. O. McCurry, assistant director, National Gallery of Canada, letter to MM, August 25, 1936, MMY.

CHAPTER 5: LEARNING

1. F. J. Moore, letter to MM, November 21, 1936, MMY.

2. MM, letter to F. J. Moore, November 27, 1936, MMY.

3. Reuben Wells Leonard Foundation, deed, December 28, 1923: $500 income from securities. Trustee: Toronto General Trusts Corporation.

4. *Rope*'s notable cast and crew included Evelyn Cook, who would become an outstanding children's writer, and stage manager Alan Jarvis, later the National Gallery's most famous director.

5. *The Varsity*, October 5, 1936.

6. On the flyleaf of my philosophy notebook, 1938, MMY.

7. John Stuart Mill, 1844, Quoted in C. W. M. Hart, "The Race Myth," *University of Toronto Quarterly* 11.2 (January 1942).

8. DMM, letter to MM, January 15, 1937, DMMT.

9. DMM, letter to MM, January 18, 1937, DMMT.

10. Peter Moore, letter to MM, January 10, 1937, MMY.

11. John Terrace, letter to MM, June 19, 1937, MMY.

CHAPTER 6: THE PROPAGANDA WAR

1. Toronto *Telegram*, January 25, 1943.

2. *CBC Annual Report* (Ottawa: Queen's Printer, 1941).

3. MM, letter to Merrill Denison, May 30(?), 1943, MMY.

4. With Lister Sinclair's *Refugee* and John Coulter's *House in the Quiet Glen*.

5. DMM, letter to MM, June 9, 1944, DMMT.

6. PWC Document 25, 2nd rev., March 23, 1944, "British Secret, U.S. Confidential," MMY.

7. *Prisoner of War Testimony*, London, October 1945. General Staff from Commander of Grenadier Regiment 987, BH Command Post, July 13, 1944, MMY.

8. Richard Deacon, *History of British Secret Service* (London: Grafton Books, 1980) 373.

9. MM, shortwave broadcast, Britain to Canada, November 15, 1944.

10. DMM, letter to MM, November 17, 1944, DMMT.

11. *History of the PPCLI* (Ottawa: Queen's Printer, n.d.) 203.

12. O. H. Mavor, letter to MM, August 18, 1945, MMY.

13. John Lehmann, *A Nest of Tigers* (London: Macmillan, 1968). My thanks to Freeman Tovell for drawing my attention to this book on the Sitwells.

14. F. J. Moore, letter to MM, March 6, 1946, MMY.

CHAPTER 7: FINDING CANADA

1. MM, letter to A. E. (Bert) Powley, February 14, 1945, MMY.
2. John Weinzweig, letter to MM, December 24, 1945, MMY.
3. Frank Chamberlain, "Under the Hat," *Radio World*, January 1946.
4. Klaus Goldschlag, letter to MM, August 27, 1945, MMY.
5. Gratien Gélinas, *Les Fridolinades: 1945–46* (Montreal: Quinze, 1980).
6. Roly Young, *Toward a Civic Theatre* (broadsheet), July 17, 1945, MMY.
7. DMM note to MM, on reverse of Young's broadsheet, July 18, 1945, MMY.
8. *Toronto Star*, November 11, 1959.
9. *Canadian High News*, 1939. Undated clipping, MMY.
10. John Holden, letter to MM, June 10, 1940, MMY.
11. DMM, letter to MM, July 22, 1943, DMMT.

CHAPTER 8: CANADA OR THE WORLD?

1. Andrew Allan, *A Self-Portrait*, intro. Harry J. Boyle (Toronto: Macmillan, 1977).
2. Alice Frick, *Image in the Mind* (Toronto: Canadian Stage and Arts Publications, 1987) 20.
3. John L. Watson, *Saturday Night*, December 6, 1949.
4. Eric Koch, letter to MM, January 6, 1948, MMY.
5. Guthrie had heard a recording before we met in 1952.
6. Watson, April 17, 1948.
7. Watson, October 28, 1948
8. See *CBC Times*, June 5, 1949.
9. *CBC Times*, April 24, 1949.
10. *Critically Speaking* was CBC Radio's weekly review of musical events, including its own programs. Chester Duncan was a Winnipeg critic. The MMY clipping is undated.
11. MM, "The Race Between the Pen and the Sword," *Saturday Night*, September 27, 1947.
12. Quoted in "Corwin at Seventy-five," a tribute to Norman Corwin, May 1, 1985, MMY.
13. See *Newsweek*, May 12, 1947.
14. Fifteen-minute programs for 274 stations. See *New York Times*, July 10, 1949.
15. "Canuck Leads Talks on Radio Education," Canadian Press, New York, August 26, 1948.
16. MM, "Which World Citizens?" *Food for Thought*, November 1948.
17. Toronto *Telegram*, March 20, 1950.
18. *Toronto Star*, June 15, 1950.
19. Saul Carson, *The New Republic*, July 8, 1950.
20. See *New York Times*, February 17, 1950.
21. Quotes from brochure for *This Is the U.N.* (New York: Tribune Productions, n.d.), MMY.
22. Carson, *The New Republic*, July 3, 1950.
23. *New York Times*, June 19, 1950.

24. New York *Herald Tribune*, June 19, 1950; New York *Daily Compass*, same date.
25. MM, "The Canadian Theatre," *The Canadian Forum*, August 1950, 108.

CHAPTER 9: TOWARD A CANADIAN THEATRE

1. Nathan Cohen, *The Critic* 1.4 (September 1950).
2. MM, letter to *The Critic* 1.5 (October 1950).
3. In "A Tribute to Dora Mavor Moore," St Lawrence Centre, November 30, 1971, MMY.
4. Quoted in Martha Harron, "A Parent Contradiction" (Toronto: Collins, 1988) 87.
5. Toronto *Wochenblatt*, December 18, 1946.
6. *Canadian Jewish Weekly*, April 10, 1947.
7. Rose Macdonald, *Telegram*, October 12, 1947; Colin Sabiston, *Globe and Mail*, October 28, 1946; Pearl McCarthy, *Globe and Mail*, December 7, 1946; Rose Macdonald, *Telegram*, November 23, 1946.
8. B. K. Sandwell, writing as "Lucy van Gogh," in *Saturday Night*, September 1947.
9. Sandwell, *Saturday Night*, March 1949.
10. Sabiston, *Globe and Mail*, December 21, 1946.
11. O. H. Mavor, letter to MM, December 23, 1949, MMY.
12. Quoted in Ronald Mavor, *Dr. Mavor and Mr. Bridie* 116.
13. Ernest Rawley of Toronto's Royal Alexandra later tried to bring the Glasgow Citizens' Theatre to Canada. In September 1950 Mavor/Bridie wrote to DMM: "Tyrone Guthrie was very keen that we should go to Canada and perhaps Australia next year but the matter has not yet come before the board. I doubt whether we could undertake it. . . ." Copy in MMY.
14. O. H. Mavor, letter to MM, January 1947, MMY.
15. *Toronto Star*, February 21, 1947.
16. Program note, *The Time of Your Life*, March 20, 1947.
17. Toronto *Telegram*, May 16, 1947.
18. *Canadian Jewish Weekly*, May 8, 1947.
19. "The kid's clever," Augustus Bridle wrote in the *Toronto Star*, October 11, 1947.
20. "On Our Stage We Speak Canadian," Montreal *Standard*, January 21, 1950.
21. *Canadian Jewish Weekly* (undated clipping), November 1947, MMY.
22. See my "Theatre in Canada," *Canadian Life*, March/April 1949; and "Why No National Theatre?" CBC Radio, August 20, 1947, pub. in *Theatrum*, September 1991.
23. *Wochenblatt*, (undated clipping), 1947, MMY.
24. Hugh Kemp, letter to MM, January 8, 1948, MMY. In fact, Kemp left Canada to become a script editor for NBC in New York. He never finished *Two Solitudes*.
25. Allan, *A Self-Portrait* 119.
26. Sabiston, *Globe and Mail*, April 2, 1948.
27. Virginia Pettit and Catherine Huntington, letter to MM, January 20, 1948, MMY.

28. *CJBC Views the Shows*, January 16, 1949.

29. Louis Calta, "Broadway to See 'To Tell the Truth,'" *New York Times* (undated clipping), January 1949, MMY.

30. Whittaker, *Globe and Mail*, October 22, 1949.

31. John Coulter, letter to DMM, August 11, 1949, quoted by Paula Sperdakos, DMMT.

32. Bill Brown, Montreal *Standard*, June 21, 1950; Cohen, "Critically Speaking," CBC Radio, January 15, 1950; Sandwell, *Saturday Night* (undated clipping), 1949. Mavor/Bridie, having read *Who's Who*, responded (December 23, 1949): "I wanted very much to like your play, but I didn't. I think that expressionist work on a framed stage is growing a bit dim. . . . You are a very good writer and you probably got away with it." Famed New York literary agent Audrey Wood was less tolerant: "While your play is well-written and thoughtful, it is predominantly a long discussion of life, the theatre, points of view, etc."

33. CBC, *Critically Speaking*, June 15, 1950.

34. Jack Karr, *Toronto Star*, January 14, 1950; Cohen, *The Critic*, September 1950; Macdonald, *Toronto Telegram*, June 14, 1950.

35. *Globe and Mail*, February 20, 1950; The Critic, April 1950; quoted by Whittaker, *Globe and Mail*, January 20, 1975.

36. Quoted in Pierre Berton, "The Man Who's Going to Make Our TV," *Maclean's*, May 15, 1952.

37. *Globe and Mail*, March 27, 1950.

38. Bob McStay, *Variety*, April 5, 1950.

39. *The Critic*, April 1950.

40. Mary Lowry Ross, *Saturday Night*, April 11, 1950.

41. Quoted in John Coulter, *In My Day*, privately printed, 1980.

Chapter 10: Into Television

1. These quotations are from early essays of mine, with no source indicated. Most recently cited in "My Adventures in Public Broadcasting," the 1986 Graham Spry Lecture for CBC Radio's *Ideas*.

2. Cited in my "What We'll Do with TV," *Saturday Night*, May 24, 1952.

3. Berton, "The Man Who's Going to Make Our TV."

4. MM, "Television . . . the Medium," *CBC Times*, February 1951.

5. MM, "What We'll Do with TV."

6. Berton, "The Man Who's Going to Make Our TV."

7. Trustee Cranham, cited in MM, "What's Television Going to Do to Us?" CBC Radio, April 1, 1952, MMY.

8. "In the first half of 1952, as compared with the first half of 1951, national advertisers as a whole reduced their expenditures in newspapers by 17 percent . . . but

increased their expenditure on TV by 87 percent." MM, address to the Canadian Retail Federation, 1953, MMY.

9. Len Turner, *Canadian TV Guide*, September 27, 1952.

10. "Radio and TV," *Buffalo Courier-Express*, September 10, 1952.

11. All quotations from my speech to UTS Alumni, October 23, 1952, MMY.

12. See Montreal *Weekend Magazine*, May 27, 1978.

13. James Montagnes, *New York Times*; Poulton, Toronto *Telegram*. Undated clippings, MMY.

14. A reporter for the Vancouver *Sun* told me (October 1952): "You won't like what I write when I get back. I've been sent here to smear you." CKEY president Jack Kent Cooke announced: "This will have to be crushed! The whole thing's ridiculous!" He soon left for the United States to become a multimillionaire.

15. Stan Helleur, Toronto *Telegram*, n.d.

16. *Globe and Mail*, December 16, 1954.

17. MM, "A Chance to Do Something Freshly Canadian," *CBC Times*, February 17, 1952.

18. MM, UTS Alumni speech, October 23, 1952, MMY.

19. Toronto *Telegram*, December 10, 1954.

CHAPTER 11: STRATFORD TO MARIPOSA

1. Tom Patterson and Allan Gould, *First Stage: The Making of the Stratford Festival* (Toronto: McClelland and Stewart, 1987) 54.

2. DMM, letter to MM, Spring (?) 1946, DMMT.

3. James Forsyth, *Tyrone Guthrie* (London: Hamish Hamilton, 1976) 214–15.

4. Forsyth, *Tyrone Guthrie* 222.

5. MM, letter to Toronto *Telegram*, June 28–29, 1959.

6. I was unaware that only days before the Stratford Festival opened, DMM — considering me lost to television — had offered Cecil Clarke the job of production manager for the New Play Society to keep him in Canada after the festival. He declined.

7. Alf Bell, letter to MM, July 28, 1953, MMY.

8. Bell, letter to MM.

9. Whittaker, "Show Business," *Globe and Mail*, January 14, 1954.

10. McStay, *Variety* (undated clipping), MMY.

11. MM, letter to Roy Loken, April 19, 1954, MMY.

12. Cecil Clarke, letter to MM, May 6, 1954, MMY.

13. MM, letter to Clarke, May 7, 1954, MMY.

14. Clarke, letter to MM, May 10, 1954, MMY.

15. Tyrone Guthrie, Robertson Davies, Grant MacDonald, *Twice Have the Trumpets Sounded* (Toronto: Clarke, Irwin, 1954) 35.

16. MM, letter to Guthrie (undated draft), October (?) 1954, MMY.

17. Stratford *Beacon-Herald*, July 15, 1954.

18. In July 1950, while I was in New York, DMM asked me to find "a director for the NPS for Jan.–Feb.–March. I am sure this outside director will give us the flip [fillip?] we need." She ignored my advice to use a Canadian, with sad results.

19. Anna Russell, *I'm Not Making This Up, You Know* (Toronto: Macmillan, 1985) 119.

20. "CJBC Views the Shows," quoted in W. E. Edmonstone, *Nathan Cohen: The Making of a Critic* (Toronto: Lester and Orpen, 1977) 217.

21. DMM, managing director's report to NPS board of governors, May 17, 1954, MMY.

22. Montreal *Herald*, October 16, 1956.

23. On NPS letterhead, undated, September 1954, MMY.

24. MM draft letter to H. Whittaker, January 21, 1955, following his review: "No-one is more aware than I of the show's shortcomings . . . but I set out to make it Canadian — and almost by definition, therefore, I invited a slower pace, less whoop-de-doo, less brass, less vulgarity . . . the antithesis of the U.S. musical method, which hits every nail loudly and raucously." I may not have sent the letter, MMY.

25. Burke Martin, *London Free Press*, January 7, 1955.

26. Davies, Kingston *Whig-Standard*; Karr, *Toronto Star*; Canadian Press.

27. Burton Richardson was the managing editor concerned. Whittaker, in the *Globe and Mail* January 14, 1955, also attacked one of the *Telegram* critics: "Despite the extraordinary perceptions of our friend Stan Helleur, the Toronto reviews of *Sunshine Town* were enough to attract the interest of Dan Petrie, ABC-TV director of the *Elgin Hour* . . . [who] wanted to do a one-hour condensation of the musical."

28. *Globe and Mail*, January 11, 1955.

29. CP telegram, 8:53 p.m., January 20, 1955, MMY.

30. Walter O'Hearn, *Montreal Star*, January 24, 1955.

31. Hugh MacLennan, *Montreal Star*, January 27, 1955.

32. Richard Newman, *London Free Press*, February 3, 1955.

CHAPTER 12: FIVE-RING CIRCUS

1. DMM, "How *Sunshine Town*?", 1955, quoted by Paula Sperdakos, DMMT, Box 78.

2. MM, Interim Report (Confidential) to NPS board, March 2, 1955, MMY.

3. I bought rights only for the duration of the Canadian run. The New York nightclub Downstairs at the Upstairs was one of several using old *Spring Thaw* material when Stan Daniels wrote from there (October 1962): "The performers were all dewy-eyed innocence, and gave the distinct impression that the number was written for them and that the ink on it was scarcely dry." MMY.

4. The snowshoe idea came from Owen Duffy, but for a sketch. I thought it much funnier as a Canadian form of ballet. The concept has often been copied.

5. MM, Interim Report (Confidential) to NPS board, June 21, 1955, MMY.

6. The theatre group was founded and led by Paddy Robertson (the "Eliza"), a former London showgirl who became a writer, broadcaster, and devoted friend of DMM. The fine cast included David Gardner, Tony van Bridge, and Sandy Webster (as Shaw). The designer was Ralph Hicklin, later a Toronto theatre critic.

7. *Globe and Mail*, April 4, 1956.

8. Annual Couchiching Conference, Proceedings, August 1956, MMY.

9. In the revised *Candide* libretto, by several hands, for the later successful Broadway revival, my use of Voltaire as narrator and role player was adopted.

10. Tyrone Guthrie, *A Life in the Theatre* (New York: McGraw-Hill, 1959) 241.

11. *Globe and Mail*, September 14, 1956.

12. *Canadian Tribune*, September 24, 1956.

13. Leon Major directed the first Canadian stage production in 1956 for the University Alumnae Players of Toronto. It won the $1,000 Dominion Drama Festival Prize.

14. Orillia, Ontario, *Newsletter*, June 16, 1960.

15. Another actor in the same 1960 CBC-TV production of *The Son* was James Doohan. After playing Kent to my Lear at the Crest Theatre later that year, he also took off for Hollywood and fame as the engineer Scotty on *Star Trek*.

16. DMM, letter to Dr. McKinnon Phillips, January 16, 1956. Quoted in MM column in Toronto *Telegram*, December 20, 1986, MMY.

17. Donald Fletcher, medical report to Phillips, March 1956. Quoted in same column.

18. Brooks Atkinson, *New York Times*, March 10, 1957.

19. James Grant, at a later time, suffered a major depression of his own.

20. For a superb summary of contemporary thought, see Kay Redfield Jamison, *Touched with Fire: Manic-Depressive Illness and the Artistic Temperament* (Toronto: Maxwell Macmillan, 1993).

21. MM, letter to Bernard Braden, September 9, 1957, MMY.

22. Tyrone Guthrie, letter to MM, July 24, 1957, MMY.

23. "Show Business," *Globe and Mail*, May 31, 1957.

CHAPTER 13: THE CRITIC

1. "For the Sake of Argument," *Maclean's*, December 1956.

2. The International Theatre Institute is an organ of UNESCO with which I had earlier been associated.

3. McStay, *Variety* (undated clipping), May 1958, MMY.

4. This blessed event gave me an insight into *King Lear* not suggested elsewhere: that Lear resented Cordelia for not being the son he had increasingly longed for.

5. *Canadian Commentator*, November 1958.

6. Malcolm Ross, ed., *The Arts in Canada: A Stock-taking at Mid-century* (Toronto: Macmillan, 1958) chapters 3 and 6.

7. MM, letter to Toronto *Telegram*, January 5, 1959.

8. *Telegram*, June 6, 1959.

9. *Telegram*, June 7, 1959

10. *Canadian Commentator*, March 1959.

11. "Nathan Cohen's Corner," *Toronto Star*, March 7, 1959.

12. George Jean Nathan, *The Critic and the Drama* (New York: Knopf, 1922) 1.

13. See MM, "The Future of Four Stratfords," *Manchester Guardian*, May 14, 1959.

14. *Telegram*, March 30, 1959.

15. *Telegram*, May 26, 1959.

16. MM, *And What Do You Do?*, a collection of verses from *Maclean's*, with cartoons by Haro (Toronto: J. M. Dent, 1960). Several of these verses have found their way into anthologies of light verse and quotations.

17. "Nathan Cohen's Corner," *Toronto Star* (undated clipping), MMY.

18. *Telegram*, August 22, 1960.

19. *Telegram*, August 24, 1960.

20. "Nathan Cohen's Corner," *Toronto Star*, June 2, 1960.

21. Tyrone Guthrie, letter to DMM, July 10, 1960, DMMT.

22. *Telegram*, October 3, 1960.

CHAPTER 14: ART AND POLITICS

1. MM, "For the Sake of Argument," *Maclean's*, February 2, 1957.

2. Blaik Kirby, "Mavor Moore: He's Show Business Octopus," *Toronto Star*, February 18, 1961.

3. MM, letter to Peter Dwyer, Canada Council, June 4, 1962, MMY.

4. Introduction to review of *Spring Thaw* in *Whittaker's Theatre*, ed. Ronald Bryden, introductions by Bryden and Boyd Neil (Toronto: The Whittaker Project 1985).

5. "Winter Almost Over, Spring Thaw Almost Here." *Toronto Star*, March 2, 1980.

6. Robertson Davies, *Peterborough Examiner*, March 27, 1961; Martin Stone, *Canadian Tribune*, April 10, 1971; Ron Evans, Toronto *Telegram*, March 30, 1961; George Marucci, *Guelph Mercury*, March 20, 1961; Bill Cowan, CJBC Radio, March 30, 1961; *Sarnia Observer*; Bob McStay, *Variety*; Bruce Richardson, *Canadian Jewish News*, April 6, 1961.

7. "Togetherness" is on the "original cast" recording of *New Faces of 1962*. A press release of May 15, 1961, cites an invitation for *Spring Thaw* to appear at the Players' Theatre, New York, "noting that four onetime stars of *Spring Thaw* are currently rising names there: Donald Harron, who has recently left *The Tenth Man* to star at this year's Stratford (Conn.) Festival; Robert Goulet, *Camelot's* Sir Lancelot; Lou Jacobi, starring in *Come Blow Your Horn*; and Norman Jewison, the brilliant television director who is to stage his first Broadway play this year."

8. Wallace Rayburn, Montreal *Gazette*, from London (undated clipping), June 1961.

9. Jean Béraud, *La Presse*, May 26, 1964. (My translation.)

10. L. B. Pearson television interview, February 26, 1962. Aired March 27, 1962, MMY.

11. *Toronto Star*, from Orillia, Ontario (undated clipping), MMY.

12. John Hirsch, letter to MM, December 20, 1960, MMY.

13. MM, letter to Peter Dwyer, Canada Council, June 3, 1962, MMY.

14. MM, letter to Alec Walton, August 24, 1962, MMY.

15. MM, "Arts Boards," draft of article, 1989, MMY.

16. Frank MacKinnon, "Honour the Founders, Enjoy the Arts" (Charlottetown: Fathers of Confederation Building Trust, 1990) 4.

17. MacKinnon 35–36.

18. It was Anthony Adamson, with his keen interest in historical sites and heritage buildings, who first suggested to me the possibility of *son et lumière* spectacles as a popular art.

19. Davies's and Finch's "Prologue" was especially commissioned for the event, MMY.

CHAPTER 15: A HUNDRED YEARS OLD

1. Quoted by Ann Dunn, *Hamilton Spectator* (undated clipping), MMY.

2. Honourable Maurice Lamontagne, speech at opening of the Third Annual Festival of the Performing Arts, Ottawa Technical High School, October 3, 1964, MMY.

3. Minutes, Meeting No. 6, Advisory Committee on the Theatre, Canadian Centre for the Performing Arts, Stratford, Ontario, September 27, 1964, MMY.

4. MM, letter to Hamilton Southam, January 28, 1965, MMY.

5. MM memorandum, "A Resident Bilingual Company for Ottawa," February 10, 1965.

6. Minutes, Standing Committee on Cultural Affairs of the National Conference on the Centennial of Confederation, Charlottetown, April 25, 1964.

7. Coulter later felt aggrieved that he had not been invited to write the libretto for the opera and sought an acknowledgement of his play as the source of the opera. See MM letter to the editor (*Globe and Mail*, January 23, 1975): "Coulter was responsible for arousing my own interest in Riel, but the opera as it developed owed more to recent biographies [etc.]. . . . The note that later appeared in the program ('with grateful acknowledgement') was in no way even a partial credit for writing the opera libretto, but an acknowledgement of the authors' collective gratitude to a great progenitor. The opera itself is a tribute to John Coulter, and I wish the old leprechaun would accept it in the spirit offered." The next day Coulter phoned me, beginning a most friendly conversation with: "This is the old leprechaun speaking."

8. A. R. M. Lower, *Canadians in the Making* (Toronto: Longmans Green, 1958) 299.

9. MM, telegram to Don Harron, MMY.

10. MM, letter to J. G. McClelland, June 24, 1965, MMY.

11. Bronwyn Drainie, *Living the Part: John Drainie and the Dilemma of Canadian Stardom* (Toronto: Macmillan, 1988) 316.

12. *Toronto Star*, August 19, 1965; Jay Walz, *New York Times*, August 22, 1965; Toho International Inc., letter to Don Harron, August 24, 1965, MMY.

13. *Toronto Star*, August 21, 1965.

14. "Yesterday the Children Were Dancing," trans. MM (Toronto: Clarke, Irwin, 1967).

15. Quoted in MM, "The Human City," *Connoisseur*, May 1973.

16. Toronto Planning Board Report, September 1962.

17. "An Assessment of Toronto's Cultural Facilities and Requirements," report by Urwick, Currie Limited, 1964.

18. George Bryant, *Toronto Star*, May 2, 1964.

19. MM, *Maclean's*, June 4, 1966.

20. Progress Report, St. Lawrence Centre for the Arts, November 8, 1966.

21. This holistic approach derived from the original Urwick, Currie report. It is spelt out in considerable detail in a memorandum I wrote to Carlton Williams, vice president of the University of Toronto, in January 1966, MMY.

22. See Eric Koch, *Inside Seven Days* (Scarborough, ON: Prentice-Hall/ Newcastle, 1986).

23. For the entire speculative list, see the *Toronto Star*, May 6, 1967.

24. As early as 1956 I had written in *Saturday Night*: "Leadership [in broadcasting] cannot be achieved by stringent business controls, for the simple reason that imagination cannot be bought by the yard. . . . Already there are signs in the CBC that due to insistence on 'proper' management the police are becoming as plentiful as the citizens, and that to protect themselves the citizens are substituting decision by committee for individual judgment."

25. MM, Report on Arts and Culture Centre, St. John's, Newfoundland, March 1967, MMY.

26. MM, letter to Floyd Chalmers, February 23, 1965, MMY.

27. Harry Somers to MM, July 30, 1965: "I've spent the whole month making small notes, absorbing, approaching from any direction, gradually formulating, allowing the instincts to roam and the intellect to corral them so that now definite shapes seem to be emerging from the fog — or I could say I'm getting pretty close to the point where I can distill my own brand of whiskey," MMY.

28. Tyrone Guthrie, letter to MM, March 24, 1966, MMY.

29. MM, letter to Floyd Chalmers, April 12, 1966, MMY.

30. MM, letter to Herman Geiger-Torel, July 21, 1967, MMY.

31. Toronto *Telegram*, September 25, 1967.

32. All press reviews September 25, 1967; Arnold Edinborough broadcast, September 30, 1967.

33. Eric MacLean, October 20; Jacques Thériault, October 23; Wendell Musgrave, October 24, 1967.

34. Peter Thurling, Toronto *Telegram*, November 25, 1967.

35. Published as *The Awkward Stage*, ed. MM (Toronto: Methuen, 1970). It created some interest abroad: see *Manchester Guardian* review, August 20, 1970.

36. Chalmers, letter to MM, August 15, 1967, MMY. I also turned down the post of head of CBC-TV drama when Fletcher Markle resigned, and instead joined the search committee that recommended John Hirsch.

37. *Toronto Star*, November 12, 1968.

38. MM, "Perspective," *Toronto Star*, January 8, 1963.

39. Edna Ruth Johnson, "Dr. Francis J. Moore, Servant of the Protestant Episcopal Church," in *The Churchman* (May 1960).

40. "Mavor Moore's Canada," *Maclean's*, November 1971.

41. Neither, according to Pearson, did Davidson. See L. B. Pearson, *Mike*, vol. 3 (Toronto: U of T Press, 1972) 191.

42. "The construction commencement ceremony for the St. Lawrence Centre for the Arts," Whittaker wrote in the *Globe and Mail*, June 18, 1968, "was a modest noontime affair. It was almost as if the battle-scarred visitors didn't want to draw attention to their hour of triumph for fear that the sniping would start again."

CHAPTER 16: CODA

1. MM, "The Decline of Words in Drama," *Canadian Literature*, ed. William New (Vancouver: U of BC Press, 1970).

2. Six Plays by Mavor Moore (Vancouver: Talonbooks, 1989) contains *The Store; Come Away, Come Away; Getting In* (also pub. Samuel French, New York); *The Pile; The Argument*, as well as a later two-act play, *The Apology*.

3. See Merle Shain, *Toronto Star*, November 21, 1968.

4. In my obituary for Cohen in the *Telegram*, I wrote: "If he were reviewing his own life? When I say I am not his judge, I use a sanctuary he would have scorned. . . . He used to refer, only half jokingly, to his 'Calvinist' upbringing — and indeed he was a Calvinist, not of religion but of art."

5. See Whittaker, "Dora Mavor Moore, Toronto Theatre's Great Lady," *Globe and Mail*, November 27, 1971.

Index